THEOLOGICAL FOUNDATIONS

VOLUME ONE

INTENTIONALITY

AND

PSYCHE

ROBERT M. DORAN

MARQUETTE
UNIVERSITY
PRESS

Library of Congress Cataloging-In-Publication Data

Doran, Robert M., 1939–
    Theological foundations / Robert M. Doran.
        p. cm. — (Marquette studies in theology ; no. 8–9)
    Includes bibliographical references.
    ISBN 0-87462-632-3 (pbk. : v. 1). — ISBN 0-87462-633-1
    (pbk. : v. 2)
    1. Theology, Doctrinal. 2. Christianity—Psychology. 3. Man
    (Christian theology) 4. Sociology, Christian (Catholic) 5.
    Catholic Church—Doctrines. I. Title. II. Series: Marquette
    studies in theology ; #8-9.
    BT78.D56 1995
    230'.01—dc20   95-41772

MARQUETTE STUDIES IN THEOLOGY No. 8

Cover design by Clare Tallon.
Photo by Andrew J. Tallon

Printed in the United States of America

MARQUETTE UNIVERSITY PRESS
MILWAUKEE

The Association of Jesuit University Presses

Contents

Preface to Volume 1

It was with some reluctance that I began in 1991 to edit many of my previously published essays, in response to requests from students and others that these papers be made more accessible. But then Andrew Tallon of Marquette University Press approached me and asked whether he could publish a collection of my articles, and then I knew that the work of editing them had not been in vain. I am very grateful.

Reviews of *Theology and the Dialectics of History* (Toronto: University of Toronto Press, 1990) and some of the responses I have received to the book in letters from readers and in comments from students have asked for further clarification on the crucial theorem of psychic conversion, and especially on its history in my thinking, and for further data that would enable readers to relate my position on society and culture to other social and hermeneutical theories. The essays in this first volume (except for the short paper with which the book concludes) trace the development of the notion of psychic conversion through the 1970s, and most of those in volume 2 show the shift to social concerns that occupied much of my attention in the 980s. As most reviewers of *Theology and the Dialectics of History* have seen, the link between the psychological and social dimensions of the book is intimate. The whole of my position on the structure of society and culture hangs or falls on the affirmation of intentionality and psyche as distinct but inseparable dimensions of human interiority.

Very relevant to the topic of this first volume is the recent discovery of an important paper by Bernard Lonergan, 'Philosophy and the Religious Phenomenon.' In this paper Lonergan affirms, not four, not even five, but six levels of consciousness, extending the structure of his analysis of consciousness not only 'upwards' to being-in-love as a distinct level (something already at least hinted at in his published work), but also 'downwards' to the working of the 'symbolic operator,' which he relates to my work on psychic conversion. This paper helped to bolster my hope that my efforts over the years have been more than an idiosyncratic speculative adventure, that they in fact advance the movement begun by Lonergan to which I have committed a large part of my intellectual energy and time.

A word should be said about the general title of these two volumes. My choice of the title was deliberately provocative. 'Antifoundationalism' has much to recommend it, when the 'foundations' that are being repudiated are grounded in the 'modern self' as object of introspective awareness or conceptualization. However, I challenge anyone to demonstrate that Lonergan's 'subject' is susceptible to the charges brought against 'foundations' by thinkers who name themselves postmodern. There is a genuine sense of the word 'foundations,' and Lonergan has begun to unpack it. I hope that I am adding something to it here; that at least is certainly my intention.

At the same time, the title could be misleading. The volumes are really ess*ays in and about* the functional specialty of foundations. They do not claim in any way to be a full statement in that functional specialty. My own statement in foundations is published in a large book, *Theology and the Dialectics of History* (University of Toronto Press, 1990), and even that statement simply builds on and so presupposes what Lonergan has contributed to this functional specialty. I wished here, however, to avoid a title that begin *Essays in*, for reasons that I hope all will easily understand.

In some ways I am happy to have the chance to polish this material in issuing it in a new edition. I was embarrassed to discover how long it took me to avoid the use of exclusive language, and in these essays I rectify that mistake whenever I am speaking in direct discourse. Furthermore, I discovered in some of the earlier essays some imprecision in my understanding of the issue of immediacy and mediation, and this I have corrected. Other than the obvious editorial changes required to create a uniform format for all of the essays in these volumes and to make the footnotes internal to each volume, very few further changes have been made. I must ask readers to be patient with the repetitions that are inevitable in a collection of essays on related topics. I have added an occasional '1993 note' where I thought that later reflections were pertinent or that more recently realized implications had to be drawn.

One of the editorial conventions that I have adopted should be explained. Lonergan's In*sight* has recently been published in a revised and expanded edition as part of his Collected Works. The trustees of Lonergan's literary estate regard this edition as standard. However, we acknowledge that for a time many readers will be more familiar with the pagination of the second (1958) edition that has been reprinted many times, most recently in paperback by Harper & Row. So all quotations from *Insight* are from the Collected Works edition, but footnote references give the page numbers of the 1958 edition first, then those of the Collected Works edition.

I wish to thank each of the publications in which these essays originally appeared for granting permission to reissue them here. Further thanks, of course, have to be extended to my students over the past twenty years for keeping alive my hope that all of this work might be useful to others. Regis College and the Lonergan Research Institute have allowed me to devote some of my time to my own work, and some of this time was used to edit these essays. Marcela Dayao of the Lonergan Research Institute put most of these essays on computer and patiently acquiesced to my requests for several printings of some of them. Frederick Crowe called my attention to Lonergan's 'Philosophy and the Religious Phenomenon.' And as always my deepest gratitude is reserved for Bernard Lonergan himself. My hope is that the publication of these essays in a collected form may further his work and help make it more accessible to a wider public.

Robert M. Doran

Acknowledgments

The following articles are reprinted here with permission:

'Paul Ricoeur: Toward the Restoration of Meaning,' *Anglican Theological Review* 55:4 (1973) 443-58.

'Psychic Conversion,' *The Thomist* 41:2 (1977) 200-36.

'Subject, Psyche, and Theology's Foundations,' *The Journal of Religion* 57:3 (1977) 267-87; Copyright 1977 by The University of Chicago. All rights reserved.

'Aesthetics and the Opposites,' reprinted by permission of the publisher from *Thought* 52, No. 205 (January, 1977) 117-33. Copyright by Fordham University Press.

'Christ and the Psyche,' *Trinification of the World: A Festschrift in Honour of Frederick E. Crowe in Celebration of His 60th Birthday*, ed. Thomas A. Dunne and Jean-Marc Laporte (Toronto: Regis College Press, 1977) 112-43.

'The Theologian's Psyche: Notes toward a Reconstruction of Depth Psychology,' *Lonergan Workshop 1*, ed. Fred Lawrence (Missoula, MT: Scholars Press, 1978) 93-141.

'Dramatic Artistry in the Third Stage of Meaning,' *Lonergan Workshop 2*, ed. Fred Lawrence (Chico, CA: Scholars Press, 1981) 147-99.

'Aesthetic Subjectivity and Generalized Empirical Method,'
The Thomist 43:2 (1979) 257-78.

'Psyche, Evil, and Grace,' *Communio* 6:2 (1979) 192-211.

'Jungian Psychology and Lonergan's Foundations: A Methodological Proposal,' *Journal of the American Academy of Religion* 47:1, Supplement (1979) 23-45.

'Jungian Psychology and Christian Spirituality,' three articles, *Review for Religious* 38:4-6 (1979) 497-510, 742-52, 857-66.

'Primary Process and the "Spiritual Unconscious,"' *Lonergan Workshop* 5, ed. Fred Lawrence (Chico, CA: Scholars Press, 1985) 23-47.

'Affect, Affectivity,' *The New Dictionary of Catholic Spirituality*, ed. Michael Downey (Collegeville, MN: The Liturgical Press, 1993) 12-14.

'Insight and Archetype' was not previously published, but underwent several revisions in the middle and late 1970s, and furnished the background for much of the material in chapter 20 of *Theology and the Dialectics of History* (Toronto: University of Toronto Press, 1990).

1 Paul Ricoeur: Toward the Restoration of Meaning

'I leave off all demands and listen.'

The philosopher Karl Jaspers recalls that Kierkegaard and Nietzsche both prophesied the emergence of an age of infinite reflection, an age in which everything is interpretation and 'anything can mean something else.'[1] Kierkegaard and Nietzsche were able so to prophesy because they knew themselves as exceptions in their own day, as precursors of this age, as *figurae* or archetypes concretely anticipating what was to become the widespread experience of their race.

The theologian John Dunne has similarly dubbed our time the 'age of apprehension,' an age in which any journey toward God must be traveled *through* and ultimately *beyond* the self.[2]

Philosophy for centuries has been gradually abandoning the study of the natural world around us to the physical and biological sciences, only to find itself ever more immersed in the task of interpreting human interiority.[3] The human sciences, at the same time, have developed conflicting approaches and conclusions, some reductive, some holistic. It appears safe to say that, given a prolonged future for our race, we still stand at the very beginning of the process of accumulating our knowledge and deepening our understanding of the inner resources, possibilities, and limits of human existence.

The almost universal influence of various critical techniques and our growing active familiarity with them have radically affected the state of religious belief in Western society. Our growing capacity for distinguishing the different patterns of our experience and cognitional awareness has had various results. For some it has sharpened the dimension appropriate to religious faith and enabled them to relate religious experience to profane life precisely by being able to distinguish the two more clearly. For others, however, it has removed this dimension altogether and revealed religion as well as conventional moralities and nonpluralistic approaches to knowledge to be culturally determined, adolescent human traits now quickly to be disposed of in favor of more mature pursuits. Religious apologists, instead of explicating the presuppositions of faith in the terms of a commonly accepted philosophy, find themselves rigorously laying bare the very possibility and pertinence of faith for an educated and sophisticated mind. And they realize that such a propaedeutic cannot be defensive; that is, it cannot violently condemn all of the understanding reached in reductive interpretations (e.g., Freudianism), which have too often demonstrated their explanatory value in certain areas. Nor can it avoid the charge of obscurantism if it fails to face the questions posed by these seemingly destructive systems of thought.

One believing person who has attempted to immerse himself in the contemporary intellectual scene and draw from it is the French philosopher Paul Ricoeur. In this essay I will try to present the problematic which Ricoeur defines and to expose his treatment of our problems of interpretation and religious belief.

1 The Notion of Philosophy and the Problem of Symbolism

Ricoeur approaches the contemporary intellectual and religious scene not as a theologian, nor as a psychologist, but as a philosopher. His treatment of religious symbolism figures as a part of a vast philosophical undertaking concerned with the task of delineating the essential structures of human existence and, more concretely, its limits and possibilities. Very roughly, we might say that the abstract structural analysis is the work of the earlier sections in his projected three-volume study of the philosophy of the will. These earlier sections are *Freedom and Nature: The Voluntary and the Involuntary*[4] and *Fallible Man*.[5] The beginnings of a more concrete study can, again roughly, be found in *The Symbolism of Evil*[6] and *Freud and Philosophy*.[7] In order to understand the significance of this concrete 'turn,' we must investigate how Ricoeur understands the philosophical task.

Ricoeur assumes that the work of René Descartes, for whom the positing of the existence of the thinking subject is a first truth which cannot and need not be verified or deduced, marks the beginning of a new tradition in philosophy. Ricoeur finds himself standing within this tradition, for which philosophy is primarily a matter of self-knowledge, of the self-appropriation of the subject.[8] But how is the self given up to philosophical reflection? Ricoeur maintains that the thinking subject is known only through the mediation of its expressions — ideas, actions, works, institutions, monuments. Philosophical reflection is to recover the act of existing, the *I am*, through reflection on the works of human beings. The *I* as such, as known, is not concretely given as an immediate datum of experience. Rather, knowledge of the self occurs only through a displacement of the home of meaning away from immediate consciousness, only through the understanding of the self's objectifications in knowledge, action, and culture.

The meaning of these objectifications or works, however, is not immediately evident nor is it univocal. Our self-expressions are capable of being variously interpreted. A privileged instance of this susceptibility to different interpretations is found in language. At least at the stage which his own thought had reached when he wrote his work on Freud, Ricoeur distinguished between those linguistic expressions which admit of only one interpretation and thus are univocal and those which contain a double meaning and thus, in this sense, are equivocal or, better, plurivocal.[9] The latter field he designates as the realm of symbolism.

If philosophy is the work of recovering in its concrete fullness the *I* at the heart of the *Cogito*, and if this retrieval can be accomplished only through the mediation of our self-expressions, philosophy must have recourse to symbols; that is, it must take as a distinct field of reflection the whole area of such expressions embracing multiple levels of meaning, and radically the area of symbolic language. Philosophy must thus become a matter of interpretation. 'I have decided to define, i.e., limit, the notions of symbol and interpretation through one another. Thus a symbol is a double-meaning linguistic expression that requires an interpretation, and interpretation is a work of understanding that aims at deciphering symbols.'[10]

2   The Conflict of Interpretations

The plurivocal nature of symbols consists in a relation of meaning to meaning. 'Symbols occur when language produces signs of composite degree in which the meaning, not satisfied with designating some one thing, designates another meaning attainable only in and through the first intentionality.'[11] Such double-meaning expressions are found in the hierophanies which are the object of study for the phenomenology of religion, in dreams, and in poetic images. Yet the power of symbolism, which *may* be rooted somewhere beyond or behind human language (e.g., in the cosmos itself or in the human psychic constitution), appears *as such* in speech. The task of interpretation is to reveal the richness or overdetermination of symbols and to demonstrate that symbols play a true role in discourse. The manifest meaning of a symbol points beyond itself to a second, latent meaning by a movement which thought can follow but never dominate. For example, the symbols figuring in any of the great religions enable the phenomenologist of religion to be drawn toward a given religion's conception of the sacred and its relation to humankind. Much of the work of a scholar such as Mircea Eliade is a matter of moving with the symbols and being drawn by them to a universe structured in a particular way and to a God or gods relating in a certain manner to the world as human beings experience it. It is the predominance of certain symbolic types, for example, which enables Eliade to distinguish religions of the 'eternal return' from religions of historically oriented 'faith.'[12] Thus the primary meaning moves us to a latent, symbolized meaning and intentionally assimilates us or draws us on to that second meaning. This process of assimilation is identified by Ricoeur as 'intentional analogy.'

As thinking becomes more concrete, it also becomes more dependent on symbols and thus more hermeneutical. Thus we may speak of a hermeneutic turn in Ricoeur's thought as he moves beyond the abstract analyses of the structures of human existence to an attempt to read human experience through a study of human expressions.[13] Such hermeneutic phenomenology differs from the neutral analyses of his earlier works and of most other phe-

nomenology in that it intrinsically points beyond itself by
means of a 'wager' which shatters the descriptive neutral-
ity of most phenomenological work. 'I wager that I shall
have a better understanding of man and the bond between
the being of man and the being of all beings if I follow the
indication of symbolic thought.'¹⁴ This wager is acknowledged again in *Freud and Philosophy*, with specific reference to the phenomenology of religion. The latter is secretly animated by an intention, a series of philosophical
decisions which lie hidden even within its apparent neu-
trality, a rational faith which employs a phenomenological
hermeneutics as an instrument for achieving the restoration of meaning which he refers to as a 'second naivete.'
Thus the implicit intention of this hermeneutic phenomenology is 'an expectancy of a new Word, of a new tidings
of the Word.'¹⁵

It is in *The Symbolism of Evil* that Ricoeur begins his
attempt to read the constitution of symbolic language by
deciphering expression, language, and text. This work also
places the horizon for the dialectical conflict he will later
attempt to mediate in *Freud and Philosophy*, the nature of
which we have yet to examine. This horizon is the problem
of the unity of human language. It is this horizon that makes
phenomenology a matter of interpretation or hermeneutic,
because of the insistence on understanding human
experience by understanding human expressions in symbol
and myth. The latter rescue human feeling from silence
and confusion. But such interpretation remains phenomenological; it does not attempt to reach *behind* the symbols
for underlying determinants but rather attempts to follow
them *forward*, to follow their indications. 'Symbols alone
give what they say.'¹⁶ 'The symbol gives rise to thought.'¹⁷
To interpret symbols phenomenologically is to reenact
them in sympathetic imagination, not through an immediate belief but through the recovery of the intentionality

of the symbol. To reenact a myth through an immediate belief would be to accept the myth as *explanatory* or etiological. To reenact it by sympathetically immersing oneself in its implicit intentionality, however, is to accept it as *exploratory*, as interpretative of us, our destiny, and our place in the cosmos.[18] It is to accept mystery. It is to 'elevate the symbols to the rank of existential concepts.'[19] This is not to say that the cosmic significance which the symbol intends is actually *given* in the symbol. If this were the case, the symbol would cease to be a symbol. Symbols are intentions without fulfillments. (This limitation will be extremely important when we discuss the more concrete reflection on religious symbols which begins from their dialectical unity-in-tension. This will be clarified in the next section.)

The phenomenology of religion may proceed either by analyzing the inherent structures of symbols and myths, or by relating them to one another either in an evolutionary perspective or by showing relations of transposition. An example of the latter is the way in which Ricoeur shows, in the last chapter of *The Symbolism of Evil*, the relations of opposition and identity between the Adamic myth and the other myths of evil. In either case three philosophical decisions are made: first, the accent is put on the *object* of investigation; second, a certain *fullness* of symbol is emphasized; third, the *intention* is that one may 'finally greet the revealing power of the primal word.'[20]

Regarding the first decision, namely, placing the emphasis on the object of investigation, the phenomenology of religion aims at disengaging the object in myth, ritual, and belief rather than discovering psychological and sociological determinants of religious behavior. The second decision, that is, emphasizing the fullness of symbol, is based on a rational faith that symbols point beyond themselves to a second meaning, *giving* what they say. This im-

plies that I who interpret am bound up in the relation of
immediate meaning to latent meaning, that I participate
in what is announced to me through the symbol. Thus the
third decision, that is, the intention to greet the revealing
power of the primal word, manifests a new desire to be
addressed and renders the phenomenology of religion a
preparation for the revelation of meaning.[21]

Several recent and very influential schools of thought,
however, forcibly impress upon us that there is a second
kind of relationship which may exist between manifest and
latent meaning. The manifest meaning may stand in a relationship not of intentional analogy, but of 'cunning distortion' to the latent meaning, that is, a relationship of
dissimulation, mystification, and illusion. In the case of
Freud, for example, the primary meaning of a symbol is a
dissimulation of basic, unsurpassable desire or instinct. The
task of psychoanalytic interpretation is, not the discovery
of a further reality beyond the symbol, a reality toward
which the symbol draws us by its own movement, but rather
the reduction of the illusion effected in consciousness by
the manifest meaning of such an expression. Religious
symbols which would lead a phenomenologist of religion
to a particular religion's concept of the sacred would be,
for psychoanalysis, but another manifestation of the
'universal obsessional neurosis of mankind' known as
religion.

These two possibilities thus give rise to conflicting
styles of interpretation, the polar extremes of which Ricoeur
calls 'the hermeneutics of suspicion' and 'the hermeneutics
of recovery.' If philosophy's task, the concrete understanding of the *I* at the heart of the *Cogito* through the mediation of our self-expressions, is to be possible at all, then
the philosopher must not only have recourse to hermeneutics — since many of these expressions are symbolic —
but must also settle the question of whether this

hermeneutic conflict can be resolved. Is one's only choice to be an option between these two styles, an option seemingly arbitrary and thus perhaps itself determined not by the exigences of disinterested inquiry or rigorous method but by the unconscious determinants of one's own psychic makeup? Or are there resources available to philosophic reflection itself which will enable a resolution or mediation of the internal variance within the field of interpretation? Is the alternative of conflicting styles definitive or provisional, real or illusory? Can philosophy discover, within the storehouse of resources properly its own, a means of resolving this tension? If not, the odds would seem to lie with the hermeneutics of suspicion, since *either* option in itself would appear arbitrary and thus itself an expression of unsurpassable instinct. The task of interpretation, and thus of the philosopher who recognizes the necessity of interpretation for the fulfillment of the reflective task, would be iconoclastic, purely and simply. The philosopher would thus 'purify discourse of its excrescences, liquidate the idols, go from drunkenness to sobriety, realize our state of poverty once and for all.'[22]

On the other hand, if the conflict can be mediated, the hermeneutics of suspicion would still remain but would be taken up into the task of recovery, which would then become, not a parallel task, exclusive of and opposed to that of demystification, but inclusive of the latter. The philosopher would then 'use the most "nihilistic," destructive, iconoclastic movement so as to *let speak* what once, what each time, was *said*, when meaning appeared anew, when meaning was at its fullest.'[23] The full act of recovery would thus be effected, not through a mere phenomenology of symbol, as in the phenomenology of religion, but by philosophical reflection in its fullest sense and in reliance upon a process of rigorous dialectic, which would include extreme iconoclasm as a moment in the restoration of meaning.

The latter possibility is favored by Ricoeur. By way of an overview of what will be exposed more fully in the remainder of this paper, we can make the following statements:

(1) With respect to symbolism and interpretation in general, Ricoeur finds the possibility of including the hermeneutics of suspicion within the hermeneutics of recovery to be grounded *objectively* in the *unity of the symbol.*

(2) As a philosophical act, it will be grounded *subjectively* in the essential role of *dialectic* within philosophical reflection. The task of philosophical reflection demands interpretation. But the hermeneutic war itself demands that reflection become also dialectic.

(3) The religious and profane spheres of meaning are to be sharply differentiated, but the interpretive, dialectical, and reflective tasks imposed by each will be analogous.

(4) With respect to the area of symbolism specifically and uniquely designated religious, the possibility of the mediation of the conflict is grounded *objectively* in the *ambiguity* of the unified sacred symbol (e.g., the eschatological symbols of Judaism and Christianity).

(5) With respect to the same area, this possibility is grounded *subjectively* in the *dialectical process* called for by such ambiguity, a process analogous to the dialectic demanded in the interpretation of profane symbolism. Thus the reflective thinker concerned with reopening a possibility of being addressed by the kerygmatic Word will take a cue from the philosopher concerned with the dialectical mediation of the hermeneutic conflict in general. The religious thinker must distinguish the expressions with which he or she is concerned from those other cultural symbols which occupy the philosopher, but the *process* of interpret-

ing the symbols of faith is analogous to the philosopher's process. Ultimately the religious thinker must move *beyond* the phenomenology of religion to a more inclusive, more complex, more dialectical mode of reflection. This process will ground both the validity of the phenomenology of religion and the viability of its implicit intention of hearing a new tidings of the Word. At the same time, however, it will incorporate the equally valid intention of demystifying hermeneutics, that of establishing the rootedness of manifest religious symbolism in the darkness of life and nature which surrounds the light of conscious awareness.

The domain peculiar to the symbolism of faith has not been immune from the attacks of the demystifiers. Nor must the religious thinker regard these attacks either as ultimately destructive intentions to be warded off or avoided at all costs, or as embarrassing revelations disclosing the ever-narrowing scope of his or her legitimate field of investigation and reflection. Rather, they can be assumed as invitations to appropriate the tension which expresses our modernity, to move beyond an anachronistic mode of reflection and expression constantly plagued by the temptation to obscurantism, to open the possibility to oneself and one's contemporaries for a post-critical encounter with the event of human speech which God has, for faith, become. The religious thinker can release the possibility for the twice-born person of modernity to hear the language of a call in which 'I leave off all demands and listen.'[24]

3　Dialectic and the Concrete Unity of Symbols

The hermeneutic task cannot remain at a phenomenological level, because of the mighty invasion into contemporary thought of the hermeneutics of suspicion. This conflicting style of interpretation reverses the three decisions made by the phenomenologist of religion. The focus of concern becomes, not the object, but the underlying determinants of human expression and behavior. The latent meaning behind human expression is not to be discovered by a movement *forward* from the expression but by a movement *back* to the realms of unsurpassable instinctual desire (as in Freud) or economic determination (as in Marx) lying behind and determining the mendacious deliverances of consciousness.[25] The intention of the phenomenology of religion to be spoken to anew by the Wholly Other is reversed in such descriptions of religion as 'the universal obsessional neurosis of mankind' or 'the opium of the people.' Such a stance, at face value, is radically opposed to the non-dialectical restoration of meaning characteristic of the phenomenology of religion. Any attempt at mediation of this controversy must be dialectical. Ultimately, as most dialectic, it must resolve not only differences in standpoint and correlative content but also differences in the underlying decisions which determine one's standpoint. Such dialectic thus will prepare the philosopher or reflective religious thinker to effect another decision which will give him or her a more inclusive standpoint. If such dialectic is possible, then the radical doubt of the hermeneutics of suspicion may prove to be beneficial and even indispensable for mature, post-critical religious belief. Whereas reflection, the recovery of the *I* at the heart of the *I think*, had to have recourse to interpretation, the hermeneutic war can be arbitrated only by a return to an expanded, dialectical, reflective critique of interpretations. While such reflection is expanded it is also more concrete, for it penetrates more profoundly into the effort to exist and the desire to be which reflection must appropriate through human expressions.

The key to such concrete reflection is found in the *unity of the symbol*. Our symbols reveal a concrete unity-intension in which the two apparently diverging lines of interpretation actually intersect. The tension which characterizes our modernity is the awareness of the unity-in-tension found in our symbols. For us to be able to think in accord with symbols, to follow their indications, we must subject them to a dialectic, discovering the intersection of diverging interpretations. Then we can return to the attitude of listening, to 'the fullness of speech simply heard and understood.'[26]

The tension localized in the mixed texture of concrete symbols is a tension of archeology and teleology. The hermeneutics of suspicion is archeological in intention. Freudian psychoanalysis, for example, provides us with an archeology of the subject. It displaces meaning away from immediate consciousness, not *ahead* toward a fuller meaning analogically bound to the meaning revealed in naive awareness, but *behind*, toward the unconscious. It is this meaning which Freudian discourse captures in interpretation, the meaning of our ultimately unknowable instincts as these are designated in our psychic lives by the ideas and the affects that represent them — for example, by dreams and neuroses, by ideals and illusions. Freud's analyses reveal the archaic, ever prior, ultimately timeless character of desire and instinct. We are drawn backward, by a detemporalizing agency, to a destiny in reverse. The muteness of such desire can be spoken only through mechanistic energy metaphors. Philosophical reflection learns from Freudian analysis that knowledge is rooted in desire and effort, and that an epistemology which studies our representations as correlative to the represented objects, no matter how 'critical' such an epistemology may be, must be supplemented by an exegesis of the desires and instincts which conscious intentionality deceptively hides from our view. It is because such desire not only is hidden but also interferes with intelligent inquiry that truth is, not a given, but a task.

But Freud's very pursuit of the *truth* concerning the mute darkness of desire, the image of his *performance* and of his own acceptance of truth as a task for him as scientist and analyst, itself should be enough to lead the philosopher to ask whether our effort to be does not reveal a further vector, a direction forward toward a goal, a second displacement of meaning away from naive awareness, but in a teleological direction. The inconsistency between Freud's *account* and his *performance* leads one to suspect suspicion. The philosopher places the concept of archeology in dialectical opposition to that of teleology. When one does so, one's reflection becomes concrete. One will discover this dialectical opposition in our symbols, myths, and rituals, and when one does so one will realize that the hermeneutic war can be resolved. The reflective thinker, instructed by the demystifying archeology of Freudian reduction and by the progressive synthesis of the forward movement of our effort to exist, returns to the spoken word and hears it, not irrationally and precritically, but as one twice-born, with an informed naivete.[27] Symbols coordinate in a concrete unity-in-tension two functions previously assumed to be opposed to one another. They repeat our childhood and the childhood of our race, but they also serve to explore our adult life.[28] Authentic symbols are regressive-progressive, archeological-teleological. Their intentional structure unifies the functions of concealing and showing, disguising and revealing. While they conceal the aims of our instincts, they disclose the process of self-consciousness.

> Disguise, reveal; conceal, show; these two functions are no longer external to one another; they express the two sides of a single symbolic function of meaning occurs only in the sphere of

the projections of desire, of the derivatives of the unconscious, of the revivals of archaism ... The opposed hermeneutics disjoin and decompose what concrete reflection recomposes through a return to speech simply heard and understood.[29]

4   The Uniqueness of Sacred Symbolism and the Death of the Religious Object

Ricoeur does not allow that his method of philosophical reflection will give us more than a frontier view of the domain of religious symbolism. In a somewhat Barthian manner he insists that even the very existence of a problematic of faith exceeds the resources of philosophical reflection. Such a problematic occurs in another dimension, that of call, kerygma, word addressed to me.

But the movement of faith toward understanding is a movement of the interpretation of events of speech, and thus must encounter a dialectic of reflection. God can be recognized by us only in the interpretation of the event of human speech which God has become. To believe is to listen to the call, but to hear this call we must interpret the message. Thus, in Anselmian fashion, we must believe in order to understand, and understand in order to believe.

God thus becomes discernible in and through a dialectic of archeology and teleology. As radical origin, God becomes discernible in the *question* of my archeology, and as ultimate goal in the *question* of my teleology.[30] Philosophical reflection itself can never assume creation and eschatology, as acts of the divine, to be any more than the horizon of its explorations of archeology and teleology. They are not fixed possessions of reflective thought, as Hegel tried to maintain. Philosophical reflection can never become absolute knowledge. The reason for this lies in the very fact which gives rise to the problematic of faith, the fact of evil. Evil will never be dissolved in dialectic. As such, it is unsurpassable, inscrutable.

The problematic of faith thus shows God to be discernible in a third way, a way not pointed to specifically by the dialectic of reflection but rather by the impossibility of the progress of reflection to the point of absolute knowledge. God becomes discernible in the *question* of evil, together with and in the symbols of reconciliation and deliverance, which qualify the manner in which eschatology is the horizon of the question of my teleology and of the teleology of the figures of the human spirit in the works of culture.

These symbols of creation, eschatology, and redemption stand today in the same need of a demystifying hermeneutics as do the symbols of culture and ethics, and the dreams, fantasies, and ideals of the individual subject. The phenomenology of religion must enter into a dialectical relationship with the psychoanalysis of religion and other forms of reductive interpretation, and this for the sake of the very authenticity of faith. For the human spirit tends, through a misconception of what it means to know,[31] to reabsorb transcendence in immanence, to transform horizon into an object which we possess and use, and to create idols rather than be content with signs of the sacred. Thus a naive metaphysics, for all its protestations to the contrary, can appear to know more about what God is than about what God is not, and religion can treat the sacred as a new sphere of objects, institutions, and powers alongside those of the economic, political, and cultural spheres. Religion becomes the reification and alienation of faith, vulnerable to the blows of a hermeneutics of suspicion, whether the latter be a process of demythologization from within religion or of demystification from without. In either case, the aim is the death of the metaphysical and religious 'object.'

Such a cultural movement, as exemplified in Freudianism, is necessary if we are to hear and read the signs of the approach of the Wholly Other. We are faced with a never-ending task of distinguishing between faith and religion — faith in the Wholly Other which draws near and belief in the religious object. The task is very difficult and demanding, mainly because it calls for such a merciless exegesis of our own reference to the sacred. Do we allow religious symbols to point to the horizon of transcendence and to do *only* this, or do we make them an idolatrous reality purely immanent to our culture and thus render them ineffective?

5 Conclusion

The task demanded by Ricoeur is particularly difficult, I believe, for one committed to the possibility of authentic sacramentality, who must at the same time admit that many of the ritual practices within his or her own community reflect indeed at least a 'universal obsessional neurosis of mankind' if not a demonic objectifying of the sacred. To speak at least of the tradition which is my own, sacramental religions are prone to the tendency to reify the sacred and capitulate to our idolizing tendencies. The combat over the sacred will necessarily be heated, it would seem, in those religious communities where, because of an insistence on sacramentality, the ambiguity of the sacred is pronounced.

The task set by Ricoeur is very demanding in another realm too, namely, that of creating a sufficiently nuanced relationship between faith and culture, religious communities and public life, authentic religion and profane institutions. Particularly in this area there is a strong tendency to objectify and use the sacred for the pursuit of goals which are not connected with the problematic of faith. 'The idols must die so that symbols may live.'[32]

The psychoanalysis of religion can be one of the roads toward the death of the religious object. It can aid us in charging the affective dynamism of religious belief to the point where the latter becomes, not simply the consolation of the child in us, but the adult power of loving in the face of hatred and death. It can help us discern that kerygmatic faith excludes a narrowly 'moral' God and a penal Christology.[33] It forces us to acknowledge that every symbol of the sacred is also and at the same time a revival of an infantile and archaic symbol, and thus to admit the ambiguity of all religious symbolism and religious experience. It can aid us in moving toward the suspension of the ethical point of view, moving beyond an ethics of righteousness, losing the immediate consolation of our own narcissism. It can purify the hermeneutics of faith to the point where the latter becomes unambiguously the symbolic exploration of ultimate relationships, of the language of a call in which 'I leave off all demands and listen.'[34] It is indeed true that the faith of the believer cannot emerge intact from such a confrontation.[35] On the other hand, Ricoeur seems to provide a solid basis for claiming that, despite the supposed origin of religious symbols in instinctual impulses, their present meaning cannot be exhausted by presenting their archeology. 'The question here is not whether a given religious symbol is genetically a psychological projection, but rather whether, irrespective of its being such a projection, what it expresses analogically discloses a genuine aspect of reality.'[36]

Finally, in a critical vein, it seems to me that three questions must be posed to Ricoeur concerning his procedure and his conclusions. These questions are posed from the standpoint of one who maintains that Bernard Lonergan's cognitional analysis[37] provides us with an invariant structure of human consciousness; that his theory of objectivity is correct (a theory missed by all of phenomenology to date, I believe); and that his later studies on meaning enable us to raise a question as to whether *understanding*, rather than language, ought to be the area where all philosophical (and theological) investigations cut across one another. These questions are by no means meant to minimize the critical significance of Ricoeur's work for philosophy and theology. Rather, they raise the possibility of a further intersubjective approximation to truth by comparing Ricoeur's problematic with that of Lonergan.

First, granted the validity of the transcendental method, that is, of deducing a priori conditions for various domains of human experience, does not this method become truly transcendental only when the *self-evident necessity* and *universality* of certain a priori structures of human consciousness are found? I am not referring here to certain logical laws,[38] such as the principles of contradiction or sufficient reason, but to the possibility of arriving at a pattern and structure of human awareness which is in principle not subject to revision. This, I would maintain, Lonergan has done with invincible forcefulness in arriving at the 'levels' of experience, understanding, judgment, and decision.[39]

Secondly, must we say that our only knowledge of transcendence is symbolic, that every attempt to know the transcendent realm in another way is inevitably idolatrous? Here Ricoeur displays a perceptualist notion of objectivity, according to which objectivity is achieved as a result of doing something analogous to 'taking a look.' Objectivity is a correlate of conceptualization for Ricoeur. But if objectivity is rather a function of judgment (e.g., the judgment 'God is'), can we not say that God is an object of nonsymbolic knowing that is not idolatrous?

Finally, what is the normative status of linguistic usage for philosophy? Is not meaning at least logically prior to language, and are not its structures independent of the contingencies of actual language? Is not actual language a vehicle of meaning rather than its logical presupposition?[40] Is not meaning a matter for understanding more radically than for language? Does not the emphasis on understanding provide philosophy with a starting point that transcends dependence on actual usage?

To repeat, these questions are not aimed against the basic thrust of Ricoeur's effort. His intention is noble, his conception of what it entails accurate, his achievement admirable. We should eagerly await the realization of his promise that there is more to come. At the same time, too, I believe we can find in Ricoeur's thought significant pointers to areas in which Lonergan's work on theological method is in need of expansion and development. I am referring particularly to the area of symbolic consciousness. In fact, the second naivete which Ricoeur's philosophy demonstrates to be both possible and desirable indicates, I believe, the region of a fourth *conversion* necessary for the foundations of theology, beyond the intellectual, moral, and religious conversions specified by Lonergan. This fourth conversion I would name 'psychic.' As a result of it, one's theological categories, positions, and system can be highly symbolic in nature; a 'poetics of the will,' such as that envisaged by Ricoeur, would be a genuine part of systematic theology as such.

Ricoeur seems to imply that philosophy is capable of *effecting* such a second immediacy by drawing upon its own resources. This I question. Philosophy by itself is not therapeutic in nature. Rather, through its work of disengaging transcendental structures, it can indicate the *possibility* of such a 'conversion.' This is precisely what Ricoeur has done. I take his work as a significant contribution to the delineation of the foundations of theology and thus to theological method as a whole.

Notes

1 Karl Jaspers, *Reason and Existenz*, trans. William Earle (New York: Noonday Press, 1968) 31.

2 See John Dunne, *A Search for God in Time and Memory* (New York: Macmillan, 1967).

3 See Bernard Lonergan, *Method in Theology* (New York: Herder and Herder, 1972) 95. A 1990 reprint has been issued by University of Toronto Press. A critical edition will be published by the same Press as vol. 12 in Collected Works of Bernard Lonergan.

4 Paul Ricoeur, *Freedom and Nature: The Voluntary and the Involuntary*, trans. Erazim Kohak (Evanston: Northwestern University Press, 1966). 1993 note: Ricoeur's hermeneutic theory developed considerably beyond the works considered in this 1973 essay. I am limiting myself here to his earlier work and focusing especially on his encounter with Freud, which was significant in my development of the notion of psychic conversion. See also chapter 3 of Robert M. Doran, *Subject and Psyche*, 2nd rev. ed. (Milwaukee: Marquette University Press, 1994).

5 Paul Ricoeur, *Fallible Man*, trans. Charles Kelbley (Chicago: Regnery, 1965).

6 Paul Ricoeur, *The Symbolism of Evil*, trans. Emerson Buchanan (Boston: Beacon, 1969). *Fallible Man* and *The Symbolism of Evil* form vol. 2 of Ricoeur's philosophy of the will. Vol. 3 on the poetics of the will is as yet unfinished.

7 Paul Ricoeur, *Freud and Philosophy: An Essay on Interpretation*, trans. Denis Savage (New Haven: Yale University Press, 1970).

8 'I assume here that the positing of the self is the first truth for the philosopher placed within the broad tradition of modern philoso-

phy that begins with Descartes and is developed in Kant, Fichte, and the reflective stream of European philosophy. For this tradition, which we shall consider as a whole before setting its main representatives in opposition to one another, the positing of the self is a truth which posits itself; it can be neither verified nor deduced; it is at once the positing of a being and of an act; the positing of an existence and of an operation of thought: *I am, I think*; to exist, for me, is to think; I exist inasmuch as I think.' Ibid. 43.

9 Ricoeur's later development has moved in the direction of acknowledging all language as symbolic. See Don Ihde, *Hermeneutic Phenomenology: The Philosophy of Paul Ricoeur* (Evanston: Northwestern University Press, 1971).

10 Ricoeur, *Freud and Philosophy* 9.

11 Ibid. 16.

12 Mircea Eliade, *Cosmos and History: The Myth of the Eternal Return*, trans. Willard R. Trask (New York: Harper & Row, 1959). See especially chapter 4.

13 This is the approach through which Ihde (see above, note 9) studies Ricoeur.

14 Ricoeur, *The Symbolism of Evil* 355.

15 Ricoeur, *Freud and Philosophy* 31.

16 Ibid.

17 Ricoeur, *The Symbolism of Evil* 347; *Freud and Philosophy* 38.

18 See *The Symbolism of Evil* 5.

19 Ibid. 357.

20 Ricoeur, *Freud and Philosophy* 32.

21 Ibid.

22 Ibid. 27.

23 Ibid.

24 Ibid. 551.

25 It cannot be denied that this is a gross oversimplification of Marx. However, it is only under this rubric that Ricoeur mentions Marx in this discussion. While he groups Freud, Marx, and Nietzsche together under the heading of the hermeneutics of suspicion, it is only Freud whom he here studies in detail.

26 Ricoeur, *Freud and Philosophy* 496.

27 Ibid.

28 For a detailed presentation of a corroborating theory from a Jungian perspective see Erich Neumann, *The Origins and History of Consciousness*, trans. R.F.C. Hull (Princeton: Princeton University Press, 1971).

29 Ricoeur, *Freud and Philosophy* 497.

30 Compare the discussions in the last two chapters of John Dunne, *A Search for God in Time and Memory*. See above, note 2.

31 At this point I am moving beyond Ricoeur, who locates the problem simply in our objectifying tendencies, to Bernard Lonergan, who maintains that the problem is that we misconceive what objectivity is. See below, Conclusion.

32 Ricoeur, *Freud and Philosophy* 531.

33 That theology is capable of such discernment apparently drawing almost exclusively upon its own resources is clear from Bernard Lonergan, *De Verbo incarnato* (Rome: Gregorian University Press, 1964) 486-593. An edited version, with English translation, will appear as vol. 8 in Collected Works of Bernard Lonergan.

34 Ricoeur, *Freud and Philosophy* 551.

[35] Ibid.

[36] Stuart C. Hackett, 'Philosophical Objectivity and Existential Involvement in the Methodology of Paul Ricoeur,' *International Philosophical Quarterly* 9 (March, 1969) 31.

[37] See Bernard Lonergan, *Insight: A Study of Human Understanding*, vol. 3 of Collected Works of Bernard Lonergan (Toronto: University of Toronto Press, 1992).

[38] Hackett would like to move this objection in this direction. To do so, I believe, is to miss the point really demanded in response to Ricoeur's insistence that reflective philosophy itself is so culturally relative that no objective certainty can be had regarding its deliverances about the *constitution* of the self.

[39] See Lonergan, *Insight*, chapters 11 and 18.

[40] This is the most cogent of the objections raised by Hackett. See p. 36 of the article referred to above in note 36. Lonergan has dealt masterfully with the question in *Method in Theology* 254-57.

2 Psychic Conversion[1]

In a recent book symptomatic and expressive of the contemporary drama of existential and religious subjectivity, psychiatrist Claudio Naranjo speaks of creating 'a unified science of human development,'[2] 'a unified science and art of human change.'[3] He attempts to disengage from the diverse techniques, exercises, and procedures of education, psychotherapy, and religion an experimental meeting ground based on a unity of concern and a common method. The various ways of growth which he examines—ranging from behavior therapy to Sufism—are, he says, contributions to *a single process of human transformation* involving (1) shift in identity, (2) increased contact with reality, (3) simultaneous increase in both participation and detachment, (4) simultaneous increase in freedom and the ability to surrender, (5) unification—intrapersonal, interpersonal, between body and mind, subject and object, human persons and God, (6) increased self-acceptance, and (7) increase in consciousness.[4] He concludes his book with the following summary of his position:

> The end-state sought by the various traditions, schools, or systems under discussion is one that is characterized by *the experience* of openness to the reality of every moment, freedom from mechanical ties to the past, and surrender to the laws of man's being, one of living in the body

and yet in control of the body, in the world and yet in control of circumstances by means of the power of both awareness and independence. It is also an experience of self-acceptance, where 'self' does not stand for a preconceived notion or image but is the experiential self-reality moment after moment. Above all, it is an *experience of experiencing*. For this is what consciousness means, what openness means, what surrendering leads into, what remains after the veils of conditioned perception are raised, and what the aim of acceptance is.[5]

My argument in this paper is twofold: first, that Bernard Lonergan's analysis of conscious intentionality not only constitutes an essential contribution to the foundational quest of a unified science and art of human change, but also provides perhaps the most embracing overall framework offered to date for the development of such a theory-praxis; and second, that the exigence for self-appropriation recognized and heeded by Lonergan, when it extends to the existential subject, to what Lonergan would regard as the fourth level of intentional consciousness, becomes an exigence for psychic self-appropriation, calling for the release of what C.G. Jung calls the transcendent function, the mediation of psyche with intentionality in an intrasubjective collaboration heading toward individuation. The release of the transcendent function is a fourth conversion, beyond the religious, moral, and intellectual conversions specified by Lonergan. I call it psychic conversion. It aids the sublation of intellectually self-appropriating consciousness by moral and religious subjectivity, and thus is an intrinsic dimension of the foundational reality whose objectification constitutes foundations in theology.

The seven characteristics of human transformation listed by Naranjo may be considered as potential effects in part of psychic conversion. But its immanent intelligibility is something different. It is the gaining of a capacity on the part of the existential subject to disengage the symbolic and archetypal constitution of moral and religious subjectivity. At a given stage in the self-appropriation of intentional consciousness, the intention of value or of the human good must come to participate in an ongoing conspiracy with the psycho-symbolic dimensions of human subjectivity. The attempt to objectify this conspiracy will result in a position complementary and compensatory to that of Lonergan and compensatory to that of Jung. First, the kind of psychotherapy inspired can and must be moved into the epochal movement of the human spirit disengaged in Lonergan's transcendental method. Only such a context preserves the genuine intentionality of Jungian psychotherapy. Secondly, however, the dynamism of transcendental method extends to this further domain of psychic self-appropriation. The finality of the methodical exigence is therapeutic. I shall begin by explicating this latter claim. Then I shall argue that intellectual conversion as articulated by Lonergan is the beginning of a response to this therapeutic exigence. In the third and fourth sections of this paper, I will speak of the psychic dimensions of the self-appropriation of moral and religious subjectivity. I will conclude with an argument for the constitutive function of the psyche in the existential subjectivity whose self-appropriation constitutes a portion of foundations in theology.

1   The Therapeutic Exigence

I assume as given an appreciation of the meaning of the term 'method' advanced by Lonergan: 'method' has

not to do with the Cartesian universal procedure for the
attainment of certitude by following fixed rules while ne-
glecting bursts of insight, moral truth, belief, and hypothesis; 'method' takes as its key the subject as subject and
thus calls for 'release from all logics, all closed systems or
language games, all concepts, all symbolic constructs to
allow an abiding at the level of the presence of the subject
to himself';[6] 'method' is horizon inviting authenticity.

I presuppose also that the dialectical-foundational
thinking which issues from such a horizon is a movement
qualitatively different from that which occupied the main-
stream of Western philosophy from Socrates to Hegel. This
latter movement seeks a control of meaning in terms of
system. It is the movement of the emergence of *logos* from
mythos, of theoretically differentiated consciousness from
an undifferentiated and precritically symbolic mentality.
This theoretic movement may archetypally be designated
heroic, in that it is the severing *in actu exercito* of the umbilical cord binding mind to maternal imagination. It
achieved its first secure triumph in the Aristotelian refinement of Socrates' insistence on *omni et soli* definitions. It
may have pronounced its full coming of age as creative
and constitutive in its Hegelian self-recognition as essentially dialectical, in its self-identification with the dialectic
of reality itself, and in a *Wissenschaft der Logik* which would
be the thinking of its own essence in and for itself on the
part of this dialectical movement of reality as *Geist*. That
Lonergan's articulation of method, with its key being the
subject as subject, captures in a radically foundational
manner the structure and dynamism of a new moment of
the historical Western mind, an epochal shift in the control and constitution of meaning, has not gone unnoticed
and is not a novel appreciation of his significance.[7] Thus
to propose to complement what can only be considered

an unparalleled achievement surely calls for more than a polite apology. Perhaps I can begin, then, by recalling that Lonergan himself acknowledges a twofold mediation of immediacy by meaning. The first is that which has occupied his attention throughout his career as scholar, teacher, and author, that which occurs 'when one objectifies cognitional process in transcendental method.' The second occurs 'when one discovers, identifies, accepts one's submerged feelings in psychotherapy.'[8] This statement would seem to imply that there are two modes or dimensions, however inseparable and interrelated, of our immediacy to ourselves, our consciousness or self-presence, in the world mediated by meaning. There is our experience of ourselves as cognitional, and there is our experience of ourselves as dispositional. These two modes, moreover, would seem to correspond more or less closely to the two primordial constitutive ways of being 'there' according to Martin Heidegger: *Verstehen* and *Befindlichkeit*.[9] They are interlocking modalities of self-presence. But Lonergan speaks not only of the mediation of these two modalities of immediacy, but also of 'a withdrawal from objectification and a mediated return to immediacy in the mating of lovers and in the prayerful mystic's cloud of unknowing.'[10] One way of formulating my question is as follows: Is this mediated return to immediacy, this second immediacy, exhausted by these two instances? Might there be a more than transient state that corresponds to this description, and that is connected with the twofold mediation of immediacy by meaning? And is it possible that both of these mediations are required if one is to approximate this state, that the mediation of cognitional or intentional process alone is not sufficient, that it must be complemented by a mediation of dispositional immediacy?

Any human subject whose world is mediated and
constituted by meaning is primordially in a condition of
immediacy to oneself as cognitional and dispositional in
that world: an immediacy to 'understanding,' that is to
cognitional process, and an immediacy to mood. The second mode of immediacy is accessible to conscious intentionality in the ever-present flow of feeling which is part
and parcel of one's concomitant awareness of oneself in
all of one's intentional operations. 'In every case Dasein
always has some mood.'[11] This dispositional immediacy is
often what we intend when we ask another, 'How are you?'
'The mood has already disclosed, in every case, Being-in-
the-world as a whole, and makes it possible first of all to
direct oneself towards something.'[12] It is this mode of immediacy that is objectified in the second mediation of immediacy by meaning, that which occurs, among other instances, in psychotherapy. What is insufficiently acknowledged by Heidegger,[13] more than hinted at by Lonergan,
and trumpeted by Jung, is that this dispositionally qualified immediacy is always imaginally constructed, symbolically constituted. Image and affect are inseparable dimensions of the undertow of psychic movement. In every case
the movement of affectivity has a symbolic significance.
But this imaginal constitution is not accessible to conscious
intentionality in the same way as is the disposition itself.
The symbolic constitution of immediacy must be disengaged by such psychotherapeutic techniques as dream interpretation and what Jung calls 'active imagination.' It is
'unconscious,' that is, undifferentiated. But when disengaged it reveals how it stands between the attitude of waking consciousness and the totality of subjectivity. This disengagement is effected by the release of the transcendent
function, by psychic conversion.[14] The dynamic structure
of the transformation of *Befindlichkeit* issuing from this
release must be integrated into the epochal movement of

consciousness effected in Lonergan's objectification of the structure of human intentionality. Its implications for theological method must be stated. Furthermore, its complementary function with respect to the objectification of intentionality will allow for the construction of a model of self-appropriation as a mediation of both the intentional and the psychic dimensions of human interiority. Self-appropriation heads toward a second immediacy, which is always only asymptotically approached. It consists of three stages: intentional self-appropriation as articulated by Lonergan; psychic self-appropriation through the release of the transcendent function, facilitating the sublation of intellectually self-appropriating consciousness by moral subjectivity; and religious self-appropriation and self-surrender of both discriminated intentionality and cultivated psyche to the *mysterium tremendum et fascinans* in the sublation of both intellectual and moral self-consciousness by differentiated religious subjectivity.[15]

Perhaps the complementary function of this model with respect to Lonergan's may be illustrated by commenting on the following statement:

> I should urge that religious conversion, moral conversion, and intellectual conversion are three quite different things. In an order of exposition I would prefer to explain first intellectual, then moral, then religious conversion. In the order of occurrence I would expect religious commonly but not necessarily to precede moral and both religious and moral to precede intellectual. Intellectual conversion, I think, is very rare.[16]

Surely there is no dispute that the three conversions are quite different events or processes. Nor need there be any argument with Lonergan's preferred order of exposition. But there may be qualifications introduced to modify some of the overtones of the assertion that, in the general case, intellectual conversion is the last and the rarest of the conversions; that, in the general case, the intellectually converted subject is the fully converted subject. In fact, the assertion is modified considerably by a further statement of the relations of sublation obtaining among the three conversions in a single consciousness. For the sublations occur in a reverse order. And sublation is understood, not in a Hegelian fashion with its intrinsic element of negativity, but along the lines suggested by Karl Rahner. 'What sublates goes beyond what is sublated, introduces something new and distinct, puts everything on a new basis, yet so far from interfering with the sublated or destroying it, on the contrary needs it, includes it, preserves all its proper features and properties, and carries them forward to a fuller realization within a richer context.'[17] On Lonergan's account, then, intellectual conversion is, in the general case, sublated by a moral conversion which has preceded it in the order of occurrence and to this extent is precritical; and both intellectual and moral conversion are sublated by a religious conversion which has preceded them and is also to this extent precritical.

But if religious conversion and moral conversion precede intellectual conversion, it would seem that, no matter how genuinely religious and authentically moral, they are infected with the cognitional myth that the real is a subdivision of what is known by extroverted looking. More precisely, precritical religious and moral conversion affect a consciousness which, from the standpoint of the cognitive function of meaning, is either undifferentiated or has achieved at best a theoretical differentiation. But beyond the common sense and theoretical differentiations of consciousness there is the exigence for differentiation in terms of interiority, the satisfaction of which is initiated by the elimination of cognitional myth which occurs in the movement toward what Lonergan calls intellectual conversion. Lonergan's account would seem to imply, then, that a consciousness in the process of fidelity to this critical and methodological exigence is then sublated by a moral and religious consciousness that is at best, from a cognitive standpoint, theoretically differentiated. Can the sublating then include the sublated, preserve all its proper features and properties, and carry them forward to a fuller realization within a richer context? Is it not rather the case that the exigence to differentiation in terms of interiority results in part from the existential inadequacy of precritical moral and religious conversion at a certain level of intellectual development, no matter how genuinely moral and religious these may be? What is there to guarantee that anything more survives the elimination of cognitional myth than a wan smile at one's former religious and moral naivete? What Lonergan calls intellectual conversion can be such a radical transformation of horizon, such an about-face, such a repudiation of characteristic features of the old, the beginning of such a new sequence, that it cannot be sublated by the old, but, if it is to be sublated at all, demands the satisfaction of a further exigence, the extension of the gains of intellectual conversion into the moral and religious domains. The sublating moral and religious consciousness must be not merely converted consciousness, but self-appropriating consciousness: existential subjectivity in the realm of differentiated interiority, and religious subjectivity in the realm of differentiated transcendence or religiously differentiated consciousness. Neither moral nor religious conversion is identical with self-appropriation at the fourth level of intentional consciousness. But a moral and religious consciousness that can sublate intellectual conversion must be a morally and religiously self-appropriating consciousness. It may well be that

> ... the end of all our exploring
> Will be to arrive where we started
> And know the place for the first time.[18]

But then the end of all our exploring will not be intellectual conversion alone, but a mediated return to immediacy through the satisfaction of a further exigence to a second mediation of immediacy by meaning, a mediation which facilitates the self-appropriation of moral and religious consciousness and the sublation of the cognitional subject by the existential and religious subject.

There are five clues provided in *Method in Theology* which I shall use to help me discuss the experience of this sublating moral and religious consciousness and the nature of its coming to pass. The clues are: (1) there *is* a second mediation of immediacy by meaning, which occurs not when one objectifies cognitional process in transcendental method, but when one negotiates one's feelings in psychotherapy; (2) feelings are the locus for the apprehension of values which mediates between judgments of fact and judgments of value; (3) feelings are in a reciprocal relationship of evocation to symbols; (4) the unified affectivity or wholeness of the converted religious subject is the fulfillment of the dynamism of conscious intentionality; and (5) with the advance in the differentiation of the cognitive function of meaning, the spontaneous reference of religious experience shifts from the exterior, spatial, specific, and human to the interior, temporal, generic, and transcendent.

The relating of these clues with Jungian psychotherapeutic insights will form the web of an argument, then, that the finality of the methodical exigence is therapeutic, and thus that this exigence intends a second immediacy, an informed naivete, the deliverance of critically self-appropriating subjectivity into a condition where 'I leave off all demands and listen.'[19]

2   The Therapeutic Function of Intellectual Conversion

Intellectual conversion is not the end of all our exploring, but the beginning of an answer to a therapeutic exigence.

We need not discuss in detail the nature of intellectual conversion. In its full sweep it is the mediation of immediacy which occurs when one answers correctly and in order the questions, What am I doing when I am knowing? Why is doing that knowing? What do I know when I do that? The answer to the first question reveals the dynamic structure, promoted by questioning, of human cognitional process. The answer to the second question reveals that this process terminates in an affirmation of the real. What I know when I faithfully pursue the process is what I intended to know when I began it: what is, being, the real. The answer to the third question reveals the structure of the real. Concomitant with answering these questions is the elimination of the cognitional myth that the real is a subdivision of the 'already out there now' and that it is to be known by looking.

There is a distinctly therapeutic function to this event. Not only is it a radical transformation of the subject in his or her subjectivity, but it is a movement toward an expanded or heightened self-knowledge precisely at a moment when such an increment is demanded because of the inadequacy of the subject's previous conscious orientation as an understanding Being-in-the-world. It is a knowing of what had previously been unknown, of the dynamic structure-in-process of the subject's cognitional activity. It is a self-conscious appropriation of what had previously been unappropriated and inarticulate, 'unconscious.'[20] The exigence for differentiation in terms of interiority has a cognitive dimension, located in the incommensurability of theoretically differentiated consciousness and common sense. But the answers to the critical questions also help to thematize an event of archetypal significance in human history, namely, the heroic severing of the umbilical cord to maternal imagination which resulted in the theoretic control of meaning, the emergence of *logos* from *mythos* on the part of the Western mind. This archetypally significant event is repeated in the ontogenetic development of the contemporary conscious subject who achieves a theoretic differentiation of the cognitive function of meaning. The answers to the critical questions tell us what we have done in insisting on *logos* in preference to *mythos* and on science in addition to common sense. They render consciousness present to itself in its heroic achievement, by thematizing that achievement which some two thousand years have brought to a certain, if ever precarious, maturity.

That the raising and answering of these questions, however, is a matter of personal decision, that interiorly differentiated cognitional consciousness is never something one simply happens upon and always something one must decisively pursue, indicates, I believe, that the therapeutic exigence met by heeding the invitation of *Insight* reflects a profound *moral* crisis. Intellectual conversion may be viewed, then, also as an answer to an ethical question, a question perhaps previously unnecessary, one not found in our historical memory, a new ethical question which we never raised before because we never had to raise it, a moral question unique to a consciousness which has brought to some kind of conclusion the demands of the theoretic or systematic exigence. The questions promoting intellectual conversion are not raised out of mere curiosity, but because of a rift in subjectivity, which, if left unattended, will bring catastrophe to the individual, to the scientific community, to the economy, to the polity, to the nations, to the world. It is the rift manifested cognitively in the split between theoretically differentiated consciousness and common sense, but also experienced psychically as the lonely isolation of heroic consciousness from all that has nurtured it, as the self-chosen separation of the knower from the primal maternal and chthonic ground of his or her being, as the alienation of the light from the darkness without which it would not be light, even as the guilt of Orestes or Prometheus, whose stories were told at the beginning of the heroic venture of Western mind. What Lonergan has captured in his articulation of intellectual conversion is, in part, a cognitional thematizing of the psychically necessary victory of the knower over the uroboric dragon of myth, of the desire to know over the desire not to know, of the intention of being over the flight from understanding. This thematization is a help toward healing the rift in subjectivity which threatens civilization with utter destruction. It is a rendering known of the previously undifferentiated structure of a differentiation which itself had already occurred.

But it is only a beginning. In large part it articulates what we have already done, clarifies what has happened, thematizes what has occurred. But it does not yet heal the rift in subjectivity. The knower remains isolated, cut off from his or her roots in the rhythms and processes of nature, separated from his or her psychic ground, alienated from the original darkness which nourished one at the same time as it threatened to smother one, guilty over the primal murder of an ambiguously lifegiving power. The difference is that one now knows what one has done, for to know what I am doing when I am knowing is also to know what the knower has done in overcoming the gods and claiming a rightful autonomy. But it is not to know the way toward wholeness, which can only come from a conscious reconciliation with the darkness; in fact, the knowledge of knowledge may even be the suspicion that all such reconciliation with the darkness is purely and simply regression, a canceling of the victory of the knower, a repudiation of a bitterly won autonomy. Yet, we must ask, was not the cognitively manifested exigence for such reconciliation what gave rise to the questions leading to intellectual conversion? And is there not a second mediation of immediacy by meaning which might complement this first? Being and knowing are isomorphic, says the self-affirming knower. If so, is it not possible that the discovery of the imaginal roots out of which the powers of intelligent grasping and reasonable affirmation have violently wrested their birthright might disclose a sphere of being which itself can not only be encountered again—for merely to reencounter it is the romantic agony—but intelligently grasped, reasonably affirmed, and delicately negotiated? Might the hero not revisit the realm of the Mothers without regression and self-destruction? Faustian, you say. Perhaps, but not necessarily so. Much, indeed all, depends on the nature of the pact agreed on before the descent, and on the character of its signers. If religious conversion has preceded intellectual conversion, the descent need not be Faustian. Faust's is not the only kenosis buried in the memory of humankind.

3   The Psyche and an Ethic of Wholeness

Central to the work of C.G. Jung is the tenacious insistence that every answer to the question of the meaning of human life must be uniquely individual if it is to have any final significance. Any answer to the question in terms simply of collective identifications is a failure to understand the question itself. The central notion of Jungian thought is the notion of individuation as an ongoing process of self-discrimination and self-differentiation from everything collective, both external and internal. Nonetheless, any facile charge of individualism, solipsism, sheer relativism or subjectivism leveled against Jung would miss the point. There are operative in Jung's thought certain directives for the process of individuation which might be called both heuristic and at least potentially transcendental. The discovery of individual meaning universally depends on their employment. These directives, phrased in a language influenced by my own attempts at restatement of Jungian psychology,[21] are: (1) conscious intentionality is potentially in a process of commerce with an available and corresponding fund of symbolic meanings constitutive of its dispositional immediacy; this fund is constituted by both personal and transpersonal factors; (2) conscious intentionality must attend to this source out of which it continually emerges anew; (3) it must also negotiate its demands intelligently, reasonably, and responsibly; (4) thereby the whole of subjectivity will be afforded an enhanced degree of life and development, as the subject continues on the journey to individuation.

The Jungian understanding of the moral crisis of the rift in subjectivity is detailed in two books by Erich Neumann, *The Origins and History of Consciousness* and *Depth Psychology and a New Ethic*. Throughout the following exposition of Neumann's position, which Jung affirms in forewords to both books, it should be kept in mind that the incommensurability of theoretically differentiated consciousness and common sense is the cognitive manifestation of the rift in subjectivity which Neumann understands in terms of a specifically psychic rift.

The theme of *The Origins and History of Consciousness* is that psychic ontogenesis is a modified recapitulation of the phylogenetic development of human consciousness. Thus

> ... the early history of the collective is determined by inner primordial images whose projections appear outside as powerful factors—gods, spirits, or demons—which become objects of worship. On the other hand, man's collective symbolisms also appear in the individual, and the psychic development, or misdevelopment, of each individual is governed by the same primordial images which determine man's collective history ... Only by viewing the collective stratification of human development together with the individual stratification of conscious development can we arrive at an understanding of psychic development in general, and individual development in particular.[22]

Thus the history both of humankind and of the individual is governed by certain 'symbols, ideal forms, psychic categories, and basic structural patterns'[23] which Jung has called archetypes and which operate according to 'infinitely varied modes.'[24] The history even of Western philosophy and science represents a series of cognitive manifestations of these archetypal patterns, which are for Neumann the ground of all meaning.

The first part of Neumann's study describes the mythic projections of these archetypal patterns. Then he goes on to argue for the psychic ontogenetic recapitulation of these symbolic patterns in the consciousness of the individual. Mythic projections reflect developmental changes in the relation between the ego—the center of the field of differentiated consciousness—and the realm of the unknown and undifferentiated archetypal base out of which differentiated consciousness arises.

> Just as unconscious contents like dreams and fantasies tell us something about the psychic situation of the dreamer, so myths throw light on the human stage from which they originate and typify man's unconscious situation at that stage. In neither case is there any conscious knowledge of the situation projected, either in the conscious mind of the dreamer or in that of the mythmaker.[25]

Moreover, the various archetypal stages of the relation between the ego and its collective psychic base form elements of the subjective development of modern men and women. 'The constitutive character of these stages unfolds in the historical sequence of individual development, but it is very probable that the individual's psychic structure is itself built up on the historical sequence of human development as a whole.'[26] That the same stages occurred at different periods in different cultures reflects their archetypal structure rooted in a common and universal psychic substructure identical in all human beings.

The developmental process begins with an original undifferentiated unity which gives way first to a separation of ego from base—the hero myth—and in these latter days of Western civilization to a very dangerous split, a rift in subjectivity. After the separation, the ego consolidates and defends its newly won position, strengthens its stability, becomes conscious of its differences and peculiarities, and increases its energy. Phylogenetically, such a consolidation is represented cognitively, I believe, by the theoretic or systematic differentiation of consciousness in Western philosophy and science. The ego even succeeds in harnessing for its own interests some of the originally destructive power of the unconscious so that the world continuum is broken down into objects which can be first symbolized, then conceptualized, and finally rearranged. Thus there emerges 'the relative autonomy of the ego, of the higher spiritual man who has a will of his own and obeys his reason,'[27] and with this, I submit, a gradual unthematized discrimination of the cognitive, constitutive, effective, and communicative functions of meaning. The end of this development is the capacity 'to form abstract concepts and to adopt a consistent view of the world'[28]—that is, the satisfaction of the theoretic or systematic exigence. Physiologically, Neumann posits, the process involves the supersession of 'the medullary man' by 'the cortical man,' involving a 'continuous deflation of the unconscious and the exhaustion of emotional components' linked with the sympathetic nervous system.[29]

My present interest is in Neumann's analysis of the cultural disease to which this altogether necessary separation of psychic systems has brought us. For the division of the two systems has become perverse. The perversion is manifested in two directions: a sclerosis of the ego, in which the autonomy of the conscious system has become so predominant as to lose the link to the archetypal base, and in which the ego has lost the striving for the wholeness of subjectivity; and a possession of the creative activity of the ego by 'the spirit,' resulting in the illimitable expansion of the ego, the megalomania, the overexpansion of the conscious system, the spiritual inflation of Nietzsche's Zarathustra. The first direction is the more common. Here, spirit is identified with instrumental intellect, consciousness with manipulative thinking. Feeling, the body, the instinctual are suppressed or, more tragically, repressed.

Consciousness is sterilized, and creativity doomed to frustration, in a culture whose institutional structures have become autonomous from the human needs they were originally constituted to meet. The transpersonal is reduced to mere illusion, to personalistic ego data; archetypes become concepts, symbols signs. Not only is ego life emptied of meaning, but the deeper layers of the psyche are activated in a destructive way so as to 'devastate the autocratic world of the ego with transpersonal invasions, collective epidemics, and mass psychoses.'[30] The affective collapse of the archetypal canon is coincident with the modern decay of values. The alternative courses open to the individual seem to be either regression to the Great Mother through external or internal recollectivization, or isolation in the form of exaggerated individualism. The contemporary relevance of Neumann's analysis for the Western way of life is all too obvious in the light of our recent and still too gradual awareness of the real character of our political life.

Following the collapse of the archetypal canon, single archetypes take possession of men and consume them like malevolent demons. Typical and symptomatic of this transitional phenomenon is the state of affairs in America, though the same holds good for practically the whole Western hemisphere. Every conceivable sort of dominant rules the personality, which is a personality only in name. The grotesque fact that murderers, brigands, gangsters, thieves, forgers, tyrants, and swindlers, in a guise that deceives nobody, have seized control of collective life is characteristic of our time. Their unscrupulousness and double-dealing are recognized—and admired. Their ruthless

energy they obtain at best from some archetypal content that has got them in its power.
The dynamism of a possessed personality is
accordingly very great, because, in its one-track
primitivity, it suffers from none of the differentiations that make men human. Worship of
the 'beast' is by no means confined to Germany;
it prevails wherever one-sidedness, push, and
moral blindness are applauded, i.e., wherever
the aggravating complexities of civilized behavior are swept away in favor of bestial rapacity.
One has only to look at the educative ideals
now current in the West.[31]

The ethical consequences of this situation as they
affect the individual in relation to the collective are detailed in *Depth Psychology and a New Ethic*. Neumann argues strongly and well that the wholeness of subjectivity,
conceived as the consequence of healing the rift described
above, is the ethical goal upon which the fate of humanity
depends.

The turning of the mind from the conscious to
the unconscious, the possible *rapprochement* of
human consciousness with the powers of the
collective psyche, that is the task of the future.
No outward tinkerings with the world and no
social amelioration can give the quietus to the
daemon, to the gods or devils of the human
soul, or prevent them from tearing down again
and again what consciousness has built. Unless they are assigned their place in consciousness and culture they will never leave mankind
in peace. But the preparation for the *rapprochement* lies, as always, with the hero, the indi-

vidual; he and his transformation are the great
human prototypes; he is the testing ground of
the collective, just as consciousness is the testing ground of the unconscious.[32]

The categorial and ontic ethic which accompanied
the separation of the psychic systems has disintegrated and
is now dead. It is an ethic which 'liberated man from his
primary condition of unconsciousness and made the individual the bearer of the drive towards consciousness.'[33] To
this extent it was not only psychically necessary but constructive. The initial phases of the development of an autonomous ego must be sustained by the demands of the
collective and its sanctions, by its juridical structures and
dogmas, its imperatives and prohibitions, even its suppres-
sions and attendant sufferings. But soon enough identification with the ethical values of the collective leads to the
formation of a façade personality, the *persona*, and to repression of everything dark, strange, unfamiliar, and
unlived, the *shadow*. The ego is cumulatively identified with
the façade, and the shadow is projected upon various scapegoats. In our time, the distance between the two systems
has become so wide that even the pseudo solution of conscious identification with the collective ethic is subtly but
publicly acknowledged as impossible. Thus Neumann can
claim: 'Almost without exception, the psychic development
of modern man begins with the moral problem and with
his own reorientation, which is brought about by means of
the assimilation of the shadow and the transformation of
the persona.'[34] As the dark and unfamiliar, the 'inferior
function,' is granted freedom and a share in the life of the
ego, identification of the ego-persona with collective value
orientation ceases. 'The individual is driven by his personal crisis into deep waters where he would usually never
have entered if left to his own free will. The old idealized

image of the ego has to go, and its place is taken by a perilous insight into the ambiguity and many-sidedness of one's own nature.'[35] Only the total personality is accepted as the basis of ethical conduct. No longer is St. Augustine's prayer of gratitude to God possible that he is not responsible for his dreams.[36]

Neumann proposes, then, the foundations of a new ethic whose aim is 'the achievement of wholeness, of the totality of the personality.' He continues:

> In this wholeness, the inherent contrast between the two systems of the conscious mind and the unconscious does not fall apart into a condition of splitness, and the purposive directedness of ego-consciousness is not undermined by the opposite tendencies of unconscious contents of which the ego and the conscious mind are entirely unaware. In the new ethical situation, ego-consciousness becomes the locus of responsibility for a psychological League of Nations, to which various groups of states belong, primitive and prehuman as well as differentiated and modern, and in which atheistic and religious, instinctive and spiritual, destructive and constructive elements are represented in varying degrees and coexist with each other.[37]

Theoretical—I interpret: categorial or ontic, as opposed to transcendental-heuristic or ontological—prescriptions for ethical conduct are declared impossible,[38] since it is 'impossible to predict the psychological form in which evil will appear in the life story of any given individual.'[39] Working through and negotiating our own individual darkness in an independent and responsible manner—becoming more fully conscious, in Jungian terms—now ranks as an ethical duty, implying that ego consciousness is regarded as 'an authority to create and control the relationship to wholeness of everything psychic.'[40] Psychic wholeness takes the place of sublimation. The latter is always 'purchased at the cost of the contagious miasma which arises out of the repression and suppression of the unconscious elements which are not susceptible to sublimation.'[41] Sublimation thus contributes to a 'holiness' which is nothing other than a flight from life. The heart of the ethical implications of the Jungian myth are contained in the following formulation of principles of value:

> Whatever leads to wholeness is 'good'; whatever leads to splitting is 'evil.' Integration is good, disintegration is evil. Life, constructive tendencies and integration are on the side of good; death, splitting and disintegration are on the side of evil ... Our estimate of ethical values is no longer concerned with contents, qualities or actions considered as 'entities'; it is related functionally to the whole. Whatever helps that wholeness which is centered on the Self towards integration is 'good,' irrespective of the nature of this helping factor. And, vice versa, whatever leads to disintegration is 'evil'—even if it is 'good will,' 'collectively sanctioned values' or anything else 'intrinsically good.'[42]

In my lengthier study of the theologically foundational role of psychic self-appropriation,[43] I have argued that it is precisely at this point that the Jungian myth is susceptible to a collapse. Neumann's (and Jung's) campaign against the collective ethic is strikingly reminiscent of St. Paul's difficulties with the Law. But the outcome is in each instance frequently just as strikingly different. It is worthy of note that, as Jung's thinking advanced, he came more to view the individuation process on the analogy of alchemy.[44] The latter is even viewed, perhaps quite correctly, as a mistaken projection onto matter of a striving for the *aurum non vulgi* of psychic wholeness. What Jung and, to my knowledge, most commentators on Jungian psychology, have missed, however, is that alchemy must be considered as one of the most remarkable failures n the history of human inquiry, a sustained insistence on asking the wrong question. And the question is wrong, not only in its projected form, but in its very origins, if indeed its origins lie where Jung placed them. For the *self*-achievement of a differentiated wholeness, while it may be the deepest desire of the human heart, is also a useless passion, completely beyond the capacity of human endeavor left to its own resources to achieve. The bitterness of Jung's *Answer to Job* is expressive of this very frustration. This is a very interesting book on Wotan, but Jung called the 'god' Yahweh.

This is not at all to deny that one must take seriously to heart everything prescribed by Neumann. We have indeed entered a new epoch in the evolution of human consciousness. It is an epoch marked by a new control of meaning in terms of interiority. It is ethically imperative on a world-historical scale that ego consciousness engage in a conscious confrontation with the forces of darkness buried in the human psyche, come to terms with these forces in truthful acknowledgment, and cooperate in their transformation and integration through acceptance and negotiation. But at this point Lonergan's transcendental analysis of moral conversion becomes equally imperative. For it is only at the summit of moral self-transcendence in the love of God, that is, in the gift of grace, that wholeness becomes something of a possibility. There alone, 'values are whatever one loves, and evils are whatever one hates,' because there alone 'affectivity is of a single piece.'[45] The problems raised by Neumann, moreover, bring to light an element that needs to be added to Lonergan's analysis of this summit: the experience of the forgiveness of sin. Only this experience, issuing from the realm of transcendence, is enough to render possible the embracing of the darkness called for by Neumann as ethically imperative for our age. The darkness has already been embraced in a kenosis quite different from Faust's, and in that divine embrace has been converted into love. Its very spontaneous tendency to separate us from the love of God has been transformed into a beneficent factor by the healing embrace of love. It is not only the hero's descent into the psychic depths that can save the world from suicide, but also the restoration in our troubled times of the genuine contemplative spirit.

4   **Religious Self-appropriation and the Psyche**

Lonergan employs various phrases, some borrowed from other authors, to describe religious conversion. With Paul Tillich, he speaks of 'being grasped by ultimate concern.'[46] With St. Paul, he speaks of God's love flooding our hearts through the Holy Spirit given to us.[47] In terms of the theoretical stage of meaning represented by Aquinas, religious conversion is operative grace as distinct from co-operative grace. But these theoretic categories are also reinterpreted in scriptural imagery. 'Operative grace is the replacement of the heart of stone by a heart of flesh, a replacement beyond the horizon of the heart of stone. Cooperative grace is the heart of flesh becoming effective in good works through human freedom.'[48] In Lonergan's own terminology, suited more to the stage of meaning when the world of interiority becomes the ground of theory, religious conversion is 'otherworldly falling in love. It is total and permanent self-surrender without conditions, qualifications, reservations.'[49] As such it is 'being in love with God,' which is 'the basic fulfillment of our conscious intentionality. That fulfillment brings a deep-set joy that can remain despite humiliation, failure, privation, pain, betrayal, desertion. That fulfillment brings a radical peace, the peace that the world cannot give. That fulfillment bears fruit in a love of one's neighbor that strives mightily to bring about the Kingdom of God on this earth.'[50]

The experience of this love is that of 'being in love in an unrestricted fashion' and as such is the proper fulfillment of the capacity for self-transcendence revealed in our unrestricted questioning. But it is not the product of our knowledge and choice. 'On the contrary, it dismantles and abolishes the horizon in which our knowing and choosing went on and it sets up a new horizon in which the love of God will transvalue our values and the eyes of that love will transform our knowing.'[51] As conscious but not known, the experience of this love is an experience of mystery, of the holy. It belongs to the level of consciousness where deliberation, judgment of value, decision, and free and responsible activity take place. 'But it is this consciousness as brought to a fulfillment, as having undergone a conversion, as possessing a basis that may be broadened and deepened and heightened and enriched but not superseded, as ready to deliberate and judge and decide and act with the easy freedom of those that do all good because they are in love. So the gift of God's love occupies the ground and root of the fourth and highest level of man's intentional consciousness. It takes over the peak of the soul, the *apex animae*.'[52]

For Lonergan, there is a twofold expression of religious conversion. Spontaneously it is manifested in changed attitudes, for which Galatians 5.22-23 provides a descriptive enumeration: 'The fruit of the Spirit is love, joy, peace, patience, kindness, goodness, faithfulness, gentleness, self-control.' But another kind of expression is directly concerned with the base and focus of this experience, the *mysterium tremendum et fascinans* itself. There is an enormous variation to be discovered in the investigation of such expression, and Lonergan correlates this variety with the predominant stages of meaning operative in self-understanding and in the spontaneously assumed stance toward reality—that is, with the manner in which one's world is mediated by meaning. He constructs a series of stages of meaning based on a cumulative differentiation of consciousness. In the Western tradition there have been three such stages of meaning, and they can be ontogenetically reproduced in the life history of a contemporary individual.

The first stage of meaning is governed by common sense. The second is familiar also with theory, system, logic, and science, but is troubled because the difference of this from common sense is not adequately grasped. The third stage is prepared by all those modern philosophies governed by the turn to the subject, which thus take their stand on human interiority. Here consciousness becomes differentiated into the various realms of meaning—common sense, theory, interiority, transcendence, scholarship, and art—and these realms are consciously related to one another. One consciously moves from one to the other by consciously changing one's procedures.

In all three stages, meaning fulfills four functions. First, it is cognitive in that it mediates the real world in which we live out our lives. Secondly, it is efficient in that it governs our intention of what we do. Thirdly, it is constitutive in that it is an intrinsic component of culture and institutions. And fourthly, it is communicative in that, through its various carriers—spontaneous intersubjectivity, art, symbol, language, and incarnation in the lives and deeds of persons—individual meaning becomes common meaning, and, through the transmission of training and education, generates history.

In the first stage, these functions are not clearly recognized and accurately differentiated. So the blend of the cognitive and constitutive functions, for example, brings about the constitution not only of cultures and institutions but also the story of the world's origins in myth. And just as the constitutive function of meaning pretends to speculative capacities beyond its range, so the efficient function of meaning pretends to practical powers which a more differentiated consciousness recognizes as magic. Religious expression at this stage is a result of the projective association or identification of religious experience with its outward occasion. The focus of such expression is on what we, by hindsight, would call *the external, the spatial, the specific,* and *the human,* as contrasted with *the internal, the temporal, the generic,* and *the divine.* What is indeed temporal, generic, internal, and in the realm of transcendence is identified as spatial, specific, external, and occurring in a realm other than that of transcendence. Thus there result the gods of the moment, the god of this or that place, of this or that person, of Abraham or Laban, of this or that group, of the Canaanites, the Philistines, the Israelites.

The key to the movement from the first stage of meaning to the second is located in the differentiation of the functions of meaning. The advance of technique will enable the association of the efficient function with *poiêsis* and *praxis* and reveal the inefficacy of magic. But more far-reaching in its implications is the differentiation of the cognitive function of meaning from the other three functions. As the key to the religious expression of undifferentiated consciousness lies in insight into sensible presentations and representations, so the limitations of such consciousness to the spatial, the specific, the external, and the human will recede to the extent that the sensible presentations and representations are linguistic.[53] This does not mean, however, that a self-conscious transposition to interiority, time, the generic, and the divine occurs. Rather we have a movement away from all immediacy in favor of objectification. The return to immediacy in terms of interiority, time, the generic, and the divine must await the emergence of the third stage of meaning.

The second stage of meaning, then, is characterized by a twofold mediation of the world by meaning: in the realm of common sense and in that of theory. The split is troubling. It was interpreted by Plato, at one point, in such a way that there seem to be two really distinct worlds, the transcendent world of eternal Forms and the transient world of appearances. In Aristotle, it led to the distinction, not between theory and common sense, but between necessity and contingence. The basic concepts of genuine—i.e., universal and necessary—science were metaphysical, and so the sciences were conceived as continuous with philosophy.

The introduction of the theoretical capacity into religious living is represented in the dogmas, theology, and juridical structures of Western religion. But just as the two tables of Eddington—'the bulky, solid, colored desk at which he worked, and the manifold of colorless "wavicles" so minute that the desk was mostly empty space'[54]—reveal the presence of a conflict between common sense and science, so in the realm of religion, 'the God of Abraham, Isaac, and Jacob is set against the God of the philosophers and theologians. Honoring the Trinity and feeling compunction are set against learned discourse on the Trinity and against defining compunction. Nor can this contrast be understood or the tension removed within the realms of common sense and of theory.'[55] And so, religiously as well as scientifically, there is demanded a movement to a third stage of meaning, the stage of the differentiation of consciousness through the appropriation of human interiority.

The sciences then come to be regarded, not as prolongations of philosophy, but as autonomous, ongoing processes; not as the demonstration of universal and necessary truths but as hypothetical and ever better approximations to truth through an ever more exact and comprehensive understanding of data. Philosophy is no longer a theory in the manner of science but the self-appropriation of intentional consciousness and the consequent distinguishing, relating, and grounding of the various realms of meaning, the grounding of the methods of the sciences, and the ongoing promotion of their unity. Theology then becomes, in ever larger part, at least in its first phase that mediates from the past into the present, an understanding of the diversity of religious utterance on the basis of the differentiation and interrelation of the realms of common sense, theory, interiority, and transcendence.

The third stage of meaning, then, is the stage of the appropriation of human interiority. The cognitive dimensions of the exigence for this appropriation have been more than satisfactorily treated by Lonergan. The result of the cognitive step in this process is intellectual conversion. I have begun to suggest what the moral dimensions would entail. That the self-appropriation of the existential subject is something quite other than that of the cognitional subject is not at all obvious from *Insight*, but the work of Lonergan after 1965 reveals a notable development in this regard, one perhaps best capsulized in '*Insight* Revisited.'

> In *Insight* the good was the intelligent and reasonable. In *Method* the good is a distinct no-

tion. It is intended in questions for deliberation. Is this worth while? Is it truly or only apparently good? It is aspired to in the intentional response of feeling to values. It is known in judgments of value made by a virtuous or authentic person with a good conscience. It is brought about by deciding and living up to one's decisions. Just as intelligence sublates sense, just as reasonableness sublates intelligence, so deliberation sublates and thereby unifies knowing and feeling.[56]

Not only, then, is there a fourth level of intentional consciousness quite distinct from the first three, but the primordial entry of the subject onto this fourth level is affective, 'the intentional response of feelings to values.' Furthermore, affective response for Lonergan is symbolically certifiable, in that a symbol is 'an image of a real or imaginary object that evokes a feeling or is evoked by a feeling.'[57] Thus moral self-appropriation will entail the negotiation of the symbols interlocked with one's affective responses to values. It will entail psychic self-appropriation. Neumann discusses the moral dimensions of this movement, while sharing in the Jungian failure to differentiate wholeness as human achievement from wholeness as God's gift. At the point in psychic self-appropriation where the issue becomes one of good and evil, the movement of appropriation shifts from the realm of interiority to the realm of transcendence, where God is known and loved. The initial move into psychic self-appropriation at the religious level, when the direction is as here indicated, occurs in the experience of the forgiveness of sin, the only genuine—in fact, the only possible—*complexio oppositorum* of good and evil. This experience brings wholeness, the affective integrity of subjectivity. With this experience, re-

ligious conversion can begin to sublate moral and intellectual conversion in the movement of self-appropriation, that
is, at the third stage of meaning.

It is not only religious expression, but religious experience itself, which is affected by the movement into the
third stage of meaning. Prior to this major breakthrough,
one's religious living is precritical, and so runs the risk of
the projection characteristic of the first stage of meaning.
It may thus be mediated in terms of what interiorly differentiated consciousness, by hindsight, calls spatial, specific,
external, and human as opposed to what is temporal, generic, internal, and transcendent. To the extent that one's
appropriation of interiority proceeds from intellectual conversion to self-appropriation at the fourth level of intentional consciousness, the spontaneous reference of religious
experience will be to what is temporal, generic, internal,
and transcendent. It will proceed as in the mode of a self-
conscious 'discernment of spirits.' Such discernment has
the same archetypal manifestations in dreams and other
symbolic productions as has any other expression of the
evaluative capacity of the existential subject. That these
expressions are not specifically acknowledged in Jungian
phenomenologies of individuation is due to a deficiency
in Jung's understanding of existential subjectivity and the
conspiracy it can engage in with the psyche.

5   Psychic Conversion as Foundational

If in addition to the mediation of immediacy by
meaning which occurs when one objectifies cognitional
process in transcendental method, there is that which occurs when one discovers, identifies, accepts one's submerged feelings in psychotherapy, then intentional self-
appropriation must be complemented by psychic self-appropriation. As related to the question of the process and

function of theology, this would mean that, whereas Lonergan has developed a method for theology based on the mediation of intentional consciousness, we must attempt to show the implications for theology of the psychic mediation. The principal implication will be a fourth conversion foundational for theology, psychic conversion, aiding the relations of sublation among the three conversions specified by Lonergan. Through the twofold mediation of immediacy theological reflection will be able to accept the possibilities which now, perhaps for the first time in its history, are available to it. For in our age not only are we confronted with the relativity of conceptual schemes of all kinds, in every area, but also, precisely because of this seemingly very uncertain and ambivalent state of affairs, the individual is given 'the (often desperate, yet maximally human) opportunity to interpret life and experiencing directly. The historical crossroads of such a time is: either the reimposition of certain set values and schemes, or a task never before attempted: to learn how, in a rational way, to relate concepts to direct experiencing; to investigate the way in which symbolizing affects and is affected by felt experiencing; to devise a social and scientific vocabulary that can interact with experiencing; so that communication about it becomes possible, so that schemes can be considered in relation to experiential meanings, and so that an objective science can be related to and guided by experiencing.'[58] What Eugene Gendlin here envisions for 'objective science' can also be the goal of theology. To envision a theology whose schemes are related to and guided by experiencing, however, does not, within the horizon provided by self-appropriation, rule out of court a theology whose concern is with 'things as they are related to one another' in favor of a theology preoccupied with 'things as they are related to us.' Rather, basic terms and relations, as psychological, are also explanatory. Such is the ultimate significance of fidelity to the methodical exigence.

The present essay, then, reflects an ongoing project to complement the work of Lonergan; it initiates a further essay in aid of self-appropriation. For beyond the intellectual conversion which occurs in self-conscious fashion when one answers correctly and in order the questions, What am I doing when I am knowing? Why is doing that knowing? What do I know when I do that? there is the self-appropriation which begins when one attentively, intelligently, reasonably, and responsibly learns to negotiate the symbolic configurations of dispositional immediacy. The latter self-appropriation is effected by the emergence in the existential subject of a mediated symbolic consciousness, in which individual, cultural, and religious symbols are treated—in what Paul Ricoeur has lucidly displayed as their archeological-teleological unity-in-tension[59]—as *exploratory* of existential subjectivity and as referring to interiority, time, the generic, and the realm of transcendence, rather than as *explanatory* or aetiological and as referring to exteriority, space, the specific, and the human. Psychic conversion is the recovery of imagination in its transcendental time-structure[60] through the psychotherapeutic elucidation of the symbols emerging spontaneously from one's psychic depths.

I share the conviction which led John Dunne to write *The Way of All the Earth*, the conviction that something like a new religion is coming into being.

> Is a religion coming to birth in our time? It could be. What seems to be occurring is a phenomenon we might call 'passing over,' passing over from one culture to another, from one way of life to another, from one religion to another. Passing over is a shifting of standpoint, a going

over to the standpoint of another culture, another way of life, another religion. It is followed by an equal and opposite process we might call 'coming back,' coming back with new insight to one's own culture, one's own way of life, one's own religion. The holy man of our time, it seems, is not a figure like Gotama or Jesus or Mohammed, a man who could found a world religion, but a figure like Gandhi, a man who passes over by sympathetic understanding from his own religion to other religions and comes back again with new insight to his own. Passing over and coming back, it seems, is the spiritual adventure of our time.[61]

The present essay reflects an effort to aid this adventure and the articulation of its truth. If theology is reflection on religion, then such articulation would be the theology appropriate to our age. Dunne says quite correctly, however, that the ultimate starting and ending point is really not one's own religion, but one's life. At present I am attempting to highlight the contributions of depth psychology to the exploration of this homeland and the significance of these contributions for religious experience and for the reflection on this experience which is theology. The project here reported on is not only complementary to the work of Lonergan, however, but in some sense compensatory, in the same way as the psyche, as it manifests itself in dreams, is compensatory to the attitude of waking consciousness. 'The relation between consciousness and unconscious is compensatory. This fact, which is easily verifiable, affords a rule for dream interpretation. It is always helpful, when we set out to interpret a dream, to ask: what conscious attitude does it compensate?'[62]

Waking consciousness, as it moves from directed attention through insight, judgment, and decision, has been the sharp focus of Lonergan's work. Since theology is a matter of knowledge and decision, such a focus has enabled him to articulate the structure of theological method. Since I accept without reservation Lonergan's account of 'what I am doing when I am knowing' and his eightfold differentiation of theological operations, the work I envision is complementary to his. But since I wish to lay emphasis on a different but equally valid source of data— which can still be grouped under Lonergan's notion of data of consciousness, since they concern interiority—the work would be compensatory to his, just as feeling is compensatory to thinking as a psychological function or as dreams are compensatory to waking consciousness as a psychic state.

If the first step in interpreting a dream is to ask, What conscious attitude does it compensate? and if the work I envision is to be understood as compensatory to Lonergan's in a sense analogous to the compensatory effect of dreams, then it is only proper to indicate what attitude or atmosphere this work would compensate.

Thus Dunne speaks of climbing a mountain in order to discover a vantage point, a fastness of autonomy. The most complete autonomy comes, he says, from the knowledge, not of external things, but of knowledge itself.

A knowing of knowing would be like a view from a mountaintop. By knowing all about knowing itself one would know in some manner everything there is to know. It would be like seeing everything from a great height. One would see everything near and far, all the way to the horizon, but there would be some loss of detail on account of the distances. The know-

ing of knowing would mean being in possession of all the various methods of knowing. It
would mean knowing how an artist thinks,
putting a thing together; knowing how a scientist thinks, taking a thing apart; knowing how a
practical man thinks, sizing up a situation;
knowing how a man of understanding thinks,
grasping the principle of a thing; knowing how
a man of wisdom thinks, reflecting upon human experience.

... At the top of the mountain, as we have
been describing it, there is a kind of madness—
not the madness that consists in having lost
one's reason, but a madness that consists in
having lost everything *except* one's reason. The
knowing of knowing, to be sure, seems worthy
of man. The only thing wrong is that man at
the top of the mountain, by escaping from love
and war, will have lost everything else. He will
have withdrawn into that element of his nature
which is most characteristic of him and sets
him apart from other animals. It is the thing in
him which is most human. Perhaps indeed he
will never realize what it is to be human unless
he does attempt this withdrawal. Even so, the
realization that he has lost everything except
his reason, that he has found pure humanity
but not full humanity, changes his wisdom from
a knowledge of knowledge into a knowledge of
ignorance. He realizes that he has something
yet to learn, something that he cannot learn at
the top of the mountain but only at the bottom
of the valley.[63]

Nobody familiar with Lonergan can read these words
about the knowing of knowing without thinking immediately of one of the most daring claims any thinker has ever
offered for his own work, true as it is: 'Thoroughly understand what it is to understand, and not only will you understand the broad lines of all there is to be understood
but also you will possess a fixed base, an invariant pattern,
opening upon all further developments of understanding.'[64]
Nonetheless, Lonergan is seeking greater *concreteness* on
the side of the subject, in the domain of 'the pulsing flow
of life.'[65] To the extent that his work aids this greater concreteness, one escapes the madness of having lost everything but one's reason. But there is much in the pulsing
flow of life that enters into one's life without providing
data for one's knowing of knowing. One may become aware
of the dark yet potentially creative power at work in the
valley and expend one's efforts, perhaps first by means of
a different kind of withdrawal—into a forest or desert, in
imitation of Gotama or Jesus, rather than up to a
mountaintop—at the negotiation and transformation of
this dark power of nature so that it is creative of one's own
life. If one succeeds in this very risky adventure, it will be
only because one will have undergone a profound conversion.

Conversion is the central theme in Lonergan's brilliant and, I believe, revolutionary recasting of the foundations of theology. And such it must be, for nobody who
has gone to the top of the mountain can accept as the
foundations of knowledge anything exclusive of what happened there. One has achieved an intellectual autonomy
as a result of which one will never be the same. But there
is a different conversion that occurs in the valley or the
forest or the desert. It is both complementary and compensatory to the conversion that takes place at the top of
the mountain, to intellectual conversion. Nor is it the same

as what Lonergan calls religious or moral conversion. I have called it psychic conversion. Its effect is a mediated symbolic consciousness, and its role in theological reflection is foundational as aiding the sublation of intellectual conversion by moral and religious conversion. Psychic conversion surrounds the other three conversions in much the same way as the 'unconscious,' according to Jung, surrounds the light of conscious waking life. More precisely, it permeates these conversions in much the same way as psyche permeates intentionality or as dispositional immediacy is interlocked with cognitional immediacy. It provides one with an atmosphere or texture which qualifies one's experiences of knowing, of ethical decision, and of prayer. This atmosphere is determined by the imaginal or symbolic constitution of dispositional immediacy. 'The imaginal' is a genuine sphere of being, a realm whose contents can be intelligently grasped and reasonably affirmed.

The complementary aspect of psychic conversion with respect to intellectual conversion appears in its role as facilitator of the working unity of intellectual conversion with moral and religious conversion. Its compensatory aspect appears primarily in its function within a *second* mediation of immediacy by meaning, and thus in the disclosure it provides that the mediation of immediacy is twofold. Second immediacy can only be approached through the complementarity of the two mediations. Psychic conversion thus corrects what I believe to be a possible implicit intellectualist bias in Lonergan's thought, especially in *Insight*. According to this implicit bias, the intellectual pattern of experience would be the privileged pattern of experience. While the emergence in *Method in Theology* of a fourth level of intentional consciousness and thus of a notion of the good as distinct from the intelligent and reasonable implicitly corrects this bias, the explicit compensation comes from highlighting the psychic dimensions of this fourth level, the level of existential subjectivity.

When I refer with Dunne to a new religion coming into being in our age, what I am indicating is in part the convergence of insights from the various world religions in the life story of many individuals who seek religious truth today. As Dunne has indicated, this search will probably be analogous to Gandhi's experiments with truth. The conversion I call psychic may provide one's criterion for evaluating these experiments and render the subject capable of reflecting on and articulating the truth discovered. It may enable one, in Dunne's phrase, to turn poetry into truth and truth into poetry. The latter poetry one may wish to include in one's theology.

One may find that the further steps in self-appropriation reveal the need for a qualification of one's previous intellectual self-appropriation. While one will not revise the structure of cognitional process which one has learned to articulate through the work of Lonergan, one may be brought to revise one's formulation of the notion of *experience* provided by Lonergan. The latter notion may be too thin, too bodiless. Having come back into the valley from Lonergan's mountaintop—or rather from one's own mountaintop—one may re-experience, or re-cognize that one experiences, in a manner for which the atmosphere of the mountaintop was too rarefied.

This, however, may also lead to further specifications of the notion of theological method which one has learned from Lonergan. One will accept the basic dynamic and operational notion of method provided by Lonergan on the basis of the structure of intentionality and of the two phases of theology as mediating and mediated; but psychic conversion may influence (1) one's choice as to what qualifies as data for theology, (2) the base from which one engages in interpretation and history, (3) the horizon determining one's view of, and influencing one's decision about, the tensions of religious and theological dialectic, (4) the bases from which one derives theological categories, positions, and system, and (5) the way in which one regards the mission of religion in the world. The functional specialties will remain, their interrelationship being determined by the structure of intentional consciousness; but their nature may be modified as a result of one's exploration of the 'objective psyche,' the home of the imaginal, the transcendental imagination, *memoria*. The task of the philosopher or theologian educated by and indebted to Lonergan may now be to descend the mountain of cognitive self-appropriation so as attentively, intelligently, reasonably, and responsibly to appropriate and articulate the rich psychic bases of human experience. Such an appropriation and articulation will make possible the advent of that fully awake naivete of the twice-born adult which Paul Ricoeur calls a second, postcritical naivete.[66]

Notes

1 I wish to acknowledge with gratitude that the term 'psychic conversion' was suggested to me by Vernon Gregson. My original term was 'affective conversion.' That Gregson's suggestion hits things off better should be obvious from the description given in this paper of the transformation referred to by this term.

2 Claudio Naranjo, *The One Quest* (New York: Ballantine, 1972) 15.

3 Ibid. 28.

4 Ibid. 122.

5 Ibid. 224.

⁶ Frederick Lawrence, 'Self-Knowledge in History in Gadamer and Lonergan,' in *Language, Truth, and Meaning*, ed. Philip McShane (Notre Dame: University of Notre Dame Press, 1972) 203.

⁷ The jacket to the book cited in footnote six, for example, refers to Lonergan's work as 'a mode of thinking which some consider axial in Jaspers' sense.' The reference is to the notion Jaspers sets forth in *The Origin and Goal of History* that 'there is an axis on which the whole of human history turns; that axis lies between the years 800 and 200 B.C.; during that period in Greece, in Israel, in Persia, in India, in China, man became of age; he set aside the dreams and fancies of childhood; he began to face the world as perhaps it is.' Bernard Lonergan, 'Dimensions of Meaning,' in *Collection*, ed. Frederick E. Crowe and Robert M. Doran, Collected Works of Bernard Lonergan, vol. 4 (Toronto: University of Toronto Press, 1988) 237-38.

⁸ Bernard Lonergan, *Method in Theology* (see above, chapter 1, note 3) 77.

⁹ Martin Heidegger, *Being and Time*, trans. John Macquarrie and Edward Robinson (New York: Harper and Row, 1962) 171-72.

¹⁰ Lonergan, *Method in Theology* 77.

¹¹ Heidegger, *Being and Time* 173.

¹² Ibid. 176.

¹³ What the Jungian analyst Marie-Louise von Franz says of the existentialists is also true of Heidegger: 'They go only as far as stripping off the illusions of consciousness: They go right up to the door of the unconscious and then fail to open it.' 'The Process of Individuation,' in *Man and His Symbols*, ed. C.G. Jung (New York: Dell Paperback, 1964) 164.

¹⁴ C.G. Jung, 'The Transcendent Function,' in *The Structure and Dynamics of the Psyche*, trans. R.F.C. Hull, vol. 8 in The Collected Works of C.G. Jung, Bollingen Series XX (Princeton: Princeton University Press, 1969) 67-91.

¹⁵ Lonergan establishes this relation of sublation among the three conversions which qualify authentic subjectivity in his thought. I

agree with this order, but suggest that psychic conversion is an enabling factor, perhaps even a necessary aid to the sublation of intellectual conversion by moral and religious conversion. Without the release
of the transcendent function, the sublation may be forever blocked by

... the conscious impotence of rage
at human folly, and the laceration
of laughter at what ceases to amuse

(T.S. Eliot, 'Little Gidding,' *Four Quartets*, [New York: Harcourt, Brace
& World, 1971] 54) which may only become more acute and even chronic
as a result of the ascent of the mountain of the understanding of understanding. The intrinsic finality of the methodical exigence is therapeutic, and thus demands the second mediation of immediacy as constitutive of self-appropriation at the level of existential subjectivity.

16 'Bernard Lonergan Responds,' in *Foundations of Theology*, ed.
Philip McShane (Notre Dame: University of Notre Dame Press, 1971)
221-22.

17 Lonergan, *Method in Theology* 241.

18 Eliot, 'Little Gidding' 59.

19 Paul Ricoeur, *Freud and Philosophy* (see above, chapter 1,
note 7) 496, 551. For a rudimentary suggestion of an attempt to relate
Ricoeur's project to Lonergan's, see my article, 'Paul Ricoeur: Toward
the Restoration of Meaning,' *Anglican Theological Review* 55 (October,
1973) 443-58 (chapter 1 in the present book.)

20 The term 'the unconscious' is ambiguous. Sometimes it is
used to mean 'the psyche,' sometimes 'the unknown,' and sometimes
the neural processes that find their psychic representation and conscious integration in images and affects. The latter use is the only genuinely adequate one. Jung seems to have consistently overlooked the fact
that consciousness and knowledge are not the same thing, and so what
is unknown he tends to call unconscious. That he was kept from this
insight by language — the German language and *Bewusstsein* in particular — at least partially excuses him, if not his English translators.
Both Freudians and Jungians would aid their cause by clarifying the
term 'the unconscious' and at times by choosing the appropriate substitute. Jungians could also rename 'the collective unconscious' as 'the
archetypal function.' This suggestion is offered to correct a potential
error of consequence for the dialogue of philosophy and depth psychology.

[21] See Robert M. Doran, *Subject and Psyche* (Lanham, MD: University Press of America, 1977; 2nd rev. ed., Milwaukee: Marquette University Press, 1994; references will be to the Marquette edition).

[22] Erich Neumann, *The Origins and History of Consciousness* (see above, chapter 1, note 28) xx-xxi.

[23] Ibid. xxii.

[24] Ibid.

[25] Ibid. 263.

[26] Ibid. 264.

[27] Ibid. 318.

[28] Ibid. 328.

[29] Ibid. 331.

[30] Ibid. 389.

[31] Ibid. 391.

[32] Ibid. 394.

[33] Erich Neumann, *Depth Psychology and a New Ethic*, trans. Eugene Rolfe (New York: G.P. Putnam, 1969) 63.

[34] Ibid. 77.

[35] Ibid. 79.

[36] Ibid. 74.

[37] Ibid. 102.

[38] Ibid. 107.

[39] Ibid. 107-108.

40 Ibid. 113.

41 Ibid. 115.

42 Ibid. 126-27.

43 Doran, *Subject and Psyche* passim.

44 Jung's alchemical researches are reported in vols. 12, 13, and 14 of his Collected Works.

45 Lonergan, *Method in Theology* 39. Lonergan has thus introduced an important and necessary qualification to an ethic of wholeness: wholeness is a function of the realm of transcendence, not of that of interiority. It is a gift of God's grace, and in a Christian context is conditioned by the experience of the forgiveness of sin. The absence of this distinction is what traps Jungian analysis in an endless treadmill of self-scrutiny leading only to a perpetually recurring psychic stillbirth.

46 Ibid. 240.

47 Ibid. 241.

48 Ibid.

49 Ibid. 240.

50 Ibid. 105.

51 Ibid. 106.

52 Ibid. 107. With the needed emphasis on the forgiveness of sin, the love of God may also be qualified as taking over the *depths* of the soul.

53 Ibid. 92.

54 Ibid. 84.

55 Ibid. 115.

[56] Bernard Lonergan, '*Insight* Revisited,' in *A Second Collection*, ed. Bernard J.Tyrrell andWilliam F.J. Ryan (London: Darton, Longman & Todd, 1974) 277. A new edition will appear as vol. ɪɪ of Collected Works of Bernard Lonergan (Toronto: University of Toronto Press).

[57] Lonergan, *Method in Theology* 64.

[58] Eugene Gendlin, *Experiencing and the Creation of Meaning* (Toronto: Free Press of Glencoe, 1962) 4.

[59] Ricoeur, *Freud and Philosophy*. See above, chapter ɪ.

[60] See Martin Heidegger, *Kant and the Problem of Metaphysics*, trans. James Churchill (Bloomington: Indiana University Press, 1962).

[61] John S. Dunne, *TheWay of All the Earth* (NewYork: Macmillan, 1972) ix.

[62] C.G. Jung, *Modern Man in Search of a Soul* (New York: Harcourt, Brace, and World, 1933) 17.

[63] Dunne, *TheWay of All the Earth* 17-19.

[64] Bernard Lonergan, *Insight* (see above, chapter ɪ, note 37) xxviii/22.

[65] Ibid. xix/13.

[66] See Ricoeur, *Freud and Philosophy* 496.

3   Subject, Psyche, and Theology's Foundations

This paper has a twofold purpose. First, I wish to show that the intentionality analysis of Bernard Lonergan may be employed in the elaboration of categories explanatory of a process of psychic self-appropriation as an aid to the self-knowledge of the existential subject. Second, I wish to suggest the implications of psychic self-appropriation for the theological method proposed by Lonergan. The movement of my argument is thus reciprocal: Lonergan enables the construction of a semantics of depth psychology; this semantics complements Lonergan's attempt to construct a method for theology. The two parts of my argument will be taken up, respectively, in the second and third major sections of the paper. The first section attempts to clarify the notions of the psyche and of the existential subject and to discuss the relation between the referents of these two terms that seems implicit in Lonergan's later work.

1   The Psyche and Existential Subjectivity

The existential subject is the subject as evaluating, deliberating, deciding, acting, constituting the world, constituting himself or herself.[1] Existential subjectivity emerges on a level of consciousness distinct from and sublating the three levels constitutive of human knowledge: experience, understanding, and judgment.[2] Existential subjectivity is consciousness at the fourth and fullest level of its potentiality: consciousness as concerned with the good, with value, with discriminating what is truly worth while from what is only apparently good.

The discussion of the existential subject as a notion quite distinct from the cognitional subject is a relatively recent development in Lonergan's thought. It is correlated with the emergence of a notion of the good distinct from the notions of the intelligent and the reasonable. 'In *Insight* the good was the intelligent and reasonable. In *Method* the good is a distinct notion. It is intended in questions for deliberation, Is this worth while? Is it truly or only apparently good? It is aspired to in the intentional response of feeling to values. It is known in judgments of value made by a virtuous or authentic person with a good conscience. It is brought about by deciding and living up to one's decisions.'[3]

The emergence of a distinct notion of the good involves a relocation of the constitutive function of the psyche in the structured process of conscious subjectivity. Psychic development is defined in *Insight* as 'a sequence of increasingly differentiated and integrated sets of capacities for perceptiveness, for aggressive or affective response, for memory, for imaginative projects, and for skillfully and economically executed performance.'[4] I shall use the term 'psyche' to refer to this set of capacities. They have a basis, Lonergan says, in 'some neural counterpart of association,'[5] but this unconscious neural basis is 'an upwardly directed dynamism seeking fuller realization, first, on the proximate sensitive level, and secondly, beyond its limitations, on higher artistic, dramatic, philosophic, cultural, and religious levels,' so that 'insight into dream symbols and associated images and affects reveals to the psychologist a grasp of the anticipations and virtualities of higher activities immanent in the underlying unconscious manifold.'[6]

In *Insight*, this set of capacities is integrated by cognitional or intellectual activities: '... the psyche reaches the wealth and fullness of its apprehensions and responses under the higher integration of human intelligence.'[7] Intellectual development sets the standard and provides the criterion for psychic, affective, and volitional development. Thus Lonergan speaks of reaching a 'universal willingness that matches the unrestricted desire to know.'[8] But in *Method in Theology*, human intelligence and the psyche, especially in its affective and symbolic capacities, are sublated and unified by the deliberations of the authentic existential subject, for the apprehension of potential values and satisfactions in feelings, along with questions for deliberation, is what mediates between cognitional judgments of fact and existential judgments of value. Thus, 'just as intelligence sublates sense, just as reasonableness sublates intelligence, so deliberation sublates and thereby unifies knowing and feeling.'[9] The development of existential subjectivity now sets the standard and provides the criterion for intellectual development,[10] and the former development is intrinsically related to the refinement of affective response.

Affectivity and symbols are no less related to one another in *Method in Theology* than in *Insight*. Feelings are said to be symbolically certifiable, and a symbol is defined as 'an image of a real or imaginary object that evokes a feeling or is evoked by a feeling.'[11] One's affective capacities, dispositions, and habits 'can be specified by the symbols that awaken determinate affects and, inversely, by the affects that evoke determinate symbols.'[12] Thus 'affective development, or aberration, involves a transvaluation and transformation of symbols. What before was moving no longer moves; what before did not move now is moving. So the symbols themselves change to express the new affective capacities and dispositions.'[13] These affective capacities and dispositions affect the existential subject, for feelings 'are the mass and momentum of his affective capacities, dispositions, habits, the effective orientation of his being.'[14] It is in intentional feeling-responses to objects and possible courses of action that values and satisfactions are first apprehended. Feelings thus are crucial in the process of deliberation that comes to term only in the decisions of the existential subject.

The transvaluation and transformation of symbols that goes hand in hand with affective development can be understood only when one realizes that symbols follow other laws than those of rational discourse.

> For the logical class the symbol uses a representative figure. For univocity it substitutes a wealth of multiple meanings. It does not prove but it overwhelms with a manifold of images that converge in meaning. It does not bow to the principle of excluded middle but admits the *coincidentia oppositorum*, of love and hate, of courage and fear, and so on. It does not negate but overcomes what it rejects by heaping up all that is opposite to it. It does not move on some single track or on some single level, but condenses into a bizarre unity all its present concerns.[15]

The function of symbols, moreover, is to meet a need for internal communication that such rational procedures as logic and dialectic cannot satisfy. 'Organic and psychic vitality have to reveal themselves to intentional consciousness and, inversely, intentional consciousness has to secure the collaboration of organism and psyche. Again, our apprehensions of values occur in intentional responses, in feelings; here too it is necessary for feelings to reveal their objects and, inversely, for objects to awaken feelings. It is through symbols that mind and body, mind and heart, heart and body communicate.'[16]

The elemental, preobjectified meaning of symbols finds its proper context in this process of internal communication. The interpretation of the symbol thus has to appeal to this context and its associated images and feelings.[17] Because of the existential significance of the symbol, Lonergan evinces a strong sympathy with those schools of dream interpretation which think of the dream 'not as the twilight of life, but as its dawn, the beginning of the transition from impersonal existence to presence in the world, to constitution of one's self in one's world.'[18]

The position of the 'later Lonergan' on the psyche, then, is that it reaches the wealth and fullness of its apprehensions and responses, not under the higher integration of human intelligence, but in the free and responsible decisions of the authentic existential subject. This position sets the stage for arguing that Lonergan's intentionality analysis can be complemented by psychic analysis and that the latter is a further refinement of the self-appropriation of the existential subject. Intentionality analysis, moreover, clarifies the finality of psychic analysis.

The argument for complementarity is bolstered by Lonergan's acknowledgment of a twofold mediation of immediacy by meaning. 'Besides the immediate world of the infant and the adult's world mediated by meaning, there is the mediation of immediacy by meaning when one objectifies cognitional process in transcendental method and when one discovers, identifies, accepts one's submerged feelings in psychotherapy.'[19] The second mediation can be understood as aiding the self-appropriation of the existential subject in much the same way as the first aids that of the cognitional subject. Intentionality analysis, as articulated in a pattern of judgments concerning cognitional fact,

moral living, and religious experience, can be complemented by depth-psychological analysis. If the latter is
engaged in within the overall context of the former, it can
critically ground moral and religious living in an expanding pattern of judgments of value that set one's course as
existential subject, and it can facilitate the sublation of an
intellectually self-appropriating consciousness by moral and
religious subjectivity. The theological pertinence of this
psychic complement to Lonergan's work will be foundational. According to the dynamic operative in Lonergan's
articulation of theological foundations, the foundational
reality of theology is the subjectivity of the theologian.
Lonergan has articulated foundational reality in terms of
religious, moral, and intellectual conversion. While the
conversions generally occur in this order, they also display
relations of sublation in the reverse order.[20] I will posit a
fourth conversion, psychic conversion, as an aspect of foundational reality. Psychic conversion is the release of the
capacity for the internal communication of symbolic consciousness. By aiding existential self-appropriation, it facilitates the sublation of intellectual conversion by moral
conversion, and of both of these by religious conversion.[21]
Foundations in theology would then lie in the objectification of cognitive, psychic, moral, and religious subjectivity
in a patterned set of judgments of cognitional and existential fact cumulatively heading toward the full position on
the human subject.

2   Toward a Semantics of Depth Psychology

My first contention is that Lonergan's intentionality
analysis enables the construction of a semantics of depth
psychology. To argue this, I will discuss first the finality of
both intentionality analysis and depth-psychological analysis under the rubric of second immediacy; second, the role

of the depth-psychological uncovering of symbolic consciousness in advancing the subject to second immediacy; third, the manner in which this uncovering can be integrated with Lonergan's intentionality analysis; and fourth, the notion of psychic conversion and its relation to Lonergan's notions of religious, moral, and intellectual conversion. I will conclude this section with a brief statement of the relation of the psychology I am suggesting to the archetypal psychology of C.G. Jung.

2.1 Second Immediacy

Method as conceived by Lonergan may be understood as the objectification or mediation of the transcendental infrastructure of human subjectivity. I will call this infrastructure primordial immediacy. The basic structure of primordial immediacy is disengaged in Lonergan's articulation of conscious intentionality. This articulation is method. Method calls for 'a release from all logics, all closed systems or language games, all concepts, all symbolic constructs to allow an abiding at the level of the presence of the subject to himself.'22 The emergence of a distinct notion of the good and especially its relation to affectivity and symbols allow us to understand psychic self-appropriation as a portion of method. In psychic self-appropriation the existential subject disengages the symbolic ciphers of the affective responses in which values and satisfactions are apprehended. From this disengagement, the subject can gauge the measure of self-transcendence operative in his or her orientation as a world-constituting and self-constituting existential subject. Psychic analysis, then, is a part of self-appropriation at the fourth level of intentional consciousness. But method in its totality is the self-appropriation of the primordial immediacy of the subject

to himself or herself in a world itself mediated by meaning. This immediacy is both cognitive and existential.

Second immediacy is the result of method's objectification of primordial immediacy, the probably always asymptotic recovery of primordial immediacy through method.
Second immediacy is 'the self-possession of the subject-as-
subject achieved as a result of the mediation of the transcendental infrastructure of human subjectivity, and so of the
objectification of the single transcendental intending of the
intelligible, the true, and the good, the self-appropriation of
the cognitional and existential subject which is the fulfillment
of the *anthropologische Wendung* of modern philosophy.'[23] From
Lonergan's statement concerning the twofold mediation of
immediacy, I infer that primordial immediacy is mediated
through intentionality analysis *and* through psychic analysis.
What is mediated by psychic analysis is the affective or
dispositional component of all intentional operations, a
component frequently and not too accurately referred to as
the unconscious.

This affective component may itself be intentional,
the apprehension of potential values and satisfactions in
feelings. In that case, psychic analysis aids the emergence
especially of existential subjectivity by mediating a capacity to disengage the symbolic or imaginal ciphers of the
intentional feelings in which values are apprehended. But
the dispositional component may also be a matter of one's
mood, of one's nonintentional feeling states or trends.[24]
Then it is what we intend when we ask another, How are
you? One may find the question quite baffling, and if one
adverts to this puzzlement over a period of time, one may
be on the way to seeking help. One may become cognizant
of being out of touch with something very important, something deceptively simple and in fact very mysterious and
profound: the dispositional aspect of one's intentional operations as a knower and doer. One has acknowledged,

however secretly and privately, that the question causes an uncomfortable confusion. One is out of touch. One does not know how one is, who one is. Because one's intentional affective responses are in part a function of one's nonintentional dispositions, one does not know where one stands, what one values, how one's values are related to one another. Finally, while the appropriation of dispositional components in psychotherapy is obviously not dependent on cognitional self-appropriation, it can also figure as a part of method, as a feature of the existential subject's heeding of the critical-methodical exigence. This exigence is at least in part therapeutic, for it is an exigence for a second immediacy, which is the fruit of the twofold mediation of primordial immediacy in cognitional analysis and in psychic analysis.

2.2 Symbolic Consciousness

In reliance on Lonergan's statement of the relation between feelings and symbols, I suggest that the dispositional component of immediacy is imaginally constructed, symbolically constituted. It is structured by imagination and expresses itself in symbols. The interpretation of these symbols is the deciphering of this component of intentionality. Nonetheless, while this component is immediately accessible to intentional consciousness as the flow of feeling which accompanies all intentional operations, its symbolic constitution can often be retrieved only by specific techniques elaborated by depth-psychological analysis. Principal among these techniques is dream interpretation. Particularly when one is out of touch with how one is, these techniques may be required in order that this dispositional component can be objectified, known, and appropriated. They reveal how it stands between the self as objectified and the self as conscious. They also enable one's self-understanding to approximate one's reality. Through these techniques, one gains the capacity to articulate one's story as it is and to guide it responsibly. One may have to reverse a cumulative misinterpretation of one's experience; this reversal will be painful, but it is escaped only at the cost of a flight from understanding, and indeed from understanding oneself. It is primarily in the existential, evaluative, and dialectical hermeneutic of one's dreams, one's own most radical spontaneity, that one recovers the individual and transpersonal core of elemental imagination which reveals in symbolic ciphers the affective component of one's intentionality.

The cognitive dimensions of method have been expressed in Lonergan's dictum, 'Thoroughly understand what it is to understand, and not only will you understand the broad lines of all there is to be understood, but also you will possess a fixed base, an invariant pattern, opening upon all further developments of understanding.'[25] Of the roots of desire and fear in human imagination, we may say something similar: Come to know as existential subject the contingent figures, the structure, the process, and the imaginal spontaneity manifested in your dreams, and you will come into possession of an expanding base and an intelligible pattern illuminating the *vouloir-dire* of human desire as it is brought to expression in the cultural and religious objectifications of human history.[26] Furthermore, elemental dream symbols are spontaneous psychic productions. By deciphering them, one gains the potential of conscripting organic and psychic vitality into the higher integration of intentionality as it raises questions of intelligibility, truth, and value. One finds, too, significant clues regarding one's own potential drift toward the loss of existential subjectivity either in triviality or in fanaticism. Dreams do not always resolve the tension they often reveal; this resolution is the task of the intentionality of the existential subject finding out for oneself that it is up to oneself to decide for oneself what one is going to make of oneself. But the symbolic manifestations of dreams can provide access to the materials one has to work with in one's self-constituting operations. Dreams will reveal a story of development or decline according as they are dealt with by existential consciousness in the dialogic process of internal communication.

2.3   Sublations

Dream interpretation can be understood in terms of Lonergan's notion of successive levels of consciousness, where the lower-level operations are sublated by the higher integrations provided by the operations that occur on subsequent levels. If being is what is to be known by the totality of true judgments,[27] then any true judgments about the symbolic ciphers of affectivity concern a sphere of being, which we may call the imaginal.[28] The differentiation and appropriation of the dispositional constituents of immediacy, then, are enabled to come to pass by a sublation on the part of conscious intentionality that is additional to the sublations explained by Lonergan. In addition to the sublation of internal and external waking sensory experience by understanding, of experience and understanding by reasonable judgment, and of experience, understanding, and judgment by existential subjectivity, there is a sublation of dreaming consciousness on the part of the whole of attentive, intelligent, reasonable, responsible, cooperative-intersubjective existential consciousness. Thus in addition to the attentive, intelligent, reasonable, and responsible appropriation of one's rational self-consciousness effected by bringing one's conscious operations as intentional to bear on those same operations as conscious, there is the attentive, intelligent, reasonable, and responsible appropriation and negotiation of one's psychic spontaneity. Such a sublation is implicit in Lonergan's reference to the approach of existential psychology, which, as we have seen, regards the dream as the dawn of life, as the beginning of the transition from impersonal existence to personal existence and self-constitution.[29] We may venture beyond Lonergan at this point and speak of an additional sublation mediating this dawn of consciousness to the existential subject. Through this sublation, the affective component of one's intentional orientation is released from muteness and confusion.

Dreams, then, may be regarded as an intelligible text or story whose meaning can be read by interpretive understanding and reasonable judgment and affirmed or reoriented by evaluative deliberation. The symbols of dreams are operators effecting internal communication, in much the same way as questions are operators promoting successive levels of intentional consciousness. The ground theme of the internal communication is the emergence of the authentic existential subject as free and responsible constitutive agent of the human world. This theme is the basic a priori of human consciousness, the intention of intelligibility, truth, and value. It promotes human experience to understanding by means of questions for intelligence, and understanding to truth by means of questions for reflection. So too it promotes truth into action, but in a thetic and constitutive manner, through questions for deliberation. The data for these questions are apprehended in intentional responses to values in feelings; the feelings structure patterns of experience; and the patterns can be understood by disengaging their imaginal ciphers and by insight into the images thus disengaged. Dream images, then, promote neural, sensitive, affective, and imaginative process to a recognizable and intelligible narrative. The narrative is the basic story of the ground theme. It can be understood; the understanding can be affirmed as correct, so that the images function in aid of self-knowledge; and beyond self-knowledge, there is praxis, where the knowledge becomes thetic: What am I going to do about it? The ultimate intentionality of the therapeutic process so conceived is thus coextensive with the total sweep of conscious intentionality. The psyche can be conscripted into the single transcendental dynamism of human consciousness toward the authenticity of self-transcendence. The imaginal spontaneity of dreams belongs to this dynamism, but it can be disengaged only by intelligent, reasonable, and decisive conscription, without which the psyche can fall prey to an inertial counterweight toward the flight from genuine humanity. This conscription must generally take place in a cooperative-intersubjective milieu, with the aid of a professional guide familiar with the vagaries of dreaming consciousness, a guide who is familiar with the dialectic of the psyche, who knows the need of healing if conscription is in some instances to take place, and who can instruct his or her dialogical counterpart on how to accept and befriend the dimensions of affectivity that need to be healed. The language of dreams is frequently so very different from that of waking consciousness that the process of negotiation usually demands that one seek such competent assistance.

2.4   Psychic Conversion

The conscious capacity for the sublation of the imaginal sphere of being is effected by a conversion on the part of the existential subject. This conversion I have called psychic conversion.[30] In this section, I will demonstrate how it meets all of Lonergan's specifications for conversion and how it is integrally related to the religious, moral,

and intellectual conversions specified by Lonergan as qualifying authentic human subjectivity.

Lonergan first began to thematize conversion in his
search for renewed foundations of theology. In a lecture
delivered in 1967, he described the new context of theology in terms of the demise of the classicist mediation of
meaning and the struggle of modern culture for a new
maieutic, only to conclude that this new context demands
that theology be placed on a new foundation, one distinct
from the citation of scripture and the enunciation of revealed doctrines characteristic of the foundation of the old
dogmatic theology. What was this new foundation to be?

Lonergan drew his first clue from the notion of
method, considered as 'a normative pattern that related to
one another the cognitional operations that recur in scientific investigations.'[31] The stress in this notion of method
is on the personal experience of the operations and of their
dynamic and normative relations to one another. If a scientist were to locate one's operations and their relations in
one's own experience, Lonergan maintained, one would
come to know oneself as scientist. And, since the subject
as scientist is the foundation of science, one would come
into possession of the foundations of one's science.

Of what use is such a clue to one seeking a new foundation for theology? Lonergan says: 'It illustrates by an
example what might be meant by a foundation that lies
not in sets of verbal propositions named first principles,
but in a particular, concrete, dynamic reality generating
knowledge of particular, concrete, dynamic realities.'[32]

Lonergan draws a second clue from the phenomenon of conversion, which is fundamental to religious living. Conversion, he says, 'is not merely a change or even a
development; rather, it is a radical transformation on which
follows, on all levels of living, an interlocked series of
changes and developments. What hitherto had been of no

concern becomes a matter of high import.'[33] Conversion of course has many degrees of depth of realization. But in any case of genuine conversion, 'the convert apprehends differently, values differently, relates differently because he has become different. The new apprehension is not so much a new statement or a new set of statements, but rather new meanings that attach to almost any statement. It is not new values so much as a transformation of values.'[34] Conversion is also possible as a change that is not only individual and personal but also communal and historical; and when viewed as an ongoing process, at once personal, communal, and historical, it coincides, Lonergan says, with living religion.[35]

Now, if theology is reflection on religion, and if conversion is fundamental to religious living, then not only will theology also be reflection on conversion, but reflection on conversion will provide theology with its foundations. 'Just as reflection on the operations of the scientist brings to light the real foundation of the science, so too reflection on the ongoing process of conversion may bring to light the real foundation of a renewed theology.'[36] Such is the basic argument establishing what is, in fact, a revolutionary recasting of the foundations of theology.

For the moment, however, my concern is not theology but conversion. The notion is significantly developed in *Method in Theology*, where conversion is differentiated into religious, moral, and intellectual varieties. What I am maintaining is that the emergence of the capacity to disengage the symbolic ciphers of the feelings in which the primordial apprehension of value occurs satisfies Lonergan's notion of conversion but also that it is something other than the three conversions of which Lonergan speaks. As any other conversion, it has many facets. As any other conversion, it is ever precarious. As any other conversion, it is a radical transformation of subjectivity influ-

encing all the levels of one's living and transvaluing one's
values. As any other conversion, it is 'not so much a new
statement or a new set of statements, but rather new meanings that attach to almost any statement.'[37] As any other
conversion, it too can become communal, so that there
are formed formal and informal communities of men and
women encouraging one another in the pursuit of further
understanding and practical implementation of what they
have experienced. Finally, as any other conversion, it undergoes a personal and arduous history of development,
setback, and renewal. Its eventual outcome, most likely
only asymptotically approached, is symbolically described
by C.G. Jung as the termination of a state of imprisonment through a cumulative reconciliation of opposites,[38]
or as the resolution of the contradictoriness of the unconscious and consciousness in a nuptial *coniunctio*,[39] or as
the birth of the hero issuing 'from something humble and
forgotten.'[40] But, like any other conversion, psychic conversion is not the goal but the beginning. As religious conversion is not the mystic's cloud of unknowing, as moral
conversion is not moral perfection, as intellectual conversion is not methodological craftsmanship, so psychic conversion is not unified affectivity or total integration of consciousness and the unconscious or immediate release from
imprisonment in the rhythms and processes of nature and
mood. It is, at the beginning, no more than the obscure
understanding of the nourishing potential of elemental
symbols to maintain and foster the vitality of conscious
living by a continuous influx of both data and energy; the
hint that one's affective being can be transformed so as to
aid one in the quest for authenticity; the suspicion that
coming to terms with one's dreams will profoundly change
what Jung calls one's ego, that is, the oftentimes too narrow, biased, and self-absorbed focus of one's conscious
intentionality, by ousting this narrowed focus from a cen-

tral and dominating position in one's conscious living and by shifting the birthplace of meaning gradually but progressively to a deeper center which is simultaneously a totality, the self.[41] Slowly one comes to discover the complexity of dreams, and thus of one's affectivity, and to affirm the arduousness of the task to which one has committed oneself. Slowly one learns that the point is what is interior, temporal, generic, and indeed at times religious, and not what is exterior, spatial, specific, and solely profane.[42] Slowly a system of internal communication is established between intentionality and one's organic and psychic vitality. Slowly one learns the habit of disengaging the symbolic significance associated with one's intentional affective responses to situations, people, and objects. Slowly one learns to distinguish symbols which indicate and urge an orientation to truth and value from those which mire one in myth and ego-centered satisfactions. Slowly one notices the changes that take place in the symbolic ciphers of one's affectivity. One becomes attentive in a new and more contemplative way to the data of sense and the data of consciousness. One is aided by this new symbolic consciousness in one's efforts to be intelligent, reasonable, and responsible in one's everyday commonsense living and in one's intellectual pursuit of truth. Some of the concrete areas of one's own inattentiveness, obtuseness, silliness, and irresponsibility are revealed one by one and can be named and quasi personified. They are complexes with a quasi personality of their own. When personified, they can be engaged in active imaginative dialogue where one must listen as well as speak. The dialogue relativizes the ego and thus frees the complexes from their counter-rigidity. Some of them, those that indicate where one needs healing, can then even be befriended and transformed. When thus paid attention to, honored, and in a very definite sense compromised with, they prove to be sources of conscious en-

ergy one never before knew were at one's disposal. Such is
psychic conversion. In itself it is not a matter of falling in
love with God or of shifting the criterion of one's choices
from satisfactions to values or of reflectively recognizing
that knowing is not looking but the affirmation of the virtually unconditioned. It is not religious conversion or moral
conversion or intellectual conversion. It *is* conversion, but
it is something other than these.

2.5   A Note on Jung's Archetypal Psychology

C.G. Jung's notion of individuation as a cumulative
process of the reconciliation of opposites under the guidance of responsible consciousness and with the aid of a
professional guide obviously bears some similarity to the
process of psychic self-appropriation that I have briefly
described. Furthermore, his insistence that neither of the
basic opposites of instinct or spirit is in itself good or evil,[43]
that moral significance attaches rather to the process of
reconciliation, is correct and illuminating. Jung's researches
help us to reject a falsely spiritualistic and narrowly egoistic tendency to locate the root of evil in instinct and the
body. Moreover, Jung is at home with a notion of elemental symbolism that is nonreductionistic and basically teleological. He would be quite in agreement with Lonergan's
description of dreams as indicating 'the anticipation and
virtualities of higher activities immanent in the underlying
unconscious manifold.'[44] Thus Jung is the principal psychological contributor to my own position. Nonetheless,
because of the intentionality analysis of Lonergan, with
which I am seeking to integrate a process of psychic analysis, I wish to suggest that there is one pair of opposites that
is not to be reconciled in the manner of the mutual
complementarity of such contraries as spirit and matter,
but that qualifies for good or for evil any such process of

reconciliation. These opposites are authenticity and unauthenticity, where authenticity is understood as self-transcendence. These opposites are contradictories, not contraries. Their conflict is revealed, not in Jung's archetypal symbols that are taken from and imitate nature's cyclical processes, but in the symbols that Northrop Frye has called anagogic and that contain and express the orientation of the whole of human action in an irreducibly dialectical fashion. It is my suspicion that the recognition of such a distinction between archetypal and anagogic symbols would necessitate a reconstruction of those further outposts of Jungian thought where the question is one of good and evil, and where the religious import of the question is revealed in one's notion and image both of the self and of God. The progressive reconciliation of the opposites that Jung calls spirit and matter and that Lonergan calls transcendence and limitation[45] takes place in what Lonergan calls the realm of interiority. But when the question is one of authenticity and unauthenticity, the resolution demands a movement into another realm of meaning, the realm of transcendence, where discriminated intentionality and cultivated affectivity surrender to the mystery of God's love and find their basic fulfillment in this surrender.[46]

3 Psyche and Theology's Foundations

In this section, I move to the second portion of my argument. It is to the effect that the semantics of depth psychology suggested by Lonergan's intentionality analysis complements Lonergan's notion of foundations in theology. I will discuss, first, the development of Lonergan's thought on foundational reality or the subject; second, the pertinence of my suggestions regarding depth psychology for Lonergan's later thought on the subject; and third, the effect that this expanded notion of the subject will have on the articulation of the functional specialty 'foundations.'

3.1   *Lonergan on Foundational Reality*

The emergence of a distinct notion of the good in Lonergan's later work effects a very significant change in his notion of the foundational reality of theology. In *Insight*, the basis of any philosophy lies in its cognitional theory. The further expansion of the basis is formulated in the philosophy's pronouncements on metaphysical, ethical, and theological issues. Now, the formulation of the basis necessarily will entail a commitment on three philosophical questions: reality, the subject, and objectivity. Lonergan has advanced his own positions on these issues in the twelfth, eleventh, and thirteenth chapters of *Insight*, respectively. One's commitments on these three issues will be positions open to development if they agree with the positions advanced in these chapters, and counterpositions inviting reversal if they are in conflict with these positions. Thus

> The inevitable philosophic component, immanent in the formulation of cognitional theory, will be either a basic position or else a basic counterposition.
>
> It will be a basic position, (1) if the real is the concrete universe of being and not a subdivision of the 'already out there now'; (2) if the subject becomes known when it affirms itself intelligently and reasonably and so is not known yet in any prior 'existential' state; and (3) if objectivity is conceived as a consequence of intelligent inquiry and critical reflection, and

not as a property of vital anticipation, extroversion, and satisfaction.

On the other hand, it will be a basic counterposition if it contradicts one or more of the basic positions.

... any philosophic pronouncement on any epistemological, metaphysical, ethical, or theological issue will be named a position if it is coherent with the basic positions on the real, on knowing, and on objectivity; and it will be named a counterposition if it is coherent with one or more of the basic counterpositions.[47]

According to the second of these basic positions, the subject becomes known when it affirms itself intelligently and reasonably. But *nothing* is known unless it is intelligently grasped and reasonably affirmed. The self-affirmation intended by Lonergan is the intelligent and reasonable affirmation of one's own intelligence and reasonableness. It is the judgment 'I am a knower,' where knowledge is the compound of experience, understanding, and judgment. Thus the basic position on the subject in *Insight* is the position on the knowing subject. The self-affirmation of the knower, along with positions on the real and objectivity, are what constitute the foundations or basis of metaphysics, ethics, and (at least philosophical) theology.

These three basic positions are reached as a result of what Lonergan later calls intellectual conversion. Intellectual conversion, according to the later Lonergan, generally follows upon and is conditioned by religious and moral conversion. There is a realism implicit in religious and moral self-transcendence which promotes the recognition of the realism of knowing. Moreover, in Lonergan's later work a primacy is assigned to the existential subject, the subject as religious and moral. The basic position on the subject includes but exceeds that on the knowing subject. It reaches to the position on the deciding, deliberating, evaluating subject. Furthermore, if the intellectual conversion which issues in the basic positions is consequent upon religious and moral conversion, then the foundation of one's metaphysics, ethics, and theology would seem to lie in the objectification of all three conversions in a patterned set of judgments concerning both cognitional and existential subjectivity. And such is indeed what happens to foundations in *Method in Theology*. The foundations of theology include but go far beyond *Insight*'s basic positions on knowing, the real, and objectivity — not by denying them but by adding that the basic position on knowing is not the full position on the human subject. The foundational reality of theology is the intellectually, morally, and religiously converted theologian. The intentionality of human consciousness, the primordial infrastructure of human subjectivity, is a dynamism for cognitional, existential, and religious self-transcendence. That subject whose conscious performance is self-consciously in accord with this dynamism is foundational reality. The objectification of this dynamism in a patterned set of judgments of cognitional and existential fact constitutes foundations in theology. Lonergan's thought thus becomes not primarily cognitional theory, but an elucidation of the drama of the emergence of the authentic subject.

3.2   Psyche and Foundational Reality

The basic position on the subject finds expression only when judgments of cognitional fact are joined with judgments of existential and religious fact. Moreover, on the basis of Lonergan's treatment of the existential subject, it is fair to say that the formulation of the position on the subject demands not only the functioning of intelligence and reasonableness grasping and affirming intelligence and reasonableness, but also a satisfactory transcendental analysis of the human good. This analysis includes a set of judgments detailing the authentic development of feelings. This development, in my analysis, is a matter of the dispositional component of primordial immediacy. If the story of the development and aberration of feelings can be told by disengaging the spontaneous symbols produced in dreams, if the habit of such disengagement is mediated to the subject by psychic conversion, if psychic conversion is foundational reality, if the objectification of conversion is the functional specialty 'foundations,' then psychic conversion is an aspect of foundational reality and an objectification of psychic conversion will constitute a portion of foundations.

There are counterpositions on the real, on knowing, and on objectivity that are incoherent with the activities of intelligent grasping and reasonable affirmation. But there are also counterpositions on the subject that are incoherent, not specifically with these activities alone, but with the emergence of the authentic existential subject. Only in this latter incoherence are they suspected of being counterpositions, for they are apprehended as articulations of countervalues in the feelings of the existential subject striving for self-transcendence, and they are judged to be such in the same subject's judgments of value. They are incoherent, not specifically with the self-transcendence intended in the unfolding of the desire to know, but with the self-transcendence toward which the primordial infrastructure of human subjectivity as a whole is headed. The subject who contains implicitly the full position on the subject is not the intelligent and reasonable subject, but the experiencing, intelligent, reasonable, responsible, religious subject. In fact, if one is looking for the full position on the human subject by scrutinizing only one's intelligence and reasonableness, one is heading for the articulation of a counterposition on the subject. One is then the victim of an intellectualist bias perhaps still too easily confirmed by the writings of the early Lonergan in those readers whose personal history has been characterized by a hypertrophy of intellectual development at the expense of the underlying neural and psychic manifolds. The emergence of the notion of the good as distinct from, though not contradictory to, the intelligent and reasonable in the writings of the post-1965 Lonergan decisively shifts the atmosphere of his work as a whole. Human authenticity is a matter of self-transcendence. Self-transcendence can be in one's knowing, in one's free and responsible constitution of the human world and of oneself, and in one's religious living as a participation in the divine solution to the problem of evil. The struggle between the dynamism for self-transcendence and the flight from authenticity provides the ground theme unifying the various aspects of this achievement.

This ground theme is invested with a distinct symbolic significance. Not only does intentionality in its dynamic thrust for self-transcendence have the potential of conscripting underlying neural and psychic manifolds into its service through the dialectical disengagement of their intention of truth and value; but the psyche insists, as it were, on stamping the entire drama with its own characteristic mark by giving it a symbolic representation, by releasing in dreams the ciphers of the present status of the drama, by indicating to the existential subject how it stands between the totality of consciousness as primordial infrastructure to be fulfilled in self-transcendence and the subject's explicit self-understanding in his or her intention of or flight from truth and value. The articulation of the story of these ciphers, the disengagement of their intelligible pattern in a hermeneutic phenomenology of the psyche, would constitute what we might call, in a sense quite different from Kant's, a transcendental aesthetic. This aesthetic would, I wager, follow Jung's phenomenology of the psyche quite closely, until one comes to the farthest reaches of subjectivity, which also constitute its center. There hermeneutic becomes dialectic, in Lonergan's quite specific sense of this word as indicating an interpretation that deals with the concrete, the dynamic, and *the contradictory*.[48] For the issue becomes that of good and evil, grace and sin, authenticity and unauthenticity. At that point psychology as a path to individuation must bow to an immanent *Ananke* and give way to religion.[49] Intentionality and the psychic manifold it has conscripted into its adventure must at this point surrender to the gift of God's love. The transcendental aesthetic issues in kerygma, proclamation, manifestation, in the return to the fullness of language simply heard and understood, in the second naivete intended in the writings of Paul Ricoeur.[50] This return is mediated by the process of self-appropriation in its entirety, by the objectification of the primordial infrastructure of intentional and psychic subjectivity in a twofold mediation of immediacy by meaning.

3.3   Psyche and the Functional Specialty 'Foundations'

The functional specialty 'foundations' would seem to have a twofold task: that of articulating the horizon within which theological categories can be understood and employed, and that of deriving the categories which are appropriate to such a horizon. What is the relationship of psychic self-appropriation to this twofold task?

I have spoken of the first task in terms of framing a patterned set of judgments of cognitional and existential fact cumulatively heading toward the full position on the human subject. Psychic self-appropriation is a contribution to this patterned set of judgments and thus to the full position on the subject. Implicit in this statement is the claim that psychic self-appropriation is a needed complement to the self-appropriation of intentionality aided by the work of Lonergan. It is even an intrinsic part of transcendental method, a necessary feature of the objectification of the transcendental infrastructure of human subjectivity. It is demanded by the task set by Lonergan, the task of moving toward a viable control of meaning in terms of human interiority.[51] The psyche is no accidental feature of the transcendental infrastructure of human subjectivity. It achieves an integration with intentionality, however, only in the free and responsible decisions of the existential subject who is cognizant of the psychic input into and reading of his or her situation. The integration of psyche and intentionality, to be sure, is not the only task confronting the existential subject. It is a task that for the most part affects one's effective freedom, and there is the more radical question which one must deal with at the level of essential freedom.[52] What do I want to make of myself? The integration of psyche with intentionality occurs in the framework established by one's answer to that question and may affect and modify this framework. But occur it must, if this more radical answer is to bear fruit in the effective constitution of oneself and of one's world.

Lonergan speaks of placing 'abstractly apprehended cognitional activity within the concrete and sublating context of human feeling and of moral deliberation, evaluation, and decision.'[53] Until cognitional activity, no matter how correctly apprehended, is so placed, it remains abstract in its apprehension. The move toward greater concreteness on the side of the subject, then, calls for a second mediation of immediacy by meaning. Only such mediation brings transcendental method to its conclusion. This is no easy task. It is at least as complicated as comprehending and affirming cognitional activity. Equally sophisticated techniques are needed for its execution. But without it the movement brought into being by Lonergan is left incomplete and those influenced by this movement are left the potential victims of an intellectualist bias. Students of Lonergan's work have not yet sufficiently attended to the shift of the center of attention from cognitional analysis to intentionality analysis, from the intellectual pattern of experience to self-transcendence in all patterns of experience as the privileged domain of human subjectivity. This shift means that the exigence giving rise to a new epoch in the evolution of human consciousness, an epoch governed by a control of meaning in terms of interiority, only begins to be met in the philosophic conversion aided by Lonergan's cognitional analysis. The radical crisis is not only cognitional but also existential, the crisis of the self as objectified becoming approximate to the self as primordial infrastructure. And the psyche will never cease to have its say and to offer both its potential contribution and its potential threat to the unfolding of the transcendental dynamism toward self-transcendence. Psychic self-appropriation is quite necessary if the concrete sublation of appropriated cognitional activity within the context of human feeling and moral decision is to take place.

Psychic analysis, then, is a necessary contribution to the maieutic that *is* the self-appropriating subject. And an articulation of psychic conversion is a constituent feature of the patterned set of judgments of cognitional and existential fact cumulatively heading toward the full position on the human subject that constitutes renewed foundations in theology.

Foundations, however, has a second task, that of deriving categories appropriate to the horizon articulated in the objectification of conversion. What is the relation of psychic self-appropriation to this foundational task?

All theological categories have a significance that has psychic and affective resonances. The *general* theological categories, those shared by theology with other disciplines, are derived from the transcendental base giving rise to the emergence of the authentic cognitional and existential subject. The narrative of this emergence can be disengaged by the deciphering of dreams. The emergence itself is the ground theme of the dialogue and dialectic between intentionality and psyche. It can be objectified in a transcendental aesthetic. The *special* theological categories, those peculiar to theology as it attempts to mediate between the Christian religion and the role and significance of that religion within a given cultural context, reflect a collaboration between God and human beings in working out the solution to the radical problem of this ground theme, the problem of evil. As the emergence of the existential subject is the drama of human existence, so the Christian religion in its authenticity is for the Christian theologian the fruit of the divinely originated solution to that drama.[54]

Psychic self-appropriation, then, is a part of the objectification of the transcendental and transcultural base from which both general and special theological categories are derived. It affects the self-understanding in terms of which one mediates the past in interpretation, history, dialectic, and the special research generated by their concerns. And it gives rise to the generation of theological categories appropriate to the mediated phase of theology, the phase which takes its stand on self-appropriation and ventures to say what is so to the men and women of different strata and backgrounds in different cultures of the world of today. It gives rise to the possibility of theological categories, doctrines or positions, and systems which are legitimately symbolic or poetic or aesthetic. It makes it possible that such categories, positions, and systems can be poetic without ceasing to be explanatory, without ceasing to fix terms and relations by one another. A hermeneutic and dialectical phenomenology of the psyche would be the objectification of psychic conversion that is a constituent feature of foundations in theology from which appropriate explanatory categories can be derived. Ray L. Hart's desire, then, for a systematic symbolics[55] is an ambition that is methodologically both possible and desirable. But its valid methodological base is found, I believe, only in the mediation of immediacy in which one discovers, identifies, accepts one's affectivity by disengaging its symbolic ciphers.

Second immediacy will never achieve a total mediation of primordial immediacy. Complete self-transparency is impossible short of our ulterior finality in the vision of God. Only in seeing God as God is will we know ourselves as we are. But there is a poetic enjoyment of the truth about us and God that has been achieved in many cultures, at many times, within the framework of many differentiations of consciousness, and related to different combinations of the various realms of meaning. The second mediation of immediacy by meaning can function in aid of a recovery of this poetic enjoyment. Even of the theologian, it may be said with Hölderlin and Heidegger:

> Full of merit, and yet poetically, dwells
> Man on this earth.[56]

Notes

See, e.g., Bernard Lonergan, 'The Subject,' in *A Second Collection* (see above, chapter 2, note 56) 69-86, with the relevant section beginning on p. 79.

[2] See ibid. 79-81. Although the schema of conscious intentionality is in this instance presented in six steps, there are four levels of intentionality for Lonergan. They are referred to as experience, understanding, judgment, and decision or existential subjectivity.

[3] Bernard Lonergan, '*Insight* Revisited,' in *A Second Collection* 277.

[4] Bernard Lonergan, *Insight* (see above, chapter 1, note 37) 456/481.

[5] Ibid.

[6] Ibid. 457/482.

[7] Ibid. 726/747.

[8] Ibid. 624/647.

[9] Lonergan, '*Insight* Revisited' 277.

[10] 'As the fourth level is the principle of self-control, it is responsible for proper functioning on the first three levels. It fulfills its responsibility or fails to do so in the measure that we are attentive or inattentive in experiencing, that we are intelligent or unintelligent in our investigations, that we are reasonable or unreasonable in our judgments. Therewith vanish two notions: the notion of pure intellect or pure reason that operates on its own without guidance or control from responsible decision; and the notion of will as an arbitrary power indifferently choosing between good and evil.' Bernard Lonergan, *Method in Theology* (see above, chapter 1, note 3) 121.

[11] Ibid. 64.

[12] Ibid. 65.

[13] Ibid. 66.

[14] Ibid. 65.

[15] Ibid. 66.

[16] Ibid. 66-67.

[17] Ibid. 67.

[18] Ibid. 69.

[19] Ibid. 77.

[20] Ibid. 241-42.

[21] See Robert M. Doran, *Subject and Psyche* (see above, chapter 2, note 21) 217-21 and chapter 6 passim.

[22] Frederick Lawrence, 'Self-knowledge in History in Gadamer and Lonergan,' in *Language, Truth, and Meaning* (see above, chapter 2, note 6) 203.

[23] Doran, *Subject and Psyche* 112-13.

[24] On intentional and nonintentional feelings, see Lonergan, *Method in Theology* 30-31.

[25] Lonergan, *Insight* xxviii/22.

[26] See Doran, *Subject and Psyche* 152.

[27] Lonergan, *Insight* 350/374.

[28] See Gilbert Durand, 'Exploration of the Imaginal,' *Spring: An Annual of Archetypal Psychology and Jungian Thought* (1971) 84-100; and Henri Corbin, 'Mundus Imaginalis, or the Imaginary and the Imaginal,' *Spring* (1972) 1-19.

[29] Lonergan, *Method in Theology* 69.

[30] Doran, *Subject and Psyche* 217-21. The present subsection is a slightly revised version of these pages.

[31] Bernard Lonergan, 'Theology in its New Context,' in *A Second Collection* 65.

³² Ibid.

³³ Ibid. 65-66.

³⁴ Ibid. 66.

³⁵ Ibid. 66-67.

³⁶ Ibid. 67.

³⁷ Ibid. 66.

³⁸ C.G. Jung, *Mysterium Coniunctionis*, trans. R.F.C. Hull, vol. 14 in The Collected Works of C.G. Jung, Bollingen Series XX (Princeton: Princeton University Press, 1970) 65.

³⁹ Ibid. 81.

⁴⁰ C.G. Jung, 'Concerning Rebirth,' in *The Archetypes and the Collective Unconscious*, trans. R.F.C. Hull, vol. 9i in The Collected Works of C.G. Jung, Bollingen Series XX (Princeton: Princeton University Press, 1971) 141.

⁴¹ C.G. Jung, 'On the Nature of the Psyche,' in *The Structure and Dynamics of the Psyche* (see above, chapter 2, note 14) 223-24.

⁴² See Lonergan, *Method in Theology* 92.

⁴³ Jung, 'On the Nature of the Psyche' 206.

⁴⁴ Lonergan, *Insight* 457/482.

⁴⁵ See ibid. 472-77/497-502. On archetypal and anagogic symbols, see Northrop Frye, *Anatomy of Criticism* (Princeton: Princeton University Press, 1957) 95-128. For the relevance of Frye's work to my own concerns, I am indebted to Joseph Flanagan, 'Transcendental Dialectic of Desire and Fear,' a paper delivered at the Boston College Lonergan Workshop, June 1976, and subsequently published in *Lonergan Workshop* 1, ed. Fred Lawrence (Missoula, MT: Scholars Press, 1978) 69-91.

46 On the realm of transcendence, see Lonergan, *Method in Theology* 83-84. 1993 note: In the original publication of this essay I added at this point an appeal to the crucified Jesus and his surrender to the one he called Abba, in his psychic significance as a symbol for the final point, if you will, in the individuation process. I continue to hold the validity of this appeal for the Christian believer, but I acknowledge too that my earlier formulation of it departed from the transcendental context of this essay. The issue of the transcendental significance of such explicitly Christian realities and symbols is a large one that I am not prepared to discuss here.

47 Lonergan, *Insight* 387-88/413.

48 Lonergan, *Method in Theology* 129.

49 Thus Jung relates a dream he had prior to writing *Answer to Job*, his most controversial work. In this dream, he is led by his father to the center of a mandala-shaped building and into the 'highest presence.' His father knelt down and touched his forehead to the floor. Jung imitated him, but for some reason 'could not bring my forehead quite down to the floor — there was perhaps a millimeter to spare.' C.G. Jung, *Memories, Dreams, Reflections*, trans. Richard and Clara Winston (New York: Vintage, 1961) 219. Jung then expected, after such a dream, severe trials, including the death of his wife, to which he was unable to submit completely. 'Something in me was saying, "All very well, but not entirely." Something in me was defiant and determined not to be a dumb fish: and if there were not something of the sort in free men, no Book of Job would have been written.' Ibid. 220. Neither, we might add, would an *Answer to Job* have been written if, in this dream, Jung had touched his forehead to the floor, when led into the highest presence, the realm of transcendence.

50 See Paul Ricoeur, *Freud and Philosophy* (see above, chapter 1, note 7). 1993 note: Here too, I originally appealed to the crucified Jesus. For my reasons for omitting this appeal, see above, note 46.

51 See Bernard Lonergan, 'Dimensions of Meaning' (see above, chapter 2, note 7).

52 See Lonergan, *Insight* 619-22/643-45.

53 Lonergan, *Method in Theology* 275.

54 1993 note: The following sentence was originally in the text at this point; I still think it valid for a Christian believer, but I am not prepared to give it the kind of transcendental significance that it seemed to carry in the original version of this paper. 'As the psyche will continue to have its say in the drama even when intentionality has proclaimed a relative autonomy from imagination, as in our day, so at the farthest reaches of the psyche there stands the image of the crucified, the anagogic symbol of universal willingness, whose surrender to the Father reveals the finality of the psyche as a constituent feature of primordial immediacy.'

55 Ray L. Hart, *Unfinished Man and the Imagination* (New York: Herder & Herder, 1968).

56 Quoted by Heidegger in 'Hölderlin and the Essence of Poetry,' in *Existence and Being*, trans. Douglas Scott (Chicago: Regnery, 1949) 270.

4 Aesthetics and the Opposites

Theology is the pursuit of accurate understanding regarding the moments of ultimacy in human experience, the referent of such moments, and their meaning for the individual and cultural life of humankind. In the last analysis, the sole foundational issue of theology is transcendence. And yet Christian theologians of both Protestant and Roman Catholic persuasions have yet to meet on the question of God, on its origins in the pure question that is the native drive of human intelligence and evaluation, and on the sources and outcome of its cumulative resolution within the fabric of human experience. The reason, I believe, is that theology's foundations are in need of further elaboration. In this paper, I will suggest an important and relatively neglected dimension of these foundations, the aesthetic dimension.

I Why Method?

A sufficiently broad anticipation of the options now confronting human consciousness would seem to provide proper persuasiveness to the opinion that the most significant movement within the theological community in the last two decades has been the gradual emergence of a preoccupation with theology's method and foundations. In retrospect it may be surmised that the preoccupation arose in response to an at first dimly conscious suspicion that something of perhaps evolutionary significance was being

demanded of human subjectivity. It may indeed be melo-
dramatic to portray the option before postmodern humankind as one of survival and extinction. Perhaps it is more
accurate, and surely more inspiring, to understand the issue as an option between survival and liberation from mere
survival, between the rigidifying of certain ranges of
schemes of recurrence and the emergence of the beginnings of new series of ranges of schemes of recurrence in
human living. The question is not biological but human,
not whether there will be life on earth, but whether there
will be human life on earth. It is a question concerned not
so much with living as with the art of living.

The questions of method and foundations in theology, oddly enough, originated in the suspicion that perhaps a qualitative mutation in the evolutionary process was
in preparation, failing which human life on earth would
cease, even if men and women were to go on living. There
is evidence that this suspicion is correct, and for this evidence we need not turn to objective studies of society and
culture, of politics and economics, though these studies
may and indeed will support the suspicion. The evidence
is given more radically in human consciousness trying to
find its way into a human future. We each know in the
depths of our being that the most endangered species is
the human individual, that the only moral problem is the
loss of self, that this loss can happen at any moment, and
that if perdured in it means the end of my human life, the
destruction of perhaps the only work of art of which I am
capable. I can at any moment switch gears, indeed switch
direction from the careful construction of my own work of
art, in favor of transference, that is, of participation in or
subservience to systems of interpersonal, psychological,
social, economic, political, cultural, educational, religious
domination. The truth that sets free, one that always has
to be wrested by an inner violence, is that I need not ca-

pitulate, that I can be linked rather to transcendent creativity, and that this link is the key to whether I will be attentive or drifting, intelligent or stupid, rational or silly, responsible or more or less consciously sociopathic. It is up to me whether I will be oppressed or free, oppressing or liberating. It lies in no one else's hands whether I will be my own person, or whether I will lose my very self. And everyone who loses self is in the very loss a sociopath, destructive of human relationships and of the striving toward that achievement of common meanings and values that is human community.[1]

The theologians who have acted on this perhaps once dim suspicion have thus turned their attention to the human self or subject. That this attentiveness has simultaneously resulted in groundbreaking efforts at clarifying theology's method and foundations ought not be surprising, though why this was the case has only recently become clear. For a method is nothing other than a self-conscious interrelating of various operations in the interests of a set of cumulative results.[2] Thus the more clearly one discriminates one's own operations — and presumably such discrimination would follow from inquiring attentiveness to oneself — the more fully one comes into possession of a method. If the one discriminating his or her operations is a theologian, then the method one comes to articulate is the method of theology. And if the operations thus discriminated are a necessary condition of theology's performance, then their articulation constitutes at least a part of theology's foundations.

If these theologians have happened to be right in their discrimination of the operations of the human self, however, their discoveries have a significance beyond theology. Indeed, to the extent that they articulate basic terms and relations defining human operations, they are laying the foundations of a new science of the art of being human. And this new science, the cumulative articulation of a collaborative enterprise, is the knowledge that will inform the new series of ranges of schemes of recurrence that is demanded if human life is to continue to unfold on this earth.

The present paper suggests a contribution to the twofold endeavor of articulating theology's method and of developing the *scienza nuova*. My debt to Bernard Lonergan is undoubtedly clear already, to C.G. Jung and Ernest Becker and, through Becker, to Otto Rank, soon to become manifest. I hope it not a presumptuous projection to predict that these guides through the labyrinthine ways of interiority will be principal among the makers of postmodern intentionality. For they came to know human desire with penetrating precision and exacting subtlety. Moreover they have opened that desire upon itself in its native spontaneity. Together, I believe, they render asymptotically possible the self-conscious recovery of intentionality which Paul Ricoeur calls a second, post-critical naivete.[3] The knowing withdrawal from deceptive self-fragmentation rendered possible by their mutual qualification one of the other is the conviction which motivates the suggestion I offer here, a suggestion consisting of hints toward a new essay in aid of self-appropriation. My subject is the human soul and the science of that soul which alone qualifies for the title 'psychology.' I suggest we recruit for theological method the discoveries of Jung and Becker and rearticulate these discoveries with the aid of Lonergan. Finally, I risk the claim of suggesting a more explicit horizon for the new science of being human than has been cleared by any of these principal contributors to human evolution taken singly. The horizon I suggest is not more inclusive than that cleared by Lonergan, but a substantial portion of the latter would be more precisely articulated if the complement I suggest were incorporated into it.

2 **Soul-Making and the Opposites**

The human subject or self is inescapably a Protean commingling of opposites. The opposites are spirit and matter, archetype and instinct, or perhaps most precisely of all, intentionality and body.[4] The mediator of their progressive integration is the human soul, or psyche, or imagination — in the present essay I am using the three terms as roughly equivalent.[5] But soul, when undifferentiated, is also the defective source of disintegration. And soul is usually undifferentiated, in fact almost always more or less not transparent to itself.

The differentiation of soul or imagination is as arduous a task as that of spirit or intentionality. For the human psyche is in one sense not a *tertium quid* in addition to body and intentionality, but the place of their meeting. And this place is not a point but a field or a dense jungle or a cavernous pit. As the place where body meets intentionality, psyche shares in both. Thus she — for soul is always *anima*[6] — is both transparent and opaque to herself, and she is somehow thus *through and through*. The writings of Lonergan display the potentialities of spirit or intentionality for self-transparency. The first portions of a Jungian analysis render soul transparent to spirit. But only the mysterious latter phase of the *opus* disclosed by Jung renders soul transparent to herself, and even then only very precariously, at least for a long period of time. *In patientia vestra possidebitis animas vestras.*

The human subject has been disclosed by Lonergan as the center and source of at least two very different kinds of operations. Those Lonergan has most clearly elucidated are cognitional. The other operations are evaluative or existential. They regard decision and action in the world. The delicacy of Lonergan's uncovering of the operations of knowing would lead us to suspect that the evaluative operations can surely be no more subtle than the cognitional. But this is not the case. For existential consciousness begins in feelings,[7] and feelings are liable to an opaqueness exceeding that of cognitional process. Moreover, self-transparency in the dimension of affectivity is seldom if ever to be achieved by reading a book, whereas there are many who can verify that Lonergan's work has performed precisely this function with respect to cognition. The mediation of affective immediacy calls upon other techniques than those employed in the self-affirmation of the knower. Many of these techniques have been elaborated by the practitioners of psychotherapy. Others survive in the accumulated wisdom of the great world religions. Ernest Becker points to the synthesis of these two sources of existential mediation of the self. But always the techniques are of soul-making,[8] the subtlest of all human arts.

But is there a way of understanding this subtle art that will enable it to be integrated with Lonergan's contribution to our knowledge of ourselves? If so, the integration would represent a kind of *coniunctio*, a marriage of the archetypally masculine (intentionality) and the archetypally feminine (psyche) within the conscious subjectivity of self-appropriating men and women.[9] Furthermore, the art of soul-making would then be the self-owning of the subject as an evaluating and existential subject, in a manner paralleling the way in which cognitional analysis results in a self-owning of the subject as intelligent and reasonable. If the latter analysis grounds that portion of theology's foundations in which there is articulated the horizon shift on knowledge which Lonergan calls intellectual conversion, soul-making would ground the articulation of the two other horizon shifts which for Lonergan constitute theology's foundational reality: moral conversion and religious conversion.[10] The subtle art of soul-making would then be as foundational for theology's future as Lonergan's explora-

tions of the knowing mind. The two movements of the
mediation of cognitive immediacy through cognitional
theory-praxis and the mediation of existential immediacy
through soul-making would somehow be of equal footing,
both for theology and for the new human science that takes
its stand on self-appropriation and that issues in a new
series of ranges of schemes of recurrence in cultural life.

This *coniunctio* is perhaps not far from Lonergan's
mind when he writes: 'Besides the immediate world of the
infant and the adult's world mediated by meaning, there is
the mediation of immediacy by meaning when one objectifies cognitional process in transcendental method *and*
when one discovers, identifies, accepts one's submerged
feelings in psychotherapy.'[11] And yet soul-making is something other than psychotherapy, even if the therapeutic
process is to date its most frequent starting place as an
explicit performance of the human subject. Soul-making
is life, not therapy, and the place of soul-making is the
dramatic stage of life: human relationships, the passages
of the subject from childhood to youth, youth to adulthood, adulthood to age, and the conscious recapitulation
of those relationships and passages that occurs when I tell
my story. As Otto Rank has made so clear in his singular
contribution to psychology's understanding of itself, we
live beyond psychology, and therapy must give way to the
soul beyond psychology.[12] Soul-making but begins when
I discover, identify, and accept previously submerged feelings. That perhaps necessary beginning — necessary at least
in this age of the rift of human intelligence from nature —
introduces into human living a new series of ranges of
schemes of recurrence that represent in effect the elaboration of soul. But surely to speak of discovering, identifying, and accepting submerged feelings in psychotherapy
does not capture the rich fabric of soul-making which begins to be woven in Jungian analysis. It is the weaving of

that fabric of withdrawal and return that constitutes the
second mediation of immediacy by meaning toward which
Lonergan is stretching in the sentence I have quoted from
his *Method in Theology*. And weaving that fabric is a more
intricate maneuver than is involved in naming feelings. It
is the much more concrete task of negotiating the figures
of one's own makeup as a self: fathers and mothers, soul
partners, lovers, heroes, friends, enemies, gods, and demons. It is in this respect akin to the Hegelian enterprise
of *Geist*'s recapturing of its own evolution, though it occurs on the plane of realism. It is telling a story, first perhaps by repeating the story that has been going forward
without one's being able to tell it as it is, but then by creating the story as one lives it, creating it in all its richness
and variety and patterns of differentiated response. Soul-
making, we said, is life and not therapy. It is living the
dream forward, as a living symbol, a symbolic man or
woman, and yet as removed from the symbol one is by a
detachment from both inner states and outer objects.

This detachment is important. Its failure is inflation,
hardly the desired outcome of soul-making. The presence
of this detachment is individuation, the self-constitution
of the human subject in his or her uniqueness as the individual, as 'only this,' with a matter-of-factness or just-soness that springs from a retrieved or second immediacy.
This immediacy must be won back from lostness in the
world of the figures one negotiates in the process of soul-
making. Its retrieval is ever precarious but is nonetheless
cumulatively solidified in the suffering of love that is the
name of this subtle art.

Despite the fact that our quotation from Lonergan
does not capture the full texture of soul-making, it bears a
significance that must be sensitively articulated. It places
the soul-making toward which Lonergan is stretching by
speaking of psychotherapy, on the same level of discourse

as the work to which he has devoted a lifetime of research, writing, and teaching. Lonergan's work is the discrimination of the intentionality of the human subject as human subject. The portion of that intentionality to whose articulation Lonergan has devoted most of his energies is human knowledge. Thus he speaks of 'objectifying cognitional process.' This is precisely what he has done in *Insight*: to raise to the level of self-recognition the operations that enter into every process of human knowledge. In this sense he is mediating, or providing the occasion for us to mediate for ourselves, our conscious immediacy to our own cognitional operations. The world itself, by the nature of our knowledge, is mediated to us by meaning. What the objectification of cognitional process does is to mediate by meaning our conscious immediacy to the cognitive operations through which the real world is mediated by meaning.

Soul-making, then, is an analogous process. What goes forward in soul-making is the mediation by meaning of a different dimension of conscious immediacy. This immediacy is not so much cognitive as dispositional. It is Heidegger's *Befindlichkeit*.[13] But even to speak of it as dispositional provides too much of a therapeutic meaning to the mediation. Perhaps the immediacy mediated by meaning in soul-making is better referred to as dramatic. Soul-making is the mediation of immediacy by a story. It is the elevation to story-telling of a story that already was going forward without being told very well. And it is also the elevation to story-making, to self-constitution, of a story that otherwise would continue without being either made or told. It is the elevation of the subject from a condition of being dragged through life to a condition of walking through life upright.[14] It is the discovery of the paradoxical yielding without which one cannot walk through life upright. It is first the elucidation and then the knowing participation in creating the drama that one's life is. Soul-making, then, is the mediation by meaning of dramatic immediacy, the immediacy of the fears and desires of a self-conscious animal haunted by the inevitability of death, but also of the dramatic component in the struggle for authenticity in one's knowing, one's doing, and one's religion.

3   Beyond Criticism and Therapy

Surely the two mediations are spoken of as separate only for the purpose of analysis. For the two immediacies, while distinct, are not separate from one another. Cognition surely figures in one's dramatic living, just as there is something dramatic about insight and the pursuit of truth. The analytic separation is important, though; Lonergan would never have written *Insight* had he concerned himself also with soul-making; and the question before a person seeking psychotherapeutic assistance is hardly Lonergan's concern, 'What am I doing when I am knowing?' But the conjunction of the two mediations, and so of the two immediacies, is the concern of this paper. That conjunction through mediation is a second immediacy, a retrieved spontaneity, a post-critical and post-therapeutic naivete. Perhaps it is closely aligned with what religious traditions have called wisdom. I suspect it is. But even wisdom need not be mediated to itself by criticism or therapy, and in most instances has not been. Moreover, most efforts at critical and therapeutic mediation have not issued in wisdom. But they have been pointing toward such a term. That pointing is itself the historical meaning of modern philosophy's turn to the subject and of psycho-analysis. The postmodern era may take its stand, then, on the achievement to which modernity, in its philosophy and depth psychology at least, has been pointing.

Before taking its stand, though, the postmodern era must reach that achievement, and what is at stake in the achievement of a post-critical and post-therapeutic wisdom is a new control of meaning, and consequently the beginning of a new epoch in the evolution of human consciousness.[15] Post-critical and post-therapeutic humanity is the beginning of new ranges of series of schemes of recurrence in human history, analogous to but superseding the schemes introduced by criticism — in, e.g., the Socratic maieutic art — and by therapy in psychoanalysis. Post-critical humanity is a retrieval of criticism as it springs from the human mind, of criticism in its roots in spontaneous intelligence and reflecting reasonableness. Post-therapeutic humanity is a retrieval of what criticism criticized, of mythic or, more broadly, symbolic consciousness, but again a retrieval *in radice*. And the root of mythic consciousness is the maternal imagination or *anima* or soul. Post-critical and post-therapeutic humanity takes its stand on this twofold retrieval of the roots of the stages of meaning that have preceded it.[16] In so taking its stand, it ushers in a new stage of meaning. Our age is as pregnant for a radically different future as was the Greece of 800-200 B.C. that saw the emergence of criticism from myth, the *miraculum Graecum*. Interestingly enough, though purely by coincidence, Jung has predicted, on the basis of dreams, another period of roughly 600 years before the new stage of meaning, or the 'new religion,' as he put it, has taken firm hold.[17] In the meantime, there will be much darkness and many explorations of blind alleys, many collapses and breakdowns, wars and rumors of war. But the temple is already being built, its foundations are laid, and its eventual construction, Jung says, is something of an inevitability. That is all that matters. The foundations of the temple consist in the two mediations of immediacy, cognitive and dramatic. The lowest level of the temple begins to build on

these foundations, demonstrating their capacity to complement one another in one movement of foundational
subjectivity. That is where we are now. The temple is in its
very beginnings, so much so that the foundations themselves need to be strengthened before building further. It
must be shown that *one* temple can be built from these
two sets of foundations that have opposed one another so
often in human history: intentionality and psyche, spirit
and soul. It must be shown that such a temple will not
collapse like a house of cards in the gentlest breeze, in fact
that it can sustain the torrential rains of an epochal change
in human conscious performance. Neither transcendental
method alone nor archetypal psychology alone can found
post-critical and post-therapeutic humanity; each needs
and implies the other, in fact, *implicates* the other by the
very nonseparability of cognition from drama and of drama
from cognition. And if post-critical and post-therapeutic
humanity is a temple, it is because transcendental method
and archetypal psychology, in their mutual implication one
of the other, both give way to the mystery beyond criticism and beyond psychology.

4   Criticism and the Soul

The philosophy of self-appropriation, when limited
to the dimension of spirit, is a matter of coming into possession of one's own infinite curiosity, one's unrestricted
impulse for correct and thorough understanding. It is, if
you want, the differentiation of the thinking function of
human consciousness. But Jung, at least, speaks of three
other functions of human consciousness: sensation, feeling, and intuition.[18] These constitute an infrastructure of
the body and the psyche. Their clarification, rendering them
more self-transparent, is another matter than possessing
one's unrestricted desire to know. In fact, even to raise the

question of this additional self-clarification, this illumination of the dark side of life, is unsettling for the self-appropriating thinking function. For the dark side, and perhaps especially feeling, where the dark side shows its own intentionality in the function of evaluation, is a threat to thinking. Darkness penetrates the domain of light, and the light does not comprehend it. The body, sexuality, intersubjectivity, time, femininity, and the dream — these are all threatening to *animus*, to intelligent intentionality in its penetrating capacities to let light shine, to differentiate, and to conquer. For it has indeed *never* conquered in this domain, and it knows that this is the case. It fears a negotiation, for that in itself would be erotic, and so it flees the question and ridicules the concern with an obscurantism that it would despise if manifested in any other dimension of human living. Its flight and ridicule widen a rift that is already the major cultural problem of our age. There are certain things that even an infinite curiosity would prefer not to be curious about, that even an unrestricted desire to know would rather not have to face. The issue is Oedipal, but in the sense of the conflict between the desire to know and the desire not to know, the intention of being and the flight from what can be understood and affirmed. Even an infinite curiosity will find certain questions unsettling.

Moreover, the questions it finds unsettling are remarkably *proximate* to the domain opened by spirit's self-appropriation. If the appropriation of spirit is the subject coming into possession of intelligent and reasonable consciousness, the appropriation of soul is the subject coming into possession of the *two* levels that surround intelligent and reasonable consciousness, namely empirical consciousness, both dreaming and waking, and existential consciousness, particularly as it primordially apprehends values in feelings.[19] Somehow the marriage of spirit and soul is ter-

ribly elusive, even though they interpenetrate so fully. One
abhors the other. They are indeed opposites.

And yet to call them opposites seems somewhat contradictory to what we said above, where *matter* was spirit's
opposite, and where soul was said to share in both matter
and spirit. This latter formulation is in fact more rigorous.
But soul *does* seem more at home with matter than with
spirit, and surely matter is more at home with her than
spirit is. Matter is not afraid of feeling, sensation, and intuition, of the light buried within the dark side. Spirit is.
Spirit fears its own corruption by the dark side — with
good reason — and knows where it cannot conquer. But,
being spirit and thus arrogant, it will not settle for negotiation. It would prefer to disown its very self, to cut short
its questioning in the name of a strange intellectualistic
bias, to cease being curious but in the name of intelligence!
It is infinitude preoccupied with being infinite. In its preoccupation it becomes finite by obscurantism, schizophrenic. Its refusal to negotiate finitude in the body is the
despair of infinitude disembodied.

And yet the advocate and ally of spirit's own self-
possession, Lonergan, has, as we have seen, himself opened
us upon *soul's* self-transparency. The breakthrough is significant. It is the essence of Lonergan's later development.
Insight alone can be an alienating book. The word 'alone'
is important. *Insight* can also be a first step into a new
epoch of human consciousness. The epoch itself will be
the overcoming of alienation within human consciousness,
and thus, viewed historically, *Insight* would not be alienating at all, but a contribution to wholeness and liberation.
In fact, perhaps one of its principal contributions is the
liberation from the illusion of a wholeness that is not self-
transcending, the futility of the project of psychological
redemption to which psychotherapy itself is too prone. But
the book is alienating if it is taken as a complete anthro-

pology. This is precisely what it is not. It is primarily a study of the intellectual pattern of experience. If taken as an anthropology, it encourages a dangerous rift of intelligence and reason from the body. If placed within the broader horizon established by complementing spirit's self-appropriation with soul's self-transparency, the book takes its rightful place as a contributor to human evolution. The movement of self-owning instituted by the author of *Insight* extends to soul, to a second mediation of immediacy by meaning, and such an extension opens upon an appropriation of a moral and religious subjectivity that are capable of sublating a self-owning spirit, an intellectually self-appropriating consciousness. Let it be noted that not all moral and religious subjectivity can sublate such a consciousness. There is a moral and religious consciousness that precedes the moment of spirit's preoccupation with owning itself. This consciousness, while converted, is not self-appropriating. Moral and religious self-appropriation are hastened into being by spirit's insistence on coming of age. This occurs through soul's self-transparency. Without it, even spirit's insistence on self-owning might become immoral and irreligious, a demonic power drive. With it, spirit's self-owning becomes spirit's self-surrender.

The surrender is to the earth. For soul is tied to body, and body is of the earth. The moral and religious consciousness that is given in soul's self-transparency is womanly consciousness, roaming the expanse of the earth, at home there, able to kiss and embrace the ground. But it is woman as wisdom, Sophia. Only woman as wisdom is transparent to herself in a second immediacy. And spirit's surrender is to wisdom, where soul performs the wedding that keeps spirit from the demonic, the wedding of spirit to body: to a moral and religious consciousness that are humble, *humilis*, of the earth, grounded, in the body, 'just this.'

5   Lonergan and the *Scienza Nuova*

The issue is of import for the cooperation of disciplines. But the disciplines must first find themselves. Lanza del Vasto has said that philosophy is lacking in the West, that those who talk about it and teach it do not know what it is about. They lack the joint 'between what they believe, what they think, what they know, what they feel, what they want and what they do.'[20] He is correct. The joint is the self, and self's joint is soul or psyche. And yet psychology in the West does not help philosophy to find psyche. What is taught in university departments of psychology surely has nothing to do with psyche. It has in fact very little to do with humankind. It would, James Hillman says, better be called statistics, physical anthropology, cultural journalism, or animal breeding.[21] If philosophy and psychology were in possession of themselves — that is, if philosophers and psychologists were moving toward self-transparency — it would be fair to speak of the import of our issue for interdisciplinary cooperation.

Perhaps all talk of interdisciplinary cooperation is an evasion of the issue, however. Are we not really talking about an entirely new science of being human? What current so-called humanistic discipline, aside perhaps from literature, would be at home with the claims here registered? Perhaps the humanistic disciplines as we have known them are themselves passé. I suspect they are. Nonetheless, it can be maintained that the issue opened by Lonergan and extended here means at least a unity-in-differentiation of three previously separate disciplines: philosophy, depth psychology, and theology. The statement is too cautious, but nonetheless true.

Theology was not mentioned above as a discipline in trouble. This is not because theology is free of the alienation from its subject that afflicts philosophy and psychology. Far from it. And who is theology's subject? The theologian: spirit and soul and body. Lonergan has provided a maieutic for theologians to employ to help them overcome alienation and the ideologies that justify it. These ideologies are usually called dogmatics or systematics. But here again, we have no more than a beginning. The method of theology is a method of *knowing*. Fair enough, since theology is knowledge. But the *atmosphere* of knowing, the drama inseparable from insight — only soul's self-transparency can provide a grid for this. And only with this is alienation overcome.

This drama, however, depends for its elucidation on an accurate understanding of insight as an activity and as knowledge. Here we locate Lonergan's contribution to the new science of the art of being human. No articulation of consciousness according to which being is laid out before it, and where the problem of knowledge is one of moving from 'in here' to 'out there,' will provide us with more than a melodrama. And the essence of melodrama as opposed to drama is that it could have been avoided by understanding things correctly from the beginning. The question of how I move from 'in here' to 'out there' in my knowledge is not the right question, does not reflect the problem which obtains between knowing and being. The problem, Lonergan has shown, is one of advancing from the real as experienced to the real as known. The real as known is being, and to reach it one does not move from interiority to exteriority, subjectivity to objectivity. One rather passes from subjectivity as experientially objective to subjectivity as absolutely objective. And this one does by letting subjectivity be normatively objective. What constitutes the normative objectivity of subjectivity is the desire to know, and the first imperative of this desire is understanding. The drama of insight is constituted within interiority, for in addition to the desire to know there is a flight from understanding. Being is a task.

This means, too, that the rejection of Cartesian subjectivity cannot be made on Cartesian terms. That is, it will not do simply to deny gratuitously the alienation of subjectivity from being which Cartesian subjects gratuitously posit. The real as experienced is not the real as known, and so cannot be affirmed as real until it is known. The affirmation of an unknown as real is naive realism. Here too there is no drama of insight. There is, in fact, not even a melodrama. There is only a kind of crude epistemological striptease. Neither Cartesian subjectivity nor naive realism consummates the marriage of knowing and being, for neither is normatively objective. Both flee understanding, and become victims of the desire not to know which is responsible both for the drama of insight and for the failure of insight into the drama of living.

Lonergan's acknowledgment of a second mediation of immediacy by meaning is tied to an appreciation of the subject and of the objectivity of subjectivity that is more nuanced than the treatment accorded these topics in *Insight*. In fact, the development of Lonergan's thought from *Insight* to *Method in Theology* is more than a matter of greater nuance in respect to interiority. It involves something of a transformation. The subject as existential is now accorded a primacy or priority of importance previously granted to the subject as cognitional. The issue of subjectivity is now the drama of living, and cognitional analysis is intended to be in aid of that drama. A new and quite distinct level of consciousness is now acknowledged. The subject's evaluations and deliberations about decision and action are no longer reducible to the questions of whether one is being intelligent or stupid, reasonable or silly, for the human good is something distinct from the intelligent and reasonable.[22] Nothing is gainsaid of cognitional analysis. It is a secure, massive, and irrevocable achievement of the human mind's knowledge of itself. But it not a sufficient anthropology, for there is more to be appropriated than one's capacity for meaning and truth.

6   Existential Consciousness as Aesthesis

The remainder is, I believe, best understood as the *aesthetic* dimension of the subject. It is this dimension that calls for a second mediation of immediacy by meaning, one that for subjects hitherto negligent of the aesthetic may begin as therapy but that more radically is soul-making. Soul is aesthesis. And soul-making is thus the recovery of aesthetic subjectivity. If values are primordially apprehended in feelings, then aesthetics is the foundation of existential subjectivity and thus of ethics and religion. Soul-making, as the recovery of the aesthetic dimension, is the post-therapeutic basis of morals and prayer. Lonergan's opening of a distinct level of consciousness that has to do with value, dialectic, and foundations as something distinct from, including, but more than and sublating meaning and truth is really an opening upon aesthetic consciousness as distinct from, including, but more than and sublating cognitional consciousness. Ethics is radically aesthetics; and the existential subject, concerned with character as his or her issue, is the aesthetic subject. Soul, beyond intelligence and reasonableness, is the key to character.

Jung was concerned with character, but ambiguously. There are romantic interpretations of his thought which seem to prescind from this concern in favor of his love of soul.[23] Jung's ambiguity appears above all in his somewhat confusing and inconsistent semantics of evil,[24] which may well conceal a hidden agenda. But character and soul are bedfellows. Character is a dance step one must work out with soul. Character emerges from 'that refining fire/ Where you must move in measure, like a dancer.'[25] And the rhythm of this movement is aesthetics. What Lonergan hints at is that the deliberating, evaluating, deciding, existential subject is also the aesthetic subject. The uppermost level of intentional consciousness is art. In its originating moment, apprehension of value in feelings, and in its terminating moment of fidelity to decision, it is radically aesthetic. Aesthetics, in its education or *Bildung*,[26] must pass through dialectic. For dialectic is a portion of the refining fire. Lonergan's positioning of dialectic as a matter of existential subjectivity is of the utmost significance. It is in fact a breakthrough in understanding this subtle movement of subjectivity. For it means that in the last analysis dialectic is a matter of the heart more radically than of the mind. Better, it is an issue of the *drama* of insight. It is as insight issues from the struggle with the flight from understanding that the refining fire is at work. To get stopped in dialectic is to suppose dialectic to be a matter principally of mind, and mind to be something whose significance is other than dramatic. Both suppositions are mistaken. The ulterior finality of mind or spirit is existential subjectivity. If this is true, then mind's dialectic is subordinate to and sublated by the dialectic of the heart in morality and religion. The dialectic of the heart moves toward the condition of complete simplicity, where the fire and the rose are one. This condition beyond the opposites, Eliot reminds us, costs not less than everything.[27] The 'everything' includes even a kind of *sacrificium intellectus*, in the sense that there is another mediation beyond the cognitional. Dialectic is in the service of a story.

We may, then, safely begin from the presumption that Lonergan's opus constitutes an irrevocable achievement on the part of the human mind's knowledge of itself and thus an essential contribution to theology's foundations.

The burden of proof surely now lies on the shoulders of one who would refute this presumption. But Lonergan's opening of consciousness upon existential subjectivity as of primary concern for itself, and thus his explorations of value, dialectic, and foundational subjectivity still constitute no more than a problem. He has opened the door to a room which he has not furnished for us, and it is the central room of our dwelling place, the living room. I do not fault him for this. To fault one whose achievement is unparalleled for what he has left to others to do is, to put it mildly, an irresponsible escape from accepting the possibility that one may oneself be one of those others. It also constitutes an unrealistic expectation even of genius. But one also must be realistic about one's self-expectations, and so I hasten to conclude with a comment about what we cannot claim or ambition to do. No thinker can furnish the living room. More precisely, I can furnish only my own dwelling place, and you yours. But I can suggest where the materials are to be found and how the task of their arrangement can most artistically be approached. In this sense the task I propose, while complementary to *Insight*, is of another order. No workbook in the dialectic of the heart can be written, no set of five-finger exercises for style and aesthesis proposed. The self-transparency of soul is of another order than that of spirit. All anyone can try to do is articulate its grammar and propose a semantics for understanding its process and implications. But even this is a task not yet accomplished with any adequacy by any author with whom I am familiar. Since it is the next task to be undertaken beyond that so artfully executed by Lonergan, I wager it is worth the attempt, however elusive, that I have suggested in this paper.

Notes

¹ The point is well and simply expressed in Lanza del Vasto's journal of his pilgrimage to India and Gandhi, *Return to the Source*:
'The policy of Gandhi is incomprehensible if one does not know that its aim is not political but spiritual victory.
'Whoever saves his own soul does not only serve himself. Although bodies are separate, souls are not. Whoever saves his own soul saves the Soul and accumulates riches that belong to all. Others have only to perceive the treasure to partake of it.' Lanza del Vasto, *Return to the Source* (New York: Pocket Books, 1974) 110-11. It seems obvious from the overall tenor of del Vasto's book that his reference to '*the* Soul' is figurative, and not an intrusion of Averroistic metaphysics into contemporary spirituality.

² 'A method is a normative pattern of recurrent and related operations yielding cumulative and progressive results.' Bernard Lonergan, *Method in Theology* (see above, chapter 1, note 3) 4.

³ Paul Ricoeur, *Freud and Philosophy* (see above, chapter 1, note 7) 496.

⁴ It is important how the opposites are conceived. For Ernest Becker, they are called self and body. This conception involves Becker, I believe, in an exaggerated dualism from which he never manages to extricate his thought. Part of Becker's point, of course, is that the dualism is inescapable, a hopeless existential dilemma, that every attempt to transcend it is a lie. I do not wish to detract from the value of Becker's profoundly moving closure of twentieth-century depth psychology on authentic religion, for I believe he is correct in his synthesis of psychoanalytic and religious insight. However, the dualism can be transcended without lying and without jeopardizing Becker's conclusions on the finality of the psychoanalytic movement, its inevitable and — considering its origins in Freud — ironic disclosure of a necessary religious spirituality at the heart of the human condition. Becker finds that 'in recent times every psychologist who has done vital work' has taken the problem of the opposites as the main problem. Ernest Becker, *The Denial of Death* (New York: The Free Press, 1973) 26. He includes in his list of psychologists Jung, who, I believe, points the way beyond the opposites. Part of Jung's technique involves reserving the term 'self' for the totality beyond the opposites, thus including body in self. Equally im-

portant is the *triple* constitution of the self, with psyche as mediating the opposites of spirit and matter. See Jung's programmatic essay 'On the Nature of the Psyche' (see above, chapter 3, note 41). The key to the issue is the nature of the symbol. Becker is unfortunately imprecise on this central question, whereas Jung offers a most accurate notion of the symbol. Part of my emphasis on Jung's importance for theology is based on his contribution to the elucidation of the symbol. In brief, Jung's notion harmonizes with Paul Ricoeur's on the *structure* of the symbol but radicalizes beyond Ricoeur the primordial place of symbolic activity in human life. See chapter 3 of my *Subject and Psyche* (see above, chapter 2, note 21).

5 I am dependent for my notion of imagination on Martin Heidegger's analysis of *Einbildungskraft* in *Kant und das Problem der Metaphysik* (see above, chapter 2, note 60). The German word is helpful: the art of forming into one. So is the *Bild* aspect of the word. I think an argument can be made that the *Einbildungskraft* of Heidegger and the psyche of depth psychology can be understood as one and the same. If I am correct, then Heidegger's *Einbildungskraft* is removed from its abstract formalism while the psyche of depth psychology is given ontological status.

6 See James Hillman's radicalizing of the Jungian notion of *anima* (and, by implication, also of *animus*) beyond contrasexuality, in 'Anima,' *Spring: An Annual of Archetypal Psychology and Jungian Thought* (1973) 97-132.

7 See Lonergan, *Method in Theology* 37-38.

8 The expression 'soul-making' is James Hillman's, but I assign to the phrase a meaning congruent with a closure of psychotherapy on spirituality that Hillman would disavow. The Dionysian quality of Hillman's work is tempting, but in the seductive manner of a soul only half made. Ultimately it must be said that Hillman, surely the most creative and original mind to emerge from the Jungian school of psychology, falls victim to and promotes the 'romantic agony,' the capitulation of intentionality to the ambiguities of a half-made psyche that Jung himself escapes potentially if not in fact by his relentless insistence on the intention of a unification of the self which Hillman seems to have abandoned as a futile enterprise. See James Hillman, *The Myth of Analysis* (Evanston: Northwestern, 1972) and *Re-Visioning Psychology* (New York: Harper and Row, 1975).

9 How this *coniunctio* is experienced in feminine consciousness remains a problem to be dealt with by a woman. It is noteworthy that Jung's original followers were predominantly women, and that the speakers at the various Lonergan workshops have been almost exclusively men. Psyche is archetypally feminine, intentionality masculine. 1993 note: See the volume *Lonergan and Feminism*, ed. Cynthia Crysdale (Toronto: University of Toronto Press, 1994).

10 On the three conversions as theology's foundational reality, see Lonergan, *Method in Theology* 267-69. Intellectual conversion would seem to coincide with intellectual self-appropriation, while moral and religious conversion obviously occur without such objectification. The art of soul-making facilitates the objectification of one's moral and religious being.

11 Lonergan, *Method in Theology* 77. Emphasis added.

12 Otto Rank, *Beyond Psychology* (New York: Dover, 1958). The conclusion of Rank's lifelong pursuit of the meaning of psychoanalysis as a human and cultural phenomenon is expressed in the following words from the preface to this extraordinary book, Rank's final and posthumously published work: 'Man is born beyond psychology and he dies beyond it but he can *live* beyond it only through vital experience of his own — in religious terms, through revelation, conversion or re-birth.' P. 16. A helpful introduction to Rank is provided by Ira Progoff, *The Death and Rebirth of Psychology* (New York: McGraw-Hill Paperbacks, 1973), chapter 7. But it is Becker who has persuasively shown the towering significance of Rank's critique of psychotherapy. I view Rank's *Beyond Psychology* as something akin to the final word on the subject. Nonetheless, neither Rank himself nor Becker seems to have appreciated the significance of Jung's contribution to the transition beyond psychology. Progoff has caught this better. Part of the problem is the tenacious insistence with which Jung's followers have created an orthodoxy of psychological redemption out of his work and thus perpetuated an illusion to which Jung's work remains vulnerable. My experience at the C.G. Jung Institute in Zürich, where I completed writing my doctoral dissertation on Lonergan and Jung, has convinced me of the acuteness of Jung's expectation that this enterprise would outlive its creative uses within a generation of its establishment. See Laurens van der Post, *Jung and the Story of Our Time* (New York: Pantheon, 1975) 4. Psychology, indeed Jung's psychology above all, is beyond Jungianism.

13 See Martin Heidegger, *Being and Time* (see above, chapter 2, note 9) 171-72.

14 The expression is from John Dunne, *The Way of All the Earth* (see above, chapter 2, note 61) 152.

15 On the relation between the control of meaning and cultural epochs, see Bernard Lonergan, 'Dimensions of Meaning' (see above, chapter 2, note 7).

16 On the stages of meaning see Lonergan, *Method in Theology* 85-86.

17 See Max Zeller, 'The Task of the Analyst,' *Psychological Perspective* 6:1 (Spring, 1975) 75, where Zeller relates a dream that was visited upon him at the very end of a three-month period in Zürich during which he was seeking to answer the question of how he was to understand what he was doing as an analyst. The dream is as follows: 'A temple of vast dimensions was in the process of being built. As far as I could see — ahead, behind, right and left — there were incredible numbers of people building on gigantic pillars. I, too, was building on a pillar. The whole building process was in its very beginnings, but the foundation was already there, the rest of the building was starting to go up, and I and many others were working on it.' Jung called the temple the new religion, said it was being built by people from all over the world, and indicated that dreams of his own and others indicated that it would take 600 years until it is built. I owe to a student of mine, Bozidar Molitor, the precious insight that the dream, so interpreted, reverses the myth of the Tower of Babel.

18 C.G. Jung, *Psychological Types*, trans. R.F.C. Hull, vol. 6 in The Collected Works of C.G. Jung, Bollingen Series XX (Princeton: Princeton University Press, 1971).

19 On the levels of consciousness: 'We are subjects, as it were, by degrees. At a lowest level, when unconscious in dreamless sleep or in a coma, we are merely potentially subjects. Next, we have a minimal degree of consciousness and subjectivity when we are the helpless subjects of our dreams. Thirdly, we become experiential subjects when we awake, when we become the subjects of lucid perception, imaginative projects, emotional and conative impulses, and bodily action. Fourthly, the intelligent subject sublates the experiential, i.e., it retains, preserves,

goes beyond, completes it, when we inquire about our experience, investigate, grow in understanding, express our inventions and discoveries. Fifthly, the rational subject sublates the intelligent and experiential subject, when we question our own understanding, check our formulations and expressions, ask whether we have got things right, marshal the evidence *pro* and *con*, judge this to be so and that not to be so. Sixthly, finally, rational consciousness is sublated by rational self-consciousness, when we deliberate, evaluate, decide, act. Then there emerges human consciousness at its fullest. Then the existential subject exists and his character, his personal essence, is at stake.' Bernard Lonergan, 'The Subject' (see above, chapter 3, note 1) 80. I have argued in *Subject and Psyche* for an extension of the sublations to include the sublation of dreaming consciousness by experiential, intelligent, rational, and existential consciousness. 1993 note: Lonergan's later affirmation of both a lower and an upper operator beyond the structure of conscious intentionality is of course most pertinent to these concerns. See especially 'Philosophy and the Religious Phenomenon,' in *Method: Journal of Lonergan Studies* 12:1 (1994) 12:2 (1994) 125-46.

20 Del Vasto, *Return to the Source* 230.

21 Hillman, *Re-Visioning Psychology* xii.

22 This is expressly acknowledged by Lonergan in '*Insight* Revisited' (see above, chapter 2, note 56) 277.

23 I refer particularly to James Hillman's disparaging of the theme of the heroic in *Re-Visioning Psychology*. But the same intonations can be heard in more orthodox Jungian publications, e.g., in Marie-Louise von Franz, *C.G. Jung: His Myth in Our Time* (New York: C.G. Jung Foundation, 1975). Jungians can too easily overlook the correct estimation of Laurens van der Post that Jung's main concern was *consciousness*, not the unconscious. See van der Post, *Jung and the Story of Our Time* 61. The fact is that raising what is dark and inferior in oneself to the same level as what is light and superior was conceived by Jung as something to be done without the surrender of the previously affirmed values, which for most of us in the West are the values inculcated by Christianity. See *ibid.* 199. Perhaps the common misconception concerning Jung on this point is related to the lack of a developed image of the father in his own psyche and in his psychology. See *ibid.* 79.

24 David Burrell has offered preliminary suggestions for cleaning up Jung's language on this point. See the chapter on Jung in Burrell's *Exercises in Religious Understanding* (South Bend: Notre Dame, 1974).

25 T.S. Eliot, 'Little Gidding,' *Four Quartets* (see above, chapter 2, note 15) 55. ·

26 See Hans-Georg Gadamer, *Truth and Method*, translation revised by Joel Weisheimer and Donald G. Marshall (New York: Crossroad, 1989) 9-19.

27 Eliot, 'Little Gidding' 59.

5 Christ and the Psyche

The archetypal psychology of C.G. Jung has aroused a great deal of interest among theologians. A recent and excellent bibliographical essay lists 442 books and articles which have concerned themselves at least in part with the relation of Jung's work to theology.[1] But the author concludes that 'scholarship on the borderlands between theology and archetypal psychology has grown tired. What it needs to avoid declining into an eremitic glass-bead-game is not so much the flair of revolutionizing ideas as the painstaking re-examination of fundamental assumptions.'[2]

With this judgment I concur, and I have argued elsewhere that the theological method of Bernard Lonergan provides a quite adequate horizon for the dialectical reinterpretation and personal employment of the Jungian maieutic on the part of the theologian.[3] The kind of critical engagement with Jung that Lonergan makes possible will help the theologian construct a portion of theology's foundations. In this paper I wish to move on from these initial methodological considerations to one particular problem of great importance; namely, the Jungian interpretation of the symbolic significance of the figure of Jesus Christ. In this examination, I will be considering some of the fundamental assumptions of both Jungian psychology and Christian theology.

My paper divides into three major sections. The first two set the problem by way of an exposition of Jung's notions of the self and individuation, and by way of an interpretation of his treatment of Christ as symbol of the self. The third section states all too briefly the methodological framework for the theologian's employment and correction of Jung, suggests all too cryptically a new formulation of the individuation process in the light of these methodological considerations, and proclaims all too poorly the symbolic and psychic significance of Jesus Christ within the framework of this revised notion of individuation.[4]

I   The Self and the Individuation Process

I.I   *Consciousness and the Unconscious*

Individuation is the process of becoming one's own self.[5] Jung proposes it as an alternative to two different paths of alienation, one in which the self retires in favor of social recognition or the *persona*, and the other in which the self is identified with a primordial image or archetype. The process of individuation occurs by way of the ego's conscious negotiation with the *complexes of the unconscious*.

Jung arrived at the notion of unconscious complexes very early in his psychiatric career. The instrument for his discovery was the association experiment, which revealed certain indicators of powerful emotions lying beyond the realm of consciousness. These phenomena were postulated by Jung to be the effects of concealed, feeling-toned complexes in the unconscious psyche.[6] These complexes are the cause of dreams as well as of disturbances in the association experiment. Jung first defined the complex as 'the sum of ideas referring to a particular feeling-toned event.'[7] He later added the notion of a nuclear element within each complex[8] and distinguished between the emotional and the purposeful aspects of the complex.[9]

The feeling-toned complex is a common phenomenon, not limited to acute or pathological states or cases.

Some, especially those connected with religious experience, even lead to long-lasting emotional stability.[10] This discovery led Jung very early to grant a greater significance to the inner content of an emotional experience than was accorded it by Freud.[11] Furthermore, complexes tend to exhibit a tenacious inner cohesiveness and stability, a unity of structure resulting from the association of feeling and idea. 'Every minute part of the complex reproduced the feeling-tone of the whole, and, in addition, each effect radiated throughout the entire mass of the associated idea.'[12]

Complexes, then, are the structural units of the psyche. Each complex has a specific focus of energy and meaning, called its nucleus. While the psyche is a whole, its parts are relatively independent of one another. The ego is its central complex, but the ego must remain in harmony with its unconscious background. This it does by negotiating the other complexes, and thus preventing them from splitting away and forming a second authority to thwart the aims of the ego. This second authority never goes away, but 'a living cooperation of all factors'[13] is possible through the process of individuation. Complexes are miniature, self-contained personalities in their own right, but this need not at all mean the disintegration of personality. In fact, there is dormant within the psyche an image of wholeness, which represents the goal of the development which is individuation. This image is progressively realized by the cumulative negotiation and integration of the complexes as they manifest themselves in dreams and other psychic phenomena.

1.2 The Personal and the Collective Unconscious

Unconscious complexes can be either personal or impersonal. Personal complexes include material which I know but of which I am not at the moment thinking; ma-

terial of which I was at one time conscious but which I
have forgotten; everything which, without attending to it,
I feel, think, remember, want, and do; and the repressed
memories made so much of by Freud.[14] They are 'those
ideas which either belonged to the ego-complex or were
split off from the ego and ignored. All personal contents,
thus, were reminiscences of events which had occurred
during life.'[15] Impersonal complexes, on the other hand,
are independent of the ego and of personal memory. They
originate from a more primordial base, and they have a
meaning common to all. The domain of personal complexes is called the personal unconscious, that of impersonal complexes the collective unconscious. The latter is a
superpersonal level of the psyche whose contents concern
humanity as such. The discovery of this universal layer of
psychic life opened for Jung and his followers prospects of
psychotherapy which extend beyond the confines of personal psychopathology. The impersonal complexes are 'the
fertile ground of creative processes,'[16] permitting the process of individuation to be a distinctly creative one, and
giving rise to the judgment that Jung's psychology is essentially one of creativity.[17] Thus the 'second authority' of
the unconscious background is not disruptive but creative
of individuated life when complexes come from or can be
related to the impersonal or collective layer, and when the
contents of this deeper dimension can be harmoniously
integrated into one's conscious development. This integration, however, is not to take place by way of identification with the impersonal complexes, for then one's conscious individuality is inundated by a primordial image
which inflates the ego to the dimensions of some kind of
Übermensch, or on the contrary destroys the ego completely
on account of its power. In the first case, one becomes 'the
fortunate possessor of *the* great truth which was only waiting to be discovered, of the eschatological knowledge which

spells the healing of the nations.'[18] Regarding the second case, Jung tells us in his autobiographical reflections of a dream he had dealing with his intimation of a second authority at the base and source of the conscious mind.

> It was night in some unknown place, and I was making slow and painful headway against a mighty wind. Dense fog was flying along everywhere. I had my hands cupped around a tiny light which threatened to go out at any moment. Everything depended on my keeping this little light alive. Suddenly I had the feeling that something was coming up behind me. I looked back, and saw a gigantic black figure following me. But at the same moment I was conscious, in spite of my terror, that I must keep my little light going through night and wind, regardless of all dangers.[19]

The little light was consciousness, understanding, 'the only light I have.'[20] The darkness was the second authority, Personality No. 2, 'with whom ... I could no longer feel myself identical.'[21] The storm 'sought to thrust me back into the immeasurable darkness of a world where one is aware of nothing except the surfaces of things in the background.'[22] The darkness of this background had to be recognized and negotiated, but not identified with. Identification would seem to be the shortest route to continual contact with the renewing power of the primordial layer of the psyche, but when one identifies with this layer it becomes storm, wind, and darkness, not life, renewal, and transformation.

> If a man is a hero, he is a hero precisely because, in the final reckoning, he did not let the

monster devour him, but subdued it, not once
but many times. Victory over the collective
psyche alone yields the true value — the capture of the hoard, the invincible weapon, the
magic talisman ... Anyone who identifies with
the collective psyche — or, in mythological
terms, lets himself be devoured by the monster — and vanishes in it, attains the treasure
that the dragon guards, but he does so in spite
of himself and to his own greatest harm.[23]

Individuation, then, is dependent upon an attitude
which finds in feeling-toned complexes, whether personal
or impersonal, occasions for deepening one's self-understanding, for becoming more conscious, for expanding
one's personality. Everything seems to depend on the delicacy of one's conscious attitude toward the unconscious
complexes. There are places where Jung suggests that individuation is a matter of the detachment from inner states
and outer objects that constitutes the mystical *via negativa*.
Thus, 'the aim of individuation is nothing less than to di-
vest the self of the false wrappings of the persona on the
one hand, and of the suggestive power of primordial images on the other.'[24] Or:

By understanding the unconscious we free
ourselves from its domination ... The pupil is
taught to concentrate on the light of the innermost region and, at the same time, to free himself from all outer and inner entanglements. His
vital impulses are guided towards a consciousness void of content, which nevertheless
permits all contents to exist ... Consciousness
is at the same time empty and not empty. It is
no longer preoccupied with the images of things

but merely contains them. The fullness of the world which hitherto pressed upon it has lost none of its richness and beauty, but it no longer dominates. The magical claim of things has ceased because the interweaving of consciousness with the world has come to an end. The unconscious is not projected any more, and so the primordial *participation mystique* with things is abolished. Consciousness is no longer preoccupied with compulsive plans but dissolves in contemplative vision.

... This effect ... is the therapeutic effect *par excellence*, for which I labor with my students and patients.[25]

1.3   The Self as Center and Totality

The key to the attainment of this detached state is the shifting of the center of gravity of the total personality from the ego, which is merely the center of consciousness, to a hypothetical midpoint between consciousness and the unconscious which Jung calls the self. 'If the transposition is successful, it does away with the *participation mystique* and results in a personality that suffers only in the lower storeys, as it were, but in its upper storeys is singularly detached from painful as well as from joyful happenings.'[26] For Western people, such an attitude can only be reached by renouncing 'none of the Christian values won in the course of Christian development,' by trying 'with Christian charity and forbearance to accept even the humblest things in one's own nature.'[27] Such an attitude can be aped only so long before it produces 'an unstable situation that can be overthrown by the unconscious at any time.'[28] The alternative to aping such an attitude is to give due consideration to the unconscious, and to integrate its contents, always keeping in mind as one does so that 'without the most serious application of the Christian values we have acquired, the new integration can never take place.'[29]

The self is conceived by Jung, however, not only as a center, but also as the totality of consciousness and the unconscious. The notion of *psychic totality* gradually became the guiding principle in all of Jung's investigations. This evolution is linked with the development of the notions of a creative transformation of energy and of a teleological orientation on the part of the psyche as a whole.[30] Jung came to understand psychic development as 'an entirely natural and automatic process of transformation,'[31] invested with an unconscious meaning which works itself out in the production, not so much of symptoms of an underlying disorder as of symbols progressively anticipating an already established goal. This goal is the self, understood as wholeness or psychic totality.

Normal development, then, inevitably entails onesidedness, if it is consciously directed at all,[32] but this onesidedness means that part of the psyche is repressed, and that an inferior part of the personality is formed, which Jung calls the shadow. 'By shadow I mean the "negative" side of the personality, the sum of all those unpleasant qualities we like to hide, together with the insufficiently developed functions and the contents of the personal unconscious.'[33] But the shadow is negative only from the standpoint of the ego. Potentially it contains the seeds of future development, of transformation, and even of a higher and more authentic form of morality. This is because, as repressed and hidden from ego consciousness, the shadow is connected more intimately than the ego with the energic forces of the psychic depths from which all consciousness emerges in the first place. Proper negotiation of the shadow is the beginning of the shift from the ego as center to the self as center, and from a state of rift between the ego and the totality to a condition of wholeness. What had previously been thought worthless contains enormous positive potentialities for psychic development, if only one knows how to tap it. The weak point of one's psychic life can be the source of potential victory, provided the latter is understood in the sense of an expanded consciousness and a deepened and more centered personality. The shadow is truly the gateway to the unconscious, the link between the ego and the depths, indeed the universal reaches, of psychic energy.

The negotiation of the shadow only introduces one to the other capacities of the unconscious: its resources for heightened personal performance, its direction toward the emergence of a future personality, its provision of both commonsense and sophisticated intellectual insight, its rich store of personal and collective memories, its autonomy as a producer of symbols of transformation, its capacity to premeditate new ideas and their combinations, its independent powers of perception, association, and prediction. The history of Jung's association with Freud[34] reveals that Jung was aware very early in his professional career that the potentialities of the unconscious are far more extensive than Freud allowed. But it was necessary for him to explore the archaic images which he relates to the archetypes of the collective unconscious before he could exploit his suspicion of a farther-reaching and more creative psychic life. Then he discovered that certain fantasies and dreams could be explained only by appealing to superpersonal motives, to something greater in us than the ego and the personal unconscious, and that these images are released by an organizing center in the psyche, a central nucleus to the entire personality, a regulating principle intent on integration and individuation; by a center which is also a goal, the self.

1.4   The Psychic and the Psychoid

The last twenty-five years of Jung's life saw his thought move far beyond medical psychology. His work became an empirical science of the human soul, and as such it becomes directly pertinent to the theologian.[35] Among the notions of his thought which were affected by this development are the archetypes of the collective unconscious.

In Jung's early work, the archetypes are not distinguished from archetypal images; namely, experienced representations of typical forms of behavior which tend to repeat themselves in the course of the living of the human drama. From their center, creative forces emerge which shape and transform life and which are ultimately responsible for genuine intellectual and artistic achievements. The ego needs the archetypes for its own continued vitality, but the archetypes also need the ego if they are to be consciously realized.

In his later work, Jung distinguishes the archetype-in-itself from the archetypal images, and he focuses more on the background of the images. He realizes more and more the incomprehensibility of the archetype-in-itself, its permanently unknown meaning.[36] The core of meaning, what the images refer to, remains unknown, as though it belonged to a realm transcendent to the psyche. This core of meaning expresses itself in metaphors which, while issuing from the realm beyond subjectivity, nonetheless are related to the life of the individual, regulate that life, stimulate psychic happenings, order them to or away from the goal of individuation, and seem to possess a foreknowledge of the envisioned terminus.[37]

Jung is led by these data to posit the presence of spirit in the psyche and to relate archetypes to this spirit factor. The collective unconscious had always consisted for Jung of vestiges of biological evolution and heredity closely connected with instinct. The archetypes had been and remain correlative to instincts. But, says Jung, they 'are not just relics or vestiges of earlier modes of functioning; they are the ever-present and biologically necessary regulators of the instinctual sphere' and stimulate images which represent the *meaning* of the instincts.[38] But these images are also numinous or spiritual or mystical in their character and effects. They can mobilize religious convictions and draw the subject under a spell from which one cannot and will not break free, so deep and full is the experience of meaningfulness one enjoys.[39] Thus, 'in spite of or perhaps because of its affinity with instinct, the archetype represents the authentic element of spirit, but a spirit which is not to be identified with the human intellect, since it is the latter's *spiritus rector*.'[40] Instinct and archetype, 'the most polar opposites imaginable,' yet 'belong together as correspondences, which is not to say that the one is derivable from the other, but that they subsist side by side as reflections in our own minds of the opposition that underlies all psychic energy.'[41]

Jung thus postulates two 'transcendental principles' quite separate from one another: spirit and instinct. Their tension is the source of psychic energy, which moves to unite them. They are mediated by the archetypal image, through which spirit becomes incarnate and instinct consciously meaningful. Spirit and instinct are not themselves psychic, but psychoid, that is, understood by relation to the psyche, but autonomous from the psyche and not subject to will as is the psyche's disposable energy. Archetypes in themselves are no longer psychic, but are transcendent principles of spirit determining the orientation of both consciousness and the unconscious psyche. Instinct is called the psychic infra-red, passing over into the physiology of the organism and merging with its chemical and physical conditions, while spirit is the psychic ultra-violet, neither physiological nor psychic. The psyche unites spirit and matter in the image.

On the basis of the hypothesis of the psychoid, Jung found himself in a position to understand somewhat better certain phenomena which had always interested him: parapsychology, extrasensory perception, and astrological correlations. He came to regard these phenomena as synchronistic, that is, as manifesting a meaningful but acausal concurrence of mind and matter. Their just-so orderedness is rooted in the psychoid parallelism of spirit and matter. The archetype-in-itself is thus an a priori ordering principle which cannot be distinguished from continuous creation understood either as a series of successive acts of creation or as the eternal presence of one creative act.[42] Synchronicity points to an ultimate unity of all existence, the *unus mundus*. The collective unconscious becomes the timeless and spaceless unity underlying empirical multiplicity, a transcendental psychophysical background containing the determining conditions of empirical phenomena. As such, it is a darkness beyond the categories of the mind, incommensurable to consciousness, less and less accessible to conscious correction and reasoning — yet the darkness, not of meaninglessness, but of a superabundance of meaning beyond the powers of rational comprehension and influence, and yet involving ego consciousness and the unconscious psyche as participants in a world-creating drama to which the individual has no choice but to submit. In this surrender one finds the self, finds one's life, but no longer claims it. One lives the 'just-so' life, without ulterior motives, without desire and without fear. In the experience of the self the dark background of the empirical world approximates consciousness. This is the experience of bounded infinity, of finite boundlessness, where the incommensurable distance of the unknown draws very near.[43]

2 Christ in Archetypal Psychology

2.1 Christ and the Archetype of the Self

Concomitant with Jung's movement to an empirical science of the soul is a development of his notion of the self. As we have seen, symbols of the self reflect a central point that does not coincide with the ego, 'something irrational, an indefinable existent, to which the ego is neither opposed nor subjected, but merely attached, and about which it revolves very much as the earth revolves around the sun.'[44] The goal of individuation is not knowing the self, but sensing it, and sensing the ego as the object of an unknown and supraordinate subject.[45] Jung calls the postulate of the self a step beyond science, yet one without which empirical psychic processes could not be understood.[46] The self is only potentially empirical, because it is the totality. Only certain symbols can convey its reality.[47]

Jung's most provocative treatment of these symbols appears in his book *Aion*.[48] This investigation 'seeks, with the help of Christian, Gnostic, and alchemical symbols of the self, to throw light on the change of psychic situation within the "Christian aeon."'[49] Many of Jung's reflections about the self in this book gravitate around the symbol of the Fishes, because Jung thinks it seriously synchronistic that astrologically Pisces is the concomitant of 2,000 years of Christian development; and around the symbol of the Anthropos, the emergent symbol of the Age of Aquarius. The Christian aeon coincides with the age of Pisces, whereas the emergent age is that of Anthropos.

For Jung the Christ image, as an Anthropos figure uniting in itself the whole of humanity, has, at least up to now, been inadequate to the task of liberating the 'true man,' just as, in the East, the Buddha image was unable to protect against the invasion of Communist ideology. This is because the Christ image, as we have known it, is too one-sided to be able to represent our wholeness. It is 'lacking in darkness and in bodily and material reality.'[50] The medieval alchemists perceived this and attempted to free from matter a divine Anthropos, 'an image of man in which good and evil, spirit and matter, were genuinely united and through which not only man but also all of nature would be made whole.'[51]

Aion discusses the relations between the traditional Christ figure and *the symbols of wholeness or of the self taken from nature.* Wholeness, Jung says, is not an abstract idea. It is empirical, in that it is anticipated by the psyche in the form of spontaneous or autonomous images. These include the quaternity or mandala symbols, whose significance as symbols of unity and totality is amply confirmed by history and empirical psychology. Wholeness confronts the subject in an a priori fashion through these images. In fact, unity and totality stand at the highest point on the scale of objective values in that their symbols cannot be distinguished from the *imago Dei.*

Why do these symbols have this value? 'Experience shows that individual mandalas are symbols of *order,* and that they occur in patients principally during times of psychic disorientation or reorientation. As magic circles they bind and subdue the lawless powers belonging to the world of darkness, and depict or create an order that transforms the chaos into a cosmos.'[52] The integration of the meaning of these symbols is painstaking work, for the disorientation of the psyche usually means that many projections must be withdrawn before the symbol can be realized. Feeling as a function of value is attached to these symbols, and only when it enters into the judgment passed on their meaning is the subject affected by the process of experiencing them.

In discussing the self in the context of the Christian aeon, Jung is preoccupied by the saturation of Christian tradition with premonitions of the conflict of Christ and Antichrist. He finds parallels to this conflict in 'the dechristianization of our world, the Luciferian development of science and technology, and the frightful material and moral destruction left behind by the Second World War.'[53] Christ is still, says Jung, the living myth of our culture, 'our culture hero, who, regardless of his historical existence, embodies the myth of the divine Primordial Man.'[54] It is Christ who occupies the center of the Christian mandala, Christ whose 'kingdom is the pearl of great price, the treasure buried in the field, the grain of mustard seed which will become a great tree, and the heavenly city.'[55] Christ, then, represents the archetype of the self, a totality of a divine kind, a glorified man, a son of God unspotted by sin, the true image of God after whose likeness our inner man is made.[56] Theologians such as Tertullian, Origen, and Augustine are quoted to substantiate this archetypal interpretation of the symbol of Christ for the Christian psyche. But for these authorities and others, the image of God in us does not reside in the corporeal human being, but in the invisible, incorporeal, incorrupt, and immortal *anima rationalis*. This God image was not destroyed by the Fall but only damaged and corrupted, and it can be restored through God's grace. Thus Christian tradition used the language of restoration in its symbols of the self or of the *imago Dei*. The renewal or transformation of the mind (see Romans 12.2) called for in Christian preaching 'is not meant as an actual alteration of consciousness, but rather as the restoration of an original condition, an apocatastasis.'[57] The recognition of the person of Christ is really the recognition of the ever-present

archetype of wholeness which had been lost from view or
never attended to. This recognition restores an original state
of oneness with the God image in the human soul.

For Jung there is no doubt that 'the original Christian conception of the *imago Dei* embodied in Christ meant
an all-embracing totality that even includes the animal side
of man.'[58] But this image of Christ soon came to lack
wholeness, since the dark side of things was excluded from
it and made into a Luciferian opponent. The figure of the
Redeemer became bright and one-sided. The dark side of
the self, the dark half of the human totality, became ascribed to the Antichrist, the devil, evil. The dogmatic figure of Christ was made so sublime and spotless that everything else turned dark beside it, so one-sidedly perfect
that it demanded a psychic complement to restore the balance. This complement was provided in Christian doctrine by the figure of Satan as Antichrist.[59]

Jung highlights what he considers a fatality inherent
in the perfectionism of the Christian disposition. It leads
inevitably, by a necessary psychological law, to a reversal
of its spirit.

> The psychological concept of the self, in part
> derived from our knowledge of the whole man,
> but for the rest depicting itself spontaneously
> in the products of the unconscious as an ar-
> chetypal quaternity bound together by inner
> antinomies, cannot omit the shadow that be-
> longs to the light figure, for without it this fig-
> ure lacks body and humanity. In the empirical
> self, light and shadow form a paradoxical unity.
> In the Christian concept, on the other hand,
> the archetype is hopelessly split into two irrec-
> oncilable halves, leading ultimately to a meta-
> physical dualism — the final separation of the

kingdom of heaven from the fiery world of the damned.

... Every intensified differentiation of the Christ-image brings about a corresponding accentuation of its unconscious complement, thereby increasing the tension between above and below.

... The ideal of spirituality striving for the heights was doomed to clash with the materialistic earth-bound passion to conquer matter and master the world. This change became visible at the time of the 'Renaissance.' The word means 'rebirth,' and it referred to the renewal of the antique spirit. We know today that this spirit was chiefly a mask; it was not the spirit of antiquity that was reborn, but the spirit of medieval Christianity that underwent strange pagan transformation, exchanging the heavenly goal for an earthly one, and the vertical of the Gothic for a horizontal perspective (voyages of discovery, exploration of the world and of nature). The subsequent developments that led to the Enlightenment and the French Revolution have produced a worldwide situation today which can only be called 'antichristian' in a sense that confirms the early Christian anticipation of the 'end of time.'[60]

The meaning of the astrological symbol of Pisces, the two opposing fishes, is related to this conflict of Christ and Antichrist in the psychic situation which prevails at the end of this aeon.

It is as if, with the coming of Christ, opposites that were latent till then had become manifest, or as if a pendulum had swung violently to one side and were now carrying out the complementary movement in the opposite direction. No tree, it is said, can grow to heaven unless its roots reached down to hell. The double meaning of this movement lies in the nature of the pendulum. Christ is without spot, but right at the beginning of his career there occurs the encounter with Satan, the Adversary, who represents the counterpole of that tremendous tension in the world psyche which Christ's advent signified. He is the 'mysterium iniquitatis' that accompanies the 'sol iustitiae' as inseparably as the shadow belongs to the light, in exactly the same way, so the Ebionites and Euchites thought, that one brother cleaves to the other. Both strive for a kingdom: one for the kingdom of heaven, the other for the 'principatus huius mundi.' We hear of a reign of a 'thousand years' and of a 'coming of the Antichrist,' just as if a partition of worlds and epochs had taken place between two royal brothers. The meeting with Satan was therefore more than mere change; it was a link in the chain.[61]

Christian tradition, then, has made Christ into only one-half of the archetype of the self. The other half it has labeled as Antichrist, Satan, evil. 'The Christian image of the self — Christ — lacks the shadow that properly belongs to it.'[62] Tradition did not allow God or Christ to be a paradox. Christians have thus fallen prey to a false spiritualism which bifurcates the self. They have preferred an ethic of perfection to one of wholeness.[63] They have in fact mistaken one-sidedness for wholeness, for Christ represents the self and Christ is one-sided. By representing

Christ as simply good and spiritual, they have placed something evil and material in opposition to him. They have, in fact, equated instinct, the dark side, with evil, while at the same time discountenancing evil as a *privatio boni*, 'a mere diminution of good and thus deprived of substance,' as simply 'the accidental lack of perfection.'[64] But if the self is not exclusively spiritual or light, its shadow turns out to be much less evil or threatening than the Christian tradition has made it out to be. The self includes the light and the dark, and individuation becomes a *mysterium coniunctionis*, a nuptial union of opposite halves.[65] The body acquires a special and, to the traditional Christian, an unexpected and alarming significance. Matter has considerable numinosity in itself, since it is part of the composite which is the totality, the self. Not to recognize this is to split oneself into two halves. The conscious half is identified with Christ, who then becomes an ego ideal rather than an archetypal image of the self. The dark half, regarded as evil, is suppressed or repressed, and, to the extent it remains conscious, is projected outside, so that the world must act out the conflict that is ultimately the moral problem of the individual.

2.2   Evil as Substantive

Jung attributes the spiritualistic perversion that he finds in the Christian tradition to the metaphysical doctrine of evil as a *privatio boni*, which, he claims, was motivated by a desire to avoid both a metaphysical dualism and an attribution of the causality of evil to God, and which for Jung succeeded in doing neither. God for Christian tradition is the *Summum Bonum*, a doctrine which for Jung is a product of the 'hybris of the speculative intellect,'[66] and the origin of the later axiom, *Omne bonum a Deo, omne malum ab homine*.[67] Jung has at least three arguments against such notions. The first is a logical argument, namely, that good and evil are a logically equivalent pair of opposites which constitute the premise for any moral judgment. They are 'coexistent halves of a moral judgment' and belong therefore to the realm of human values. We are the authors of human value judgments, but not of the facts submitted to our moral judgment, except in a very limited sense.[68]

The second argument is theological (in the loose sense). Evil is said by Basil to have no substance but to arise from a 'mutilation of the soul,' and yet really to exist. Its relative reality, then, has a ground in a real mutilation which itself must have an equally real cause, even if this be nothing more than carelessness, indifference, and frivolity. To posit such psychic causes does not reduce evil to nothing but shifts it to the plane of psychic reality. The latter is 'very much easier to establish empirically than, say, the reality of the devil in dogma, who according to the authentic sources was not invented by man at all but existed long before he did. If the devil fell away from God of his own free will, this proves firstly that evil was in the world before man, and therefore that man cannot be the sole author of it, and secondly that the devil already had a "mutilated" soul for which we must hold a real cause responsible.'[69]

The third argument is existential, and it concerns our experience of conflicts of duty. Real moral problems result from those situations where we seem to be required to satisfy irreconcilable obligations, where a choice cannot be arrived at by rational discrimination, let alone in dependence on precedent, precepts, and commandments. Such dilemmas are terminated, Jung says, not by a decision, but by uncontrollable natural forces. Jung finds psychological benefit and accuracy in attributing such forces to the will of God, in that they 'ought not to be regarded as an arbitrary wishing and willing, but as absolutes which one must learn how to handle correctly.'[70] 'God' is here to be understood in the sense of *daimôn*, that is, of 'determining power which comes upon man from outside, like providence or fate.'[71] While we can obey or reject the *daimôn*, obedience is more than following one's own opinion, and rejection destroys more than one's own invention.[72] There are evils necessarily concomitant upon the resolution of all conflicts of duty, and if it is true that the resolution of such conflicts is due to the will of God, then these evils must be ascribed to God as to their cause.

Jung prefers to the Christian doctrine of God as *Summum Bonum*, then, the Gnostic conceptions of good and evil as, respectively, the right and left hands of God, with the right hand pertaining to rationality and the masculine, and the left hand to emotionality and the feminine. While the Christian notion of *privatio boni* took hold in the struggle against Manichean dualism, the Gnostic conception of the reality of evil does not endanger the unity of God. Jung is also sympathetic with the Ebionite notion of the two sons of God, the elder being Satan, and the younger Christ. 'Only with Christ did a devil enter the world as the real counterpart of God.'[73]

3   **Toward a Metascience of Depth Psychology: The Orders of Elemental Symbolism**

Christ and Satan are treated by Jung as archetypal symbols, on the same plane as, for example, the royal king and queen of alchemical lore who symbolize the androgynous nature of the psyche, or the golden flower of Taoist literature which Jung interprets as symbolizing the wholeness of individuated life.[74] Archetypal symbols are taken from nature and imitate nature, albeit in a generic and highly associative manner. They reflect a wholeness in nature, and can effect a wholeness in us insofar as we are

nature. When Christ and Satan are understood as archetypal symbols, both are necessarily incomplete, for one is
light and the other darkness. Neither reflects a wholeness
in nature such as is symbolized in the nuptial *coniunctio* or
in the golden flower rooted in the earth but displaying its
singular perfection to the world of light and sun and air.
On the archetypal level, only a conjunction of Christ and
Satan would seem to reflect the wholeness of nature that
comes to expression in the associative clusters of archetypal symbols. They need one another if they are adequately
to represent the self, the wholeness, that is the goal of the
individuation process. Christ for Jung is necessarily inadequate as a symbol of the self or Anthropos, for he is without sin and darkness. Only the reconciliation of God's two
sons, of the hostile divine brothers, of the warring fishes
who constitute the sign of Pisces which has prevailed over
the Christian aeon, will provide the symbolization of individuated totality that will satisfy Jung's postulate of a progressive reconciliation of opposites cumulatively heading
toward the realization of the self.

Jung's speculation is more developed in an earlier
work, 'A Psychological Approach to the Dogma of the Trinity,'[75] where the Trinity is presented as an incomplete symbol, lacking the fourth element which could make it whole.
The fourth element is the devil, the dark or evil side of
God. The fuller implications of such a position are revealed
in Jung's perhaps most controversial work, *Answer to Job*.[76]
While Jung begs his reader to pay attention to a preface in
which he assures us that he is writing not theology but
psychology, the work cannot be ignored by the theological
community. Statements such as the following reflect Jung's
passionate convictions concerning what constitutes adequate symbolizations of the deity.

Job ... was an ordinary human being, and therefore the wrong done to him, and through him to mankind, can, according to divine justice, only be repaired by an incarnation of God in an empirical human being. This act of expiation is performed by the Paraclete; for, just as man must suffer from God, so God must suffer from man. Otherwise there can be no reconciliation between the two.[77]

Again:

Redemption or deliverance has several important aspects, the most important of which is the expiation wrought by Christ's sacrificial death for the misdemeanors of mankind. His blood cleanses us from the evil consequences of sin. He reconciles God with man and delivers him from the divine wrath, which hangs over him like doom, and from eternal damnation. It is obvious that such ideas still picture God the father as the dangerous Yahweh who has to be propitiated. The agonizing death of his own son is supposed to give him satisfaction for an affront he has suffered, and for this 'moral injury' he would be inclined to take a terrible vengeance. Once more we are appalled by the incongruous attitude of the world creator towards his creatures, who to his chagrin never behave according to his expectations. It is as if someone started a bacterial culture which turned out to be a failure. He might curse his luck, but he would never seek the reason for the failure in the bacilli and want to punish them morally for it. Rather, he would select a more favorable culture medium. Yahweh's behavior towards his creatures contradicts all the requirements of so-called 'divine' reason whose possession is supposed to distinguish men from animals. Moreover, a bacteriologist might make a mistake in his choice of a culture medium, for he is only human. But God in his omniscience would never make mistakes if only he consulted with it. He has equipped his human creatures with a modicum of consciousness and a corresponding degree of free will, but he must also know that by so doing he leads them into the temptation of falling into a dangerous independence. But Yahweh is forgetting his son Satan, to whose wiles even he occasionally succumbs. How then could he expect man with his limited consciousness and imperfect knowledge to do any better? He also overlooks the fact that the more consciousness a man possesses the more he is separated from his instincts (which at least give him an inkling of the hidden wisdom of God) and the more prone he is to error. He is certainly not up to Satan's wiles if even his creator is unable, or unwilling, to restrain this powerful spirit.[78]

Again:

To believe that God is the Summum Bonum is impossible for a reflecting consciousness.[79]

Again:

The inner instability of Yahweh is the prime cause not only of the creation of the world, but also of the pleromatic drama for which mankind serves as a tragic chorus. The encounter with the creature changes the creator.[80]

Again:

> Yahweh's decision to become man is a symbol of the development that had to supervene when man becomes conscious of the sort of God-image he is confronted with. God acts out of the unconscious of man and forces him to harmonize and unite the opposing influences to which his mind is exposed from the unconscious. The unconscious wants both: to divide and to unite. In his striving for unity, therefore, man may always count on the help of a metaphysical advocate, as Job clearly recognized. The unconscious wants to flow into consciousness in order to reach the light, but at the same time it continually thwarts itself, because it would rather remain unconscious. That is to say, God wants to become man, but not quite. The conflict in his nature is so great that the incarnation can only be bought by an expiatory self-sacrifice offered up to the wrath of God's dark side.
>
> At first, God incarnated his good side in order, as we may suppose, to create the most durable basis for a later assimilation of the other side. From the promise of the Paraclete we may conclude that God wants to become *wholly* man; in other words, to reproduce himself in his own dark creature (man not redeemed from original sin) ... The incarnation in Christ is the prototype which is continually being transferred to the creature by the Holy Ghost.[81]

Here too Jung expresses his enthusiasm for the dogma of the bodily assumption of the Virgin Mary into heaven, since it reveals, he believes, the integration of matter and femininity, and thus of the dark side, into the Godhead.

What we have said, then, of Jung's treatment of the symbolic significance of Christ may also be said of that of the Trinity. If the symbol of a triune God is treated on the archetypal plane, and thus as a symbol taken from nature and imitating nature, it is necessarily a symbol of incompleteness. It seeks its fourth, for quaternity does indeed seem to be the numeric symbolism of natural wholeness, which finds its expression in rotary and cyclical movements which are usually divided into four phases.[82]

David Burrell has accepted the archetypal incompleteness of Trinitarian symbolism, but has proposed a different 'rounding off' from that postulated by Jung, one which would also affect the evaluation of the symbolic significance of Christ as archetype of the self.

> So far as the Christian symbol of the Trinity is concerned, it does in fact seem to invite a fourth member. Christian tradition holds out the missing place to be filled by each one who is adopted into sonship ... Without denying that trinity is symbolically inferior to quaternity, one can see in the deficient symbol of the Trinity a way of displaying the fact that the Christian revelation is not a mere announcement but an invitation. God presents himself as lacking what only the faithful respondent can fill. Or more explicitly yet, what only the community of the faithful can make up for, as it fills out 'the fullness of him who fills the whole creation' (Eph 1.23).[83]

The question faced by neither Burrell nor Jung is whether archetypal symbols, that is, symbols of wholeness taken from and imitating nature, are to be treated as criteria for judging the symbolic adequacy of statements about the divine. It is clear, I believe, that for Jung the divine is to be found within nature, and exclusively there, and is to be liberated from the darkness of matter in the form of the divine Anthropos, the image of man which unites good and evil, spirit and matter, masculine and feminine. The drama of redemption is reversed: we redeem God from unconsciousness more radically than God redeems us from sin. Jung's own personal belief is revealed in posthumously published lecture notes compiled by disciples and entitled 'Is Analytical Psychology a Religion? Notes on a Talk given by C.G. Jung.'[84] In these notes dating from 1937 Jung reveals affinities with the later radical theology of Thomas J.J. Altizer, who, it is significant, wrote his doctoral dissertation on Jung. One quotation will suffice:

> Life has gone out of the churches, and it will never go back. The gods will not reinvest dwellings that once they have left. The same thing happened before, in the time of the Roman Caesars, whose paganism was dying. According to legend, the captain of a ship passing between two Greek islands heard a great sound of lamentation and a loud voice crying: *Pan megistos ethneken,* Great Pan is dead. When this man reached Rome he demanded an audience with the emperor, so important was his news. Originally Pan was an unimportant nature spirit, chiefly occupied with teasing shepherds; but later, as the Romans became more involved with Greek culture, Pan was confused with *to pan,* meaning the All. He became the *demiurgos,* the *anima mundi.* Thus the many gods of paganism were concentrated into one God. Then

came this message. "Pan is dead." Great Pan,
who is God, is dead. Only man remains alive.
After that the one God became one man, and
this was Christ; one man for all. But now that
too is gone, now every man has to carry God.
The descent of spirit into matter is complete.[85]

On such an assumption, of course, only symbols
taken from nature and imitating nature can reflect the
wholeness of the All that is God. There is no further dimension of symbolism beyond the archetypal, for there is
nothing further to be symbolized. What is to be done is to
win through to the wholeness that can make one a carrier
of God, of a quadripartite God in whom evil is as real and
as effective as good. At this point Jung brings us into theological difficulties of the greatest import for the life of religion, difficulties not unlike those experienced in the earliest centuries of the Christian church. How is the Christian theologian to meet these difficulties?

It will not do, I believe, in this day and age for the
theologian simply to declare that symbolic thinking must
give way to the analogical thinking of metaphysics when
one intends to speak in a scientific manner about the divinity and Christian revelation. Nor is it even sufficient,
though certainly it is appropriate, to point to the implicit
realism of scriptural imagery, a realism which in the course
of theological development eventually, indeed within three
centuries, achieved expression in propositions which transcended imaginative representation and, because of this
transcendence, were able to clarify doctrinal questions in
a way that symbolic thinking could never do.[86] I do not
wish to deny the place of metaphysics in theology[87] nor to
play down the significance of the emergence of an explicit
though noncritical realism concomitant with the development of the Trinitarian and Christological doctrines. Such

systematic and historical emphases could well show that, on many issues, Jung has begged the question or entirely missed the point, and more radically could demonstrate the need of a rigorous maieutic to control the vagaries of symbolic thought. But I wish to suggest that this maieutic must be more in keeping with the realm of interiority upon whose symbolic manifestations Jung has done so much to open us by his painstaking and courageous explorations of the labyrinthine paths of psyche. There is an emerging control of meaning in terms not of theory or system or metaphysics but of interiority,[88] and Jung has made no small contribution to its elaboration. His contribution, however, does not adequately account for the fact that human interiority is not only psyche but also and primarily intentionality; namely, a capacity for self-transcendence in knowing, doing, and religion, a capacity whose fulfillment alone constitutes authentic selfhood. Intentionality and psyche are distinct dimensions of interiority, and this twofold constitution must inform any adequate symbols of the self. Moreover, it is intentionality analysis that provides the basic framework for the integration of psyche into the new maieutic. The theologian's principal problem in confronting Jung is one of method.

I am suggesting, then, that archetypal psychology is transformed when it is sublated by intentionality analysis, but that the sublation and transformation do not remove from psychology its own intrinsic explanatory power. By this power symbolic terms and relations are fixed by one another at the symbolic level itself, without the need for moving into a nonsymbolic realm of discourse to achieve explanatory existential or theological significance, even though the possibility of this metaphysical transposition remains intact.[89] Intentionality analysis will result in a transformed science of depth psychology, and the changes it will introduce on Jung's notion of the self and hence of the symbolic significance of the person of Christ for the human psyche are enormous.

This reconstruction of depth psychology will reveal among other things that there are three and not two orders of elemental psychic symbols: personal, archetypal, and anagogic. The difference and relations among these three orders of symbols are best understood from a clarification of the notion of the unconscious.

Bernard Lonergan has indicated that 'the unconscious' frequently is used to refer to what is or has been conscious but not objectified.[90] This aspect of subjectivity, I believe, would better be called 'the undifferentiated.' But what is truly unconscious is all energy in the universe that is not present to itself, the energy that emerges into new forms in accord with emergent probability, but not in accord with the potentially intelligent emergent probability that is human consciousness.[91] Proximately to consciousness, this energy takes the form of neural-physiological process in the body. More remotely, it is universal energy, the entire nonconscious cosmos.

Energy begins to become conscious when it becomes psychic energy, and the latter emerges in the dream. With Jung, we may distinguish between the ego or differentiated consciousness of the subject and the totality of subjectivity, the self. The latter is a triple compound, however, of differentiated consciousness, the twilight of what is conscious but not objectified, and the strictly unconscious energy of neural-physiological process. These constitute the limits of the self at any time. When neural-physiological energy enters into consciousness in the dream, a portion of the strictly unconscious dimension of the self has become conscious. Its symbolic language may be personal. The personal unconscious includes repressed elements as well as elements that have never been conscious in either a differentiated or undifferentiated fashion. As the personal unconscious of an intelligent subject, it is permeated by intelligence. Its revelations will frequently appear as insightful commentaries on the waking life of the subject. Other dreams, properly referred to as archetypal, will reflect more universal and generalizable motifs of personal development and decline. The symbols of these dreams are taken from and imitate nature, and are thus archetypal. The energy from which these dreams emerge is what constitutes 'nature' and is also what alone should be called the collective or, better, impersonal or objective or cosmic unconscious. It is the potency also for some of the dreams that are synchronistic with or prophetic of outer events.

Finally, there are certain dreams, recorded I trust in the annals of all the higher religions, that can be said to originate with an experienced directness from the absolute limit of the process of going beyond that is God. Such dreams are hermeneutic of the divine call to an ever more converted mode of living or to the execution of specific tasks. In them, the energy that is the cosmic and then the personal unconscious is the transparent medium of creative and redemptively healing power. The symbols of such dreams are anagogic. They are not so much mimetically emergent from within nature or energy or history, as the whole meaning of nature, energy, and history is contained within them[92] and is offered in a revelatory fashion to the consciousness of the dreaming subject as his or her ultimate dramatic context of existence. These dreams are no longer a mere commentary on life or imitation of nature; they are rather the context or system of relationships that constitutes the ineffable mystery that is the final meaning of existence, the context within which all of life is contained and which now offers itself to the subject in the form of a concrete call. Intentionality analysis will reveal that there is a totality of meaning about such symbols that reflects the final limit of the dialectic of human desire, the

dialectic between unconditional love or universal willingness and cosmic hate, the dialectic that is at once the final
and the basic option of every human subject. Joseph
Flanagan, to whom I am indebted for introducing me to
Northrop Frye's distinction between archetypal and
anagogic symbolic meaning, remarks that 'in the anagogic
phase of meaning, a single symbol can become so concentrated in meaning as to contain within itself an unlimited
feeling of desire or dread. The classical examples of this in
the Western literary universe are the symbols of Christ and
Satan.'[93] If we may still speak of anagogic symbols as the
emergence of the unconscious into consciousness, we do
so only indirectly, that is, with reference to the psychoid
medium of anagogic dreams and to our own absolutely
spiritual unconscious, and not with reference to the first
and quite personal agent of such dreams.[94]

Such an account of the unconscious is not sufficient
to explain our dreams, however. Coupled with and interlocking in scissors-fashion with energy-become-psychic is
a symbolic function that belongs to human intentionality.
This symbolic function joins with and constitutes the human psyche as the psyche of a potentially intelligent, reasonable, responsible, agapic, but also incarnate subject, a
subject who is within nature but destined for a goal which
transcends the whole order of nature or proportionate being. Anagogic symbols witness to the transcendent origin
and destiny of such a subject. They express 'a mystery that
is at once symbol of the uncomprehended and sign of what
is grasped and psychic force that sweeps living human
bodies, linked in charity, to the joyful, courageous, wholehearted, yet intelligently controlled performance of the
tasks set by a world order in which the problem of evil is
not suppressed but transcended.'[95] As symbolizing our
'orientation into the known unknown,' they unlock the
transforming dynamism of human sensitivity and 'bring it

into harmony with the vast but impalpable pressures of the pure desire, of hope, and of self-sacrificing charity.'[96] Intentionality analysis will reveal that the dialectic of good and evil cannot be overcome by an apocatastatic reconciliation of opposites but only by the divine transformation of evil into good that is redemption. Good and evil will not be among the opposites of spirit and matter, or transcendence and limitation,[97] reconciled by psyche, for evil in its roots is basic sin, and basic sin is a non-event that can be understood only by an inverse insight: the only point to the non-self-transcendence of the potentially self-transcending subject or self is that there is no point to it.[98]

One final point must be added to round off what is nonetheless a very incomplete sketch of a metascience of archetypal psychology. Jung knew, and psychotherapy can bear out, that the joining of spirit and matter in psychic imagery can be destructive as well as constructive, even morally evil as well as good.[99] I find no way in which the vistas opened for us by the work of Jung can be understood in terms of scientific psychology alone. The themes treated by Jung do not find in his work the universal context within which alone they can be understood. We seem to be led by the process of discovery to which Jung introduces us to adopt an explanatory standpoint that is beyond the scientific disengagement of a purely immanent process of subjective psychological development and breakdown. The only adequate horizon for understanding psychic data seems to demand not only the sublation of depth psychology by intentionality analysis but also the sublation of both psychology and method by the process of *the discernment of spirits*. The triply compounded subject or self (spirit or intentionality, psyche, and matter or limitation) is a participant through intentionality in dimensions of reality that transcend the subject's individuality but that affect the subject's emergence or failure of emergence into authentic selfhood.

Archetypal images, then, are the recurrent and often cyclical symbols taken from nature that enable the transcultural communication of the human drama to take place, the associative clusters that refer to and evoke human action as a whole and especially as it displays the story of a conflict between desire and reality.[100] Anagogic symbols are no longer parts of a whole, however associative and generic, but the containers of the whole of human action, the symbolic correlatives of a religiously transformed universal viewpoint, symbols that seem to be and say (rather than show) or to negate the Logos, the shaping word of the universe and of history.[101] Christ and Satan function, not in an archetypal fashion, so that they need one another, but in a supremely anagogic, and so dialectical, manner for the Christian psyche, and even for the secular psyche of Western people. It is not their coincidence that will symbolize the wholeness that is the destiny of the self, but only the glorious body that had once been overcome by the power of darkness, sin, and death, and that is now raised to life by the transcendent power of the Father.[102] The goal of individuated totality is transcendent, not immanent, and is understood only by a theology that reflects on the living religion that alone enables human subjectivity to emerge from the endless treadmill of self-analysis to which it is diabolically condemned by a psychology that refuses to transcend the realm of rotary, cyclical, quadripartite symbols of the eternal return.[103] This psychology, in insisting on the hegemony of these symbols rather than on that of symbols of liberation from the eternal return, witnesses in its own unique way to the fact that, once God is admitted on intelligent and reasonable grounds, even the intellectual tangles resulting from fundamental counterpositions on the human subject's intentionality are 'not merely a *cul-de-sac* for human progress,' but a 'reign of sin, a despotism of darkness; and men are its slaves.'[104]

The psyche of the human subject is to be articulated with an intentionality whose natural desire is for the vision of God,[105] but whose potentiality for the actualization of this finality is radically and, within the order of nature, irretrievably disempowered by the surd of basic sin. Individuation is to be reinterpreted as the conversion of the human psyche to participation in the universal willingness that alone expresses the natural finality of subjectivity. Symbols of the self are, most properly, symbols that reflect the existential status of the total subject at any point in its pilgrimage. But Christ may function indirectly as a symbol of the self in several ways. The Crucified, for example, may be the symbol of the life and truth and love that are victimized by my refusals to be a pure and naked desire for God,[106] and also the symbol of the universal willingness that alone matches the unrestricted character of intentionality's thrust toward total agapic self-transcendence.[107] The Risen One may be the symbol of the self I will be when I know even as I am known. The figure of Satan, on the other hand, may function as the symbol of the radical refusal to be a pure and naked desire for God, and of the self I will be if I continue to deny the truth of who I am. The meeting between Christ and Satan is not a link in the chain of nature's cyclical and rotary movements, but the expression of the final irreconcilability of universal willingness with the non-event of basic sin's refusal to answer the divine call.

Jung's later speculations on alchemical symbolism and his pathological outbursts in *Answer to Job* reflect the decadence to which the romantic imagination is subject in its last phase, when it refuses to submit in truth and in tautly stretched love to the death-dealing powers of the autumn of life. Frye tells us that a central image of the last or *penseroso* phase of romance is that of 'the old man in the tower, the lonely hermit absorbed in occult or magical studies.'[108] It is as though Jung embodied in his person the entire *mythos* of romance, but no other *mythos,* and principally not the apocalyptic *mythos* whose symbols are anagogic and whose relation to the demonic is not that of potential complementarity but that of dialectic,[109] of the presence or absence of the converted subjectivity that makes its way, in fear and trembling, in the darkness of a repentant faith, but also with the resilience of a hope that has broken through the great mandala, toward the ulterior finality of the self in the direct vision of God.

Notes

[1] James W. Heisig, 'Jung and Theology: A Bibliographical Essay,' *Spring: An Annual of Archetypal Psychology and Jungian Thought* (1973) 204-55. A significant treatment that appeared after this essay is the chapter on Jung in David Burrell, *Exercises in Religious Understanding* (see above, chapter 4, note 24).

[2] Heisig, 'Jung and Theology' 232.

[3] See my *Subject and Psyche* (see above, chapter 2, note 21).

[4] What is needed is a thorough rewriting of the foundations of the science of depth psychology from the standpoint of Lonergan's generalized empirical method. This endeavor would proceed by furthering the portions of Jung's psychology which are in harmony with Lonergan's method and reversing those portions which are in dialectical conflict with the horizon provided by this method. In this paper, I am severely limited to indicating one area, albeit a central and crucial one, in which Jung stands in need of the correction that can result from an adequate epistemological, metaphysical, and theological base for understanding our psychic depths and their strange and elusive imaginal manifestations.

[5] 'Individuation means becoming an "individual," and, in so far as "individuality" embraces our innermost, last, and incomparable

uniqueness, it also implies becoming one's own self. We could therefore translate individuation as "coming to selfhood" or "self-realization." C.G. Jung, 'The Relations between the Ego and the Unconscious,' in *Two Essays on Analytical Psychology*, trans. R.F.C. Hull, vol. 7 in Collected Works of C.G. Jung, Bollingen Series XX (Princeton: Princeton University Press, 1966) 173.

[6] Information on the association experiment and the complexes is provided in Henri F. Ellenberger, *The Discovery of the Unconscious: The History and Evolution of Dynamic Psychiatry* (London: Penguin, 1970) 691-94, and in Liliane Frey-Rohn, *From Freud to Jung: A Comparative Study in the Psychology of the Unconscious*, trans. Fred E. Engreen and Evelyn K. Engreen (New York: C.G. Jung Foundation, 1974) 13-40. It should be pointed out that consciousness for Jung is itself a complex, whose center is the ego. In general, consciousness for Jung is ego consciousness, whereas the unconscious is everything that lies beyond the ego's differentiated realm. We shall later be pointing to a different and, I believe, more accurate and far-reaching notion of both consciousness and the unconscious. For the moment, though, we are concerned only with Jung.

[7] C.G. Jung, 'The Associations of Normal Subjects,' in *Experimental Researches*, trans. Leopold Stein in collaboration with Diana Riviere, vol. 2 in Collected Works of C.G. Jung, Bollingen Series XX (Princeton: Princeton University Press, 1972) 72.

[8] C.G. Jung, 'On Psychic Energy,' in *The Structure and Dynamics of the Psyche* (see above, chapter 2, note 14) 11.

[9] C.G. Jung, 'A Review of the Complex Theory,' in ibid. 92-104.

[10] C.G. Jung, 'Dementia Praecox,' in *The Psychogenesis of Mental Disease*, trans. R.F.C. Hull, vol. 3 in Collected Works of C.G. Jung, Bollingen Series XX (Princeton: Princeton University Press, 1960) 43.

[11] See Frey-Rohn, *From Freud to Jung* 20-21.

[12] Ibid. 23.

[13] Jung, 'The Relations between the Ego and the Unconscious' 174.

14 C.G. Jung, 'On the Nature of the Psyche,' in *The Structure and Dynamics of the Psyche* 185.

15 Frey-Rohn, *From Freud to Jung* 34.

16 Ibid. 35.

17 James Hillman, *The Myth of Analysis* (see above, chapter 3, note 8) 34.

18 Jung, 'The Relations between the Ego and the Unconscious' 169.

19 C.G. Jung, *Memories, Dreams, Reflections* (see chapter 3, note 49) 88.

20 Ibid. The identification here of consciousness with understanding is Jung's, not mine.

21 Ibid. 89.

22 Ibid. 88.

23 Jung, 'The Relations between the Ego and the Unconscious' 170.

24 Ibid. 174.

25 C.G. Jung, 'Commentary on "The Secret of the Golden Flower,"' in *Alchemical Studies*, trans. R.F.C. Hull, vol. 13 in Collected Works of C.G. Jung, Bollingen Series XX (Princeton: Princeton University Press, 1970) 44-45. This essay of Jung's I find the finest statement of the existential meaning of individuation, one far more compatible with the framework provided by a generalized empirical method than Jung's later formulations. But it presents a vision which Jung did not seem to have the philosophical and theological horizon to sustain in any consistent fashion. Unfortunately, Jung's contact with alchemy was also launched by his encounter with 'The Secret of the Golden Flower,' and there was a romantic strain in Jung's disposition which he could not resist and which led to his eventual capitulation to what, I believe,

is a fundamentally and dialectically different manner of thinking from what is reflected in this essay.

26 Ibid. 45-46.

27 Ibid. 48.

28 Ibid.

29 Ibid.

30 See Frey-Rohn, *From Freud to Jung* 43-71

31 C.G. Jung, *Symbols of Transformation*, trans. R.F.C. Hull, vol. 5 in Collected Works of C.G. Jung, Bollingen Series XX (Princeton: Princeton University Press, 1967) 59.

32 See C.G. Jung, 'The Stages of Life,' in *The Structure and Dynamics of the Psyche* 388.

33 C.G. Jung, 'On the Psychology of the Unconscious,' in *Two Essays on Analytical Psychology* 66, note 5.

34 See chapter 5 of Jung, *Memories, Dreams, Reflections*, and *The Freud/Jung Letters: The Correspondence between Sigmund Freud and C.G. Jung*, ed. William McGuire, trans. Ralph Manheim and R.F.C. Hull, Bollingen Series XCIV (Princeton: Princeton University Press, 1974).

35 The import of this fact, recognized by many (including Jung), seems to be best understood by Evangelos Christou, *The Logos of the Soul* (Vienna-Zürich: Dunquin Press, 1963). Unfortunately Christou died before completing this penetrating study, one of the few serious efforts at Jungian metapsychology to appear to date.

36 See C.G. Jung, 'The Psychology of the Child Archetype,' in *The Archetypes and the Collective Unconscious* (see above, chapter 3, note 40) 156.

37 See Jung, 'On the Nature of the Psyche' 204, 209.

38 Ibid. 201.

39 See ibid. 206.

40 Ibid.

41 Ibid.

42 See C.G. Jung, 'Synchronicity: An Acausal Connecting Principle,' in *The Structure and Dynamics of the Psyche* 417-531.

43 See Jung, *Memories, Dreams, Reflections* 325.

44 Jung, 'The Relations between the Ego and the Unconscious' 240.

45 Ibid.

46 Ibid.

47 C.G. Jung, *Psychological Types* (see above, chapter 4, note 18) 460.

48 C.G. Jung, *Aion: Researches into the Phenomenology of the Self*, trans. R.F.C. Hull, vol. 9ii in Collected Works of C.G. Jung, Bollingen Series XX (Princeton: Princeton University Press, 1968).

49 Ibid. ix.

50 Marie-Louise von Franz, *C.G. Jung: His Myth in Our Time* (see above, chapter 4, note 23) 135.

51 Ibid. 136. Dr. von Franz continues: 'At bottom it is the image of man in the Aquarian Age which is being formed in the collective unconscious. The astrological image of the Aquarian period is an image of man which, according to Jung, represents the Anthropos as an image of the Self, or of the greater inner personality which lives in every human being and in the collective psyche ... The task of man in the Aquarian Age will be to become conscious of his larger inner presence, the Anthropos, and to give the utmost care to the unconscious and to nature.' Note the equivalence of 'good and evil' with 'spirit and matter.'

52 Jung, *Aion* 31-32.

53 Ibid. 36.

54 Ibid.

55 Ibid. 36-37.

56 Ibid. 37.

57 Ibid. 40.

58 Ibid. 41.

59 Ibid. 41-43.

60 Ibid. 42-43.

61 Ibid. 43-44.

62 Ibid. 45.

63 See Erich Neumann, *Depth Psychology and New Ethic* (see chapter 2, note 33).

64 Jung, *Aion* 41.

65 Jung's final study of the individuation process as a *mysterium coniunctionis* appears in a book by that title. See above, chapter 3, note 38.

66 Jung, *Aion* 46.

67 Ibid.

68 'These facts are called by one person good and by another evil. Only in capital cases is there anything like a *consensus generalis*. If we hold with Basil that man is the author of evil, we are saying in the same breath that he is also the author of good. But man is first and foremost the author merely of judgments; in relation to the facts judged, his responsibility is not so easy to determine. In order to do this, we

would have to give a clear definition of the extent of his free will. The psychiatrist knows what a desperately difficult task this is.' Ibid. 47-48.

69 Ibid. 48.

70 Ibid. 27.

71 Ibid.

72 Ibid.

73 Ibid. 61.

74 For the royal pair, see *inter alia*, Jung, *Mysterium Coniunctionis*. For the Taoist symbolism of the golden flower, see Jung, 'Commentary on "The Secret of the Golden Flower," esp. 22-25.

75 C.G. Jung, 'A Psychological Approach to the Dogma of the Trinity,' in *Psychology and Religion: West and East*, trans. R.F.C. Hull, vol. ii in Collected Works of C.G. Jung, Bollingen Series XX (Princeton: Princeton University Press, 1969) 107-200.

76 C.G. Jung, 'Answer to Job,' in ibid. 355-470. Marie-Louise von Franz tells us that this was the work of Jung's which satisfied him the most; that he would rewrite all the others if he could, but would leave this one as it is. If this is true, it provides us with a significant hermeneutical key to the interpretation of Jung's entire corpus. See von Franz, *C.G. Jung: His Myth in Our Time* 161. On the supposition that *Answer to Job* so successfully expresses what Jung wanted to say, von Franz's book may well be as accurate a reflection of the final meaning of Jung's work as we have available to us at present.

77 Jung, *Answer to Job* 414.

78 Ibid. 414-15.

79 Ibid. 419.

80 Ibid. 428.

81 Ibid. 456-57.

82 See Northrop Frye, *Anatomy of Criticism: Four Essays* (see above, chapter 3, note 45) 160.

83 David Burrell, *Exercises in Religious Understanding* 231.

84 'Is Analytical Psychology a Religion? Notes on a Talk given by C.G. Jung,' in *Spring: An Annual of Archetypal Psychology and Jungian Thought* (1972) 144-48.

85 Ibid. 146-47.

86 See Bernard Lonergan, 'The Origins of Christian Realism,' in *A Second Collection* (see above, chapter 2, note 56) 239-61; more fully his *De Deo trino*, I. Pars Dogmatica (Rome: Gregorian University Press, 1964) 15-112. An edition of *De Deo trino*, with Latin and English on facing pages, will appear as vol. 9 in Collected Works of Bernard Lonergan (Toronto: University of Toronto Press).

87 See Bernard Lonergan, *Philosophy of God, and Theology* (Philadelphia: Westminster, 1973). The lectures that form this book will be included in vol. 14 in Collected Works of Bernard Lonergan (Toronto: University of Toronto Press).

88 On the notion of the control of meaning, see Lonergan, 'Dimensions of Meaning' (see above, chapter 2, note 7).

89 My argument is given in some detail in my *Subject and Psyche*. See also my article, 'Psychic Conversion' (above, chapter 2).

90 Bernard Lonergan, *Method in Theology* (see above, chapter 1, note 3) 34.

91 On emergent probability, see Bernard Lonergan, *Insight* (see above, chapter 1, note 37) 121-28/144-51; on intelligent emergent probability, ibid. 209-11/234-37.

92 On anagogic symbolic meaning, see Frye, *Anatomy of Criticism* 115-28.

93 Joseph Flanagan, 'Transcendental Dialectic of Desire and Fear' (see chapter 3, note 45) 78.

94 On the notion of the spiritual unconscious and its relation to the work of Freud and Jung, see Roger Woolger, 'Against Imagination: The *Via Negativa* of Simone Weil,' *Spring* (1973) 256-72.

95 Lonergan, *Insight* 723-24/745.

96 Ibid. 723/744.

97 See ibid. 469-79/494-504.

98 Several notions are to be distinguished sharply when dealing with the problem of evil. Lonergan, for example, accurately distinguishes moral impotence, basic sin, moral evil, and physical evil. Only basic sin is a *privatio boni* in the sense in which this expression is metaphysically intended to indicate a lack and only a lack. More strictly, it is a non-event where intelligence would expect an event. Jung fails to distinguish the various components that constitute the problem of evil.

99 See Jung, 'On the Nature of the Psyche' 205-206.

100 See Frye, *Anatomy of Criticism* 104-15.

101 See ibid. 115-28.

102 It may be not insignificant for this discussion that Jungian psychology lacks a developed study of the symbol of Father, a symbol intrinsically related to *intentionality* as opposed to, but capable of sublating, psyche. The absence of an appreciation for the symbolic significance of Father has also been noted by Laurens van der Post, *Jung and the Story of Our Time* (see above, chapter 4, note 12) 78-79.

103 'There are two fundamental movements of narrative: a cyclical movement within the order of nature, and a dialectical movement from that order into the apocalyptic world above. (The movement to the demonic world below is very rare, because a constant rotation within the order of nature is demonic in itself).' Frye, *Anatomy of Criticism* 161-62.

104 Lonergan, *Insight* 692/714.

105 See Lonergan, 'The Natural Desire to See God,' in *Collection* (see above, chapter 2, note 7) 81-91.

106 See Sebastian Moore, *The Crucified Jesus is No Stranger* (New York: Seabury, 1977).

107 On universal willingness, see Lonergan, *Insight* 623-24/646-47.

108 Frye, *Anatomy of Criticism* 202.

109 The dialectical character of the meaning of Christ and of Satan is studied carefully by Frederick E. Crowe, 'Dialectic and the Ignatian Spiritual Exercises,' *Lonergan Workshop* 1, ed. Frederick Lawrence (Missoula, MT: Scholars Press, 1978) 1-26.

6 The Theologian's Psyche: Notes Toward a Reconstruction of Depth Psychology

The need for a dialectical and metascientific critique of the thought of C.G. Jung and, perhaps even more, of the praxis of Jungian analysis, can hardly be overestimated. The need becomes even more apparent when we recognize that Jung seems now to be beginning to be visited by the fate that awaits all more or less comprehensive genius: that of giving rise to diverse and even dialectically opposed interpretations.[1] The dialectical reflection I have in mind would be similar in scope, purpose, and depth of insight to Paul Ricoeur's philosophical interpretation of Freudian psychoanalysis. Obviously, the present paper is no place for so massive an enterprise, yet I hope it conveys the general contours I would think such a critical interpretation would take. But more immediately, my concern is the function that a reconstructed depth psychology can play in theology.

Jung has by no means been ignored by the theological community. A recent bibliographical essay lists 442 books and articles devoted at least in part to the relations between archetypal psychology and theology.[2] In an even more recent study it has been claimed not without reason that 'Jung's work promises to prove as reliable a handmaid for doing theology today as more metaphysical schemes proved in the past.'[3] I have argued elsewhere that the gen-

eralized empirical method of Bernard Lonergan provides
the horizon needed for the critical reinterpretation of the
Jungian maieutic and for its critical employment on the
part of the theologian, and that such a critical engagement
with Jung will help the theologian construct a part of
theology's foundations.[4] I have also suggested how a dialectical critique of Jung will modify his psychology's interpretation of the symbolic significance of the person of Jesus
Christ and of the Trinity and his convictions regarding what
constitutes adequate symbolization of the deity.[5] In the
present paper I wish to expand on my previous methodological considerations, to suggest more explicitly the ontological referents of a revised notion of the unconscious,
and to show how a theory of elemental symbolism can be
developed from the articulation of psyche and intentionality, to fill a vacuum left in those notions of psychic symbolism such as Jung's that lack an adequate explicit or even
implicit grounding in basic assumptions about intentionality. In the course of the paper, I shall attempt an initial
reconstruction of a central paper of Jung's.

I   **Method and Psyche**

1.1   Psyche and the Functional Specialty 'Foundations'

I assume a familiarity on the part of the reader with
Lonergan's thought on generalized empirical method and
on the place of foundations among the eight functional
specialties of theology. Foundations has the twofold task
of objectifying the horizon within which theological doctrines are presented, systematic theology is developed, and
religious communication is attempted; and of generating
the appropriate general and special categories for this
mediated phase of theology.[6] The general categories are
those shared by theology with other disciplines, while the

special categories are those proper to theology. As a methodologist, Lonergan restricts himself to 'indicating what qualities are desirable in theological categories, what measure of validity is to be demanded of them, and how are categories with the desired qualities and validity to be obtained.'[7] The base of interiorly and religiously differentiated consciousness will provide theology with categories that are in some measure transcultural, not in their explicit formulation, but in the realities formulated. These categories will possess the utility of models 'built up from basic terms and relations that refer to [these] transcultural components in human living and operation and, accordingly, at their roots they will possess quite exceptional validity.'[8] Their derivation, finally, will flow from the explicit objectification of the basic terms and relations of the structure of the self-transcending intentionality of the theologian and from the articulation of the same theologian's dynamic state of religious and Christian subjectivity. There will be five sets of special theological categories, which we may roughly list as: religion, the religious community in history, divinity, revelation, and redemption.[9]

Now the claim that Jung's interpretation of Christian symbols is a matter of both positive and critical concern for the theologian interested in generating or deriving categories that will be operative in systematic theology raises fundamental methodological difficulties which we must confront head-on, albeit initially and heuristically, at the outset of our investigation. For systematics is properly conceived by Lonergan as an explanatory discipline rather than as a descriptive exercise.[10] That is to say, the basic terms and relations of systematic theology will aim to propose hypotheses as to the relations of things to one another rather than more or less sophisticated descriptions of things in their relations to us.[11] Now the basic terms and relations of the systematic theology that took its stand on a faculty psychology were metaphysical. But metaphysical terms and relations are not basic but derived sets of categories for a systematics based on intentionality analysis. Here the basic terms and relations will be psychological, and the psychological base is described as follows: 'General basic terms name conscious and intentional operations. General basic relations name elements in the dynamic structure linking operations and generating states. Special basic terms name God's gift of his love and Christian witness.' Derived terms and relations, on the other hand, 'name the objects known in operations and correlative to states.'[12] But Jung's interpretation of Christian symbols, on this account, would seem to be pertinent neither for basic nor for derived terms and relations. For Jung's psychological concern is not that of Lonergan's intentionality analysis. That is, he is not engaged in naming conscious and intentional operations, nor is he concerned with the links among these operations that generate the states of intelligence in act, reason in act, originating value in act. Furthermore, Jung frequently insists that his interpretation of Christian symbols does not claim to name the objects correlative to the psychological states which these symbols reflect.[13]

How can we claim, then, that there is a pertinence of archetypal psychology, however critically modified it may be, for the functional specialty 'foundations'? Moreover, even if such a pertinence could be established, how could it claim to be anything more than descriptive? Is it not the intrinsic limitation of symbolic consciousness that it is incapable of explanatory power? Does not explanation ensue only when insight into the images produces formulations which prescind from imaginative representation? Does not explanation depend upon freedom from the vagaries of imagination? Is it not true, for example, that the Athanasian rule regarding the divinity of the Son and his consubstantiality with the Father possesses implicit explanatory significance only because it is a proposition about propositions and thus a proposition that has freed itself from the imaginative representations of earlier and more primitive Christologies?[14]

Such is the problem, and our answer will be that Jung's maieutic of the psyche can be critically modified by Lonergan's intentionality analysis in such a way as to provide access to an explanatory account of symbolic consciousness. It is this account, this reflection of *a self-appropriation of one's own symbolic consciousness*, that will allow the derivation of categories that are at one and the same time symbolic yet invested with explanatory significance. In psychic self-appropriation, symbolic terms and relations are derived which fix one another in an explanatory way, just as in the self-appropriation of intentionality general basic terms (operations) and relations linking the operations and generating states come to fix one another in the elaboration of a transcendental or generalized empirical method. The theological pertinence of Jung's psychology is that, when transposed and transformed into an element within generalized empirical method, it complements intentionality analysis by mediating in explanatory fashion the dramatic or aesthetic component of the pursuit of intelligibility, truth, and value, and it thus enables the derivation of explanatory categories which, even while explanatory, nonetheless are symbolic.

But what happens to archetypal psychology in the light of the transposition it undergoes when it becomes a portion of the self-appropriation that is generalized empirical method? It will be decisively changed by this transposition in that the worldview or myth issuing from Jung's writings will be corrected on certain fundamental accounts. Nonetheless, this change will be nothing other than a reversal of the counterposition in Jungian writings, and a

consequent development and enrichment of Jung's very
real discoveries into a horizon which, it would seem, he
may have at times intended without ever achieving or being given it, or, if he was brought to it, without ever formulating it satisfactorily. What is this horizon?

1.2   Converted Subjectivity

Foundations articulates the basic horizon from which
the theologian engages in doctrines, systematics, and communications. It does so by objectifying the three conversions which constitute the basic horizon or foundational
reality. These three conversions are religious, moral and
intellectual.[15] Religious conversion, the fruit of God's gift
of love, generally precedes moral conversion, while intellectual conversion is generally the fruit of both religious
and moral conversion.[16] Nevertheless, intellectual conversion is then sublated into a higher unity by moral conversion, and both intellectual and moral conversion are
sublated into the higher integration provided by religious
conversion. Thus:

> Because intellectual, moral, and religious con-
> versions all have to do with self-transcendence,
> it is possible, when all three occur within a
> single consciousness, to conceive their relations
> in terms of sublation. I would use this notion
> in Karl Rahner's sense rather than Hegel's to
> mean that what sublates goes beyond what is
> sublated, introduces something new and dis-
> tinct, puts everything on a new basis, yet so far
> from interfering with the sublated or destroy-
> ing it, on the contrary needs it, includes it, pre-
> serves all its proper features and properties, and

carries them forward to a fuller realization within a richer context.

So moral conversion goes beyond the value, truth, to values generally. It promotes the subject from cognitional to moral self-transcendence. It sets him on a new, existential level of consciousness and establishes him as an originating value. But this in no way interferes with or weakens his devotion to truth. He still needs truth, for he must apprehend reality and real potentiality before he can deliberately respond to value. The truth he needs is still the truth attained in accord with the exigencies of rational consciousness. But now his pursuit of it is all the more secure because he has been armed against bias, and it is all the more meaningful and significant because it occurs within, and plays an essential role in, the far richer context of the pursuit of all values.

Similarly, religious conversion goes beyond moral. Questions for intelligence, for reflection, for deliberation reveal the eros of the human spirit, its capacity and its desire for self-transcendence. But that capacity meets fulfillment, that desire turns to joy, when religious conversion transforms the existential subject into a subject in love, a subject held, grasped, possessed, owned through a total and so an other-worldly love. Then there is a new basis for all valuing and all doing good. In no way are fruits of intellectual or moral conversion negated or diminished. On the contrary, all human pursuit of the true and the good is included within and furthered by a cosmic context and purpose and, as well, there now ac-

crues to man the power of love to enable him
to accept the suffering involved in undoing the
effects of decline.[17]

Now there would seem to be one profound and far-
reaching difference between intellectual conversion, on the
one hand, and moral and religious conversion, on the other
hand. For intellectual conversion, in the technical sense in
which Lonergan uses this term, seems to be coextensive
with the self-appropriation of one's cognitive being. It is
not identical with intellectual or cognitive self-transcendence, for, if it were, not only intellectual conversion but
knowing itself would be very rare. Intellectual conversion
affects directly, not knowing, but the objectification of what
I am doing when I am knowing, why doing that is knowing, and what I know when I do that.[18] Thus:

> Intellectual conversion is a radical clarification,
> and consequently, the elimination of an exceed-
> ingly stubborn and misleading myth concern-
> ing reality, objectivity, and human knowledge.
> The myth is that knowing is like looking, that
> objectivity is seeing what is there to be seen
> and not seeing what is not there, and that the
> real is what is out there now to be looked at ...
> To be liberated from that blunder, to discover
> the self-transcendence proper to the human
> process of coming to know, is to break often
> long-ingrained habits of thought and speech.
> It is to acquire the mastery in one's own house
> that is to be had only when one knows pre-
> cisely what one is doing when one is knowing.
> It is a conversion, a new beginning, a fresh start.
> It opens the way to ever further clarifications
> and developments.[19]

Moral and religious conversion, on the contrary, are coextensive with a state of moral and religious self-transcendence, but not with moral and religious self-appropriation. Moral conversion 'changes the criterion of one's decisions and choices from satisfactions to values,' whereas religious conversion 'is being grasped by ultimate concern. It is other-worldly falling in love. It is total and permanent self-surrender without conditions, qualifications, reservations.'[20] Such decisive transformations can be effected without the subtle capacity for detailing what has occurred that accompanies intellectual conversion. Intellectual conversion marks initiation into a distinct realm of meaning, the realm of interiorly differentiated consciousness.[21] Moral and religious conversion generally occur without such differentiation. They are self-transcendence at the fourth level of intentional consciousness, but without self-appropriation at this fourth level.[22] Intellectual conversion, however, is more than self-transcendence at the first three levels of intentional consciousness. It is the understanding of understanding that is reflectively grasped as virtually unconditioned and then affirmed in the judgment 'I am a knower.'[23] It is not knowing, but the position on knowing that constitutes a part of the explicit base of a critically verified philosophy.[24] It is properly referred to by Lonergan as a conversion that may be called a personal philosophic experience.[25]

Now initiation through intellectual conversion into interiorly differentiated consciousness as a realm of meaning distinct from common sense and theory is also an introduction to a third historical stage of meaning in the Western tradition. 'In the first stage conscious and intentional operations follow the mode of common sense. In a second stage besides the mode of common sense there is also the mode of theory, where the theory is controlled by a logic. In a third stage the modes of common sense and

theory remain, science asserts its autonomy from philosophy, and there occur philosophies that leave theory to science and take their stand on interiority.'[26] This initiation
occurs through a basic clarification of operations that had
occurred also in the first two stages of meaning, namely,
the operations involved in knowing. This clarification in
the mode of interiority is simultaneously intellectual conversion. But also among the operations that occurred in
the first two stages of meaning are the operations of morally and religiously converted subjects. As we have seen,
these operations occurred *in actu exercito* and may have
given rise to the kinds of clarification that issue from common sense and theoretical objectifications, but they were
not objectified by interiorly differentiated consciousness.
As occurring but not objectified, they did not in fact need,
include, or sublate intellectual conversion. What needs,
includes, and sublates intellectual conversion is self-appropriating moral and religious consciousness. The question arises, then, as to whether an objectification characteristic of the third stage of meaning is possible regarding
the operations of moral and religious subjectivity. What
would constitute moral and religious self-appropriation as
distinct from moral and religious conversion? The key to
our answer is to be found, I believe, in a fourth conversion. I call it psychic conversion. Psychic conversion, when
joined with the three conversions specified by Lonergan,
enables us to locate the foundational role of a transformed
archetypal psychology.

First, then, I must specify what I mean by psychic
conversion. Then I must show why it is the key to moral
and religious self-appropriation, and briefly indicate its role
in the sublation of intellectual conversion by moral conversion and of intellectual and moral conversion by religious conversion.

1.3 *Psychic Conversion*

Like intellectual conversion, psychic conversion is an entrance into the third stage of meaning. It can occur before or after intellectual conversion, but its correct objectification depends on intellectual conversion. What then is psychic conversion and what does it effect in and for the subject?

The movement into interiorly differentiated consciousness occurs through an objectification of the data of consciousness. Consciousness is the subject's presence to himself or herself in all the operations of which he or she is the subject. But there are two interlocking modalities to the data of consciousness: a cognitive modality and an affective or dramatic modality. Cognitional analysis mediates the first, whereas what we might call imaginal analysis mediates the second. Imaginal analysis can take many forms, and in our own day one of its principal manifestations occurs in those forms of psychotherapy which link affective or dramatic subjectivity with the spontaneous images and symbols originating from the psychic depths in dreams and in various stages of hypnagogic experience. One way, then, to the mediation of the affective or dramatic component of the data of consciousness is through the interpretation of dreams.

Beyond cognitional analysis, however, there is intentionality analysis. The concern of intentionality analysis is not limited to the cognitive moments of our conscious being but extends beyond the levels of experience, understanding, and judgment to a fourth level of consciousness, the level of evaluation, deliberation, decision and action or praxis. Lonergan refers to consciousness at this fourth level as existential subjectivity. Moral and religious conversion affect such subjectivity. Thus it is more accurate to speak of the first component of the data of consciousness as an intentional component, the component which intends self-transcendence in both knowing and doing.

Furthermore, the affective or dramatic or aesthetic component is best understood as psychic, for it is this component that is illuminated when we understand our dreams correctly. There is a drama to insight, to the further questions that intend truth, and to the process of evaluation, deliberation, and decision that seeks to discriminate what is truly worth while from what is only apparently good. The dramatic or psychic component, while pertinent for and attending every aspect of intentionality, becomes particularly central and crucial at the level of existential subjectivity, for such subjectivity is concerned with value, and values are apprehended in feelings, which themselves are certified by symbols. Thus:

> Intermediate between judgments of fact and judgments of value lie apprehensions of value. Such apprehensions are given in feelings. The feelings in question are not the ... nonintentional states, trends, urges, that are related to efficient and final causes but not to objects. Again, they are not intentional responses to such objects as the agreeable or disagreeable, the pleasant or painful, the satisfying or dissatisfying. For, while these are objects, still they are ambiguous objects that may prove to be truly good or bad or only apparently good or bad. Apprehensions of value occur in a further category of intentional response which greets either the ontic value of a person or the qualitative value of beauty, of understanding, of truth, of noble deeds, of virtuous acts, of great achievements. For we are so endowed that we not only ask questions leading to self-transcen-

dence, not only can recognize correct answers constitutive of intentional self-transcendence, but also respond with the stirring of our very being when we glimpse the possibility or the actuality of moral self-transcendence.[27]

And:

Not only do feelings respond to values. They do so in accord with some scale of preference. So we may distinguish vital, social, cultural, personal, and religious values in an ascending order. Vital values, such as health and strength, grace and vigor, normally are preferred to avoiding the work, privations, pains involved in acquiring, maintaining, restoring them. Social values, such as the good of order which conditions the vital values of the whole community, have to be preferred to the vital values of individual members of the community. Cultural values do not exist without the underpinning of vital and social values, but none the less they rank higher. Not on bread alone doth man live. Over and above mere living and operating, men have to find a meaning and value in their living and operating. It is the function of culture to discover, express, validate, criticize, correct, develop, improve such meaning and value. Personal value is the person in his self-transcendence, as loving and being loved, as originator of values in himself and in his milieu, as an inspiration and invitation to others to do likewise. Religious values, finally, are at the heart of the meaning and value of man's living and man's world.[28]

Further:

> A symbol is an image of a real or imagi-
> nary object that evokes a feeling or is evoked
> by a feeling ...
>
> The same objects need not evoke the
> same feelings in different subjects and, in-
> versely, the same feelings need not evoke the
> same symbolic images ... There is in the hu-
> man being an affective development that may
> suffer aberrations. It is the history of that pro-
> cess that terminates in the person with a deter-
> minate orientation in life and with determinate
> affective capacities, dispositions, and habits.
> What such affective capacities, dispositions,
> habits are in a given individual can be speci-
> fied by the symbols that awaken determinate
> affects and, inversely, by the affects that evoke
> determinate symbols ...
>
> Affective development, or aberration, in-
> volves a transvaluation and transformation of
> symbols. What before was moving no longer
> moves; what before did not move now is mov-
> ing. So the symbols themselves change to ex-
> press the new affective capacities and disposi-
> tions ... Inversely, symbols that do not submit
> to transvaluation and transformation seem to
> point to a block in development.[29]

Symbols, moreover, fulfill a need that logic cannot
satisfy, the need for internal communication.

Organic and psychic vitality have to reveal
themselves to intentional consciousness and,
inversely, intentional consciousness has to secure the collaboration of organism and psyche.

Again, our apprehensions of values occur in intentional responses, in feelings: here too it is necessary for feelings to reveal their objects and, inversely, for objects to awaken feelings. It is through symbols that mind and body, mind and heart, heart and body communicate.

In that communication symbols have their proper meaning. It is an elemental meaning, not yet objectified ... It is a meaning that fulfills its function in the imagining or perceiving subject as his conscious intentionality develops or goes astray or both, as he takes his stance to nature, with his fellow men, and before God. It is a meaning that has its proper context in the process of internal communication in which it occurs, and it is to that context with its associated images and feelings, memories and tendencies that the interpreter has to appeal if he would explain the symbol.[30]

I have quoted so extensively from Lonergan in order to demonstrate that he provides most of the material for indicating what I mean by psychic conversion. Psychic conversion is the release of the capacity for the internal communication of symbolic consciousness. It is effected when one gains the habit of negotiating one's dreams as ciphers of the dramatic component that attends one's intentional operations as a knowing and acting subject. Its progressive and cumulative result is an integrated affectivity which expresses itself as a complementarity of intentionality and psyche, the conscription of psyche into intentionality's orientation toward intelligibility, truth, and value, and at the same time the synchronizing of intentionality's projects with the potentialities of one's developing affectivity. The development of affectivity, and

especially its increasing capacity for objectivity or detachment, is reflected in the movement from the permeation
of one's dreams by the bizarre to their bearing the aesthetic qualities and directness that reflect increasing individuation.[31]

I have argued elsewhere that psychic conversion
meets all the specifications for conversion laid down by
Lonergan, and yet that it is different from the religious,
moral, and intellectual conversions which he has treated.[32]
In the same work, I have indicated that psychic conversion
extends the relations of sublation that obtain among the
levels of consciousness to include the sublation of dreaming consciousness and its imaginal sphere of being by
empirical, intelligent, rational, and existential consciousness. Rather than repeat these arguments here, I will proceed to the argument that psychic conversion is the key to
moral and religious self-appropriation.

1.4   Existential Self-appropriation

The basis of my position is clear already. Briefly the
argument may be summarized in the following five steps:

(1) aesthetic subjectivity is the basis of moral and
religious subjectivity;

(2) our affective responses to symbols and, inversely,
the symbolic images evoked by our feelings are what form
and structure aesthetic subjectivity;

(3) this reciprocal relationship of affectivity and symbol manifests itself in elemental fashion in our dreams;

(4) the capacity for negotiating these elemental symbols is the fruit of psychic conversion;

(5) psychic conversion thus enables the appropriation of the aesthetic base of our moral and religious responses. This aesthetic base enables in turn an explicit reading of the intentionality of the heart that is existential sub-

jectivity. The capacity for this reading is moral and religious self-appropriation.

Since a detailed presentation of each of these steps would involve a great deal of repetition, let me simply build on what we have already seen.

Attendant upon the component of intentionality moving toward self-transcendence in our raising of questions for intelligence, truth, and deliberation, there is a dramatic component to the data of consciousness that is revealed in feelings. The conflict between the desire to know and the flight from understanding, and between making values or satisfactions the criterion of our decisions, constitutes a drama of the emergence or failure of emergence of the authentic subject. The desire to know, Lonergan tells us, can invade the very fabric of our dreams,[33] that is, it affects not only the intentionality of the intelligent intelligibility that is spirit, but also the psychic and bodily undertow that conditions all incarnate spirit. The dreams of an intelligent incarnate spirit will be permeated with intelligence and meaning. That our dreams are ciphers of our intentionality is due to the psychic component that attends intentionality in its pursuit of meaning, truth, and value. For we pursue or fail to pursue the objectives of intentionality, not as pure spirits, but as spiritual, psychic, and bodily subjects. What discloses itself in dreams is the status of our desire, and our desire is not pure instinct, but the polymorphic desire of an incarnate spirit. The drama of our intentionality is the drama of the conflict between detachment and disinterestedness in our desire to know and in our constitution of ourselves and the world, on the one hand, and the attached and interfering desire of our sensitivity, our individual and group bias, and our flight from further theoretical and philosophic questions that Lonergan calls general bias, on the other hand. It is this dialectic of desire that reveals itself in our dreams.[34] The dialectic of desire as affectively experienced is aesthetic subjectivity.

While the dialectic of desire attends and is pertinent to every level of intentional consciousness, its specific importance reveals itself only when we come to consider the fourth level, existential subjectivity, where the issue is value, and where what is at stake is character. In fact, it may be said that the dialectic of desire attends the pursuit of meaning and truth precisely because meaning and truth are themselves values and because their realization calls for a decision on the part of the existential subject for self-transcendence in one's cognitive being. It is for existential subjectivity that values as such are the issue, and, as we have seen, the base of the value experience lies in an affectivity structured in terms of and certified by symbolic consciousness. This aesthetic subjectivity, the dialectic of desire, is the base of our moral and religious being.[35] Thus the access to the dialectic of desire, an access provided by psychic conversion, will enable us to appropriate our subjectivity at this fourth level of its intentional consciousness.

If psychic conversion is the key to moral and religious self-appropriation, then the sublation of intellectual conversion by moral conversion and of intellectual and moral conversion by religious conversion is greatly aided and facilitated by psychic conversion. As we have seen, intellectual conversion is attendant upon intellectual self-appropriation, whereas moral and religious conversion are independent of and prior to moral and religious self-appropriation. In fact, there would seem to be a dynamic moving the subject from intellectual self-appropriation to moral and religious self-appropriation, if indeed Lonergan is correct about the relations of sublation that obtain among the three conversions that for him constitute foundational reality. For self-appropriation at the level of one's cognitive being, it would seem, can be securely sublated into existential (moral and religious) consciousness only to the extent that such consciousness has been subjected to as rigorous a maieutic as has intelligent and reasonable consciousness. If I am correct in emphasizing the aesthetic base of existential consciousness, then the key to this maieutic is psychic conversion. Thus, while psychic conversion, in its occurrence, is at least in principle independent of any of the three conversions specified by Lonergan, being simply the release of the capacity for the internal communication of symbolic consciousness, its role in foundational reality is specified by the aid it provides in the task of sublating intellectual conversion into one's commitment to all value and both of these commitments into the surrender of cognitive and affective being into the hands of God.

1.5   The Three Orders of Elemental Symbols

There are three different kinds of dream symbols: personal, archetypal, and anagogic. The differences and relations among these three orders of symbols are best approached from a discussion of the unconscious.

The unconscious is one of the most ambiguously employed notions in the human sciences. I believe that the key to the precise and legitimate employment of the terminology of the unconscious lies in a careful discrimination of the notion of energy.

As Lonergan has indicated, frequently the expression 'the unconscious' is used to refer to what is or has been, in fact, conscious but not objectified.[36] This aspect of subjectivity, I believe, would better be called 'the undifferentiated.' But what is truly unconscious is all energy in the universe that is not present to itself, the energy that emerges into new forms and laws in accord with emergent probability but not in accord with potentially intelligent emergent probability.[37] Proximately to consciousness, this energy takes the form of neural-physiological process in the body. More remotely, it is universal energy, the entire nonconscious cosmos.

Now energy begins to become conscious when it becomes psychic energy, and psychic energy emerges in the dream. With Jung, we may distinguish between the ego of the conscious subject and the totality of subjectivity, conscious and unconscious, that Jung calls the self.[38] But in terms of our discussion of energy, when neural-physiological energy enters into consciousness through the dream, a portion or aspect of the unconscious dimension of the self has become conscious. Many of these dream symbols are personal. They come from what Jung calls the personal unconscious, which includes all that is forgotten and repressed by consciousness as well as elements that have never before been conscious in either a differentiated or undifferentiated fashion. But other dreams reflect more universal and generalizable motifs of development and decline. These dreams, as well as those that are either synchronistic with or prophetic of outer events, are the products of the emergence into consciousness of an energy that is impersonal or superpersonal. Their images imitate nature in their reflection of generic motifs of life, death, and rebirth. They are archetypal images, and the energy that is their ground corresponds to what Jung calls the collective or impersonal unconscious or, less happily, the objective psyche. Finally, there are certain dreams, recorded in the annals of all the great world religions, that can be said to originate with an experienced directness from the realm, not of ego-transcendent energy nor even of what we are here calling impersonal or superpersonal energy, but of absolute transcendence, from the absolute limit of the process of going beyond that is God. Such dreams are hermeneutic of the divine call. In them, the energy that is the cosmic and then the personal unconscious is the transparent medium of creative and redemptive power. The symbols of such dreams are properly called anagogic, in that, rather than their being mimetically expressive of nature or even of history, the whole meaning of nature and history is contained or summed up within them and offered in a revelatory fashion to the consciousness of the dreaming subject as his or her ultimate dramatic context of existence. These dreams are no longer a commentary on life or an imitation of nature, but the context or system of relationships that constitutes the ineffable mystery that is the final meaning of existence, the context within which all of life is contained and which now offers itself to the subject in the form of a concrete call. There is a totality about such symbols that reflects the final limit of the dialectic of human desire, the dialectic of unconditional love and cosmic hate that is at once the final and basic option of every human subject. Thus Joseph Flanagan correctly remarks that 'in the anagogic phase of meaning, a single symbol can become so concentrated in meaning as to contain within itself an unlimited feeling of desire or dread. The classical example of this in the Western literary universe are the symbols of Christ and Satan.'[39] If we may still speak of anagogic symbols as the emergence of the unconscious into consciousness, such an affirmation does not refer to the first, direct, and quite personal agent of such dreams, but only to the energic materials that they employ.[40]

2   Jung and Method

2.1   *The Way of Individuation: Jung*

Individuation, the process of becoming one's own self[41] can be set within the context determined by the incorporation of psychic conversion into the foundational reality proposed by Lonergan. It then becomes *the psychic and aesthetic correlative of the self-appropriation of intentionality.*

In 1946 Jung wrote an essay that has since come to be regarded as programmatic for the future developments of archetypal psychology. This essay is entitled 'On the Nature of the Psyche.'[42] A recent survey of the development of the notion of the archetypes since Jung's own work spotlights this essay as the springboard of the later refinements.[43] In the present section I propose to employ this essay to demonstrate in a very initial fashion how Jungian psychology can be reconstructed from the horizon established by generalized empirical method.

Jung presents the process of individuation as a progressive and cumulative reconciliation of opposites. The opposites are named spirit and matter or instinct. The operator of their ongoing integration is the psyche. The integration or reconciliation of the opposites is portrayed in the dramatic form of psychic images and symbols.

'On the Nature of the Psyche' begins by refuting the contention of some turn-of-the-century psychologists that only what is conscious is the proper concern of the psychologist. For example, Wilhelm Wundt objected to the hypothesis of the unconscious on the grounds that the notion of unconscious representations without a subject is an anomaly. For Jung this objection is easily met by speaking, not of representations, but of *complexes* or contents. These are to be thought of, not as inborn ideas but as patterns of behavior, not as perceptions but as forms of behavior, as 'sketches, plans, or images which, though not actually "presented" to the ego, are yet just as real as Kant's hundred thalers.' Jung calls them archetypes.[44] They are 'fundamentally analogous forms of perception that are to be found everywhere.'[45]

These impersonal complexes constitute, at least for the moment, the hypothesis of the unconscious psychic which forms a matrix or background to ego consciousness. This background Jung characteristically refers to as 'a preconsciousness.'[46] In this context he introduces the notion of threshold. A threshold divides ego consciousness from the entire psychic background. 'The indispensable raw material of all knowledge — namely psychic reactions — and perhaps even unconscious "thoughts" and "insights" lie close beside, above, or below consciousness, separated from us by the merest "threshold" and yet apparently unattainable.' This psychic system 'may possibly have everything that consciousness has, including perception, apperception, memory, imagination, will, affectivity, feeling, reflection, judgment, etc., all in subliminal form.'[47] In this sense, 'the possibility of an unconscious subject becomes a serious question.'[48]

A less reified and inchoately more differentiated hypothesis would speak, however, not of an unconscious subject, but of the dissociation or dissociability of the psyche into complexes. Dissociation can result from one of two quite different occasions: the repression of originally conscious contents because of their incompatibility with ego consciousness, and (more often for Jung) the functioning of processes that never entered into ego consciousness at all because the ego could not assimilate them. In either case, the complexes may possess the energy to cross the threshold, and if so they *do* affect ego consciousness and are reflected in the symptoms known to psychopathology.[49]

The notion of the threshold is a metaphor originally used in psychological studies of sensation. When introduced into psychology it raises the possibility that 'there is a lower as well as an upper threshold for psychic events, and that consciousness, the perceptual system par excellence, may therefore be compared with the perceptible scale of sound or light, having like them a lower and upper limit.'[50] Moreover, it may be that we can extend this notion of threshold to the outer limits, not of ego consciousness alone but of the psyche in general, so that there are '"psychoid" processes at both ends of the psychic state.'[51]

The hypothesis of the unconscious can be verified only if there are unconscious contents that can be integrated into consciousness by an interpretive method. The dream has been one of the principal mediators of this integration, but whereas for Freud dream contents are exclusively linked with the instinctual sphere, for Jung their specifically psychic component has lost the compulsive character of instinct and can be applied in different ways by 'the will.' It can even function, under the direction of 'the will,' in ways 'contrary to the original instinct.'[52] The psychic, then, is 'an emancipation of function from its instinctual form and so from the compulsiveness which, as a sole determinant of the function, causes it to harden into a mechanism. The psychic condition or quality begins where the function loses its outer and inner determinism and becomes capable of more extensive and freer application, that is, where it begins to show itself accessible to a will motivated from other sources.'[53]

So much for the lower limits of the psyche. What about the upper limit of these psychic phenomena emancipated from physiological compulsion? Jung is reticent on the issue. 'With increasing freedom from sheer instinct,' Jung says, 'the *partie supérieure* (the psychic) will ultimately reach a point at which the intrinsic energy of the function ceases altogether to be oriented by instinct in the original sense, and attains a so-called "spiritual" form.'[54] This would seem to be due to the fact that the instinct in question is *human* instinct, which 'may easily mask a sense of direction other than biological, which only becomes apparent in the course of development.'[55]

The psychic, then, for Jung is a sphere of disposable energy, intermediate between physiological determinism and spirit. The psychic is intrinsically linked with both of these extrapsychic spheres, reaches ever further into each of them, and links them with one another under the guidance of the 'the will,' which is familiar with other goals besides the instinctual.

Is the unconscious for Jung, then, psychic at all, or is it psychoid? Is not the psyche even for Jung coextensive with consciousness? Does not the term 'the unconscious' refer to those physiological processes which have not entered, and in some cases cannot and will not enter, into the sphere of disposable energy where energy becomes at once psychic and conscious? Jung is forced to deal with this question, but in doing so he sets up a model which includes in the unconscious the personalistic fringes of consciousness, the Freudian findings, and the psychoid functions.

The first two sets of 'contents' of the unconscious, so conceived, are psychic, but in a manner quite different from the contents of ego consciousness. They include undifferentiated and unintegrated feeling-toned complexes which can recede ever further from ego consciousness. As they do so, they assume an ever more archaic, mythological, and even at times numinous character. With increasing dissociation, they seem 'to sink back to a more primitive (archaic-mythological) level, to approximate in character to the underlying instinctual pattern, and so assume the qualities which are the hallmark of instinct: automatism, nonsusceptibility to influence, all-or-none reaction, and so forth.'[56] Yet they are not psychoid but psychic. They are little luminosities endowed with an 'approximative consciousness.'[57] They correspond, in fact, to 'tiny conscious phenomena.'[58] Thus the psyche *is* after all consciousness, but its contents are, says Jung, partly conscious and partly unconscious. The psyche is a 'conscious-unconscious whole' whose lower reaches begin with emancipation from instinct.

But now further clarifications are in order, for Jung distinguishes between the personal and the collective unconscious. The collective unconscious consists of vestiges of biological evolution and heredity closely connected with instinct. There is an image with fixed qualities that corresponds to every instinct. Insofar as the human animal functions instinctively, he or she is equipped with such instinct types or instinctually related imaginal patterns. But, says Jung, these types or archetypes 'are not just relics or vestiges of earlier modes of functioning; they are the ever-present and biologically necessary regulators of the instinctual sphere' and represent 'the *meaning* of the instincts.'[59] Jung claims to have found at least an indirect access to these instinctual patterns in human activity through the gradual discovery of certain well-defined themes in the dreams and fantasies of his patients. These themes manifest and render capable of conscious recovery the process which Jung named individuation. Among the most salient characteristics of these images are the following: 'chaotic multiplicity and order; duality; the opposition of the light and dark, upper and lower, right and left; the union of opposites in a third; the quaternity (square, cross); rotation (circle, sphere); and finally the centering process and a radial arrangement that usually followed some quaternary system ... The centering process is, in my experience, the never-to-be surpassed climax of the whole development, and is characterized as such by the fact that it brings with it the greatest possible therapeutic effect.'[60] These fantasies and dreams guided by unconscious regulators 'coincide with the records of man's mental activity as known to us from tradition and ethnography.'[61] Furthermore, the whole centering process seems ruled by 'a dim foreknowledge not only of the pattern but of its mean-ing.'[62] On the basis of such experience, Jung postulated that 'there are certain collective unconscious conditions which act as regulators and stimulators of creative fan-tasy-activity and call forth corresponding formations by availing themselves of the existing conscious material.'[63] The regulators are the archetypes which, Jung says, may be in the end identical with the human instinctual pat-terns.[64] Yet when they appear in imaginal form, they are endowed with an element of spirit, in that their character is numinous or spiritual or mystical. They can mobilize religious convictions and draw the subject under a spell from which one cannot and would not break free, so deep and full is the experience of meaningfulness one enjoys.[65]

Nonetheless we are not to draw the conclusion that the effects of archetypal experience are always positive. Such experience can be healing or destructive, since spirit, as represented in the archetypal image, has *as such* no moral significance. Spirit and instinct 'belong together as corre-spondences, ... subsist side by side as reflections in our own minds of the opposition that underlies all psychic energy,'[66] but *'instinct is not in itself bad any more than spirit is good. Both can be both.'*[67]

2.2   *Individuation and Generalized Empirical Method*

It seems to me necessary to introduce here the dis-tinctions we have already established in our methodologi-cal comments, so as to make clear the relation of Jung's presentation to our own formulations. What Jung encour-ages us to suggest is, first, that there is an upper and a lower threshold dividing ego consciousness from the un-differentiated, and a further upper and lower threshold dividing the whole of consciousness (understood in terms of self-presence and including both ego consciousness and the whole realm of the undifferentiated) from processes that, to use Jung's terms, are psychoid, that is, nonpsychic but understood by analogy with the psyche. The upper threshold divides psyche from spirit, the lower psyche from matter. Our terminology would alter Jung's formulation to the following: perhaps beyond the structure of consciousness, at both ends of the spectrum that stretches from the dream to the highest reaches of existential consciousness in agapic love and in the mystic's cloud of unknowing, there are processes that, at the lower end, are literally and entirely unconscious and, at the upper end, are purely spiritual. Our 'spectrum of the structure of consciousness' is Jung's 'psyche in general,' our 'unconscious' is Jung's lower psychoid aspect, while his higher psychoid aspect would refer to what I would call spiritual processes that originate independently of the conscious subject they may affect. These spiritual processes are the domain referred to by what Christian spirituality has come to call the discernment of spirits. The 'psyche in general' for Jung means what we, following Lonergan, would call the subject.

Thus when Jung speaks of the unconscious he means sometimes what we also mean by the unconscious, sometimes what we have chosen to call the undifferentiated, and sometimes the upper psychoid realm that is spirit. In failing to distinguish these realms as sharply as they should be discriminated, Jung posits a notion of the totality of subjectivity or the self that is inflationary, that extends beyond what our stricter terminology would allow: so much so that in one place Jung refers to the self as 'a borderline concept, expressing a reality to which no limits can be set.'[68] Such a description may hold for the self's reachings into the upper and lower psychoid spheres, but should not, strictly speaking, be used of the self, which is 'just this.'[69] For Jung, moreover, the hypothesis of the unconscious seems to refer in part to an aspect of the psyche, whereas for us the psyche is the beginning of consciousness, and the unconscious is both extrapsychic and, except for the personal unconscious, even in a sense extrasubjective. For Jung's psychic unconscious, I substitute the term 'the undifferentiated,' or what Lonergan calls the 'twilight of what is conscious but not objectified.'[70] And I reserve the term 'the unconscious' for what is altogether beyond the lower reaches of the disposable psychic energy at any point in time, that is, for what Jung calls the psychoid in its lower or physico-chemical dimensions. The introduction of the directing power of will, moreover, approaches our notion of the dialectic of desire. Psyche then becomes 'essentially conflict between blind instinct and will (freedom of choice).'[71] The dialectic of desire is more complicated than this, but this conflict would represent at least one of its dimensions.

As we can see, Jung understands the process of individuation as a progressive and cumulative reconciliation of the opposites of spirit and matter or instinct. The medium of their reconciliation is psychic energy. Spirit and matter are, as such, both psychoid. The archetype is an intrinsic constituent of spirit, but it is at the same time the meaning of the instinctual counterpole. It displays this meaning through the archetypal images released in the psyche of the dreaming subject. These images will display the process of the reconciliation in the form of a story or narrative whose intelligent recapitulation constitutes the recovery of individuation through meaning. The images seem to reflect a foreknowledge of the goal or of certain steps along the way to the goal. And yet the coincidence of spirit and matter can be destructive as well as therapeutic, even morally evil as well as good. Clearly we are opened upon intellectual difficulties of great proportions which cannot be resolved within the framework of scientific psychology alone. We seem to be led by the very process of discovery to a standpoint that is beyond psychology, beyond the scientific disengagement of a purely immanent process of subjective psychological development. The context seems to be set by this analysis for integrating psychology not only with intentionality analysis but also with spirituality, and especially with the tradition of the discernment of spirits.

But can we be more precise on the notions of the collective unconscious and the archetypes? I believe we can again draw upon the methodological considerations of the first portions of this paper for a more satisfactory formulation of the discoveries of Jung than Jung himself was able to provide for them.

The collective unconscious, then, like the personal unconscious, should be considered as psychoid, not as psychic. Whereas the personal unconscious is all energy in the neural-physiological bodily process of the subject that is not present to itself, the collective unconscious is the same energy insofar as it carries a potential for releasing images of transpersonal elemental meaning. The collective or, better, impersonal or perhaps even cosmic unconscious is *at bottom* all energy in the universe that is neither psychic energy and thus at least inchoately conscious, nor nonconscious energy in the bodies of conscious subjects considered simply as personal. Impersonal energy, as well as that which constitutes the personal unconscious, can come into consciousness by becoming psychic energy, i.e., by emerging into the dream. In the dream's images there are revealed not only the repressed and forgotten meanings and evaluations that often show themselves in the displaced fashion highlighted by Freud and accounted for by the processes of neural interaction, but also at times variations on a ground theme of the emergence of the authentic subject. These variations are transpersonal and thematic in their impact and meaning, and since the ground theme is a crosscultural one, the variations on the theme and even at times the symbols through which the variations will be narrated are found crossculturally and are discovered to have been operative in other ages and perhaps even at times in quite archaic cultures.

Furthermore, Jung's work shows us that the emergence of the authentic subject is a matter of the concrete reconciliation and integration of the opposites of spirit and matter. Spirit in the subject is intelligent, reasonable, and responsible consciousness, the single transcendental intention of intelligibility, truth, and value, the unrestricted desire to know and the capacity for a universal willingness. Matter is limitation. Spirit in the subject is a participant, I suggest, in purely spiritual processes that transcend the subject's individuality but that, through this participation, affect the subject's emergence or failure of emergence into authenticity. The images released in the psyche through the reconciliation, not of spirit in the subject and matter in the subject simply as personal, but of spirit and matter that both transcend the purely personal world of the subject and involve the subject as a participant in their interaction, are Jung's archetypal images. On our account, though, it would be more accurate to speak of some of these images as archetypal and of others as anagogic. Archetypal images are the recurrent and often cyclical symbols taken from nature that enable the communication of the human drama to take place; they are the associative clusters that refer to and evoke human action as a whole and especially as it displays the story of a conflict between desire and reality. Anagogic symbols are no longer parts of a whole, however associative, as are archetypal images, but the containers of the whole of human action, symbols that seem to be or reflect or negate the Logos, the shaping word of the universe and of history.[72] Again, as Joseph Flanagan has indicated, Christ and Satan function symbolically in an anagogic rather than archetypal fashion for the Christian psyche and even for the secular psyche of Western people.[73]

2.3   *Individuation and the Problem of Evil*

Jung does not treat the symbolic significance of Christ and of Satan in Christian tradition as anagogic symbols, but makes of them archetypal symbols on the same plane as, e.g., the royal king and queen of alchemical lore who symbolize for Jung the androgynous nature of the psyche,[74] or the golden flower of Taoist literature which Jung interprets as symbolizing the wholeness of individuated life.[75] Such symbols are taken from nature and imitate nature, albeit in a generic and highly associative manner, which allows them to reflect a wholeness in nature. If Christ and Satan are considered as archetypal rather than anagogic, however, they are necessarily incomplete, for one is light and the other darkness. Neither reflects a wholeness in nature such as is symbolized in the nuptial *coniunctio* or even in the golden flower. On the archetypal level, only a conjunction of Christ and Satan would seem to reflect the wholeness of nature that the associative clusters that are archetypes symbolize. And this is precisely how Jung treats these two symbols, as needing one another if they are adequately to represent the self, the wholeness, that is the goal of individuation. Christ for Jung is necessarily inadequate as a symbol of the self, for he is without sin and darkness. Only the reconciliation of God's two sons, of the hostile divine brothers, will provide for Jung the symbolization of individuated totality that will satisfy his postulate of a progressive reconciliation of opposites cumulatively heading toward the realization of the self.

Implicit in this conceptual scheme, of course, is the arrangement of good and evil among the opposites to be reconciled by the imaginal processes of the psyche. In a sense, then, it may be said that Jung is not faithful to the insight expressed in 'On the Nature of the Psyche,' where spirit and matter, both in the subject and beyond the subject but involving the subject as a participant in their interaction, were seen best to represent or summarize the understanding of the opposites reconciled by psychic energy,[76] and where it is clearly stated that neither of the opposites so conceived is in itself good or bad. 'Both can be both.'[77] More precisely, we can make several further criticisms. First, and somewhat *ad hominem*, the postulate of the reconciliation of spirit and matter necessarily moves Jung into specifically metaphysical and theological territory where he is not at home. Secondly, there is a quite definite distinction between 'good and bad' on the one hand, and 'good and evil' on the other. And thirdly, the adequate treatment of the problem of evil calls for several distinctions which never seem to have been recognized by Jung. I have in mind the sort of distinctions Lonergan draws among moral impotence,[78] basic sin, and moral evil.[79] At the root of all these criticisms, though, is the need for clarification of the notion of the self, and I limit myself to this task in the present context.

2.4   *What is the Self?*

Jung has much to say about symbols of the self, but tells us not enough about what it is that these symbols symbolize. What, from the standpoint of generalized empirical method, is the self? Is it not the subject? Do not the symbols of wholeness which for Jung symbolize the self reflect the totality of subjectivity in its concern for receptive attentiveness to the data of sense and of consciousness, for meaning, for truth, for value, and for the absolutely transcendent origin and goal of nature and of history? This will be my option, that the self, under the aspect of totality, is the subject as the latter has been disengaged by Lonergan, and as Lonergan's analysis is complemented by the additional sublation effected by psychic conversion. And the most notable thing about this self or subject is that it can be authentic or inauthentic; that its authenticity consists in self-transcendence in knowing, in doing, and in religion; and that it truly knows itself only when it reflectively recognizes that it is authentically itself solely in the self-transcending intention of intelligibility, truth, and value.[80] This total self or subject transcends the limits of differentiated consciousness or ego and reveals its ego transcendence in dreams that originate from the personal unconscious. But beyond the personal unconscious and even beyond the self, there extends the vast reach of the cosmos, which is not only ego-transcendent but self-transcendent. The self, then, finds its lower limit at the threshold that divides the personal and collective unconscious from the non-self. The upper limit of the self is constituted by another and quite different threshold, one which marks the boundary between the highest intention of agapic love on the part of existential subjectivity and the spiritual processes that can be divined only by religious discernment. Nonetheless, despite the thresholds which limit the self or subject to being 'just this,' its lower and upper self-transcendent reachings make of it a tension of limitation and transcendence, and its genuineness consists in negotiating this tension.[81]

Generalized empirical method, then, allows us to substitute the intentionality categories of limitation and transcendence for Jung's characterization of the intrasubjective opposites as matter and spirit. Let us keep matter and spirit as our formulation for the self-transcendent opposites in whose interaction the self is an intrinsic participant, in fact, an instrumental operator of integration or of disintegration, but let us speak of limitation and transcendence as articulating the way matter and spirit become the opposites in the intentional subject or self.

Psyche, then, becomes one dimension of this totality of subjectivity, a dimension which is manifest at each level of intentional consciousness in the dramatic and affective component of all empirical or inattentive, intelligent or stupid, reasonable or silly, responsible and constructive or irresponsible and sociopathic consciousness. But what qualifies the subject as subject is intentionality, the orientation to self-transcendence at each level, and the successive sublations of lower levels by higher ones in the pursuit of authenticity. And what qualifies the psychic component of this intentional striving as authentic or inauthentic is the manner in which it participates in the negotiation of the tension of limitation and transcendence and the extent to which it shares in the detachment and disinterestedness, the universality and cosmic context, of the single transcendental intending of the intelligible, the real and true, and the good. The self, the totality of subjectivity, is both genuine and authentic to the extent to which the organic, psychic, and intentional systems are operating, first, in harmony with one another; second, in the interests of cognitive, moral, and religious self-transcendence; and third, for the promotion of the religiously discerned integration of spirit and matter as this integration is issued into being by world-constituting and self-constituting projects on the part of the developing, self-transcending subject.

This transposition of the Jungian notion of the self into the categories of an intentionality analysis complemented by the maieutic of the psyche which such an analysis renders possible highlights the most important fact about the self: that it can be self-transcending cognitively, existentially, and religiously, or that it can flee understand-

ing and shun truth in the name of any one or some or all of
the counter-philosophies which deny its capacity for meaning and objectivity; that it can allow its action in the world
to be governed by dramatic, egoistic, group, or general
bias; and that it can hide from and eventually come to
hate the call to holiness which alone reveals its ulterior
finality. This dialectic of the self-transcendence and the
self-containment of the self is not properly emphasized by
Jung; nor does he pay sufficient attention to the fact that
symbols which open up upon the authentic self are visited
upon subjects whose intentional orientation is away from
meaning, truth, and value, only for the sake of calling them
to radical conversion. This latter fact may not completely
escape Jung, but it is not brought to the center and core of
his articulation of the process of rendering conscious the
individuation that is the psychic meaning of total human
development. By bringing this fact to its proper place in a
theory of individuation, we provide the only adequate context for discussing the problem of evil. This discussion
would show us clearly, I believe, that good and evil cannot
be among the opposites generally qualified as transcendence and limitation, the opposites whose progressive reconciliation constitutes the process of individuation. To place
them among the opposites involves a category mistake on
the part of Jung, and insofar as understanding is central to
human development and misunderstanding an obstacle
to such development, Jung's category mistake is also an
obstruction to the individuation process which he labored
so diligently to understand, formulate, and promote, and
which he correctly judged to be, not only a psychological
but indeed a moral and religious imperative of our time.

3 **Conclusion**

Lonergan's intentionality analysis and Jung's psychology take on an explicitly dialectical relation to one another when the subject must negotiate the evil one avows of oneself. But the underlying dynamics which come to the fore in the area of moral and religious authenticity are present in either case from the very beginning, so that the entire relation of these two conceptions of human development and transformation may be considered dialectical. Lonergan describes and explains throughout his work the exigences of what in his later writings is called self-transcendence. These exigences, which constitute the law of the subject as intentional, are less consistently glimpsed and even less heartily affirmed by Jung, despite the access he provides the subject to trustworthy ciphers in their regard. There is, I submit, operative in Jung's thought a less than adequate notion of what makes for wholeness, despite his correct insistence on the centrality of the issue.

The further and mysterious outposts of Jungian thought constellate a number of problems for the theologian: the problem of method; the question of the relation between psychology and religion; the proper way to speak about good and evil; the relation of symbols of the self to images of God; the nature of wholeness; and the contribution of psychic deliverances to a theological doctrine of God. The theologian is not helped by the fact that Jung's forays into explicitly theological territory most evidence the need for a dialectical critique of Jung's entire corpus. I have no desire to deny or undermine the extraordinary significance of Jung for theology, and I share, though perhaps for other reasons, the frequent complaints of Jungians that theology has yet to appreciate this significance.[82] I share, too, the assessment of David Burrell, already cited, that 'Jung's work promises to prove as reliable a handmaid

for doing theology today as more metaphysical schemes
proved in the past.' But, Burrell adds, 'Every such interpretative scheme must be carefully monitored and critically employed, yet that defines the theologian's task.'[83]
The beginning of this critical monitoring must focus on
the religious significance of the process of individuation,
which is simultaneously lived and discovered under the
auspices of a Jungian analysis. For, as Burrell says, in this
journey one will not fail to meet God.[84] But one will also
meet much that is not God and that even is against God.
The crux of the matter is the negotiation of evil, and so
the ultimate monitoring of the theologian is existential and
religious before and even while it is speculative or intellectual. In terms of the tradition that is my own, the Roman
Catholic and Ignatian tradition, it is best conceived as discernment of spirits.

One further statement of Burrell's deserves mention
and approval: 'Rather than Jung's explicit statements about
God, it is his language conveying the pursuit of individuation which offers the most fruitful model for discovering a
religious way of speaking.'[85] The resources of this model
need to be carefully disengaged by the religious thinker
equipped with sharper tools of philosophical analysis than
those enjoyed by Jung. Easy adaptation of religion to analytical psychology — a temptation encouraged by Jung's
religious suggestiveness — is to be disparaged on both religious and psychological grounds, to say nothing of
method. It is here, again, that the theologian's monitoring
of Jung's work and praxis both begins and ends: what is
the relation between the process of individuation as articulated in analytical psychology and that of religious development and transformation as objectified in that portion of theological foundations dealing with religious and
moral conversion? The relation is intimate, yet it is clearly
not one of identity. That genuine religious conversion, as

this is understood by Christian theology, can and I dare
say does sometimes occur within the course of a Jungian
analysis, I do not wish to deny. But my focus in this paper
has been on the respective formulations of an analytical
psychology of individuation and a foundational-theologi-
cal objectification of conversion. The languages depart over
the issue of evil, and, before this, over the notion of the
self. For Christian faith, Jung's articulation of the problem of evil — and so his formulations of the self and of
wholeness — are unacceptable. This, I find, is an inescapable conclusion, one I have wanted to avoid but have not
been able to while still remaining faithful to my understanding of what Christianity, as a religion proclaiming
redemption from evil, means. For analytical psychology this
conviction probably remains hopelessly tied to the 'Old
King' of a declining age, to the splitting of opposites symbolized by the astrological sign of Pisces, and to that portion of Christianity which must be relinquished as we move
toward a new and more universal religion.[86] But I find
that to relinquish this portion of Christianity in favor of
Jung's apocatastatic model of the *integration of evil and good*
is not only to relinquish Christianity in toto but to regress,
to pursue avenues previously traveled in the history of religions, avenues which from our present vantage point can
only be termed blind alleys in the evolution of religious
consciousness. So many of Jung's insights into the psychological aberrations of some Christian spirituality are
unfortunately attended by a recommended alternative that
is no less an aberration, and that perhaps even exceeds in
illusion the mistake it was intended to replace. The ultimate relation of the Christian religion to Jung's myth is
irretrievably dialectical. One cannot entertain both in their
respective totalities without internal self-contradiction. No
final resolution is possible except through dialectic.

There are, nonetheless, definite parallels between individuation and the self-appropriation to which Lonergan's work invites us. The principal similarity is of course that both are processes of self-knowledge and self-transformation. Jung's writings no more than Lonergan's can be understood without a change being effected in the subject studying them. 'The only test available for Jung's science is that to which we put a road map: does it succeed in getting us there? A working meaning for the term *individuation* is reserved for those who allow themselves to submit to its demands.'[87] But despite the relative lack of attention paid to the positive significance of symbolic consciousness in Lonergan's formulations, he is working from and promoting a more accurate understanding of the totality that is the self than is Jung. What Jung provides to a subjectivity tutored by Lonergan is access to the symbolic ciphers of the psyche regarding the economy of the subject's pursuit of the authenticity of self-transcendence. Lonergan offers the theologian essentially what he offers anyone who reads him: an avenue to the intentionality that, among other things, founds theology. Jung presents to such a subject a complementary access to symbolic ciphers of personal development and transformation. The contribution is not only not negligible but serves to offset the one bias that Lonergan may not purge us of, the intellectualist bias that would regard the intellectual pattern of experience as a somewhat privileged domain of self-transcending activity.[88]

The relationship is further complicated, however, by the fact that Jung's model of wholeness, one of *ego*-transcendence, is not also one of *self*-transcendence but ultimately one of self-enclosure. Jung fails to appreciate how significant it is to the process of becoming, or living our way into the self, that the self is an intentional self, intent on and capable of affirming true meanings and making good decisions — where 'true' and 'good' denote self-transcendence as the criterion of one's genuineness as a knower and as a moral agent. Philosophically, Jung is a Kantian. Furthermore, his remarkably thorough knowledge of the human psyche is not matched by a sufficiently penetrating knowledge of the spirit which psyche mediates with the body in the movement toward wholeness. Thus the self-transcending dynamism of the psyche is only inconsistently glimpsed and affirmed by Jung. This dynamism is an orientation toward intentionality, a potential readiness for conscription into the eros of the pure question intent on meaning, truth, and value. But an explicit conscription cannot take place without psychic conversion, and this conversion is neither identical with nor unrelated to the intellectual, moral, and religious conversions which condition authenticity. The lines between psyche and spirit are not clearly drawn by Jung, nor does his articulation of their dialectic completely escape a romanticist resolution in the capitulation of intentionality to nature's rhythms. Such romanticism, however, is not conversion and consequently falls short of authenticity.

The relation of psyche and spirit or transcendence can be put very succinctly: psyche is the whole realm of the imaginal, while spirit or transcendence is the domain of operations intent on intelligibility, truth, and value. Ultimately only the intentionality of spirit is responsible for authenticity or inauthenticity, for it is this intentionality which qualifies a person as good or evil. Again we find the focus for the most important bit of monitoring that must be done by the theologian if Jung's work is to realize its theological fruitfulness. I am inauthentic when I am not what the very constitution of my intentionality prompts me to be: contemplatively attentive, intelligent in my inquiry for meaning, reasonable in my exigence for truth, and responsibly self-transcending in my decisions. Psyche's images are the most accurate ciphers of my relative self-transcendence or self-enclosure. They are, as such, utterly trustworthy, humbling, demanding, and evocative. But to pursue them for their own sake is to lose one's very self. A romanticist conception of individuation is a hopeless *cul-de-sac*. It dooms one to the endless treadmill of self-analysis that is psychology.[89] Psychology is not life — a fact recognized in all depth-psychological analyses of the transference phenomenon, yet missed in the theoretical or metapsychological constructions of all the leading depth psychologists save Otto Rank.[90] Ultimately it must be said that Jung does not provide a road map for getting us there, if 'there' is individuated *life*, and the reason lies in the problems constellated at those furthest outposts of his thought that he has pointed us to in his paper 'On the Nature of the Psyche.'

Notes

1 Compare, e.g., Morton Kelsey, Dreams: *The Dark Speech of the Spirit. A Christian Interpretation* (New York, Doubleday, 1968) and *Encounter with God: A Theology of Christian Experience* (Minneapolis: Bethany, 1972) and John A. Sanford, *Dreams: God's Forgotten Language* (Philadelphia and New York: Lippincott, 1968) with James Hillman, *The Myth of Analysis* and *Re-Visioning Psychology* (see above, chapter 4, note 8).

2 James W. Heisig, 'Jung and Theology: A Bibliographical Essay' (see above, chapter 5, note 1).

3 David Burrell, *Exercises in Religious Understanding* (see above, chapter 4, note 24) 232.

4 Robert M. Doran, *Subject and Psyche* (see above, chapter 2, note 21).

5 Robert M. Doran, 'Christ and the Psyche' (chapter 5 above).

⁶ At some point I want to attempt to indicate more precisely the role of foundations in the work of interpretation, history, and dialectic. For our present purposes, it is sufficient that we work with Lonergan's notion of an indirect influence of foundations on interpretation, history, and dialectic, and a direct influence on doctrines, systematics, and communications. See Bernard Lonergan, *Method in Theology* (see above, chapter 1, note 3) 268. 1993 note: Chapter 20 of my *Theology and the Dialectics of History* (Toronto: University of Toronto Press, 1990) attempts to express some nuances on the relation of foundations to theology's first phase. See also the papers 'Self-knowledge and the Interpretation of Imaginal Expression' and 'Psychic Conversion and Lonergan's Hermeneutics' in volume 2 of this set, *Theology and Culture*.

⁷ Lonergan, *Method in Theology* 282.

⁸ Ibid. 285.

⁹ Ibid. 290-91.

¹⁰ See Bernard Lonergan, *Insight* (see above, chapter 1, note 37) index under 'Description and explanation.' Strictly speaking, Lonergan leaves it to the theologian to determine the explanatory status of his or her categories. See *Method in Theology* 285. It is obvious, however, that Lonergan judges that the theologian whose subjectivity has been tutored through the cognitional and existential analysis of *Insight* and *Method in Theology* will be in possession of more than a model with exceptional foundational validity.

¹¹ The argument that such is Lonergan's conception of an ideal for systematic theology is bolstered by his recent and persuasive suggestion that such a philosophy of God as that proposed in chapter 19 of *Insight* be included within systematics. See Bernard Lonergan, *Philosophy of God, and Theology* (Philadelphia: Westminster, 1973).

¹² Lonergan, *Method in Theology* 343.

¹³ See, for example, C.G. Jung, 'Answer to Job' (see above, chapter 5, note 76) 360-62.

¹⁴ 'Terminalis denique ratio non solum omnem transcendit imaginem sed etiam quodammodo omnem intelligibilitatem in imag-

ine perspectam. Sicut enim equationes campi electromagnetici a Maxwell inventae ita ex imaginibus ortae sunt ut tamen nulla sit imago quae iis correspondeat, ita etiam regula ab Athanasio posita nisi conceptus et iudicia non respicit. Eadem enim de Filio quae de Patre dicuntur, excepto Patris nomine. Quod non solum ab imaginibus praescindit sed etiam in nullo imaginabili vel perspici vel intelligi potest.' Bernard Lonergan, *De Deo trino.* I. Pars dogmatica (Rome: Gregorian University Press, 1964) 86. A new edition, with Latin and English on facing pages, will appear as vol. 9 in Collected Works of Bernard Lonergan (Toronto: University of Toronto Press).

15 See Lonergan, *Method in Theology* 267-69, 142.

16 Ibid. 267-68. 'I should urge that religious conversion, moral conversion, and intellectual conversion are three quite different things. In an order of exposition I would prefer to explain first intellectual, then moral, then religious conversion. In the order of occurrence I would expect religious commonly but not necessarily to precede moral and both religious and moral to precede intellectual. Intellectual conversion, I think, is very rare.' 'Bernard Lonergan Responds,' in *Foundations of Theology* (see above, chapter 2, note 16) 233-34.

17 Lonergan, *Method in Theology* 241-42.

18 Ibid. 25.

19 Ibid. 238-40.

20 Ibid. 240.

21 See ibid. 81-85, 272.

22 See ibid., chapter 1.

23 See Lonergan, *Insight*, chapter 11.

24 Ibid. 385-90/410-15.

25 See Bernard Lonergan, 'The Subject' in *A Second Collection* (see above, chapter 3, note 1) 79.

26 Lonergan, *Method in Theology* 85.

27 Ibid. 37-38.

28 Ibid. 31-32.

29 Ibid. 64-66.

30 Ibid. 66-67.

31 See ibid. 65.

32 See *Subject and Psyche* 219-21.

33 Lonergan, *Insight* 4/28.

34 Paul Ricoeur distinguishes three levels of creativity of symbols and relegates dreams to the lowest, that of 'sedimented symbolism: here we find various stereotyped and fragmented remains of symbols, symbols so commonplace and worn with use that they have nothing but a past. This is the level of dream-symbolism and also of fairy tales and legends; here the work of symbolization is no longer operative. At a second level we come upon the symbols that function in everyday life; these are the symbols that are useful and are actually utilized, that have a past and a present, and that in the clockwork of a given society serve as a token for the nexus of social pacts; structural anthropology operates at this level. At a higher level come the prospective symbols; these are creations of meaning that take up the traditional symbols with their multiple significations and serve as the vehicles of new meanings. This creation of meaning reflects the living substrate of symbolism, a substrate that is not the result of social sedimentation ... This creation of meaning is at the same time a recapture of archaic fantasies and a living interpretation of this fantasy substrate. Dreams provide a key only for the symbolism of the first level; the "typical" dreams Freud appeals to in developing his theory of symbolism do not reveal the canonical form of symbols but merely their vestiges on the plane of sedimented expressions. The true task, therefore, is to grasp symbols in their creative moment, and not when they arrive at the end of their course and are revived in dreams, like stenographic grammalogues with their "permanently fixed meaning."' Paul Ricoeur, *Freud and Philosophy* (see above, chapter 1, note 7) 504-506. Ricoeur here undervalues the symbolization of the dream, which, when attended

to and cultivated, more often responds as a critic of Ricoeur's second-level symbols and as an agent of his third-level symbols than as a dumping ground for his first-level symbols. Dreams both tell and promote a story, and the story they tell and promote is the story of the dramatic component of the life of the intentional subject. Had Ricoeur turned to Jung rather than to Hegel for the teleological counterpart to the Freudian archeology of the subject, he might have discovered this to be the case. It is Jung's lasting significance to have discovered and at least begun to make precise a teleology of the subject working from the data of dreaming consciousness. See Gerhard Adler, *The Living Symbol: A Case Study in the Process of Individuation* (New York: Pantheon, 1961).

35 See Robert M. Doran, 'Aesthetics and the Opposites' (see above, chapter 4) and 'Aesthetic Subjectivity and Generalized Empirical Method' (see below, chapter 9).

36 'It is much better to take full cognizance of one's feelings, however deplorable they may be, than to brush them aside, overrule them, ignore them. To take cognizance of them makes it possible for one to know oneself, to uncover the inattention, obtuseness, silliness, irresponsibility that gave rise to the feeling one does not want, and to correct the aberrant attitude. On the other hand, not to take cognizance of them is to leave them in the twilight of what is conscious but not objectified. In the long run there results a conflict between the self as conscious and, on the other hand, the self as objectified.' Lonergan, *Method in Theology* 33-34. Lonergan adds: 'This twilight of what is conscious but not objectified seems to be the meaning of what some psychiatrists call the unconscious.' Ibid. 34, note 5. He then gives references to books by or about Jung, Karen Horney, and Wilhelm Stekel. The implications in regard to Jung are, we shall see, partly correct but incomplete. For Jung, consciousness is not self-presence in intentional operations, but the ego, i.e., a complex characterized by relative differentiation and the capacity for objectification and control. The unconscious for Jung includes what Lonergan would call what is conscious but not objectified, but it includes much else besides.

37 See Lonergan, *Insight* 121-28/144-51; 209-11/234-37.

38 See inter alia C.G. Jung, 'The Relations between the Ego and the Unconscious' (see above, chapter 5, note 5).

[39] Joseph Flanagan, 'Transcendental Dialectic of Desire and Fear' (see above, chapter 3, note 45) 78. I am indebted to Flanagan for introducing me to Northrop Frye's distinction of archetypal and anagogic meaning, which I have transposed into the context of my own concerns in this paper. See Frye, *Anatomy of Criticism* (see above, chapter 3, note 45), especially the second essay, 'Ethical Criticism: Theory of Symbols,' 95-128.

[40] In addition Roger Woolger has spoken of a spiritual unconscious and of its relation to Jung's collective and personal unconscious. See Roger Woolger, 'Against Imagination: The *Via Negativa* of Simone Weil' (see above, chapter 5, note 94). Woolger's concern is not with anagogic images, but with the condition beyond all imagery, the condition of the mystic's cloud of unknowing. For the transition from imaginal negotiation to the *via negativa*, there is demanded the stretching of the psyche to harmony with a cosmic or universal willingness. For a discussion of Woolger's notion see below, chapter 15.

[41] See C.G. Jung, 'The Relations between the Ego and the Unconscious' 173.

[42] See above, chapter 5, note 14.

[43] See Naomi R. Goldenberg, 'Archetypal Theory after Jung,' *Spring: An Annual of Archetypal Psychology and Jungian Thought* (1975) 199-220. Ms Goldenberg says of the new generation of Jungians: 'Their psychology stems mainly from the direction Jung took in "On the Nature of the Psyche," in which the relations among psyche, spirit and matter are explored.' Ibid. 212.

[44] Jung, 'On the Nature of the Psyche' 165-66. See also Liliane Frey-Rohn, *From Freud to Jung* (see above, chapter 5, note 6) 34-35. In the 1946 essay, Jung's concern is almost exclusively with the impersonal complexes or the collective unconscious.

[45] Jung, 'On the Nature of the Psyche' 165.

[46] Ibid. 168. Jung consistently rejects the exclusive use of the term 'subconscious' or 'subconsciousness.' See, e.g., 'Phenomenology of the Spirit in Fairy-Tales,' in *The Archetypes and the Collective Unconscious* (see above, chapter 3, note 40) 239.

47 Jung, 'On the Nature of the Psyche' 172. Obviously the unconscious is being considered here as one system, with as yet no differentiation having been introduced among what we have named the undifferentiated and the personal and collective unconscious in the strict sense in which we have distinguished these three aspects of the background.

48 Ibid. 165.

49 Ibid. 175.

50 Ibid. 176.

51 Ibid.

52 Ibid. 181. In a footnote Jung tells us that his reference to the will 'is purely psychological and has nothing to do with the philosophical problem of indeterminism.' Ibid. Here we see Jung a victim of the strictures of the second stage of meaning, where theory is the supreme differentiation of cognitional consciousness. In the stage marked by interiorly differentiated consciousness, the Aristotelian division of the sciences presupposed by this remark of Jung's no longer obtains. Now philosophy has given way to method; and method's task is the ongoing unification of the sciences. Philosophy become method 'is neither a theory in the manner of science nor a somewhat technical form of common sense, nor even a reversal to Presocratic wisdom. Philosophy finds its proper data in intentional consciousness. Its primary function is to promote the self-appropriation that cuts to the root of philosophic differences and incomprehensions. It has further, secondary functions in distinguishing, relating, grounding the several realms of meaning and, no less, in grounding the methods of the sciences and so promoting their unification.' Lonergan, *Method in Theology* 95. On such a supposition, Jung's statement may be reformulated as follows: The psychic, as opposed to the physiological or purely instinctual, marks the entrance of previously compulsive drives into the sphere of conscious intentionality, where what has so become conscious can be understood intelligently, affirmed reasonably, and negotiated freely and responsibly. This relationship to intentionality characterizes the psychic as opposed to the physiological or organic.

53 Ibid. 181-82.

54 Ibid. 182.

55 Ibid.

56 Ibid. 187.

57 Ibid. 189-90.

58 Ibid. 199.

59 Ibid. 201.

60 Ibid. 203.

61 Ibid.

62 Ibid. 204.

63 Ibid.

64 Ibid. 205. It is obvious that Jung has a quite nonreductionistic notion of instinct, in contrast with, e.g., Freud. James Hillman has capitalized on this notion of instinct in his development of the notion of soul-making. For Jung there are five basic instinctual groups: hunger, sexuality, the drive to activity, reflection, and creativity. 'The first four are comparable to Konrad Lorenz' major groups: feeding, reproduction, aggression, and flight ... Lorenz does not mention the fifth instinct, creativity; but then he speaks from observations of animal behavior, while Jung speaks from the study of people.
'If we accept the hypothesis of a creative instinct, then this instinct, too, must be subject to psychization. Like other drives, it can be modified by the psyche and be subject to interrelation and contamination with sexuality, say, or activity. (But neither one's sexual drive, nor productive activity in the world, nor reflective consciousness, nor contentious ambition is the ground or manifestation of one's creativity.) Moreover, as an instinct, the creative is able to produce images of its goal and to orient behavior toward its satiation. As an instinct, the creative is a necessity of life, and the satisfaction of its needs a requirement for life. In the human being, creativity, like the other instincts, requires fulfillment. According to Jung's view of man, activity and reflection are not enough; there is a fifth component as basic in man as hunger and sexuality, the *quintessentia* of creativity ... (Jung's) major concern in

both his therapy and his writing was with the manifestations and vicis-
situdes of the creative instinct and with disentangling it from the other
four.' James Hillman, *The Myth of Analysis* (see chapter 4, note 8) 33-34.
That the creative instinct is coextensive with the process that leads to
individuation is obvious from Hillman's list of the conceptions Jung
uses to deal with it: 'the urge to wholeness, the urge toward individuation or personality development, the spiritual drive, the symbol-mak-
ing transcendent function, the natural religious function, or, in short,
the drive of the self to be realized.' Ibid. 34. To employ the word 'instinct' in this regard is to highlight the physiological and biological dimensions of an incarnate spirit.

[65] Jung, 'On the Nature of the Psyche' 205.

[66] Ibid. 206.

[67] Ibid. Emphasis added.

[68] C.J. Jung, *Psychology and Alchemy*, vol. 12 of Collected Works
of C.G. Jung, trans. R.F.C. Hull, Bollingen Series XX (Princeton:
Princeton University Press) 355.

[69] One is reminded here of Paul Ricoeur's complaint about the
impreciseness of Jung's language: 'Psychoanalysis is limited by what
justifies it, namely, its decision to recognize in the phenomena or culture only what falls under an economics of desire and resistances. I
must admit that this firmness and rigor makes me prefer Freud to Jung.
With Freud I know where I am and where I am going; with Jung everything risks being confused: the psychism, the soul, the archetypes, the
sacred.' *Freud and Philosophy* 176.

[70] Lonergan, *Method in Theology* 34.

[71] Jung, 'On the Nature of the Psyche' 183.

[72] See Frye, *Anatomy of Criticism* 95-128. I am suggesting that
some such distinction as Frye's between archetypal and anagogic symbols is crucial for understanding the domain of reality upon which we
are opened by Jung's discoveries.

[73] The pertinence of the distinction of anagogic and archetypal
symbols for our present discussion appears precisely here. I have dis-

cussed the implications of the distinction in 'Christ and the Psyche' (above, chapter 5).

74 See C.G. Jung, *Aion* (see above, chapter 5, note 48).

75 See C.G. Jung, 'Commentary on "The Secret of the Golden Flower" (see above, chapter 5, note 25), esp. 22-25.

76 'Opposites are extreme qualities in any state, by virtue of which that state is perceived to be real, for they form a potential. The psyche is made up of processes whose energy springs from the equilibration of all kinds of opposites. The spirit/instinct antithesis is only one of the commonest formulations, but it has the advantage of reducing the greatest number of the most important and most complex psychic processes to a common denominator.' Jung, 'On the Nature of the Psyche' 207. In treating the opposites, the logical distinction of contraries and contradictories escapes Jung. Spirit and matter are contraries, good and evil contradictories.

77 Ibid. 206.

78 Lonergan, *Insight* 627-30/650-53.

79 Ibid. 666-68/689-91.

80 Besides the aspect of totality, Jung includes under the notion of the self also the aspect of the center. The self is simultaneously the wholeness of subjectivity and the center of subjectivity. This later aspect is, I believe, most profoundly treated by Jung in 'Commentary on "The Secret of the Golden Flower." Our transposition of the notion of the self into the context of generalized empirical method does not neglect this second aspect. I have called attention to Lonergan's contribution to the shift to this center by speaking of the therapeutic function of intellectual conversion. See *Subject and Psyche*. In a similar vein, Vernon Gregson speaks of Lonergan's work as intentionality therapy. See Vernon Gregson, 'A Foundation for the Meeting of Religions: A Christian View of Religion as Spirituality.' Paper for the annual meeting of the American Academy of Religion, Chicago, 1975. Intellectual conversion joined with and complemented and sublated by psychic conversion will orient the subject toward this center.

81 Lonergan, *Insight* 469-79/494-504.

82 See Marie-Louise von Franz, *C.G. Jung: His Myth in Our Time* (see above, chapter 4, note 23) 188-89.

83 Burrell, *Exercises in Religious Understanding* 232.

84 Ibid. 221.

85 Ibid. 184.

86 See chapter 9 of von Franz's book mentioned above in note 82.

87 Burrell, *Exercises in Religious Understanding* 185.

88 Lonergan's later emphasis on healing as a development from above downwards, foreshadowed in the relationship between loving and knowing discussed in *Method in Theology*, represents a clear breakthrough on his part beyond this possible bias. See Bernard Lonergan, 'Healing and Creating in History,' in *A Third Collection*, ed. Frederick E. Crowe (Mahwah, NJ: Paulist, 1984) 100-109.

89 See Ira Progoff, *The Death and Rebirth of Psychology* (New York: McGraw-Hill, 1973) 288.

90 'Man is born beyond psychology and he dies beyond it but he can live beyond it only through vital experience of his own — in religious terms, through revelation, conversion or re-birth.' Otto Rank, Beyond Psychology (see above, chapter 4, note 12) 16.

7   Dramatic Artistry in the Third Stage of Meaning

1   Method and/or Theology

To speak or write about the construction of a new Christian vision is in large part to exercise one's mind and heart in methodological reflection. But to contribute directly to a new Christian vision is to engage in theology proper, and obviously in that phase of theology that attempts direct discourse, discourse *in oratione recta*, where 'the theologian, enlightened by the past, confronts the problems of his own day.'[1] At one point, however, the distinction between doing theology and doing method is not sharply disjunctive. That point occurs in the functional specialties of dialectic and foundations, where the theologian is doing method *in* theology.

Let me explain. Bernard Lonergan asks the readers of *Method in Theology* 'not to be scandalized because I quote scripture, the ecumenical councils, papal encyclicals, other theologians so rarely and sparingly. I am writing,' he says, 'not theology but method in theology. I am concerned not with the objects that theologians expound but with the operations that theologians perform.'[2] But in dialectic and foundations the operations that theologians perform and the horizon governing their performance become the objects that theologians expound. And so in dialectic and foundations doing theology becomes, in part, doing method. Conversely, in the chapters on dialectic and foundations, Lonergan is doing not only method but, at one point, theology itself. He is urging a horizon within which theological operations are to be performed. He is objectifying that horizon and qualifying it as normative. To this extent he is doing dialectic and foundations, and not simply writing about what it is to do these two functional specialties. He is actually performing and getting us to perform operations that theologians perform.

Thus, in summary, we might say: (1) When the operations that theologians perform and the horizon within which they perform them become the objects that theologians expound, the theologian becomes a methodologist, and does so without ceasing to be a theologian; (2) conversely, when the methodologist recognizes that the process from data to results that constitutes both the whole of theology and each of its functional specialties is qualified by (first phase) or founded in (second phase) the basic horizon of the theologian, and when he or she offers methodological counsel on the resolution of the resultant difficulties by proposing a normative horizon, he or she has become a theologian without ceasing to be a methodologist. In brief, normative horizon is both a theological and a methodological issue.

The paper that follows is intended as a contribution, then, both to method and to theology. It would clarify the basic horizon of a contemporary empirical theology. It not only speaks about the construction of a new Christian vision, but offers a contribution to that vision. It is written at that juncture where the operations that theologians perform and the horizon within which they perform them become the objects that theologians expound. Its concern is the normative horizon for theological operations in a methodical Christian theology, for which an understanding of the revelation of God in Jesus Christ is inextricably bound up with one's explanatory understanding of oneself. For in such a theology the basic terms and relations are psychological.[3]

2 Psychic Conversion and the Third Stage of Meaning

2.1 The Developing Position on the Human Subject

The foundational theologian is engaged in the task of assembling a patterned set of judgments of cognitional fact and of existential fact cumulatively heading toward the full position on the human subject. Foundations, then, is in one sense as open-ended as are the other functional specialties. But from Lonergan we have learned at last that open-endedness and relativism are not synonymous, and nowhere does this lesson strike home with greater clarity and persuasiveness than in the work of the foundational theologian. In fact, a case may be made that only by engaging in foundations does the lesson strike home at all. If one's movement out of classicism or rationalism or deductivism or even a far more adequate version of the theoretical stage in the control of meaning does not enter upon a personal appropriation of interiority, if it does not take one into foundations, one seems inevitably to regress, to surrender on the level of one's intelligence and rationality, and even more disastrously on the level of one's responsibility — to surrender to one or many of the current philosophic fads that take their basic stand on a despair over the human mind or the human heart. Then the last word is given, perhaps, to talk of language games and family resemblances, or to normless views of historicity and cultural pluralism, or to confusions of consciousness with knowledge, of truth with concepts, of processive development with formless process, of the notion of being with the idea of being, of the development of knowledge through incremental judgments with an exclusively eschatological notion of truth. If human knowing and human loving are, even if only as obediential potency, *capax Dei*, if this capacity is the only satisfactory explanation of an unrestricted intentional quest, then there is indeed reason to maintain that the full position on the human subject is not about to become some secure, well-rounded possession of methodologists and theologians. But the judgments one cumulatively assembles on the human subject in the course of a lifetime and their ever more refined patterning into an ever developing position *will* be judgments of fact. The fact in question will be either cognitional or existential. The developing of the pattern of judgments will be a progressive integration of one's judgments of cognitional fact with one's judgments of existential fact. Many of these judgments have already found their way into the pattern that has been woven by Lonergan and by the students of his writings. The pattern includes the reconciliation of the irreversible self-affirmation of the knower with the primacy of existential fact, the subtle articulation of positions on religious, moral, and intellectual conversion, the developing position on the human good, the recognition of the manners and degrees and cognitive, moral, and affective normativity of self-transcendence, and the privileged position, from the standpoints of both cognitional subjectivity and existential subjectivity, that is to be accorded to the change in one's being that occurs when one surrenders and deepens one's surrender to the love of God.

In my doctoral dissertation,[4] I argued that the transition from the Lonergan of *Insight* to the Lonergan of *Method in Theology* may be understood as a development beyond cognitional analysis to an intentionality analysis that includes cognitional analysis but sublates it into a position on the subject that is differentiated from that which emerges in *Insight* by the addition of a fourth level of consciousness determined by a most significant change in Lonergan's notion of the human good. The evidence for this interpretation seems fairly straightforward, but its implications for a developing position on the human subject are only gradually emerging. One of the implications that I have already tried to establish is that the emergence of a new notion of value permits, in a way not explicitly opened by Lonergan's treatments of either depth psychology or myth in *Insight*, the sublation-by-appropriation of symbolic consciousness into transcendental method.[5] This sublation occurs by reason of a conversion that I call psychic conversion. Psychic conversion is the release of the capacity for internal communication especially through the recognition, understanding, and responsible negotiation of the elemental symbols that issue from the psychological depths especially in one's dreams. These symbols are dramatic indicators of one's existential subjectivity. They can aid one in an explanatory understanding of moral and religious subjectivity.

In the present paper, I wish to show how psychic conversion enables a higher viewpoint on the duality inherent in the human subject of which Lonergan makes so much in *Insight*, and how it is essential to a reflective overcoming of this duality. The higher viewpoint permits a mediation of the dialectic of spiritual freedom and spiritual unfreedom, a mediation that can function in the third stage of meaning as an adequate cipher of basic alienation and of liberation from basic alienation. Since all other forms of alienation flow from basic alienation,[6] psychic conversion will further the socially, economically, culturally, and politically emancipatory and therapeutic potential of generalized empirical method, as well as its effects on one's personal freedom. It will thus function in an understanding and negotiation of the dialectic of history.

The central notion in my position will be the tension of limitation and transcendence that qualifies the genuine person.[7] The key to clarifying this tension lies in the meaning of the experiential imperative: be attentive. The criteria for this imperative, with which the upward movement of an authentic and nonalienated consciousness begins,[8] are affective, artistic criteria. These criteria are sublated by the criteria of intelligence, reasonableness, and responsibility but, here as elsewhere, sublation is not negation but means 'that what sublates goes beyond what is sublated, introduces something new and distinct, puts everything on a new basis, yet so far from interfering with the sublated or destroying it, on the contrary needs it, includes it, preserves all its proper features and properties, and carries them forward to a fuller realization within a richer context.'[9] Moreover, the gaining of such criteria will be understood, not as the result of a development from below upwards, but as a gift that proceeds in a healing fashion from above downwards, from the complex mediation of transformative love with the dimensions of human consciousness that are preoccupied with the intention of value.[10]

We must discuss, then, the nature and functioning of these affective, artistic criteria and their mediation to the subject. I must postpone a discussion of the effect of my position on what, without some such explanatory framework as I am presenting here, risks becoming yet another regressive emphasis both at the superstructural level of contemporary theology in the forms of remythologizing and of the theology of story, and at the everyday level in the form of an unmediated, fundamentalist spirituality. But what is at issue is the fact that 'intrinsic to the nature of healing, there is the extrinsic requirement of a concomitant creative process. For just as the creative process, when unaccompanied by healing, is distorted and corrupted by bias, so too the healing process, when unaccompanied by creating, is a soul without a body ... A single development has two vectors, one from below upwards, creating, the other from above downwards, healing.'[11] In religious matters the neglect of the creative vector is fundamentalism. It can take many forms. In both religion and theology, the neglect of the creative vector will be in the long run simplistic, regressive, ineffectual, nonredemptive. It is the conjunction of the two vectors that is at stake when I speak of psychic conversion. Psychic conversion will be an intrinsic factor in enabling the healing process of transformative love to be accompanied by a concomitant creative process.

Our way into the issue will be by way of what happens to what in *Insight* is called the dramatic pattern of experience[12] when the intentional primacy of existential subjectivity is acknowledged.

2.2   *Existential Intentionality as Dramatic Artistry*

Lonergan has acknowledged that the notion of the good that appears in *Method in Theology* is different from that proposed in *Insight*: 'In *Insight* the good was the intelligent and reasonable. In *Method* the good is a distinct notion. It is intended in questions for deliberation: Is this worthwhile? Is it truly or only apparently good? It is aspired to in the intentional response of feeling to values. It is known in judgments of value made by a virtuous or authentic person with a good conscience. It is brought about by deciding and living up to one's decisions. Just as intelligence sublates sense, just as reasonableness sublates intelligence, so deliberation sublates and thereby unifies knowing and feeling.'[13] The emergence of a distinct notion of the good has also issued in an acknowledgment of the primacy of existential subjectivity, of the fourth level of intentional consciousness.[14] What I wish to establish is that the primacy of existential intentionality is also the primacy of the dramatic pattern of experience.

Patterns of experience are sequences of sensations, memories, images, conations, emotions, and bodily movements that are subjected to an organizing control by one's interest, attention, purpose, direction, striving, effort, intentionality. As such, patterns of experience are the psychic correlative of intentional operations, where psyche is implicitly defined in terms of 'a sequence of increasingly differentiated and integrated sets of capacities for perceptiveness, for aggressive or affective response, for memory, for imaginative projects, and for skillfully and economically executed performance.'[15] My position is simply this: the concern of existential intentionality — value, the good, real self-transcendence, being an originating value, a principle of benevolence and beneficence — links up with the psychic pattern of the dramatic subject. The success of the dramatic subject is ascertained in terms of his or her fulfillment of the purpose, direction, concern of the dramatic pattern — to make a work of art out of one's living. It is the authentic existential subject who is concomitantly a dramatic artist, and it is the inauthentic existential subject who is an *artiste manqué*, a failed artist.[16] Existential authenticity and dramatic art are respectively the intentional and psychic obverse and reverse of the same precious coin.

There is, then, a dramatic pattern of experience, a sequence of sensations, memories, images, conations, emotions, and bodily movements that are organized by one's concern to make a work of art out of one's living, to stamp life with a style, with grace, with freedom, with dignity. The dramatic pattern is operative in a preconscious manner, through the collaboration of imagination and intelligence in the task of supplying to consciousness the materials one will employ in structuring the contours of one's work of art. These materials emerge into consciousness in the form of images and accompanying affects. The images meet the demands of underlying neural manifolds for conscious representation and integration. From a pre-psychological point of view, these underlying manifolds are purely coincidental. They find no systematization at the purely biological level. They are a function of an energy that is properly psychic, that is, of a surplus energy whose formal intelligibility cannot be understood by laws of physics, chemistry, or biology, but only by irreducibly psychological understanding. The images and affects in which this surplus energy finds its systematization emerge into consciousness at the empirical level, the first level of consciousness, the level whose functioning is governed by one's fidelity or infidelity to the transcendental precept 'Be attentive.'[17] Nonetheless, there is a prior functioning of intelligence and imagination in the dramatic pattern of experience, reaching into the preconscious and unobjectified dimension of one's subjectivity for the images one will employ in weaving the pattern and contours of one's work of dramatic art.

It is this preconscious collaboration that concerns us. The intelligence and imagination that cooperate in a preconscious manner to select images for conscious attention, insight, judgment, and decision may or may not themselves be authentic intelligence and imagination. To the extent they are authentic, they have been liberated effectively by religious, moral, and intellectual conversion — liberated from the dramatic bias that would overwhelm the light of consciousness with the darkness of elementary passions; liberated from the individual bias that would grant to the satisfaction of one's ego a privileged and eventually solitary place in the list of motives that govern one's decisions and performance and that would arbitrarily brush aside the questions that challenge such an allegiance to oneself; liberated from the group bias that would identify the human good with what is good for one's intersubjective group or social class or nation; liberated from the general bias that neglects the questions and refuses the insights that would arise from an intelligence that takes its stand on the inherent dynamism of its own love of intelligibility, truth, and value.[18] An authentic dramatic artist has been healed by conversion in such a manner that the prior collaboration of intelligence and imagination in the selection for conscious discrimination of the images that are needed for the insightful, truthful, and loving construction of a work of dramatic art can go forward in inner freedom. This freedom manifests itself in an affective detachment from inner states and outer objects and situations that matches the detachment of authentic intentionality. The story of the gaining of this detachment and of one's failures and setbacks in its regard, as well as of one's affective engagement in the world of dramatic and existential meaning, is what is unfolded in symbolic form in one's dreams. The dreams of a developing dramatic artist detail imaginally how one is faring in the progressive integration of body and intentionality, of limitation and transcendence, that constitutes the flourishing of the human person. The psyche is the promoter and the mirror of the progressive dialectic of this integration. An unsuccessful dramatic artist, on the other hand, stands in need of healing from bias, whether the bias be dramatic, egoistic, group, or general bias or some mixture of these. His or her dreams reflect a need of healing. Effective freedom is intrinsically a function of the unbiased collaboration of intelligence and imagination in the admission to conscious discrimination of images linked with appropriate affects and oriented to the artistic production of the 'first and only edition' of oneself.[19] The basic criteria of the authenticity of the project of one's living, then, as expressed in the transcendental imperatives linked with the four levels of conscious intentionality — be attentive, be intelligent, be reasonable, be responsible — have psychic concomitants that make up the dramatic pattern of one's experience. There are aesthetic, imaginal, affective promoters, ciphers, even criteria of authenticity.

Lonergan's acknowledgment of the primacy of existential intentionality shifts the ultimate burden of his thought from cognitional analysis to an intentionality analysis that sublates the knowledge of knowledge into a more embracing elucidation of the drama of the emergence of the authentic person. The latter is concomitantly a successful dramatic artist. Such a shift entails a sublation of the intellectual pattern of experience by the dramatic pattern, and of the knowing of knowing by the knowing of existential intentionality. The intellectually patterned sequence of sensations, memories, images, conations, emotions that subjects these elements to the organizing control of a concern for explanatory understanding of data can no longer be granted a strict primacy in the relations among the various patterns of experience, for the subject as existential and dramatic sublates the subject as cognitional or intellectual. The dramatic pattern of experience, the psychological concomitant of existential intentionality, must integrate at the level of sensation, image, memory, emotion, and conation the interplay of all other patterns of experience, including the intellectual. If one is psychically differentiated to operate in the intellectual pattern, then this pattern too is sublated by the concerns of the dramatic artist/existential subject, in the same way that knowing is sublated by decision. This means that, from the standpoint of self-appropriation, cognitional analysis is sublated by an intentionality analysis that acknowledges not only the existence but even the primacy in all conscious subjects of the fourth level of intentional consciousness. This sublation of the knowing of knowing by the knowing of existential intentionality is perhaps the cutting edge at the present time of the developing position on the subject that is transcendental method. But the knowing of existential intentionality is also the knowing of dramatic artistry, an appropriation of the dramatic pattern of experience, an appropriation that is rendered possible by psychic conversion. Psychic conversion thus advances the developing position on the subject. It renders possible the sublation of the knowledge of knowledge by the knowledge of existential intentionality, the sublation of cognitional self-appropriation by moral and religious self-appropriation.[20]

2.3   The Dramatic Pattern in the Third Stage of Meaning

The more differentiated one's consciousness, the more complex becomes the task of dramatic artistry. As it is the existential subject who shifts from common sense to theory to interiority to art to scholarship to transcendence by shifting the procedures of intentional consciousness, so the intentional shifts are accompanied by a concomitant adaptation of the stream of sensations, memories, images, emotions, conations, and bodily movements under the direction of the dramatic artist. It is the task of dramatic artistry to govern the interplay of the various patterns of experience. Thus the psyche of an intentionally more differentiated consciousness must be a more differentiated psyche. Differentiation in the various realms of meaning is joined with differentiation in the patterns of experience organized and controlled by these realms of meaning. Intentional and psychic differentiation, it seems, are mutually complementary.

Now *Insight* is a set of exercises through which one enters on differentiation in the realm of interiority. Such differentiation begins with intellectual self-appropriation. This self-appropriation is a form of conversion, the intellectual conversion of the self-affirming knower. But *Insight* is an initiation not only to a realm of meaning, but also to a stage of meaning.[21] Such initiation, it seems, is always dramatic.[22] We can, I trust, all testify to the complex emotional impact of *Insight*. One of the constants of this impact is its psychologically taxing quality, no matter what the extent of the enthusiasm generated by Lonergan's genuinely exciting invitation. The sequence of sensations, memories, images, emotions, conations does not adapt easily to the invitation and challenge of *Insight*. Not only does any knowledge in the intellectual pattern of experience make a bloody entrance, but the psychic tension is increased when the demand made upon the stream of sensitive consciousness is to adapt itself to an exercise in which the intellectual pattern is brought to bear in explanatory fashion upon itself and upon its relation to other patterns in which the sensitive stream is spontaneously more at home. Moreover, the sensitive stream is confronted with a demand that it subordinate its spontaneous home to a higher specialization of human intelligence than even the most intelligent common sense. The intentional subordination of common sense to a generalized empirical method that thinks on the level of history is concomitantly a psychic self-surrender of sensitive spontaneity to what it can only perceive at first as a terrifying abyss. The call and demand of Lonergan in *Insight* is or can be psychologically upsetting and even physically unnerving.

With the emergence of an insistence on Lonergan's part on the primacy, indeed the hegemony, of existential subjectivity, the story of sensitive spontaneity in the way of self-appropriation enters a new episode. In some ways, the newness is experienced with relief. For one thing, affectivity now receives a privileged acknowledgment as the home of value. For another, affectivity and symbol no longer find their integration in knowledge, but both cognitional and psychic subjectivity come to rest in good decisions. The suspicion that *Insight*, for all its brilliance, necessity, and truth, was not the last word on self-appropriation is confirmed, and the confirmation is welcomed by the psychological stream of sensitive experience. The constraint imposed upon aesthetic liberation from biological purposiveness by self-appropriation in and of the intellectual pattern seems to be a temporary exigence, a needed constraint until the questions of cognitional theory, epistemology, and metaphysics have been thoroughly answered, but that need not be maintained as primary pattern when the artistry of the dramatic subject becomes what it is time to attend to as one follows Lonergan from cognitional self-appropriation to existential self-appropriation. The relief, moreover, is not apt to be deceptive, for if one has truly followed Lonergan to the intelligent and reasonable position on the subject in *Insight*, one needs no persuasion that 'the very wealth of existential reflection can turn out to be a trap.'[23].

But the task of dramatic artistry has become a more complicated one. For with intellectual conversion one has entered upon a third stage of meaning, where meaning is controlled not by practical common sense nor by theory, but by a differentiation of consciousness in the realm of interiority. Existential subjectivity in the way of self-appropriation must sublate a cognitional subjectivity that has been transformed, converted, from counterpositional allegiances to self-affirmation of its own normative intelligence and reasonableness. This means that the knowledge of existential subjectivity must sublate the knowledge of knowledge. So with the entrance into a new stage of meaning, one's dramatic pattern of experience now has to become a sequence of sensations, memories, images, emotions, conations, and bodily movements that includes but does not remain identical with that sequence to which one was introduced in the course of one's intellectual maieutic. An even tauter stretching of sensitive spontaneity is called for, a more demanding discipline, a more profound surrender that is at the same time a more wide-ranging adaptability and flexibility, a greater degree of freedom. The task is monumental. It is an extension to psyche of differentiation in the realm and stage of interiority. Its successful execution would be a high achievement of human artistry, the differentiation of a dramatic pattern of experience that sublates the other patterns subject to the organizing control of the other realms of meaning, and that does so in the third stage of meaning, that is, not simply *in actu exercito* but with a reflexive control. Existential self-appropriation is, in Lonergan's analysis, not itself conversion, as is intellectual self-appropriation, but a reflection on religious and moral conversion that allows them to sublate intellectual conversion. But is the dramatic differentiation that existential self-appropriation is intrinsically linked to, even dependent upon, not itself in need of a conversion if it is to succeed? This is what I have argued in speaking of psychic conversion.

2.4   Dreams and Dramatic Artistry

Psychic conversion is the gaining of the capacity on the part of the existential subject for the internal communication that occurs in the conscious and deliberate negotiation of one's own spontaneous symbolic system, that is, of the images for insight, judgment, and decision that are admitted to consciousness by the subject in the dramatic pattern of experience. The key to psychic conversion, I believe, is the dream, for in the dream symbols are released in a manner unhindered by (yet perhaps reflective of) the dramatic, individual, group, and general bias of waking consciousness's guardianship. The dream is the story of intentionality, a story told by sensitive consciousness. It is a cipher of authenticity and of its immanent sanctions. It performs this function precisely as the operator of the higher system of sensitive consciousness in its function of integrating what otherwise is a coincidental manifold on the level of neural demand functions.[24] Transcendental method or intentionality analysis, then, is the key to understanding the function of the dream. Conversely, the dream is an indication of the drama of one's existential intentionality.

Lonergan has dealt with the dream in *Insight* in the context of his discussion of dramatic bias. The emergence of a distinct level of existential consciousness in his later work calls for a further nuancing of the position of *Insight* on the dream. In *Insight* Lonergan relies on the Freudian notion of the dream's manifest and latent content, according to which there is a deceptiveness to the dream. This is a notion which Jung, who was more open to a nonreductive interpretation of human spirituality, did not accept. I agree with Jung in his rejection of the Freudian distinction, since I find that this distinction is based on an inadequate notion of symbolism. As we shall see, there are problems also with Jung's theory of symbolism, problems perhaps rooted in an implicit epistemological idealism endemic to the romantic mentality from which Jung never broke free.

The basic context set by *Insight* remains valid. Thus, biased understanding and distorted censorship prevent the emergence into consciousness in waking life of the images that would give rise to unwanted but needed insights that would correct and revise one's current viewpoints and behavior. The bias also causes the dissociation of the affects of persona and ego from their proper imaginative schemata and their attachment by association to other and incongruous imaginative schemata. Furthermore, unconscious complexes are formed, consisting of repressed and needed materials. What, then, happens in the dream? Might it be that there the distorted censorship — that is, the inauthentic collaboration of imagination and intelligence — is relaxed enough that neural demand functions can and do find their proper conscious complement in psychic images that, were they to be adverted to by the waking subject, would indeed provide materials for the insights that are needed in the dramatic artistry of life? Basically, I believe this to be the basic principle for the interpretation of dreams. In dreams, the complexes speak as they are. They show what they do or do not want. What preponderates in dreamland is not one's dramatic pattern of experience, but the neural demand functions and their systematizing complexes. In a genuine person successfully making a work of art out of his or her life, neural demand functions are also being granted waking entrance into consciousness in an appropriate manner, but in an inauthentic person fleeing the insights that are needed for dramatic artistry, they are being repressed from representation in consciousness. The repressed materials and the repressing dramatic subject emerge as they are in the dream. The dream is a commentary on the quality of one's dramatic artistry. It manifests whether or not in waking consciousness the dramatic subject is or is not allowing the emergence of the imaginative schemata that would give rise to needed insights. The sentiments of repressed complexes do not emerge in a disguised fashion in the dream, but speak quite plainly of their plight, of what is happening to them, of their distorted object relations. In the dreams of the biased subject, the expressions of repressed complexes are alien to the conscious performer; they emerge into consciousness with their objects; they sometimes interfere with sleep; they violate the aesthetic liberation of consciousness. This is the point of Jung's insistence on the compensatory function of the dream.[25] Dreams will be increasingly an ally, a complement, of the subject open to insight, and increasingly even an enemy of the subject who does not want the insights one needs if one is to make a work of art out of one's own living. In their function of meeting neural demands that have been neglected in the wear and tear of conscious living, dreams always provide imaginative schemata that can be negotiated by waking consciousness in such a way that neural demand functions are met in a harmonious, integrated, congruous fashion. But there is no disguise to the content of the dream. It is a natural phenomenon which displays the linkage of image and affect in both the conscious and unconscious complexes, and displays them as they are. It shows what in fact each of these complexes wants and does not want. If the dramatic subject does not want insight, the dream displays this rejection. If the persona is burdened with incongruous affects, the dream displays the incongruity. If one's subterranean life has been made the victim of the repression of conscious insight, the dream displays its plight, its crippled condition, its anger, its violence, its perversion.

The course of one's dream story, then, will reflect the quality of the ongoing relationship of waking consciousness with neural process in the task of the art of living. For the person fleeing the insights needed for artistic living and thus repressing from consciousness the imaginative schemata that would integrate in a harmonious fashion one's neural demand functions with the conscious orientation of dramatic living, dreams will increasingly reflect, but not in a disguised fashion, the inhibitions that a distorted and biased dramatic pattern of experience has placed on neural demand functions. The dreams of a biased subject will manifest the violence that the flight from understanding has perpetrated upon the neural-physiological materials. The dreams of the subject who wants insight and truth will become continuous with and complementary to the dramatic artistry of living, and will reflect the orientation to integration that qualifies such a subject. The dreams of the biased subject will be increasingly discontinuous with and compensatory to the attitude of waking consciousness, which, in its flight from understanding, has done violence to the psychoneural base. The discontinuity is in the interests of providing a compensatory corrective to the attitude of waking consciousness. These dreams, if one would attend to them, would let one know that one is indeed biased and would inform one of the sanctions of one's scotosis. But the chances of a biased subject paying attention to such a message are minimal, and the disharmoniousness of dreamland with waking consciousness increases to the point of bizarreness as the neural demand functions are further neglected through one's flight from understanding. The dream is a cipher of the authenticity or inauthenticity of the waking subject. Dreams are liable to be attended to only by the subject who wants needed insights even if they correct and revise current viewpoints and behavior. The dreams of such a subject will reflect, even if through prolonged struggle and crisis at key points in one's life, an increasing harmony and artistic creativity in one's dramatic living. But the dreams of the subject fleeing needed insights will reflect rather the violence done to the underlying materials by the biased waking collaboration of intelligence and imagination in preventing these materials from emerging into consciousness in such a way as to promote artistic living. The dreams of the person who wants the light of truth, no matter how corrective it may be, will be increasingly themselves works of art, as truth takes its effect in his or her life. The dreams of the person who loves the darkness of bias will be increasingly bizarre and incongruous, but not deceptive. There is no opposition between manifest content and latent content in the dreams either of the subject who honors neural demand functions and integrates them imaginatively and intelligently by conscripting them into his or her desire for insights needed for living, or of the subject fleeing understanding. The content in the latter case is incongruous, and becomes increasingly so the more desperate the appeal expressed in the incongruity, and the more the appeal is resisted by the subject who is fleeing the insights that would lead to change; the incongruity itself is an appeal for help, an appeal that, were it to be heeded, would itself be the beginning of therapy.[26]

2.5   Bias and Conversion

Because the dramatic bias that excludes helpful images by virtue of elementary aggressivity and affectivity is itself conditioned by the dialectic of community that is complicated by individual, group, and general bias, the reorientation of the preconscious collaboration of intelligence and imagination to the exercise of a constructive rather than repressive censorship is a complex task indeed. Fundamentally, it means overcoming bias in all of its forms. Such a precarious victory, we know from Lonergan, is possible only through religious, moral, and intellectual conversion. As I understand the relations of the conversions to the biases, religious and moral conversion affect principally individual and group bias, while intellectual conversion is needed to overcome general bias. Because dramatic bias is or can be joined to any of the three biases of practical common sense or to any combination of them, it is effectively corrected only by the sustained operations of conscious intentionality in its triply converted state, where a scheme of recurrence is established that sets up a defensive circle to prevent the systematic interference of any form of biased intentionality. In the ideal case, as one develops in the converted life, the interferences of bias are rendered increasingly less probable, increasingly more co-incidental.

Psychic conversion is both a function of and an aid to the sustained intentional authenticity of the religiously, morally, and intellectually converted subject. As resulting from the therapeutic movement of the other three conversions from above downwards, psychic conversion is a function of their dominance in one's intentional orientation. But as enabling a recurrent scheme of collaboration between neural demand functions and conscious discrimination, it is an aid to the creative development of subjectivity from below upwards. Psychic conversion is what enables one recurrently to *attend to* the imaginal deliverances of dramatic sensitivity. It is a function of the other three conversions, for without these one's intentional consciousness is biased against the emergence of materials for insight. But it is also an aid to growth and development in the other three conversions, for it provides to an antecedently willing intentionality the materials that this intentionality needs if the insights are to occur that will function in offsetting the shorter and especially longer cycles of decline in human living. It is the defensive circle set up by a triply converted intentionality to prevent the systematic interference of bias in the projects of the dramatic/existential subject. Psychic conversion also facilitates the sublation of intellectual conversion by moral and religious conversion, since it allows the latter two conversions to be transposed into the post-critical context of self-appropriation in the realm of interiority, and thus to be mediated to the subject in a manner demanded by the third stage of meaning, where meaning is controlled by differentiation in the realm of interiority. In its function as an aid to this sublation, psychic conversion mediates a dramatic pattern of experience for interiorly self-differentiating consciousness. It mediates dramatic artistry in the third stage of meaning, and thus intimately affects the self-appropriation of the fourth level of intentional consciousness, the level of moral and religious response.

2.6   Psychic Conversion and the Experiential Imperative

It needs to be emphasized that psychic conversion also throws light on the transcendental precept corresponding to the first level of intentional consciousness: Be attentive. Attentiveness is a function of one's willingness for insight, truth, and responsible change: that is, of religious, moral, and intellectual conversion. Conversion is a therapeutic movement from above downwards, enabling the movement from below upwards in one's conscious performance to be complete and creative. Conversion affects one first at the fourth level of intentional consciousness; thus Lonergan can say that usually religious conversion occurs first, then moral conversion, and thirdly intellectual conversion.[27] Psychic conversion would be a further extension downwards, into the unconscious neural base, of the therapy of consciousness that begins when one falls in love with God, that continues as this love promotes value over the satisfactions of individual and group egoism, and that extends further when one of the values promoted is truth, and so when the subject moves from the general bias of common sense and from the philosophic counterpositions on knowing, the real, and objectivity, to cosmopolis and to the basic philosophic positions that cosmopolis needs, implies, and in a more tutored state explicitly supports.[28]

The willingness introduced by religious conversion and extending to moral and intellectual conversion affects the censorship, the prior collaboration of intelligence and imagination in the admission to consciousness of the images that are needed for a sustained and creative development of one's being in harmony with one's self-transcendent orientation to intelligibility, truth, the real, and the good. The willingness introduced by religious conversion and extending downwards to psychic conversion renders one watchful, vigilant, expectant, contemplative: in a word, attentive. Attentiveness first permits the intelligible emergent probability of world process to become recurrently and not coincidentally intelligent, truthful, responsible emergent probability in and through the mediation of human consciousness. And so we have perhaps the starting point of a contemporary mediation through transcendental method of the biblical insight that the whole of creation groans in expectation, waiting for the liberation of the children of God.

3   Genuineness in the Third Stage of Meaning

In this section, I wish to relate the preceding discussion to Lonergan's treatment of genuineness,[29] the equivalent in *Insight* of what in his later work is called authenticity. Three steps are necessary: first, a statement of the relation of psychic conversion to sensitive desire as integrator and operator of development;[30] second, a delineation of the effective constituents of genuineness in the third stage of meaning; and third, a suggestion that will be amplified in the final section of this paper to the effect that the notion of psychic energy is relevant to our concern.

3.1   *Psychic Conversion and Sensitive Desire*

Genuineness promotes the harmonious cooperation of the self as it is and the self as it is apprehended to be.[31] In itself, however, it is an admitting into consciousness of the tension between limitation and transcendence that attends human development. There is a tendency to resist this conscious admission, a tendency rooted in the conflict between a sensitive desire to remain as one is and the dynamism of intentionality's pure desire to know and to love, which has its own psychological counterpart in the finality of corresponding underlying neural and psychic manifolds.[32]

The conflict is resolved only through a sensitive or affective self-transcendence that matches, accompanies, permeates, sustains the detachment of intelligent, reasonable, and responsible intentionality, and that, as 'universal willingness,'[33] is the condition of the sustained possibility of authentic consciousness. We resist this sensitive purification, and for reasons that are not hard to find.[34] Yet this resistance is what prevents the genuineness that would promote the harmonious cooperation of the self as it is and the self as it apprehends itself to be. This resistance is biased. It distorts the collaboration of imagination and intelligence in their dramatically patterned function of providing images that would enable insight into one's being. Sustained authentic dramatic intrasubjective collaboration, then, would seem to be a function of a purification of sensitive desire. While such a purification is itself a function of all four conversions, my principal concern is to relate it to psychic conversion.

Psychic conversion aids the mediation of the drama of sensitive spontaneity in its dialectical relationship to the authentic finality of the subject. By mediating this drama, it promotes a self-possessed detachment in the realm of affectivity — a detachment that, in the limit, not only matches but sublates and sustains the detachment of the pure, disinterested, unrestricted desire to know that one has come to affirm in the self-affirmation of the knower and in the positions on being and objectivity.[35] Psychic conversion, as a function of religious, moral, and intellectual conversion, promotes a purification of sensitive desire through mediating to intentional consciousness the story of sensitive spontaneity on the move. The higher system of intellectual conversion is both integrator and operator of one's development in the third stage, and in its latter function it promotes its own sublation into moral and religious subjectivity by provoking the questions that lead to the self-appropriation of the fourth level. Psychic conversion is the key to this further development. The sensitive purification that it promotes is yet a higher systematization of human life.

> There are three conditions which often look alike
> Yet differ completely, flourish in the same hedgerow:
> Attachment to self and to things and to persons,
>   detachment
> From self and from things and from persons; and, growing
>   between them, indifference
> Which resembles the others as death resembles life,
> Being between two lives — unflowering, between
> The live and the dead nettle. This is the use of memory:
> For liberation — not less of love but expanding
> Of love beyond desire, and so liberation
> From the future as well as the past.[36]

When the detachment of intentionality has entered upon the stage of self-appropriation, affective self-transcendence too must be submitted to a thoroughgoing maieutic of self-mediation. As affective self-transcendence confers on dramatic existential living its aesthetic or artistic character, so psychic conversion is the source of this dramatic

artistry for the subject whose development has brought
him or her into the third stage of meaning.

3.2   *Consciousness and Genuineness*

There is a strange law to human development, according to which the more consciously a development occurs, at least to a given point, the greater risk it incurs of
losing the simplicity and honesty, the perspicacity and sin-
cerity, that we associate with genuineness. Consciousness
and genuineness seem to be at odds. For genuineness is a
matter of the harmonious cooperation of the self as apprehended and the self as it is, and the very development of
the powers of apprehension can mean either correct or
mistaken understanding of the starting point of development in the subject as one is, of the term in the subject as
one is to be, and of the process from the starting point to
the term. If these apprehensions are correct, 'the conscious
[self as apprehended] and unconscious [self as it is] components of the development are operating from the same
base along the same route to the same goal. If they are
mistaken, the conscious and unconscious components, to
a greater or less extent, are operating at cross-purposes.'[37]
Moreover, the apprehensions may be minimal or extensive.

> They are minimal when they involve little more
> than the succession of fragmentary and sepa-
> rate acts needed to carry out the successive
> steps of the development with advertence, in-
> telligence, and reasonableness. They are more
> or less extensive when one begins to delve into
> the background, the context, the premises, the
> interrelations, of the minimal series of con-
> scious acts, and to subsume this understand-

ing of oneself under empirical laws and philosophic theories of development.[38]

If other things are equal, the minimal apprehensions
are more liable to be free of error than the apprehensions
through which one tries to match the self as it is by a self
as it is known. Other things may, of course, not be equal,
and then 'errors have become lodged in the habitual background whence spring our direct and reflective insights,'
so that, 'if we relied upon our virtual and implicit self-
knowledge to provide us with concrete guidance through
a conscious development, then the minimal series, so far
from being probably correct, would be certainly mistaken.'[39]

In the latter case, then, genuineness depends on a
more or less extensive self-scrutiny that would bring the
self as it is apprehended into harmony with the self as it is.
This self-scrutiny reaches its limit in the third stage of
meaning, where it takes the twofold form of (1) the introspective method of intentionality analysis, and (2) a depth
psychology that has been transformed by and integrated
into method.[40] This twin maieutic promotes the harmony
between the self as it is and the self as it is known. As the
subject's development enters the third stage of meaning,
then, the needed self-scrutiny (1) is systematized in intellectual conversion and (2) is carried further by means of
psychic conversion. Through intellectual conversion, the
generalized or transcendental structure of what Jean Piaget
calls the cognitive unconscious[41] (the knowing self as it is)
becomes objectified, and through psychic conversion, the
energic compositions and distributions of the affective
unconscious (the affective self as it is) become known and
are integrated with and promote the intentionality disclosed
in transcendental method. Because it is through the affective self as it is that values are apprehended and responded

to, psychic conversion enables or at least initiates a mediation of moral and religious subjectivity.[42] Through these third-stage conversions, what was conscious in a twilight state but not objectified — objectification may even have been resisted — becomes known. Genuineness in the third stage of meaning, then, promotes the harmonious cooperation of the self as it is and the self as it is objectified, known, apprehended through self-appropriation. It promotes a second naivete, a second immediacy, a naivete that in the limit returns to 'speech that has been instructed by the whole process of meaning,'[43] an informed, post-critical, post-therapeutic naivete.

Psychic conversion, then, enables the emergence of a post-critical and post-therapeutic dramatic/existential pattern of experience that can sustain and sublate the tension introduced into sensitive consciousness by an affirmation of the philosophic basic positions and by the thorough and effective critique of common sense through which one subordinates the imperiousness of practicality to the sanctions of the transcendental precepts. Just as there is cognitive self-transcendence without the self-appropriation of cognitive process that is intellectual conversion, so there is affective self-transcendence without the self-appropriation of affectivity that occurs through psychic conversion. As the former, so the latter is precritical. A post-critical and post-therapeutic self-transcendence of cognitive structure and of affective energic compositions and distributions has been mediated by self-appropriation.

The therapeutic character of the methodical maieutic, however, is not adequately explained in terms of mediation alone. More precisely, mediation, if it is effective, is also transformation. The higher system it introduces is not merely integrator but also operator of development. Mediation is conversion, a change in the subject, 'a change of direction and, indeed, a change for the better. One frees oneself from the unauthentic. One grows in authenticity. Harmful, dangerous, misleading satisfactions are dropped. Fears of discomfort, pain, privation have less power to deflect one from one's course. Values are apprehended where before they were overlooked. Scales of preference shift. Errors, rationalizations, ideologies fall and shatter to leave one open to things as they are and to man as he should be.'[44] If consciousness is to be open to things as they are and to ourselves as we should be, it must be converted. The extent of the conversion is the extent of the openness, as one might expect from the correspondence of the therapeutic movement from above downwards and the creative movement from below upwards in human consciousness.

3.3   Psychic Energy

The openness of an intellectually and psychically converted consciousness permits the post-critical and post-therapeutic entrance into third-stage consciousness of a basic law of limitation and transcendence.[45] The tension of limitation and transcendence is characteristic of all development in the concrete universe of being proportionate to human experience, human understanding, and human judgment. But in human beings the tension itself becomes conscious. Wherever it is found in the universe, the tension is rooted in potency, that is, in the individuality, continuity, coincidental conjunctions and successions, and nonsystematic divergence from intelligible norms, that are to be known by the empirical consciousness of a mind intent on explanatory understanding.[46] Potency is the root of tension because it is the principle both of limitation and of the upwardly but indeterminately directed dynamism of proportionate being that Lonergan calls finality.[47] Now the principle of limitation of the lowest genus of proportionate being is prime potency, and since each higher genus is limited by the preceding lower genus, prime potency is the universal principle of limitation for the whole range of proportionate being.[48]

Prime potency grounds energy, which, Lonergan writes, 'is relevant to mechanics, thermodynamics, electromagnetics, chemistry, and biology.'[49] Thus, he asks, 'Might one not say that the quantity of energy is the concrete prime potency that is informed mechanically or thermally or electrically as the case may be?' And he asks for an answer to this and other questions 'such that prime potency would be conceived as a ground of quantitative limitation and general heuristic considerations would relate quantitative limitation to the properties that science verifies in the quantity it names energy.'[50]

The notion of energy as also psychic is not without its difficulties, but it has been defended by C.G. Jung,[51] approved, it would seem, by the physicist Wolfgang Pauli,[52] and is defensible in terms of Lonergan's exposition of explanatory genera and species. Nonetheless,

> ... when one mounts to the higher integrations
> of the organism, the psyche, and intelligence,
> one finds that measuring loses both in signifi-
> cance and in efficacy. It loses in significance,
> for the higher integration is, within limits, in-
> dependent of the exact quantities of the lower
> manifold it systematizes. Moreover, the higher
> the integration, the greater the independence
> of lower quantities ... Besides this loss in sig-
> nificance, there is also a loss in efficacy. Classi-
> cal method can select among the functions that
> solve differential equations by appealing to
> measurements and empirically established
> curves. What the differential equation is to clas-

sical method, the general notion of development is to genetic method. But while the differential equation is mathematical, the general notion of development is not. It follows that, while measurement is an efficacious technique for finding boundary conditions that restrict differential equations, it possesses no assignable efficacy when it comes to particularizing the general notion of development.[53]

The loss of significance and efficacy to the quantitative treatment of what remains a quantity is most apparent in human beings, where 'the higher system of intelligence develops not in a material manifold but in the psychic representation of material manifolds. Hence the higher system of intellectual development is primarily the higher integration, not of the man in whom the development occurs, but of the universe that he inspects.'[54] The human psyche as integrator develops in an underlying manifold of material events, but the same psyche as operator is oriented to the higher integration of the universe in and through human intentional consciousness.

It is this tension between psyche as integrator of physical, chemical, cytological, and neurological events and psyche as operator of the higher integration of the universe in human intelligence, affirmation, and decision that is the sensitive manifestation of the law of limitation and transcendence as this law becomes conscious in human development. In fact, it is through psychic energy as integrator and operator that this law *does* first become conscious. The genuineness that would accept the law into consciousness and live from it, then, is promoted by a mediated recognition of psychic energy as integrator and operator of one's own development.

4   Psychic Energy and Elemental Symbols

4.1   Transformation of and by Symbols

Freud and Jung entertained what eventually were to become dialectically opposed understandings of psychic energy and of its functioning in personal development. For Freud, psychic energy would seem to be reducible to a biological quantum. It is always, in all its manifestations or object relations, explained by moving backwards. Its real object is sexual, and it institutes other object relations only by being displaced from the sexual object. There is one basic and unsurpassable desire. Dreams, works of art, linguistic expressions, and cultural objectifications dissimulate this desire. They do not witness to a polymorphism of human desire, a capacity to be directed in several autonomous patterns of experience, but rather always disguise the unsurpassable biological instinct from which they originate. Displacement can be either neurotic or healthy. It always occurs through the agency of one or more mechanisms: repression, substitution, symbolization, sublimation. In each instance the primary process, governed by the pleasure principle, is superseded by a secondary process whose principle is the harsh Anankê of reality.

The seat of psychic energy, then, that is, the unconscious, is on this account never related directly to the real world. It must be adapted by the reality principle, and submit in stoic resignation to things as they are. Therapy enables this healthy, adult stoicism, this adaptation to a cruel fate.

For Jung, on the contrary, specifically psychic energy is a surplus energy from the standpoint of biological purposiveness. It is, in Lonergan's terms, a coincidental manifold at the biological level. Its original orientation is neutral, undetermined, undifferentiated. It is not aboriginally sexual, tied to a destiny in reverse,[55] but can be directed to a host of different objects. Moreover, it can be transformed. The transformation of energy is not displacement, even by sublimation, for psychic energy has no determinate object from which to be displaced. Thus Jung frequently takes issue with the Freudian notion of mechanisms of displacement, and sharply distinguishes his own notion of transformation from even the seemingly least reductive Freudian mechanism, sublimation.[56] Sublimation is a bending of instinctual desire to a suitable form of adaptation to reality. In essence it is a self-deception, 'a new and somewhat more subtle form of repression,' for 'only absolute necessity can effectively inhibit a natural instinct.'[57] Transformation, on the other hand, is itself a thoroughly natural process — that is, a process that occurs of itself when the proper attitude is adopted toward the process of energic composition and distribution (complex formation) that depth psychologists call the unconscious.[58] This proper attitude initially may be characterized as one of compassionate and attentive listening, of an effort to befriend the neglected dimensions of one's subterranean existence. Attentiveness, therapeutically tutored, puts one in touch with the upwardly but indeterminately directed dynamism that Lonergan calls finality. Healing thus complements creativity. Jung designates the fuller being[59] to which finality is directed as wholeness, which he characterizes as the unconscious meaning and purposefulness of the transformation of energy.[60]

The Jungian explanation of symbols provides a quite direct access to the transformation of energy in the service of this unconscious meaning and purposefulness. I find it most instructive to compare the early and later Jung on fantasy and dream.[61] More or less in agreement with Freud, the early Jung indicated that fantasy thinking and dreaming represent a distortion in one's relation to reality, an intrusion — welcome or unwelcome — of the nonrealistic unconscious psyche into the domain of the reality principle or ego.[62] Fantasies and dreams are thinly but subtly disguised instances of wishful thinking, symptoms of the primary process, needing only the suspicious hermeneutic of reduction in order to be revealed for what they are.[63] But in Jung's later work, fantasies and dreams are not distorted forms of thinking, or illegitimate relations to reality, but spontaneous products of a layer of the subject that has its own distinct meaning and purpose.[64] Fantasies and dreams, moreover, have a function: they cooperate in the interests of the transformation of energy in the direction of the wholeness of the personality.[65]

The development in Jung's thought is from symptom to symbol. If dreams and fantasies are symptoms of neurotic difficulty, they reveal the formation of substitutes for sexual energy. But if they have a meaning of their own as symbols of the course of occurrences or conjugate acts at the psychic level of finality, then they are to be interpreted as integrators and operators of a process of development, that is, of the transformation of psychic energy in the direction of the fuller being that Jung calls wholeness. As an integrator and operator of development, the spontaneous or elemental symbol is efficacious. It does not merely point to the transformation of energy like a sign; it *gives what it symbolizes*; it is not just a symbol of transformation, but a transforming symbol. If for the moment I may neutralize a religiously charged word, we might call the symbol as integrator and operator sacramental.

Because we have made reference to Lonergan's notion of finality, it is interesting to note in this context that Jung speaks explicitly of the necessity of adopting a teleological point of view in the science of the psyche. The question to be asked of the elemental symbol is not so much, What caused this distortion in the relation to reality? as it is, What is the purpose of this symbolic expression? What is it intending? Where is it heading? The intelligibility is to be discovered in the higher system of human living that systematically assembles and organizes the psychic materials.[66] There is not, however, an either/or dichotomy to be entertained between the causal point of view and the teleological approach. Jung understood that these two scientific orientations are complementary to one another. Both are necessary if the symbol, precisely as symbol, is to be correctly understood. The causal point of view displays the system of energy composition *from which* energy has passed over into a new distribution. The teleological point of view reveals the direction of the new distribution. Where Jung differs from Freud is that the new distribution is not a faulty substitute for the primal system, but a new and autonomous system in its own right, invested with energy that has become properly its own. It takes over something of the character of the old system, but radically transforms this character in the process. To employ explanatory categories from Lonergan, we might say that, just as potency is a principle of limitation for the realm of proportionate being, even as finality urges world process to new genera that are not logically derivative from former genera, so psychic energy is a principle of limitation for that domain of proportionate being that is human development, even as its finality urges human development to new patterns, capacities, and differentiations that are not logically derivative from former constellations.

The elemental symbol, then, is not for Jung an inferior form of thinking, the symptom of a maladaptation to reality, but is rather 'the best possible description or formulation of a relatively unknown fact.'[67] The relatively unknown fact is the self as it is and the self as it is becoming, in its various dimensions.

The process of development toward wholeness, when engaged in consciously and deliberately, Jung calls individuation. Psychic energy as the principle of the upwardly but indeterminately directed dynamism of finality is initially undifferentiated as far as its specific focus or objective is concerned. But it is generically directed to a wholeness that is moved toward by individuation. Its elemental symbolic productions effect its ongoing transformation in this direction. Wholeness is a generic goal that becomes specifically differentiated through the process of individuation.[68]

The complementarity of the causal and the teleological points of view in the interpretation of elemental symbols corresponds to the transformation of an *object* into an *imago*. On a purely causal interpretation, the appearance or suggestion of a maternal symbol in a dream or fantasy, for example, signifies some unresolved component of infantile Oedipal sexuality, some disguised or displaced form of the primal Oedipal situation. On a teleological interpretation, the same symbol may point not just *back* to one's childhood or infancy, but also *ahead* to further development. It may be, not a symptom of infantile fixation, but a symbol of the life-giving forces of nature. It may have a more than personal meaning, a significance that Jung calls archetypal. One may be regressing to the mother, but precisely for the sake of finding memory traces that will enable one to move forward. In this case, 'mother' is no longer an object or a cause of a symptom but, in Jung's term, an *imago*, that is, a cluster of memory associations through whose aid further development may take place.[69] What was once an object of one's reachings may become a symbol of the life that lies ahead. The energy once invested in an object is now concentrated in a symbol which transforms the original investment in such a way as to propel one to an adult future. The cathexis of psychic energy has been transferred — by transformation, not by displacement — from an object to the 'relatively unknown fact' that is expressed in the symbol. Psychic energy has been channeled into a symbolic analogue of its natural object, an analogue that imitates the object and thereby gains for a new purpose the energy once invested in the object.

4.2 *Intentionality and the Transformation of Energy*

To say that the transformation of psychic energy is a natural and automatic process does not mean that wholeness, the reconciliation of opposites, is its inevitable result. We have already called attention to the requisite attitude on the part of consciousness if the individuation process is to proceed from generic indetermination to specific and explanatory differentiation. Jung himself insisted on the need for a freely adopted conscious attitude toward the psychological depths and their symbolic manifestations if individuation is to occur.[70] The same may be gathered from Lonergan's discussion of the collaboration of imagination and intelligence in presenting to conscious discrimination the images needed for insight, judgment, and decision.[71] Earlier I called the proper attitude one of therapeutically tutored attentiveness. Such contemplative listening is a function of the effective introduction into one's operative intentionality of the universal willingness that matches the unrestricted spontaneity of the desire for intelligibility, the unconditioned, and value. 'There is to human inquiry an unrestricted demand for intelligibility. There is to human judgment a demand for the unconditioned. There is to human deliberation a criterion that criticizes every finite good.'[72] The transformation of psychic energy may well be a natural and automatic process, but the direction it will assume is dependent on the orientation of the higher system of intentionality in which the psyche itself finds its integration. Thus, too, the science of depth psychology depends on a maieutic of intentionality.

The unrestricted demand of inquiry, judgment, and deliberation constitutes what Lonergan calls the transcendent exigence of human intentionality. 'So it is ... that man can reach basic fulfillment, peace, joy, only by moving beyond the realms of common sense, theory, and interiority and into the realm in which God is known and loved.'[73] Religious conversion and its development in spirituality is what brings one into this realm of transcendence. As fulfillment of intentionality and simultaneously as participation in the divinely originated solution to the problem of evil, religious conversion is the beginning of the therapeutic movement from above downwards that proceeds through moral and intellectual conversion to the psychic conversion that effects the therapeutically tutored attentiveness that represents the proper attitude to the symbolic deliverances of psychic finality. In this way, the divinely originated solution to the problem of evil penetrates to the sensitive level of human living. In the limit, it is to be expected that what will occur in the unfolding of the story told in one's dreams will be the transformation of one's spontaneous symbolic process so that it matches more and more the exigences of the divinely originated solution. For the transformation of sensitivity and spontaneous intersubjectivity wrought by development in the realm of transcendence penetrates to the physiological level of human subjectivity.[74] The divinely originated solution to the problem of evil is a higher integration of human living that will be implemented by a converted intentionality, an intentionality that has been transformed by the supernatural or transcendent conjugate forms of faith and hope and charity.[75] But because the solution is a harmonious continuation of the emergent probability of world process, it must penetrate to and envelop the sensitive level with which the creative movement of intentionality from below upwards begins. Spontaneous psychic images function in human consciousness in a manner analogous to the role of questions for intelligence, reflection, and deliberation. As questions promote the successive sublations of lower levels of consciousness by higher levels, so psychic images, when attended to under the influence of an antecedently willing collaboration of imagination and intelligence, promote the sublation of neural demand functions by waking empirical consciousness, which in turn is sublated by intelligent, rational, and existential consciousness.

The transformation of energy under the influence of the transcendent conjugate forms introduced into intentional consciousness by religious conversion will enter a dimension or stage that was not adequately differentiated by Jung. As we saw above, Jung was extremely sensitive to the transformation of energic compositions and distributions from personal object relations to archetypal *imago* relations. But beyond the archetypal stage of energic transformation, there is an anagogic stage.[76] It represents the envelopment of sensitivity by the divinely originated solution to the problem of evil. In this stage, transformed and transforming symbols are released that correspond to the unrestricted intentionality of human intelligence, human judgment, and human deliberation. Anagogic symbols simultaneously reflect and give the conversion of human sensitivity itself to participation in the divinely originated solution to the problem of evil. They correspond to what Lonergan calls 'the image that symbolizes man's orientation into the known unknown.'[77] Lonergan aptly explains their function: '… since faith gives more truth than understanding comprehends, since hope reinforces the detached, disinterested, unrestricted desire to know, man's sensitivity needs symbols that unlock its transforming dynamism and bring it into harmony with the vast but impalpable pressures of the pure desire, of hope, and of self-sacrificing charity.'[78] These symbols make of the divinely originated solution 'a mystery that is at once symbol of the uncomprehended and sign of what is grasped and psychic force that sweeps living human bodies, linked in charity, to the joyful, courageous, wholehearted, yet intelligently controlled performance of the tasks set by a world order in which the problem of evil is not suppressed but transcended.'[79] Through anagogic symbols, the divine solution becomes living history in a deeper, more personal manner. Through their agency, 'the emergent trend and the full realization of the solution [includes] the sensible data that are demanded by man's sensitive nature and that will command his attention, nourish his imagination, stimulate his intelligence and will, release his affectivity, control his aggressivity, and, as central features of the world of sense, intimate its finality, its yearning for God.'[80] In fact, since the higher system of intentionality is primarily the higher integration, not of the subject in whom development occurs, but of the universe of being that the subject knows and makes, it may be said that elemental anagogic symbols not only intimate but also promote the finality of the universe. The participation of sensitivity in the divinely originated solution to the problem of evil that occurs through anagogic symbols, when sustained by the harmonious cooperation of the therapeutic movement from above downwards with the creative development from below upwards, would then have to be understood as the fulfillment of the process of conversion in the retrieved genuineness of the subject in the third stage of meaning.

Notes

[1] Bernard Lonergan, *Method in Theology* (see above, chapter 1, note 3) 133.

[2] Ibid. xii.

[3] Ibid. 343.

[4] Robert M. Doran, *Subject and Psyche* (see above, chapter 2, note 21).

[5] It will appear from this paper that this sublation is implicitly prepared even by *Insight*. Furthermore, it can be argued that even in *Method in Theology* its possibility is still implicit.

[6] Lonergan, *Method in Theology* 55.

[7] Bernard Lonergan, *Insight* (see above, chapter 1, note 37) 472–79/497–504.

[8] Bernard Lonergan, 'Healing and Creating in History' (see above, chapter 6, note 88).

[9] Lonergan, *Method in Theology* 241.

[10] Lonergan, 'Healing and Creating in History.'

[11] Ibid. 107–108.

[12] Lonergan, *Insight* 187–89/210–12.

[13] Bernard Lonergan, '*Insight* Revisited' (see above, chapter 2, note 56) 277.

[14] Bernard Lonergan, 'The Subject' (see above, chapter 3, note 1) 79–84.

[15] Lonergan, *Insight* 456/481.

16 See Ernest Becker, *The Denial of Death* (see above, chapter 4, note 4) 176-207.

17 On the levels of consciousness and their corresponding sanctions for one's authenticity as a human subject, see inter alia Lonergan, *Method in Theology* 3-25; on the dramatic pattern *Insight* 187-206/210-31.

18 On the relationship of the dialectic of community to the inner dialectic of the subject, see Lonergan, *Insight* 218/243.

19 Lonergan, 'The Subject' 83.

20 In contrast with the position of Lonergan, I would want to say that it is not moral and religious conversion as such that sublate intellectual conversion, but moral and religious self-appropriation, i.e., the knowledge of existential intentionality. Psychic conversion is an aid to this knowledge. Thus it is psychic conversion that enables the sublation of intellectual conversion by a self-appropriating moral and religious subject.

21 See Lonergan, *Method in Theology* 85-99.

22 See Jean Piaget, 'The Mental Development of the Child,' in *Six Psychological Studies*, trans. Anita Tenzer and David Elkind (New York: Random House, 1967) 60-70 for a description of the drama that accompanies the adolescent's budding familiarity with systematic thinking.

23 Lonergan, 'The Subject' 85.

24 Lonergan, *Insight* 189-91/212-14.

25 See, e.g, C.G. Jung, 'The Practical Use of Dream-Analysis,' in *The Practice of Psychotherapy*, trans. R.F.C. Hull, vol. 16 in Collected Works of C.G. Jung, Bollingen Series XX (Princeton: Princeton University Press, 1970) 153.

26 It must be kept in mind that the factors that operate in the aberration of the censorship are manifold and complex. Lonergan has recognized this complexity by referring to the dominance of the dialectic of community over the dialectic of the dramatic subject. See *Insight* 218/243. This means, of course, that there are extreme cases of people

who never really had a chance themselves, whose failed artistry is a function not so much of inauthenticity as of victimization. As a civilization nears 'the catalytic trifle that will reveal to a surprised world the end of a once brilliant day' (*Insight* 210/235), such cases are liable to become more numerous. The reversal of personal decline in such instances is increasingly more improbable. So too, I believe, the need for and the availability of an extraordinary remedy from the realm of transcendence increases as the longer cycle of social decline moves toward the day of reckoning. It is to be kept in mind, however, that even extraordinary remedies are subject to the distorting influence of human religious inauthenticity.

27 Lonergan, *Method in Theology* 243.

28 On cosmopolis see Lonergan, *Insight* 238-242/273-67.

29 Ibid. 475-79/499-504.

30 On integrator and operator see ibid. 464-65/489-91.

31 Lonergan speaks of genuineness as 'the necessary condition of the harmonious cooperation of the conscious and unconscious components of development.' Ibid. 477/502. The context of this reference indicates to me that his later refinement is more precise, according to which there is a need to avoid a conflict between what one spontaneously is and what one has objectified oneself to be. See *Method in Theology* 34.

32 For a description of the conflict see *Insight* 476-77/501-502. As we shall see, the tension is rooted in the conjugate potency that Jung calls psychic energy, which is simultaneously the integrator of underlying physical, chemical, cytological, and neurological manifolds and an operator not only of the higher integration of the human subject through universal willingness but of the higher integration of the universe of proportionate being through understanding, judgment, decision, and love.

33 Ibid. 623-24/646-47.

34 See ibid. 473-74/498-99. The opposition is even more concretely understood when one brings in Lonergan's insistence on the primacy of a fourth level of consciousness. For then not only is the universe of being to be known by intelligent grasp and reasonable affir-

mation, but also it is to be promoted in its upwardly directed dynamism by responsible decision.

35 Ibid., chapters 11-13.

36 T.S. Eliot, 'Little Gidding' (see above, chapter 2, note 15) 55.

37 Lonergan, *Insight* 475/500.

38 Ibid. 476/500.

39 Ibid. 501.

40 For the general structure of this transformation and integration, see Doran, *Subject and Psyche*.

41 See Jean Piaget, *The Child and Reality: Problems of Genetic Psychology*, trans. Arnold Rosin (New York: Grossman, 1973) 31-48.

42 See Robert M. Doran, 'Subject, Psyche, and Theology's Foundations' (above, chapter 3) and chapter 1 of *Subject and Psyche*.

43 Paul Ricoeur, *Freud and Philosophy* (see above, chapter 1, note 7) 496.

44 Lonergan, *Method in Theology* 52.

45 Lonergan, *Insight* 472-75/497-99.

46 On potency, see ibid. 432-433/457-58; on central potency (individuality) and conjugate potency (other aspects of the empirical residue) ibid. 437/462; on a coincidental manifold of conjugate acts (occurrences) as potency for a higher integration by an emergent conjugate form, ibid. 438/463-64.

47 Ibid. 442-51/467-76.

48 Ibid. 442-43/467-68.

49 Ibid. 443/468.

50 Ibid. 444/469.

51 C.G. Jung, 'On Psychic Energy,' in *The Structure and Dynamics of the Psyche* (see above, chapter 2, note 14) 3-66.

52 See C.G. Jung, 'Synchronicity: An Acausal Connecting Principle,' ibid. 419-519, at 514.

53 Lonergan, *Insight* 463/488.

54 Ibid. 469/494. Again, in the light of the later expansion of the analysis of consciousness to the fourth level, 'intellectual development' as used throughout Lonergan's treatment of human development in chapter 15 of *Insight* must include the existential development of the subject as originating value.

55 Ricoeur, *Freud and Philosophy* 452.

56 For a representative critique of the notion of sublimation, see C.G. Jung, 'Analytical Psychology and the "Weltanschauung,"' in *The Structure and Dynamics of the Psyche* 365.

57 Ibid.

58 Jung, of course, initially agreed with Freud that psychic energy is displaced from sexual object relations to other distributions, but he soon abandoned this notion in favor of the natural process of transformation. His early agreement with Freud on the notion of sublimation can be seen in some original 1909 footnotes to a paper Jung revised and expanded in 1949. See 'The Significance of the Father in the Destiny of the Individual,' in *Freud and Psychoanalysis*, trans. R.F.C. Hull, vol. 4 of Collected Works of C.G. Jung, Bollingen Series XX (Princeton: Princeton University Press, 1961) 320-21, notes 21 and 22.

59 See Lonergan, *Insight* 445/471.

60 Compare Lonergan, ibid. 477/501: '*Unconsciously operative* is the finality that consists in the upwardly but indeterminately directed dynamism of all proportionate being.' Emphasis added. The context is the tension of limitation and transcendence in human development.

61 Approximately, the early Jung is the Jung prior to the 'confrontation with the unconscious' detailed in chapter 6 of the autobiographical *Memories, Dreams, Reflections* (see above, chapter 3, note 49).

62 'Ego' is here used differently from the way Lonergan employs the term (*Insight* 191/214), where the ego *is* a daydreamer or fantasizer, and not in a particularly helpful manner.

63 On the hermeneutic of suspicion, see Ricoeur, *Freud and Philosophy* 32-36. Jung's early interpretation of fantasies and dreams is still present in the book that generally is acknowledged as Jung's definitive break with Freud, the 1912 work *Wandlungen und Symbole der Libido*. An English translation of the work by Beatrice M. Hinkle, *Psychology of the Unconscious,* appeared in 1916 (New York: Moffatt Yard). What appears in Jung's Collected Works (Volume 5), however, is the extensive revision of 1952, *Symbole der Wandlung.* The revision obviously puts forth the later interpretation of fantasies and dreams. The English translation by Hull is entitled *Symbols of Transformation* (see above, chapter 5, note 31).

64 The dream 'is a typical product of the unconscious, and is merely deformed and distorted [i.e., not constituted] by repression. Hence any explanation that interprets it as a mere symptom of repression will go very wide of the mark.' Jung, 'Analytical Psychology and the "Weltanschauung"' 365.

65 Jungian analyst John Weir Perry has argued persuasively that this is the case even — or especially — with the fantasies of psychotics. See Perry's *The Far Side of Madness* (Englewood Cliffs, NJ: Prentice-Hall, 1974) 28-30. If Perry is correct, he has contributed another facet to the critique of the usual treatment of schizophrenia that has been offered by Thomas Szasz and R.D. Laing.

66 See Lonergan, *Insight* 264-67/289-92.

67 C.G. Jung, *Psychological Types* (see above, chapter 4, note 18) 474.

68 Compare Lonergan: '...the course of development is marked by an increasing explanatory differentiation. The initial integration in the initial manifold pertains to a determinate genus and species; still, exclusive attention to the data on the initial stage would yield little knowledge and less understanding of the relevant genus and species. What is to be known by understanding is what is yet to come, what may be present virtually or potentially but as yet is not present formally or actually. Accordingly, if one attends simply to the data on each succes-

sive stage of a development, one finds that the initial integration can be understood only in a generic fashion, that subsequent integrations are increasingly specific intelligibilities, that the specific intelligible differentiation of the ultimate stage attained is generated in the process from the initial stage.' *Insight* 452-53/478.

69 Paul Ricoeur's notion of the archeological-teleological unity-in-tension of the concrete symbol helps me understand the complex constitution and function of the dream. See Ricoeur, *Freud and Philosophy* 494-551. The tense unity of regressive and progressive aspects is rooted in what Ricoeur calls the overdetermination of the symbol, a factor which in turn I would root in the coincidental character of psychic energy from a biological standpoint.

70 See C.G. Jung, 'The Relations between the Ego and the Unconscious,' in *Two Essays on Analytical Psychology* (see above, chapter 5, note 5) 123-241.

71 Lonergan, *Insight* 187-96/210-20.

72 Lonergan, *Method in Theology* 83-84.

73 Ibid. 84.

74 Lonergan, *Insight* 741-42/763.

75 Ibid. 696-703/718-25.

76 Jung's failure to distinguish the archetypal from the anagogic leads, in the last analysis, to a displacement of the tension of limitation and transcendence that is every bit as erroneous as Freud's reductionism. On displacement of the tension as failure in genuineness, see ibid. 478/503.

77 Ibid. 723/744.

78 Ibid.

79 Ibid. 723-24/745.

80 Ibid. 724/745.

8 Insight and Archetype: The Complementarity of Lonergan and Jung

The generalized empirical method of Bernard Lonergan and the archetypal psychology of C.G. Jung are contributions to the systematizing of a qualitative leap in the evolution of human consciousness. The leap is into a third stage of meaning, where meaning is controlled, not by mythical imagination, not by practical common sense, not by theory, but by a subjectivity that has been mediated to itself by a reflexive process of self-appropriation. Through this process the subject discovers the capacities and the normative exigencies of his or her own intention of meaning, truth, being, and value, and comes to govern his or her cognitional and existential praxis on the basis of this discovery. Such an understanding of the present juncture in the history of consciousness is, of course, dependent on Lonergan.[1] What I wish to add is an account of how Jung contributes, not only to our understanding of the new stage in conscious evolution but also to the very emergence of a consolidating systematization of the various conscious occurrences that give rise to this stage of meaning,[2] once the Jungian maieutic of psychic energy is subjected to the dialectical method that emerges from Lonergan's intentionality analysis.

The present paper, then, is best viewed as a postcritical[3] statement of the articulation of two comple-

mentary mediations of subjectivity, where the complementarity in question has issued from dialectic. The dialectic
has already reversed counterpositions in Jung's formulations of psychic reality.[4] The postcritical statement incor-
porates the positive gains of the dialectic into a developing
position on the human subject.

1   Energy and Human Desire

The reflective praxis of self-appropriation issues in a
semantics of the dialectic of human desire. The dialectic
itself is the humanly conscious form of the tension of limitation and transcendence that qualifies all development in
the universe proportionate to human experience, understanding, and judgment. The tension is rooted in potency
as ground of both limitation and finality, and ultimately in
the prime potency that grounds energy.[5] The tension of
limitation and transcendence becomes conscious when
energy becomes psychic, and a matter of existential responsibility when psychic energy becomes human, that is,
when it can achieve its highest integration only by being
sublated by the cognitive intention of being and the existential intention of value. The humanly conscious tension
is qualitatively more pronounced than the psychic tension
of limitation and transcendence in the other animals, because in its human realization psychic energy is not only
an integrator of underlying material events and an operator of the subject's spiritual development but also and primarily a factor in the integration of the very universe of
being intended in human knowledge and action.[6] In human desire, psychic energy is sublated by the spirituality
of knowledge and decision, and thus becomes conscripted
into the intelligent and reasonable, responsible and loving
intention of a universe of being to be known or to be realized through the self-transcendent dynamism of human

intentionality. The extent of this conscription of psychic energy by spirituality is the extent of a sensitive detachment that matches the detachment of intentionality in its pure desire to know and to love. This sensitive detachment is the precondition of the individuated wholeness that for Jung was the objective of the conscious negotiation of psychic teleology.[7]

The phrase 'the semantics of desire' is found in Paul Ricoeur's refined and delicate articulation of the place of Freudian psychoanalysis in the philosophy of self-appropriation.[8] But to speak of *a semantics of the dialectic of desire* is to extend the meaning of the term 'desire' so that it includes not just the biological purposiveness highlighted with such single-minded intensity by Freud but also the sensitive psychological component of intentionality in the various autonomous realms of meaning specified by Lonergan.[9] The realms of meaning find their psychic components in what Lonergan calls patterns of experience.[10] Desire thus includes even the pure, disinterested, detached orientation that in *Insight* is the desire to know[11] and that in *Method in Theology* is extended to the intention of value.[12] Nonetheless, Ricoeur has argued convincingly that the problems posed by Freud and by those associated positively or negatively with him must be faced by a philosopher intent on the reflective task of self-appropriation. I would extend this argument and make of psychic process in all its forms an element that must be articulated in a developing position on the human subject.[13] This means that the science of depth psychology will become a constituent part of transcendental method, which I understand as a developing and potentially comprehensive science of the human subject as subject. I propose that we attempt to understand the relationship between Lonergan's science of intentionality and the science of the psyche by investigating first what I would call the elemental sym-

bolic significance of Lonergan's work itself — that is, its
meaning for the evolution of energy into participation in a
third stage of meaning.[14]

2   Axial Humanity

The theme of axial humanity elaborated by Karl Jaspers and Lewis Mumford is familiar enough, I trust, that
the arguments offered by these two insightful and sensitive thinkers need no summary treatment here.[15] But an
interpretation of the significance attached by Lonergan to
this notion can serve to focus the present argument.[16] The
Greek discovery of mind in the period extending from
Homer to Aristotle issued in a new control of meaning in
terms of realism, science, and philosophy. The control of
meaning, moreover, determines an epoch in the history of
human consciousness, a stage of meaning; and a change
in the control of meaning represents an axis in this history.
The figure of Socrates in the Platonic dialogues is the classic
figura midwifing the theoretic control of meaning, that is,
the second stage of meaning. The classicist formulation of
this maieutic, however, is Aristotle's, and especially as he
formulates an ideal of science in his *Posterior Analytics*.
There, science is contrasted with opinion, necessity with
contingency, theory with praxis, wisdom with prudence;
and as the first members of each disjunction trumpet the
new control of meaning, so the second reflect merely the
best that the old could hope to aspire to. While the Aristotelian understanding of theory was to be overthrown by
modern science, the significant point for our purpose is
that the Aristotelian formulation splits both the universe
and the human mind that knows the universe. The Greek
discovery of mind, for all its necessity and achievement,
left in its wake a rift in subjectivity, a split consciousness.
Modern science was not prepared to heal this split until

its methodological gains were to be extended to the study of the subject.

The rift is even more dramatically understood, I believe, if we appreciate the fact that the theoretic control of meaning was a break, not just from opinion about contingency and from mere prudence in action, but more radically from mythic consciousness. We can sense the drama of the emergence of the second stage of meaning if we compare the ethos of the Aristotelian corpus with that of the Homeric epics. Then it becomes clear that what happened in Greece between 800 and 200 B.C.E. was the establishment of a new economy of interiority, the emergence of a new mode or form of being human. The drama was violent. It rephrased the interplay of spirit and psyche, intentionality and energy, the masculine and the feminine, theory and poetry. The drama is nowhere more poignantly reflected than in the tragedies written during this time. The Oedipus trilogy is a projection of its frequent failure and yet of the capacity for a new though tragic nobility even through the failure; and the Orestes trilogy is an acknowledgment that the drama might issue in a truce, but that the truce was on woman's terms — though woman was now Athena, wisdom, precisely because of the drama. These plays, I believe, could have been written only then, reflecting as they do the dream life of human subjects in an axial period of the history of consciousness.[17]

The control of meaning so classically expressing itself in the works of Aristotle is referred to by Lonergan as the beginning of the second stage of meaning in Western consciousness.[18] Lonergan has recounted how this epochal shift underwent a revolutionary transposition in modern science, where the disjunctions posited by Aristotle are negated. Lonergan, too, has provided us with an insight into the kind of insight that in Greece first emerged as a recurrent operation; with an understanding of the kind of understanding that there became our formal achievement; with an appropriation *in* the intellectual pattern of experience *of* the intellectual pattern that there differentiated itself from the dramatic, mythical, and biological patterns that both preceded it and remained to threaten it. But this insight into insight is itself the end of this cultural epoch in the history of human consciousness.

As insight in the intellectual pattern was axial, so too is insight into insight. The end of one stage of meaning is coincident with the beginning of another. The theoretic control of meaning has given way to another form of consciousness. Where intellectual history will place the beginning of the third stage of meaning is still uncertain. Was it in Descartes's affirmation of the apodicticity of subjectivity as the foundation of philosophy? In Kant's rendition of philosophy's questions as concerned with what the subject can know, what the subject ought to do, and what the subject can hope for? In Hegel's proclamation that the dialectical movement of *Geist* is both the absolute method of knowing and the immanent soul of its content? In Kierkegaard's midnight cry that the dialectic is the becoming of the individual? In the triumph of the therapeutic announced by Freud, developed further by Jung, and relativized by Otto Rank? My own position is that these occurrences are still potency for the new form. What has been building for some time is a movement toward the declaration on the part of subjectivity that it alone is the source of objectivity. And this breakthrough, as definitively systematized in the work of Lonergan, is an entrance into a new stage of meaning, an intellectual conversion, a new epoch in the history of consciousness, the formal beginning of a new series of ranges of schemes of recurrence in the world process whose immanent intelligibility is an emergent probability that becomes intelligent intelligibility in human consciousness. The new control of meaning, moreover, rests upon the critical recovery of what has gone before. The principal agents of the retrieval have, I believe, been Lonergan and Jung: the latter of the primordial control of meaning by the maternal imagination of humankind, and the former of her son, who long ago in Greece violently and perhaps a bit bizarrely but perhaps also miraculously severed the umbilical cord to the psyche — only at the gravest peril to himself — and who must now negotiate a reconciliation with the darkness of the imaginal womb.

Lonergan and Jung, then, both promote human consciousness into the new epoch. But they must be brought to bear on one another. They are *figurae* of the factors that have been warring for nearly 3000 years. They are opposites. Dialectic can resolve their contradictoriness, so that they join in a transcendental aesthetic that is approached by both of them from opposite quarters, an aesthetic that is to be understood as the culmination of reflective philosophy. The unity of the opposites is that condition of retrieved simplicity that Paul Ricoeur calls a second naivete.[19] The second stage of the control of meaning is thoroughly exhausted. It has no more resources. Theoretical intelligence has reached the end of the first half of its life, and the second now hangs in the balance. The alternatives are sharply placed in relief by Mumford: either a posthistoric humanity in which intelligence regresses to a programmed rigidity, or a world-cultural humanity dependent on intelligence finding its way to a second half of life by taking the necessary self-reflective turn to the center in order to discover itself.[20] Without this discovery, the history of a creative intelligence that promotes human life is finished. Intelligence will simply grow old, and not very gracefully.

I am affirming, then, that *our* time is axial, and I am concerned with its elemental symbolic significance. What

is *our* story? What are *we* dreaming? What story binds together Lonergan and Jung, insight and archetype, intentionality and desire, interlocking them in mutual
complementarity, and formulating what comes to expression in this interlocking? Might it be a story which reverses
the myth of the Tower of Babel? Despite their differences,
there is something about the work of Lonergan and Jung
which encourages such an interpretation. We have evidence
that such a story has already been dreamt, and I find the
dream and Jung's interpretation of it stirring. We are indebted to Jungian analyst Max Zeller for sharing it with
us. It goes as follows:

> A temple of vast dimensions was in the pro-
> cess of being built. As far as I could see —
> ahead, behind, right and left — there were in-
> credible numbers of people building on gigan-
> tic pillars. I, too, was building on a pillar. The
> whole building process was in its very begin-
> nings, but the foundation was already there,
> the rest of the building was starting to go up,
> and I and many others were working on it.[21]

Zeller was visited by this dream while in Zürich in
1949, trying to discover for himself a satisfactory answer to
the question of what he was doing as a Jungian analyst.
This dream occurred two nights before he was to leave
Zürich. Jung's interpretation of it speaks of a new religion.
What Zeller dreamt of is the temple that is being built in
our time, a temple whose foundations have already been
laid. 'We don't know the people,' said Jung, 'because, believe me, they build in India and China and in Russia and
all over the world.' Six hundred years will elapse, he added,
before the temple is built. But 'this new religion will come
together as far as we can see.'[22]

It is not accidental, as anyone familiar with dreams knows, that this particular dream occurred to one intent on the question which the dream provided images for answering. For the desire to know, Lonergan reminds us, can invade the very fabric of our dreams.[23] Nor is it accidental that the question to which the dream provided such images was intent on the meaning of the profession of Jungian analyst. For it is the symbolic function of universal energy become psychic, or of what Jung not too happily called the collective unconscious, that is the basis of the gathering of the dispersed peoples reflected in the dream. The great motifs of the human drama are transcultural. Jung's discovery is a contribution to the appropriation of this common humanity and thus to the reversal of the myth of the Tower of Babel. His contribution to the temple of the 'new religion' is foundational.[24]

So too, though, is Lonergan's contribution. For transcendental method and the collective unconscious or elemental symbolic function are quite germane to one another, as complementary as masculine and feminine, intentionality and psyche. Jung's discovery is as transcendental as Lonergan's, Lonergan's as collective or universal as Jung's. Transcendental method and the collective unconscious pertain, by definition, to universal humanity. They are constants of the human self, permanent features of all human subjectivity. Their discovery and articulation issues in a control of meaning for an increasingly planetized earth, in the epoch of what Mumford calls world-cultural humanity. Wherever there is human subjectivity, there is a constant elemental symbolic function with constant motifs as well as the capacity to release new symbolic reflectors of the economy of interiority under the dominance of a preconscious collaboration of imagination and intelligence searching for imaginal materials for conscious insight, reflection, and evaluation.[25] And so wherever there is human subjectivity, there is also experiencing of the data of sense and of consciousness; there are inquiry, insight, formulation, reflection, the commitment of affirmation, and the awful fact of existential responsibility. These givens, where articulated or objectified in self-appropriation, are the foundations of the temple. Their interlocking in the mode of self-appropriation is the commitment of the subject to the task of building the temple, to the story of our time.

The fuller structure of the universal human self, it would seem, can be known in heuristic fashion by integrating what Jung disclosed with what Lonergan uncovered, by interlocking archetype and insight, and by finding in this interlocking some resources of the symbolic function that Jung himself never rendered explicit. Let us accept this as a hypothesis, and let us put it to the test.

3   The Anthropos

Consciousness is the presence of the subject to himself or herself in all of the operations of which he or she is the subject: dreaming, sensing, perceiving, imagining, feeling, inquiring, understanding, reflecting, affirming, denying, evaluating, deliberating, deciding, acting. Consciousness is not knowledge. Knowledge is a matter of correct understanding. Consciousness is also and consequently not self-knowledge, which is a matter of the correct understanding of oneself. Nonetheless it is only conscious beings who perceive, question, understand, formulate, reflect, and affirm — who know. Consciousness is thus the necessary condition, though not the guarantee, of fully human knowledge. And consciousness conditions self-knowledge in yet another way, because it provides the very data that one must understand and affirm if one is to know oneself. Among these data are the operations of knowing and the states and direction of feeling. Moreover, as I may know without knowing what it is to know, so I may feel without knowing what I feel. Psychotherapy, like Lonergan's cognitional theory, in part renders known what was already conscious.

But, says Jung, in addition to consciousness there is the unconscious. I interpret the unconscious to be energy at its physical, chemical, and biological levels, opaque energy, in need of a higher integration by at least the sensitive consciousness of the psyche if it is to come into the light. The unconscious is energy in the dark, energy at a level prior to and surrounding the opening to the light that is found in sensitive consciousness. The unconscious is all energy that is not present to itself. In principle at least, the unconscious is all energy in the universe save that which becomes present to itself as psychic energy in animal and human consciousness. Proximately, it is neural-physiological process in the human organism. Remotely, it is the world.[26]

The universe, then, in which human consciousness finds itself is not static but in process; this process has given rise to successive higher integrations in the form of explanatory genera and species, unities and intelligibilities, laws that unify otherwise coincidental manifolds; and among these unities is human intelligence itself.[27] It may be, moreover, that the sciences arrange themselves in a pattern isomorphic to the process and its emergent forms. So Lonergan would argue that chemistry is an autonomous science from physics. The laws of physics are not abrogated in chemistry, feature in chemistry, but are sublated into a higher viewpoint containing other laws that systematize data that remain coincidental from the standpoint of physics. So too chemistry leaves unexplained certain phenomena in the universe of being, but not in such a way that its laws or those of physics are left behind or abrogated in the further laws known by the biological sciences. And there are data of sensitive consciousness that are purely coincidental from the standpoint of biology but that are unified in the insights of sensitive psychology, even though the laws of biology, chemistry, and physics are part of the complete scientific understanding of sensitive life. Finally, human being provides a manifold of data left unexplained by the science of sensitive consciousness. These are the data on men and women as selves and as concerned with their own self-constitution, and as knowers in whose intelligent activity the universe itself attains a higher systematization. Thus there are the data of consciousness: operations of inquiry, insight, reflection, judgment, evaluation, decision, love, and religion; the data on the difference between being intelligent and stupid, reasonable and silly, responsible and irresponsible, loving and selfish; and the data of self-constitution that give rise to the judgment that, within the limits provided by the givens known by other sciences, it is up to me which of these alternatives I will be. I will never understand such data by studying physics, chemistry, biology, or even sensitive psychology. To understand them, I must raise questions concerning the data of human consciousness. Such attention and inquiry will give rise to a science that accounts for data on human living that are left unexplained by other sciences. This science is a knowledge of the human subject as human subject. It is moving toward the full position on the human subject.

Now the unconscious in itself, as all energy that is not present to itself, would be known by the physical, chemical, and biological sciences. But the unconscious as known by depth psychology is not a matter of physics, nor of chemistry, nor of biology. It is this same reality, but as pertinent for human living, that is, as reaching a higher integration under the dominance of sensitive, intelligent, rational, and existential consciousness. Its pertinence discloses itself in the most rudimentary form of human consciousness, the dream. In the dream, the universe known by physics, chemistry, and biology — the unconscious universe — reaches toward an ulterior finality. It initiates something of an experiment with human consciousness, an entrance into subjectivity. In the dream as in sensitive waking consciousness, the energy of the cosmos becomes psychic energy. The psyche, Jung said, is at bottom world.[28] But as psyche it is world for itself, energy rudimentarily transparent to itself, the universe as operator of its own development, as posing a question to the human subject endowed with the capacity of being not merely present to himself or herself, but of being so in intelligence, in reasonableness, in responsibility, in erotic and agapic love. The universe can become love in human consciousness, and its entrance into this capacity, its expression of this finality, occurs in the dream. The universe is at the mercy here of the human subject, for everything depends on what one does with one's dreams. I can be completely oblivious of them, as most white Westerners are. I can reject them as insignificant. I can interpret them naively or superstitiously or projectively. Or I can live the dream forward intelligently, truthfully, deliberately, erotically, agapically. Then the universe is promoted to a higher integration, to a fuller being. But if the dream is forgotten or rejected, ridiculed or denied, an evolutionary blind alley or false start or even complete breakdown and collapse has been suffered. The universe depends on the subject to promote its upwardly but indeterminately directed dynamism, its finality. Now that it has issued in human consciousness, its future depends on human consciousness: the world depends on the subject for its higher integration, for the determination of its direction, the definition of its finality, and the execution of its desire.

Such a perspective is related to Lonergan's and to Jung's. It is somewhat different, for Lonergan is not primarily concerned with understanding the psyche, and Jung is quite seriously deficient on a notion of human intentionality. My position heuristically integrates Jung's incredible familiarity with the human psyche with Lonergan's masterful treatment of intentionality. The position, basically stated, is that the psyche promotes the universe to the fuller being it will find in human knowledge and action. That the position is consistent with Lonergan's should be clear to one familiar with his notion of emergent probability. That it shares some features with Jung's account is evident in two directions: it includes a notion of the unconscious broad enough to embrace both the personal and the crosscultural or collective dimensions of psychic energy insisted on by Jung, and it orients everything toward consciousness as Jung himself did. But Lonergan's notion of intentional consciousness clarifies and discriminates this orientation well beyond Jung's achievement.

4   The Subject and Symbols

The human subject, as far as we know, is the last of the unities or aggregates to emerge in the world process known in part by physics, chemistry, biology, and sensitive psychology. The subject is characterized by conscious capacities not found in other species of conscious beings, by capacities for questioning, insight, explanatory understanding, affirmation of truth, moral commitment, responsible decision, freely adopted postures of eros and agape, reverential worship. Human success or failure depends on the recurrence or failure of recurrence of these operations that are the subject's unique capacity. In this sense, world process continues its upwardly directed dynamism in the operations of human subjectivity. The subject continues the process of the emergence of the world to new forms, unities, intelligibilities: those of human conscious living. Primary among them are human cultures, which are, properly speaking, not 'things'[29] but processes of self-constitution on a social scale.

Our analysis has argued that the point of contact between the unconscious energy of prehuman cosmic process and the intelligent intelligibility of human subjectivity is to be located in psychic energy. Psychic energy finds expression in the elemental symbols of our dreams. A symbol, then, is the place of the conscious meeting of past and future, origin and destiny, limitation and finality. Symbols synthesize into a tense unity the texture of human time, indeed of the primordial time that constitutes the possibility of all human immediacy and institutes the structure of this immediacy. Symbols are the rich texture in which nature and freedom, matter and spirit commingle. They are the products of transcendental imagination in its function of instituting primordial human time, where the future beckons the having been into presence, thus constituting the present.[30] The present is the subject's temporality as a tense unity of project and possibility. The dream symbol is what evokes, indeed even creates, this unity, or in its absence calls one back to it. Project is future and spirit, finality and transcendence, while possibility is past and matter, origin and limitation. Project is consciousness, possibility the unconscious. Project is anticipation, possibility is memory. Psychic energy is their meeting ground. The dream proposes both to make of the possible a project, and to insure that the project remains possible.

No other project than one that is possible, no other future than that which has a past, no other destiny than that which has an origin, no other human spirit than that in synchronicity with matter prevails. All other projects are folly, alienation, and destructiveness. The intentionality of an incarnate spirit thus depends upon psychic energy's symbolic productions as defensive circles safe-guarding its own authenticity. Intentionality split from psyche represents the schizoid condition of onesided hy-pertrophy to which the human subject is susceptible. It is a displacement of the tension of limitation and transcen-dence in favor of transcendence. Perhaps there is no dis-ease more contagious among humanly conscious animals than this splitness, no condition more precarious than the self-transcendent dynamism of spiritual intentionality in union with a human body.[31] Intentionality and the body are genuine opposites, as opposite as future and past, spirit and matter, consciousness and the unconscious, transcen-dence and limitation. The integration occurs through ne-gotiating the symbolic process of the psyche's dreams.[32]

Dreaming consciousness, then, the place where the universe expresses its capacity to become agape, provides the conditions for the subject becoming one. The dream founds our tense conscious unity, and its process intends our wholeness, the integrity of our project, which consists in our synchronicity with a universe that transcends us and in our harmony with the absolutely transcendent ground of this universe. The task of that intentional con-sciousness which extends upward beyond the dream through attentiveness, intelligence, reasonableness, respon-sibility, and love is to live the dream forward, to make of a possibility a project while guaranteeing that all projects are indeed possible, to make of matter spirit while incar-nating spirit in matter, to make of the universe conscious finality, to make of the past a story with a future. Such living and making are what Jung called synchronicity in human experience.[33] Any other living and making is a more or less acute form of alienation.

5   **Contemplation**

Alienation conditions human suicide, which is the ultimate expression of evolutionary breakdown. But synchronistic living and making, where alienation is transcended, are by no means a simple matter of spontaneity and uninhibited immediacy. For the world in which we live is mediated to us by meaning, and it is really the conscious operations of meaning to which we are immediate. But meaning can be true or false, whole or partial, genuine or distorted, and immediacy to operations of false, partial, or distorted meaning by no means transcends alienation. Synchronistic living and making, genuine just-soness, depends on the discrimination of mind and heart, thought and feeling, spirit and psyche, that is the objective of the third stage of meaning. It is a disciplined spontaneity, a tutored immediacy, a second naivete.[34] The operator of such discipline is the releasement (*Gelassenheit*) that Heidegger calls *Denken*,[35] Lonergan attentiveness. Let us call it contemplation. Contemplation alone will save the world from suicide.

But let us focus, not on survival but on artistic living, aesthetics, pattern, and totality. Then we move beyond the drama constituted by final alienation to the role of contemplation in the aesthetic production of the dramatic form of conscious living. The body provides the content to which spirit gives form. It does so in our dreams. The content is the tense unity of possibility and project, past and future, limitation and transcendence. The future as such has no content until it becomes the present, and this it does only by the body's living its way into it. But, as we know, there are some lives which can only be designated formless. The present is present by content, and thus cannot be without materials. But it can be formless, and formlessness is the consequence of the subject's cognitive and existential ignorance or neglect of the content. Content there is, for there has been the past, but form there is not, for the subject does not know or does not want to know what the past has been. One tells no story, nor does one create one. Not knowing the past, one is ignorant of possibility. Rejecting the past, one refuses possibility. And without possibility one creates no project, knows no future. Life without project is formless, a *massa confusa*, a *prima materia*.

One begins to know what has been by listening to it. When we listen to the past, matter becomes conscious. In our dreams we are forced to listen. We have no choice until we awake. Then, of course, we are conscripted on all sides by voices claiming our powers of listening, and so we forget what the universe uttered when the body spoke through the psyche to intentionality. We listen, and all we hear is noise. It makes no sense, for we have forgotten the code which would tell us what the noise means. And so we go about our daily business, create futile projects with no possibility, project futures with no past, divorce consciousness from the emergent process of the universe. And we have the temerity to proclaim, as one impossible project succeeds another's collapse, that it is the world that is absurd. The only absurd element in the universe is intelligent consciousness that has forgotten what intelligence is and where it belongs in the universe, a consciousness that constitutes long-range or short-range projects that are impossible from the outset, and futures into which there is no body to move, a consciousness that displaces the tension of limitation and transcendence in either direction or that, in manic-depressive fashion, oscillates from one displacement to its opposite. Intelligence is the capacity to respond to the universe in my self-constitution and in the constitution of the human world. Any contrary exercise of intelligence is really quite stupid. But if I have forgotten to listen to the universe, my intelligence is no response, but a bitter and resentful monodrama.

The contemplative spirit retrieves and heals memory, and in so doing projects a possible future into which a body can move. Contemplatives, synchronistic people, alone project a destiny commensurate with their origin and move toward that destiny as conscious beings. The path between origin and destiny is narrow, not straight but winding, and daily. Only a heart like a stream of water can keep to it, follow it to its end, even skip and laugh and dance along the way. And to come to this heart is the discipline of listening. The subject who does not listen in *Gelassenheit*, releasement, attentiveness, to psyche is from the beginning inauthentic consciousness, and will never be truly intelligent, reasonable, and responsible. The first of Lonergan's transcendental precepts[36] calls for attentiveness. It is the imperative least elucidated by Lonergan. Its other name is contemplation, its activity receptivity, its prime data dreams, and its function the provision of the possibility without which the projects of intelligence, reason, and decision are folly and degradation.

6 The Dimensions of Elemental Symbols

From an existential point of view, there would seem to be seven kinds of dreams. I would consider the following list a set of ideal types,[37] classifying different ways in which underlying neural manifolds are integrated by the psychic representation granted them in dreams.

There are, then, (1) dreams that merely represent physiological disturbance or satisfaction. These dreams usually occur when one is in the deepest sleep; they are thus seldom subject to recall, and are for all practical purposes devoid of any existential or dramatic significance.

The other six varieties of dreams, however, present materials for the shaping of the project of one's life.

There are two instances of existential dreams where the figures and scenes are personal, that is, taken from the acquaintances and localities one is familiar with in one's waking existence, and where the theme relates directly to current events in one's existential living or to past events that have not yet been satisfactorily appropriated. But these dreams do not relate these events to themes of more universal significance. One of these instances of personal existential dreams tends to be fairly straightforward and almost literal (2), the other symbolic (3). Both literal and symbolic personal dreams indicate real existential possibilities or even demands.

Symbolic personal dreams are moving in the direction of archetypal significance, but what characterizes a dream as archetypal (4) is that the figures and scenes, whether familiar or strange, are constituted into themes that reflect universal human development and decline and that do so in a manner permeated with an aura of mystery. Archetypal figures, scenes, and themes are contained and defined by nature. Both personal and archetypal dream symbols are imitative analogues of nature. A maternal symbol, for example, means, not one's own mother, but the life-giving or destructive powers of nature. But as archetypal, the symbol is set into a context of reenactment of fundamental themes endemic to a human being as a natural entity. The process of one's existential living receives a mythical significance in archetypal dreams.

Beyond the archetypal dimension of symbolism, there is an anagogic significance. Anagogic dreams (5) set the symbols they employ in a context of transnatural relatedness. Their meaning is supernatural, more ineffable than archetypal meaning. Nature is contained in and transformed by such symbols.

Dreams may be not only existential interpreters of one's concrete situation, however, but either prophetic of (6) or synchronistic with (7) outer events. Prophetic dreams may be either literal or symbolic, and the symbolism may be personal, archetypal, or anagogic. Prophetic dreams foretell an event that will occur in the external drama of human life. Synchronistic dreams, on the other hand, which again may be either literal or symbolic, report an external event that is occurring at the same time as it is being dreamt.

The three varieties of symbolism — personal, archetypal, and anagogic — call for further comment. Symbols become archetypal in proportion to the extent that they reflect, not personal object relations, but universal *imago* relations whose specificity in any given case depends on the personal object relations they imitate. Thus, for example, a maternal symbol in a dream is archetypal when it means, not the personal mother, but the forces of nature in their life-giving or destructive quality, and when this *imago* relation is endowed with a universal natural significance that is experienced in a deeply emotional way. But whether the maternal symbol will give life or will destroy depends on one's negotiation of the personal mother. This is the significance of Jung's unjustly maligned notion of the collective unconscious. It may be that this term of Jung's contributes to misunderstanding, making us think of some 'already down there now real' to be known by looking down. But there has perhaps been no more valuable scientific psychological hypothesis advanced in the brief history of depth psychology than this notion of the collective unconscious, however much it may need to be redeemed from Jung's romanticism and shoddy thinking. Its significance is reflected in Max Zeller's dream; it provides the potential for reversing the Tower of Babel myth. It is the instrument of crosscultural communication, the psychic basis of common humanity.

What both personal and archetypal dream symbols reveal is the unfolding of dramatic artistry. They present to intentional waking consciousness the images needed for insight, reflection, and evaluation, in the service of making a work of art out of one's living. The relation of dreams to the task of dramatic artistry is a matter not yet adequately nuanced by any depth psychologist, including Jung. My typology starts with Jung's articulation as a given, and with his correction of Freud as an advance.[38] But I move beyond Jung by locating his sensitivity to the *mundus imaginalis* within a context defined in part by our previously stated position on the human subject or *anthropos*.

Thus, in fundamental harmony with Jung, I find that the symbols of our dreams are unusually sensitive and trustworthy in their reporting of how it stands between my conscious intentionality and the complex of forces which constitute nonconscious matter, between project and possibility, task and aboriginal vocation. Existential dreams are both integrators and operators of this economy. They are neither pure reflections of solely physiological process, as dreams of the night may be and often are, nor are they merely the uncritical establishers of conscious task and project. But all depends on what intentional consciousness does with them, and consciousness is free within limits to do anything it chooses. What it needs to do is to negotiate the dream as a significant datum of consciousness in its own right, as a reflector of the economy that obtains or could obtain between project and possibility, transcendence and limitation. Dreams are the language of energy become psychic in a subject of intelligent, reasonable, responsible, erotic, and agapic activity. They are to be sublated by intelligent, truthful, responsible, and loving consciousness and embodied in the world through decision in their regard. They are to be listened to by waking intentional consciousness. They are part of one's life, if one is visited by them. They are the data of the *mundus imaginalis*, which, as a domain that can be intelligently grasped and reasonably affirmed, constitutes a sphere of being.[39] We are responsible for our existential dreams. They are to be understood, affirmed, and decisively negotiated by our critical consciousness. They are visited upon our capacity for understanding, truth, and decision.

What, then, constitutes a dream as archetypal is the extent to which it reflects and affects one as *anthropos* emergent from nature and embedded within nature. Archetypal dreams, which are the stuff of myth, employ symbols that are taken from nature and imitate nature. The most archetypal dreams of all are integrators and operators of what is going forward in the natural development or evolution of the economy of subjectivity. We think here of the Greek tragedies that were composed at the time of the emergence of the second stage of meaning, or of Max Zeller's dream signaling the emergence of the third stage. Dreams which blend archetypal and personal elements reflect one's personal involvement in this evolution.

The evolution of consciousness may be understood as a creative development from below upwards, in continuity and conformity with the emergent probability that is the immanent intelligibility of world process. But in addition to a creative vector from below upwards in individual lives and in history, there is a healing movement from above downwards,[40] a movement that begins with the complex mediation of divine love with the existential intention of value and that proceeds from religious and moral conversion to the healing of cognitive operations that Lonergan calls intellectual conversion.[41] The necessary correction on Jung of which mention was made earlier is possible within the framework of Lonergan's affirmation of the complementarity of healing and creating. Thus, the conversion process from above downwards eventually will

bring one's intentional orientation into contact with the
psychic energy in which the upwardly but indeterminately
directed dynamism that Lonergan calls finality first becomes conscious. This contact becomes a correspondence
of synchronicity through a fourth conversion that I have
elsewhere called psychic conversion. But this correspondence is effectively realized only through the overcoming
of bias in all its forms. Then the symbolic operators of
psychic development and the questions for meaning, truth,
and value that are the operators of intentional development will function together in the promotion of a single
creative vector of subjective development from below upwards. The healing of consciousness to the point of realizing a therapeutically tutored attentiveness to the symbolic
deliverances of psychic energy thus not only complements
the creativity of the psyche and of intentionality but even
releases the creative process itself by making it possible
that the symbolic images of psychic process can be sublated
by the successive levels of conscious intentionality.

As we have seen, Jung discovered that what occurs
in the transformation of energic compositions and distributions involves a movement from object relations to *imago*
relations. What was once an object of one's energic
reachings — for example, the personal mother — becomes,
if successfully negotiated as one moves from childhood
through youth into middle life, a symbol of the life that
lies ahead, an *imago* that gives one the nourishing energy
to move forward in the creation of one's work of dramatic
art. The energy once invested in an object is now concentrated in a symbol, which transforms the original investment so as to promote one's movement into an adult future. The movement from object relations to *imago* relations is strictly synchronized with the real status of the
object in one's life. If one has not successfully negotiated
an object relation, the *imago* that imitates the object will

not be helpful but hostile, even destructive. But the important point for our present heuristic analysis is that it is the transformation from object relations to *imago* relations that accounts not only for personal symbols but also for archetypal symbols. In either case, psychic energy has been channeled into a symbolic analogue of its natural object, an analogue that imitates the object and thereby gains for a new purpose the energy once invested in the object.

What Jung did not grasp, however, is that, while the transformation from personal object relations to personal and archetypal *imago* relations corresponds to the creative development from below upwards, there is another transformation of and by symbols that harmonizes with the therapeutic movement from above downwards. When this healing is conversion, and so when it begins with the gift of divine love at the height of consciousness, the dimension of the symbolic that corresponds to it and reflects it is to be distinguished from the archetypal. For the symbols that are integrators and operators of this development, while they are taken from nature, do not imitate nature as do archetypal symbols, but point to, intimate, even promote the transformation of nature itself into a new creation. Such symbols are anagogic. They can be understood only from a theological point of view, for which the objective of individual and historical development is transcendent and the course of one's personal development is radically determined by one's participation in the divinely originated solution to the problem of evil.[42] Because Jung lacked an adequate understanding of intentionality, he fared poorly in treating the problem of evil and perhaps never came to understand the central symbols of the Christian tradition in their anagogic, not archetypal, significance. The unrestricted spontaneity of our desire for intelligibility, the unconditioned, and the good is a transcendent exigence, a natural desire to see God.[43] To it there correspond symbols through which the divinely originated solution to the problem of evil penetrates to the sensitive level of human living. There is a transformation of psychic energy under the influence of the supernatural or transcendent conjugate forms or habits of faith and hope and charity.[44] Through it psychic energy enters a dimension not clearly specified by Jung, the anagogic dimension in which symbols are released that match the unrestricted intentionality of human intelligence, reflection, and deliberation. Anagogic symbols simultaneously reflect and give the conversion of human sensitive consciousness to participation in the divinely originated solution to the problem of evil. They correspond to what Lonergan calls 'the image that symbolizes man's orientation into the known unknown.'[45] Lonergan explains their function: 'Since faith gives more truth than understanding comprehends, since hope reinforces the detached, disinterested, unrestricted desire to know, man's sensitivity needs symbols that unlock its transforming dynamism and bring it into harmony with the vast but impalpable pressures of the pure desire, of hope, and of self-sacrificing charity.'[46] These symbols make of the divinely originated solution 'a mystery that is at once symbol of the uncomprehended and sign of what is grasped and psychic force that sweeps living human bodies, linked in charity, to the joyful, courageous, wholehearted, yet intelligently controlled performance of the tasks set by a world order in which the problem of evil is not suppressed but transcended.'[47] It is in such fashion that the figure of Christ has functioned symbolically for the Christian psyche.[48] It is in such fashion, likewise, that the annals of all the major world religions record experiences of sensitive spontaneity under the transforming influence of the divine solution. There is an intelligibility to the anagogic that is generically different from that of the archetype. Jung's confusion was to collapse the anagogic into the archetypal.

The appropriate alternative is to understand the anagogic as the final hermeneutic determinant of the meaning and value of all other symbolic deliverances, including archetypal symbols.

Notes

[1] On the third stage of meaning, see Bernard Lonergan, *Method in Theology* (see above, chapter 1, note 3) 93-96.

[2] I understand all emergent process in the universe, including the emergence, consolidation, and survival of new forms of consciousness, according to Lonergan's understanding of emergent probability. Thus occurrences of a potentially new kind remain purely coincidental until systematized by an emergent form at the new level. In the case of consciousness, a new stage of meaning remains potential until a systematization has emerged that can consolidate an otherwise purely coincidental manifold of occurrences. The occurrences that are potentially a third stage of meaning are conscious human operations of inquiry and understanding, reflection and judgment, that take as their object the human subject in his or her subjectivity. Thus, for example, the various modern philosophies involved in the turn to the subject and the psychologies that seek a scientific understanding of the energic compositions and distributions of affectivity are instances of occurrences that potentially can be systematized into a new series of ranges of schemes of recurrence in cognitive and existential praxis, into a new control of meaning whose basic terms and relations are located in interiorly differentiated consciousness. My understanding of the third stage of meaning thus already shows the influence of Lonergan's mediation of conscious intentionality within world process. On emergent probability as immanent intelligibility of world process, see Bernard Lonergan, *Insight* (see above, chapter 1, note 37) 115-28/138-51. For its extension to conscious human operations, ibid. 209-11/234-37. For its metaphysical constitution, ibid., chapter 15. On the present as kairos for the emergence of the third stage, ibid. 386/411.

[3] The term 'postcritical' needs some clarification. I use it to refer to any language that is sufficiently informed by the maieutic of a

third-stage control of meaning that, in the limit, it is no longer an articulation of a problematic but a formulation on the basis of an understanding of human interiority that has already been grasped as virtually unconditioned. Complete self-transparency is obviously not possible. But incremental judgments of fact about oneself are, and a sufficient number of these produces a differentiation in the realm of interiority.

4 See, for example, Robert Doran, 'Dramatic Artistry in the Third Stage of Meaning' (see above, chapter 7). On positions and counterpositions, see Lonergan, *Insight* 387-88/413. On symbols and positions-counterpositions, ibid. 531-49/554-72.

5 See ibid. 442-51/467-76; 472-75/497-99.

6 See ibid. 469/494. On systems as simultaneously integrators and operators of development, see ibid. 464-65/489-91.

7 Jung perhaps came closest to so formulating the process and objective of individuation in a 1929 essay, 'Commentary on "The Secret of the Golden Flower" (see above, chapter 5, note 25). Ironically, the Chinese alchemical text that Jung explores in this essay sparked an interest in alchemy that was to lead him to an increasingly less comprehensive account of human development, until at the end we find a quite different formulation involving a displacement of the tension of limitation and transcendence in favor of psychic energy as integrator, at the expense of its function as operator in conjunction with intentionality. What Lonergan enables us to understand is that psychic wholeness is a byproduct of authentic intentionality. Wholeness, then, is to be understood in terms of self-transcendence, not in terms of self-containment. Such a qualification, of course, will mean a quite extensive refinement of the adequacy of mandala symbols as par excellence symbols of individuated totality. They reflect psychic energy as integrator, but are not the best symbols of psychic energy as operator of development. On human intentionality as spirituality, see Lonergan, *Insight* 514-20/538-43.

8 Paul Ricoeur, *Freud and Philosophy* (see above, chapter 1, note 7) 5-7.

9 Lonergan, *Method in Theology* 81-85, 272.

10 Lonergan, *Insight* 181-89/204-12.

11 Lonergan, *Insight* 348-50/372-75; 3-4/27-29.

12 Lonergan, *Method in Theology* 34-35.

13 I have specified the precise locus of the insertion of this concern into a developing position on the subject in the first chapter of *Subject and Psyche* (see above, chapter 2, note 21). Chapter 3 of the same book relates my proposal to the results of Ricoeur's study of Freud.

14 Already I am presupposing that Jung's insight into various autonomous compositions and distributions of psychic energy is more satisfactory than the Freudian reductionistic theory of libido. But, as we shall see, Jung's insight must itself be expanded beyond archetypal symbols, if the genuineness of the subject is to be promoted by depth-psychological analysis. I understand the promotion of genuineness as the immanent intelligibility normative of any truly therapeutic process. On genuineness, see Lonergan, *Insight* 475-79/499-502.

15 See Karl Jaspers, *The Origin and Goal of History*, trans. Michael Bullock (New Haven: Yale, 1953) 1-21 and passim; and Lewis Mumford, *The Transformations of Man* (New York: Harper Torchbooks, 1956) 57-80.

16 Bernard Lonergan, 'Dimensions of Meaning' (see above, chapter 2, note 7).

17 I am somewhat influenced in my interpretation by Erich Neumann, *The Origins and History of Consciousness* (see above, chapter 1, note 28).

18 Lonergan, *Method in Theology* 93-96.

19 See Ricoeur, *Freud and Philosophy* 496.

20 See Mumford, *The Transformations of Man*, chapters 7 and 8. The expressions 'first and second half of life' are reflections writ large of Jung's understanding of individuation. See C.G. Jung, 'The Stages of Life,' in *The Structure and Dynamics of the Psyche* (see above, chapter 2, note 14) 387-403.

21 Max Zeller, 'The Task of the Analyst' (see above, chapter 4, note 17) 75.

22 Ibid. The reference to six hundred years is a striking reminder of Lonergan's insistence on the detachment that must permeate a specialization of human consciousness that thinks on the level of history. See *Insight* 238-42/263-67.

23 Lonergan, *Insight* 4/28.

24 I suggest that we interpret Jung's expression 'new religion' to mean a community of meaning founded on the self-appropriation of the resources of subjectivity that is the basis of the new stage of meaning. Jung's contribution to this mediation has, of course, profound religious significance, but perhaps not exactly the significance that Jung's sometimes inflated expressions would claim.

25 See Lonergan, *Insight* 187-206/210-31.

26 This is a more precise use of the terms 'consciousness' and 'the unconscious' than is found in Jung's work, where 'consciousness' means the ego and where 'the unconscious' includes not only opaque energy but also what, on my analysis and following Lonergan, is better viewed as what is conscious but not objectified. See Lonergan, *Method in Theology* 34, note 5.

27 See Lonergan, *Insight* 254-57/280-83; 262-67/287-92; 437-42/463-69.

28 C.G. Jung, 'The Psychology of the Child Archetype,' in *The Archetypes and the Collective Unconscious* (see above, chapter 3, note 40) 173.

29 On the notion of the thing, see Lonergan, *Insight*, chapter 8. On intelligent emergent probability, see ibid. 209-11/234-37.

30 See Martin Heidegger, *Kant and the Problem of Metaphysics* (see above, chapter 2, note 60).

31 See Ernest Becker, *The Denial of Death* (see above, chapter 4, note 4).

32 No fundamental ontology which does not treat the psyche's role in constituting our conscious unity can provide an adequate philo-

sophical anthropology. Perhaps no philosopher has come closer to realizing this than Martin Heidegger, were it not for the twofold fact that (1) Heidegger does not acknowledge that the transcendental imagination constituting *Dasein*'s temporality as Being-in-the world is the psyche; and (2) the tension of the opposites is so acute precisely because the notion of being that is *Dasein* is *not* bounded by the horizon of time established by the sensitive psyche. See Lonergan, *Insight* 379-80/403-404; 514-20/538-43.

33 See C.G. Jung, 'Synchronicity: An Acausal Connecting Principle,' in *The Structure and Dynamics of the Psyche* 417-519.

34 See Ricoeur, *Freud and Philosophy* 496.

35 See Martin Heidegger, *Discourse on Thinking*, trans. John M. Anderson and E. Hans Freund (New York: Harper and Row, 1966) and *What is Called Thinking?* trans. Fred D. Wieck and J. Glenn Gray (New York: Harper and Row, 1968).

36 See Lonergan, *Method in Theology*, chapter 1.

37 'The ideal-type ... is not a description of reality or a hypothesis about reality. It is a theoretical construct in which possible events are intelligibly related to constitute an internally coherent system. Its utility is both heuristic and expository, that is, it can be useful inasmuch as it suggests and helps formulate hypotheses and, again, when a concrete situation approximates to the theoretical construct, it can guide an analysis of the situation and promote a clear understanding of it.' Ibid. 227.

38 Jung's correction of Freud is fundamentally over the notion of psychic energy. I have treated it as such in 'Dramatic Artistry in the Third Stage of Meaning' (see above, chapter 7).

39 On spheres of being, see Bernard Lonergan, '*Insight* Revisited' (see above, chapter 2, note 56) 274.

40 See Bernard Lonergan, 'Healing and Creating in History' (see above, chapter 6, note 88).

41 On religious, moral, and intellectual conversion, see Lonergan, *Method in Theology* 237-44.

⁴² On the problem of evil and a divinely originated solution that is continuous with world process, see Lonergan, *Insight*, chapter 20.

⁴³ See Lonergan, *Method in Theology* 84-85; see also 'The Natural Desire to See God,' in *Collection* 81-91.

⁴⁴ See Lonergan, *Insight* 696-703/718-25.

⁴⁵ Ibid. 723/744.

⁴⁶ Ibid.

⁴⁷ Ibid. 723-24/745.

⁴⁸ See Sebastian Moore, *The Crucified Jesus Is No Stranger* (New York: Seabury Press, 1977).

9 Aesthetic Subjectivity and Generalized Empirical Method

The generalized empirical method proposed by Bernard Lonergan effects a mediation through self-appropriation of the subject's intelligent, reasonable, and responsible intentionality. More precisely, the work of Lonergan is a quite thorough maieutic of intelligent and reasonable consciousness, of what Lonergan would call the second and third levels of conscious intentionality,[1] and a significant pointer to the other levels. The developing articulation of the dynamics of the fourth level, the level of responsible or existential consciousness, is currently a principal concern of many of Lonergan's students. What constitutes self-appropriation of the level of consciousness concerned with evaluation, deliberation, decision, and action? The present paper proposes to advance discussion of this issue.

The core of my argument is to the effect that the self-appropriation of existential subjectivity depends on a maieutic of consciousness distinct from but complementary to that proposed by Lonergan, a second mediation of the subject as subject, a psychic mediation of one's dramatic artistry, of the aesthetic subjectivity whose concern is to make a work of art out of one's living.[2]

The aesthetic and dramatic dimension of our being attends the operations which occur at all levels of conscious intentionality. There is a drama not only to one's self-constitution as existential subject and to one's constitution of the world through decisive action but also to one's pursuit of intelligibility and truth.[3] The drama is more than adverted to in Lonergan's repeated references in *Insight* to the struggle between the desire to know and the flight from understanding.[4] The mediation I am proposing, then, is an objectification of the whole of conscious intentionality in its dramatic dimension. Nevertheless, its special importance emerges only when one asks whether there is an access to the data of interiority that will allow self-appropriation at the level of existential subjectivity to be as complete, as thorough, and as explanatory as that which Lonergan renders possible at the levels of intelligent and reasonable subjectivity. Thus it is not without reason that Lonergan's discussion of feelings[5] occurs, not when he is explicating our cognitive operations, even though these too are permeated by affectivity, but when he is articulating his notion of the human good, of the concern for value that is the distinctive mark of the fourth, existential level of consciousness.

It will be obvious from my argument that I believe that the archetypal psychology of C.G. Jung contains the seeds of a potential contribution to the aesthetic mediation that is the focus of my concern. But Jung proves useful only as a consequence of a dialectical encounter between his phenomenology of individuation and Lonergan's heuristic account of human development.[6] As it stands, without such a dialectic, Jung's project is mired in the quicksands of romanticism, in a short-circuiting of the finality of the subject due to an inadequate treatment of the problem of evil. But to discover the relation of the self-transcendence of intentionality to the psyche is to obviate the difficulties raised by Jung, whose extraordinary familiarity with the psyche was not matched by an appreciation of the self-transcendent dynamism of the imperatives of authentic consciousness.[7]

I   Aesthetics and the Existential Subject

In this section I propose to argue from Lonergan's analysis of the role of feelings at the fourth level of consciousness and from his discussion of the relationship of symbols to feelings, first, that aesthetic subjectivity in the form of dramatic artistry is the psychic correlative of moral and religious intentionality (1.1); second, that aesthetics is the basis of ethics (1.2); third, that aesthetic or dramatic self-appropriation is the key to self-appropriation at the fourth level (1.2); and fourth, that these three conclusions ground a methodological affirmation of a psychic conversion through which aesthetic self-appropriation becomes possible (1.2).

1.1   Aesthetic Subjectivity and Moral and Religious Intentionality

The existential subject, then, is the subject as evaluating, deliberating, deciding, acting, and in one's actions constituting the world and oneself. Existential consciousness is a level of consciousness distinct from but sublating the three levels of consciousness constitutive of human knowing. It is consciousness as concerned with the good, with value, with the discrimination of what is truly worth while from what is only apparently good.

The discussion of the existential subject as a notion quite distinct form the cognitional subject is a relatively recent development in Lonergan's thought. It reflects the emergence of a notion of the human good as distinct from the notions of the intelligent and the reasonable. Lonergan acknowledges this development and the attendant recognition of the role of feelings in existential subjectivity.

In *Insight* the good was the intelligent and the
reasonable. In *Method* the good is a distinct
notion. It is intended in questions for deliberation. Is this worthwhile? Is it truly or only
apparently good? It is aspired to in the intentional response of feeling to values. It is known
in judgments of value made by a virtuous or
authentic person with a good conscience. It is
brought about by deciding and living up to
one's decisions. Just as intelligence sublates
sense, just as reasonableness sublates intelligence, so deliberation sublates and thereby
unifies knowing and feeling.[8]

Feelings, then, and with them the whole of the psyche,
are no longer integrated by knowledge, as in *Insight*, but
by self-constituting existential subjectivity. In *Insight*, the
psyche 'reaches the wealth and fullness of its apprehensions
and responses under the higher integration of human
intelligence.'[9] In *Method in Theology*, both human
intelligence and the psyche are sublated and unified by
the deliberations of the existential subject, for affective
apprehensions of potential values mediate between cognitive judgments of fact and existential judgments of value.
The new notion of the good, then, involves a relocation of
the significance of the psyche for generalized empirical
method.

The import of this relocation becomes more pronounced when we consider the relationship of symbols to
the feelings in which values are first apprehended. 'A symbol is an image of a real or imaginary object that evokes a
feeling or is evoked by a feeling.'[10] One's affective capacities, dispositions, and habits 'can be specified by the symbols that awaken determinate affects and, inversely, by the
affects that evoke determinate symbols.'[11] Thus 'affective

development, or aberration, involves a transvaluation and transformation of symbols. What before was moving no longer moves; what before did not move now is moving. So the symbols themselves change to express the new affective capacities and dispositions.'[12] And affective capacities and dispositions, as we have seen, initiate one's existential response to potential values and satisfactions. They are the effective orientation of one's being.[13]

The transformation and transvaluation of symbols, then, goes hand in hand with one's affective development. But it can be understood only when one realizes that symbols follow other laws than those of rational discourse.[14] The function of symbols is to meet a need for internal communication that rational procedures cannot satisfy.[15] The elemental, pre-objectified meaning of symbols finds its proper context in this process of internal communication. The interpretation of the symbol thus has to appeal to this context and to its associated images and feelings.[16]

Such an interpretation of symbols and of their relation to feelings and to the intention of value is obviously significant for one's evaluation of the significance of dreams. Thus Lonergan manifests a clear sympathy for those schools of dream interpretation that think of the dream 'not as the twilight of life, but as its dawn, the beginning of the transition from impersonal existence to presence in the world, to constitution of one's self in one's world.'[17] Later I shall argue for the privileged position of the dream in the task of internal communication that is the proper role of symbols for human consciousness. For the moment, though, I wish simply to correlate what I mean by aesthetic subjectivity with the dimension of our being marked by the reciprocal influence of symbols and feelings in our initial response to values. Aesthetic subjectivity is the psychic correlative of our intentional existential orientation in the world mediated by meaning.[18] Already it would ap-

pear that a disciplined exploration of one's psychic being
would complement intentionality analysis and would mediate one's self-appropriation especially of the existential
level of one's being. Through such an exploration, one
would be investigating the aesthetic or dramatic dimension of one's moral and religious responses. There must be
a psychological contribution to the position on the subject, one that would aid especially moral and religious self-
appropriation and that would facilitate the sublation of an
intellectually self-appropriating consciousness by moral and
religious subjectivity.[19] Such a mediation would contribute to the articulation of what Lonergan calls foundational
reality,[20] that is, to the basic explanatory and dialectical
position on the subject.

*1.2   Aesthetics, Ethics, Self-appropriation, and Psychic
       Conversion*

Lonergan has articulated foundational reality in
terms of religious conversion, moral conversion, and intellectual conversion. But neither religious nor moral conversion is a matter of religious or moral self-appropriation. Neither is a matter of explanatory self-knowledge, as
is intellectual conversion.[21] The position on foundational
reality would seem to demand some explanatory understanding of religious and moral conversion.[22] In effect, what
I am suggesting amounts to the affirmation of a psychic
conversion that would be the base of moral and religious
self-appropriation, that would play the same function in
explanatory existential self-knowledge as the aesthetic dimension of subjectivity itself plays in the decisions of the
concrete existential subject. As aesthetic subjectivity is the
ground of moral and religious response, by being the locus of the apprehension of values, so aesthetic self-appropriation is the ground of moral and religious self-appro-

priation. Authentic self-appropriation in an explanatory mode is conditional upon the release of the capacity to disengage in explanatory fashion the orientation of one's spontaneous symbolic system on the move. This release is psychic conversion. As contributing to explanatory existential self-understanding, it aids the sublation of intellectual conversion by a moral and religious conversion that are advancing in a mediated possession of themselves, that is, the moral and religious subjectivity of interiorly differentiated consciousness in the third stage of meaning.[23]

2 The Mediation of Aesthetic Subjectivity

In an attempt to grasp the immanent intelligibility of an explanatory mediation of aesthetic subjectivity, I suggest that we begin with an interpretation of Lonergan's writings and of what we are about in studying his work. Let us regard the thought of Lonergan as the mediation by meaning of the intentional operations to which we are immediately present, that is, of which we are conscious. Lonergan provides us with at least one statement that encourages such an interpretation. 'Besides the immediate world of the infant and the adult's world mediated by meaning, there is the mediation of immediacy by meaning when one objectifies cognitional process in transcendental method and when one discovers, identifies, accepts one's submerged feelings in psychotherapy.'[24] Obviously the immediacy mediated by meaning in these two processes is not that of the infant, who lives exclusively in a world of immediacy, but that of the adult, of the subject who lives in a world mediated and constituted by meaning and motivated by value. The immediacy that itself is mediated by meaning in transcendental method is our immediacy to our own intentional operations by which the world itself is mediated and constituted by meaning, and the immediacy that is mediated by meaning in psychotherapy is our immediacy to our submerged feelings in the same world mediated and constituted by meaning.

Transcendental method and psychotherapy are similar processes, then, insofar as they render known what previously was conscious but not objectified. In the one case this is the structure of intentional cognitional operations, in the other the energic compositions and distributions that are one's feelings.[25] Nonetheless, there is a significant difference between the two processes, for transcendental method aims at an explanatory self-understanding, where the terms and relations of intentional process fix one another. Psychotherapy is neither so thorough nor so explicitly explanatory in its objective. Nonetheless, as we shall see, it *does* provide us with a clue to our solution. Perhaps a heuristic structure of psychotherapies would point the way to a mediation of explanatory knowledge of the aesthetic and dramatic components of our being.[26] Basic to this heuristic structure would be a distinction between primordial immediacy and second immediacy.

Primordial immediacy is the experiential infrastructure of conscious human performance. It is the subject as dreaming, experiencing, inquiring, understanding, conceiving, formulating, reflecting, judging, deliberating, evaluating, deciding, acting: the subject as subject. Its basic structure has been disengaged by Lonergan's intentionality analysis. It is a primordial immediacy in that in all of these operations we are present to ourselves, immediate to ourselves operating — conscious. Second immediacy is the mediated recovery of primordial immediacy through explanatory self-appropriation, through transcendental or generalized empirical method, which, strictly speaking, mediates not only cognitional process but the process and structure of intentionality as a whole. It is the asymptotic result of objectifying the subject. But because of the origin of the fourth level of intentional consciousness in the affective apprehension of values by feelings, explanatory self-appropriation of existential consciousness will be dependent upon an explanatory mediation of affectivity, of aesthetic subjectivity, of dramatic artistry. And because the levels of cognitional consciousness are continuous, not only in an upward moving direction with existential consciousness, but also in a downward moving direction with dreaming consciousness, it seems reasonable to propose that the dream's significance reaches up to existential subjectivity, indeed that it might be the key to the knowledge not only of existential consciousness but also of the aesthetic and dramatic dimension that permeates the single thrust of intentional consciousness to intelligibility, truth, reality, and value.[27]

The negotiation of one's dreams may begin in a psychotherapeutic context, but their finality and ultimate significance must be extended beyond the narrow confines of ordinary psychotherapy and into the context provided by the third stage of meaning, whose base is transcendental method as articulated by Lonergan. Then it will be acknowledged that the same dreams that provide some forms of psychotherapy with a principal source of data on the client are in fact dramatic ciphers in a symbolic mode of the emergence or failure of emergence of authentic intentionality.[28] From the standpoint of my position on psychic conversion, the negotiation of dreams is basically the mediation of the drama that permeates the struggle between the dynamism for self-transcendence and the inertial counterweight of self-absorption, and particularly as this drama affects our sensitive consciousness. Dreams provide materials for one's work of dramatic artistry, images for insight, reflection, and decision in the forging of a work of dramatic art. They provide access to the plots and themes that are operative in both one's cognitional structuring and one's decisive shaping of the world. They provide to consciousness an accessibility to the sometimes otherwise mute intentionality of the subject. They interpret the subject in his or her dispositional immediacy in the world mediated by meaning, his or her affective and so real self-transcendence.

Jung calls the capacity of waking consciousness to negotiate the imaginal configurations of dreams the transcendent function.[29] Transposing Jung's insight into the framework of a generalized empirical method as proposed by Lonergan, we might say that, when the transcendent function becomes habitual, it enables the existential subject to receive, interpret, affirm, evaluate, and negotiate symbolic materials for the drama of one's emergence as an authentic subject. I regard the transcendent function so understood to be conditioned by psychic conversion.

The function of psychic conversion within generalized empirical method may be understood, then, in terms of the relations of sublation that obtain among the various levels of consciousness. Lonergan has spoken of the sublation of the sensitive stream by understanding, of sensitivity and understanding by reasonable judgment, and of experience, understanding, and judgment by existential subjectivity. The operators of these successive sublations are, respectively, questions for intelligence, questions for reflection, and questions for deliberation. But prior to waking experience, there is dreaming consciousness. It is in the dream that we first become conscious. And so in addition to the sublations specified by Lonergan, there is the sublation of the dream by waking consciousness through memory, and then by understanding, judgment, and decision. The dream is a set of symbols arranged in a dramatic sequence, whose meaning can be read by interpretive understanding and reasonable judgment, and in whose regard decisive action can be taken by the existential subject. Dream symbols are operators effecting the internal communication of organism, psyche, and mind. The ground theme of the internal communication is set by the concerns of the dramatic artist to make a work of art out of his or her life, by the inescapable task of the existential subject as free and responsible constitutive agent of the human world. This ground theme is the basic a priori of human consciousness. It is this theme that promotes human experience to understanding by means of questions for intelligence, and understanding to truth by means of questions for reflection. So too, this basic a priori promotes knowledge into action, but in a thetic and constitutive manner, through questions for deliberation. The data for these questions are apprehended in feelings; the feelings are linked with symbols; and the symbols that tell the story of the dramatic base of our existential performance are unlocked in our dreams. This narrative can be understood, the understanding can be affirmed as correct, and the self-knowledge thus gained can be employed in the ongoing constitution of one's world and concomitantly of oneself. Such is the basic scheme of the contribution of psychic conversion to our development. The ultimate intentionality of psychic conversion is thus coextensive with the total sweep of conscious intentionality. Through psychic conversion, the psyche is conscripted into the single transcendental dynamism of human consciousness toward the authenticity of self-transcendence.

It may be, too, that psychic conversion throws special light on the first of the transcendental precepts that Lonergan links with the levels of consciousness: Be attentive. Psychic conversion allows us to speak of attentiveness as contemplation, letting-be, listening, responsivity, active receptivity. With the release of the transcendent function, dream interpretation consists in the attentive reception of dreams as already interpretive of the subject in his

or her dramatic artistry; in insight into what is thus received; in the reflective judgment that the insight is correct; and in the responsible negotiation of this self-knowledge in the thetic projects of the existential subject.

3   The Unconscious and the Dream

The psyche of the dreaming subject frequently is
called the unconscious. More properly, though, it is better
conceived as the beginning of consciousness. What is
unconscious is all energy in the universe that is not present
to itself. Energic compositions and distributions at the
neural level are elevated to consciousness in the systematization and representation granted them by the dream. At
this point energy becomes psychic energy. It is informed
not just physically, chemically, and botanically, but psychologically. The underlying neural manifold so integrates
its own physical and chemical aggregates as to promote its
elevation to the higher integration of the dream. The dream
thus discloses in sensitive consciousness a complex of underlying physiological transformations. It integrates these
transformations by granting them psychic representation
in the form of elemental symbols. These symbols then can
find their own higher integration as they are sublated into
waking consciousness through memory, into intelligent
consciousness by insight, into truthful consciousness by
reflective understanding of the adequacy of one's insight,
and into responsible consciousness by decisions which in
turn will operate further transformations of the underlying sensitive manifold. Dream symbols thus provide materials for one's work of dramatic art.
    Our understanding of psychic energy is still quite
rudimentary. We know that there are different kinds of
dreams or, better, different kinds of symbols that integrate
underlying physiological transformations. We can list at

least seven ideal types. The first have to do with dreams of the night, the other six with dreams of the morning.[30]

Dreams of the night will not concern us here, for the reasons that (1) they involve merely a psychic integration of physiological processes, (2) they are very seldom subject to recall, and (3) they are usually devoid of existential or dramatic significance. Dreams of the morning, however, have to do with the materials presented to one's dramatic pattern of experience for the shaping of a work of living artistry. The figures and themes of these dreams may take six distinct forms. Two of these are personal, one archetypal, one anagogic, one prophetic, and one synchronistic.

Personal dreams of the morning may be either primarily symbolic or almost entirely literal in their meaning. What qualifies them as personal is that the figures in these dreams are taken from the acquaintances of one's own dramatic existence, and that the themes relate directly to this existence. But in some instances the figures and places are symbolic of complexes or undercurrents in one's own psychological interiority and in other instances they mean the actual personages and locations they represent. Moreover, the dream does not attempt to read the events in one's existential living against a background of more universal significance. Thus, in a fundamentally literal personal dream, one meets one's boss, with whom in waking life one has an unspoken strained relationship. In the dream one bites the bullet and begins to assert oneself and one's own intentions in a more forthright manner. The dream is quite direct. Nor is it in all likelihood a matter of Freudian wish fulfillment, but is better interpreted as an indication of a real existential possibility, desirability, necessity. A bit more symbolically, a graduate student struggling through a make-it-or-break-it course from an extremely demanding teacher dreams of being pursued, hunted by the professor, who is intent on killing or decisively wounding him. More symbolically still, a man is about to cross a bridge suspended over a dangerous chasm, but just before he sets foot on the bridge it collapses into the ravine below. It is not time to attempt a transition, to 'cross the great water.'[31]

Dreams become archetypal to the extent that the symbolic figures that constitute them, whether they be taken from one's personal waking life or are strangers, assume a more universal and usually mysterious significance permeated with a deeply resonant emotion. The themes of archetypal dreams are taken from the more or less universal mythical reflections of human possibility embodied in the traditional lore of many widely divergent nations and cultures. Certain symbols lend themselves easily to archetypal significance and interpretation: water, fire, maternal symbols, animals. But these symbols, as in personal symbolic dreams, are imitative analogues of the natural figures they represent. A maternal symbol means, not one's personal mother, but the life-giving or destructive powers of nature. And the symbol is set into a context in which it participates in a story that is clearly mythical in its significance. In such dreams, the process of one's existential living is interpreted against the backdrop of more or less universal human themes of development and decline.

Anagogic dreams differ from archetypal dreams in that the context in which they set the symbols they employ is an ultimate context of human redemption or loss. Anagogic symbols may be taken from nature but their meaning is supernatural. Thus a Christian mystic may dream on the night between Holy Thursday and Good Friday of a conflict that represents the drama of human salvation being remembered and celebrated by his church community at this time. The meaning of anagogic dreams is even more ineffable than that of archetypal dreams. Contemplation of the ultimate mystery alone begins to be an appropriate existential response, for such dreams are most likely to be interpreted as originating more or less directly from the realm of absolute transcendence. While a correct philosophical theology will regard God as the first agent in every event, and thus also in every dream, there are some dreams in which the process of universal instrumentality[32] engages the individual subject directly as a principal actor in world constitution or discloses to this subject immediately an ultimate context of love and awe.[33]

Prophetic dreams may be either literal or symbolic, and the symbolism may be personal, archetypal, or anagogic. What these dreams do is actually foretell an event that will occur in the external drama of human life. Synchronistic dreams, which also may be either literal or symbolic, reflect an external event that is occurring at the same time as it is being dreamt. In either prophetic or synchronistic dreams, there is not so much a challenge to a decision as the reporting of a fact.

As indicated above, our scientific understanding of the energic processes that are integrated in these different varieties of dreams is extraordinarily incomplete. Obviously what is occurring is that unconscious neural-physiological process is finding a higher integration in psychic representation. It is entering into consciousness, and will find yet higher forms of conscious integration to the extent that the dream is remembered, understood correctly, and responded to in attitude or, as the case may be, decision. But, despite our relatively inchoate understanding of psychic energy, it is possible to indicate heuristically the method that must be employed in studying it. The method is genetic, for the basic heuristic assumption is development. A study of development demands an appreciation of the upwardly but indeterminately directed dynamism of the world of possible experience, understanding, and judgment. Such dynamism is finality as a present fact heading for fuller being, more specifically differentiated perfection. Finality is unconsciously operative in neural process, but is elevated to consciousness in the dream and is conscripted into the conscious intention of a living work of art by the psychically converted subject genuinely engaged in the dramatic pattern of experience.[34]

4 The Transcendental Imagination

There are many correspondences between the imaginal configurations mediated through psychic conversion and the Kantian-Heideggerian transcendental imagination.[35] But the latter is transposed out of the formalism of German philosophy and into the context of a maieutic of concrete subjectivity. For Heidegger, the transcendental imagination institutes primordial time, not only as the form of inner sense, but as the very constitution of the immediacy of understanding and mood that is *Dasein*. But the time structure of imagination, and thus of our concern for the world, is fragile and disproportionate. Thus existential psychiatry would regard neurosis as the victory of a temporal disproportion. Anxiety weights the disproportion in favor of the future, guilt in favor of the past. In either case, the spontaneity of the subject is paralyzed. At the extremes of either disproportion, the subject utters the 'I am nothing' of depression or the 'I am everything' of inflationary schizophrenia, and not the 'I am this' of self-possession. The recovery of the primordial time structure of one's subjectivity is thus therapeutic. It involves a progressive and cumulative reconciliation of the duality of human subjectivity.

The opposites are, I believe, best formulated by Lonergan, for whom there is a tension in all development between limitation and transcendence.[36] In human development, this tension is conscious. It is a tension between the self as one is and the self as one is to be. It is appropriately negotiated by correct apprehensions of the starting point, the term, and the process between them at any stage of one's development, so that there is a correspondence between the facts of one's development and one's apprehension of these facts. Coincident respectively with limitation and transcendence, one may, at least descriptively, list past and future, body and intentionality, matter and spirit, instinct and archetype, potentiality and project, origin and outcome, the unconscious and consciousness. The psyche is essential to the establishment of the reconciliation of these related dualities.[37] It functions by releasing images that integrate underlying biological manifolds but that are also the materials for insight, reflection, and decision in the forging of a work of dramatic art. The images reflect in a personal, archetypal, or anagogic fashion the present economy of the duality of the subject. The reconciliation of the duality, however, is not to be conceived of as a removal. The opposition is ineluctable.[38] But it is destructive of dramatic artistry only when it is displaced by bias and consequent misunderstanding. As Paul Ricoeur insists in *Fallible Man*[39] and Lonergan in his treatment of genuineness,[40] the disproportion is ontological, not psychological. It is the disproportion of infinitude and finitude in the human subject.

The discovery and cultivation of the psychic mediator of limitation and transcendence may begin in psychotherapy, but because its fruition is in the dramatic stage of life, the process of a differentiated psychic self-transparency is better understood as a matter of aesthetics than of psychotherapy. If values are apprehended in feelings, aesthetic subjectivity lies at the basis of existential subjectivity, of morals and religion. Lonergan's opening of generalized empirical method upon a fourth, existential level of consciousness concerned not with intelligibility or truth but with value is also an opening of method onto aesthetic consciousness. Ethics is radically aesthetics, and the existential subject for whom the issue is one of personal character is at base the aesthetic subject, the dramatic artist.

Notes

1 On the levels of consciousness, see *Method in Theology* (see above, chapter 1, note 3) chapter 1. Lonergan there discusses four levels. Consciousness is so structured as to move by questioning from experience of the data of sense and of the data of consciousness (the empirical level) to insight into the experienced data and conceptualization and formulation of one's insights (the intelligent level), and then to reflection on the adequacy of one's understanding and to judgment in accord with the adequacy reflectively grasped (the reasonable level), and finally to deliberation, decision, and action, that is, to constitution of the world and of oneself (the responsible or existential level). In the lecture 'The Subject' (see above, chapter 3, note 1) 69-86 esp. 80, Lonergan adds a lower level of dreaming consciousness, and in *Philosophy of God, and Theology* (see above, chapter 5, note 87) 38, he adds a highest level of religious love. 1993 note: The posthumously published paper 'Philosophy and the Religious Phenomenon' (*Method: Journal of Lonergan Studies* 12: 1 [1994] xx-xx) is the most direct indication of an expansion beyond *Method*'s four levels of intentional consciousness.

2 It is obvious, then, that I am employing the term 'aesthetic subjectivity' in a manner quite different from the usage of Hans-Georg Gadamer (*Truth and Method*, see above, chapter 4, note 26). For Gadamer, the term is pejorative, and designates an immediacy of taste that would empty the work of art of its distinctive claim to truth. In my usage, the term also designates an immediacy of feeling, but to a world already mediated and constituted by meaning. As such, it is not simply the immediacy of empirical consciousness to data of sense, but permeates all of the levels of conscious intentionality disclosed by Lonergan.

Thus insights, judgments, and decisions are all dramatic events; permeating their quality as intentional operations is a dispositional character, a quality of feeling, of 'mass and momentum,' of energic compositions and distributions, without which 'our knowing and deciding would be paper thin.' Lonergan, *Method in Theology* 30-31. When I speak of aesthetic subjectivity, I am referring to the following facts: 'Because of our feelings, our desires and our fears, our hope or despair, our joys and sorrows, our enthusiasm and indignation, our esteem and contempt, our trust and distrust, our love and hatred, our tenderness and wrath, our admiration, veneration, reverence, our dread, horror, terror, we are oriented massively and dynamically in a world mediated by meaning. We have feelings about other persons, we feel for them, we feel with them. We have feelings about our respective situations, about the past, about the future, about evils to be lamented or remedied, about the good that can, might, must be accomplished.' Ibid. 31.

³ That feeling permeates not only existential consciousness but also cognitive levels is clear from the illustrative instance of insight with which Lonergan opens the first chapter of *Insight*: Archimedes running naked from the baths of Syracuse, crying excitedly, 'I've got it!' See Lonergan, *Insight* (see above, chapter 1, note 37) 3/27.

⁴ For example, ibid. 199-203/223-27; xi-xii/5-6.

⁵ Lonergan, *Method in Theology* 30-34.

⁶ Lonergan, *Insight* 458-79/484-504.

⁷ For Lonergan, the self-transcendent capacities of the levels of intentional consciousness are normative for authenticity. Corresponding to each level is a precept, and the complex of imperatives constitutes the law of human nature. The imperatives or 'transcendental precepts' are: Be attentive, Be intelligent, Be reasonable, Be responsible, and with God's grace, Be in love. See *Method in Theology* 20. The failure of the Jungian project is summarized by Paul J. Stern, *C.G. Jung: The Haunted Prophet* (New York: Dell, 1976) 256-57: 'The myth of the emergence of the God-man was the culmination of Jung's quest for the great synthesis that would resolve his inner duality. This quest also led Jung to propound a variety of other syntheses: the fusion of religion and empiricism in analytic psychology; the coupling of ego and unconscious in the archetype of the self; the confluence of spirit and matter in the

symbols of alchemy; the blending of the singular and the universal in the collective unconsciousness.

'But in the last analysis Jung's search for the Holy Grail of conjunction failed. His syntheses did not eventuate in genuine union; they were makeshift soldering jobs, contrived amalgamations, rather than transcendent integrations of the opposites.

'In the intellectual realm, Jung's great synthesis remained very much at the level of mere verbal operations whose superficialities were concealed by an impressive array of erudition. Jung's often-noted lack of lucidity, his turgid style, the leakiness of his logic, his inability to distinguish between hypotheses and facts are as many telltale signs of this lack of integration.' Stern balances this harsh judgment with an appropriate recognition of Jung's intimations of forthcoming differentiations and integrations of human consciousness. I view Jung as a precursor of a very important movement in the evolution of consciousness, a movement that he could not himself systematize because of his inadequate conceptualizations concerning the intentionality of the human spirit. I have suggested elsewhere that the root of Jung's problem lies in misplacing the opposites, a fact that appears most obviously in his hopelessly jumbled treatment of the problem of evil. See 'Dramatic Artistry in the Third Stage of Meaning' (above, chapter 7) and 'The Theologian's Psyche: Notes toward the Reconstruction of Depth Psychology' (above, chapter 6). See also 'Aesthetics and the Opposites' (above, chapter 4).

8   Bernard Lonergan, '*Insight* Revisited' (see above, chapter 2, note 56) 277.

9   Lonergan, *Insight* 726/747. The psyche is implicitly defined in terms of 'a sequence of increasingly differentiated and integrated sets of capacities for perceptiveness, for aggressive or affective response, for memory, for imaginative projects, and for skillfully and economically executed performance.' Ibid. 456/481.

10   Lonergan, *Method in Theology* 64.

11   Ibid. 65.

12   Ibid. 66.

13   Ibid. 65.

14 'For the logical class the symbol uses a representative figure. For univocity it substitutes a wealth of multiple meanings. It does not prove but it overwhelms with a manifold of images that converge in meaning. It does not bow to the principle of excluded middle but admits the *coincidentia oppositorum*, of love and hate, of courage and fear, and so on. It does not negate but overcomes what it rejects by heaping up all that is opposite to it. It does not move on some single track or on some single level, but condenses into a bizarre unity all its present concerns.' Ibid. 66.

15 'Organic and psychic vitality have to reveal themselves to intentional consciousness and, inversely, intentional consciousness has to secure the collaboration of organism and psyche. Again, our apprehensions of values occur in intentional responses, in feelings; here too it is necessary for feelings to reveal their objects and, inversely, for objects to awaken feelings. It is through symbols that mind and body, mind and heart, heart and body communicate.' Ibid. 66-67.

16 Ibid. 67.

17 Ibid. 69. This represents a different evaluation of the function of the dream from that proposed by Lonergan in *Insight* 194-96/217-20.

18 That there must be such a psychic correlative is argued also by Lonergan in *Insight*: '... man's concrete being involves (1) a succession of levels of higher integration, and (2) a principle of correspondence between otherwise coincidental manifolds on each lower level and systematizing forms on the next higher level. Moreover, these higher integrations on the organic, psychic, and intellectual levels are not static but dynamic systems; they are systems on the move; the higher integration is not only an integrator but also an operator; and if developments on different levels are not to conflict, there has to be a correspondence between their respective operators.

'... on the intellectual level the operator is concretely the detached and disinterested desire to know. It is this desire, not in contemplation of the already known, but headed towards further knowledge, orientated into the known unknown. The principle of dynamic correspondence calls for a harmonious orientation on the psychic level, and from the nature of the case such an orientation would have to consist in some cosmic dimension, in some intimation of unplumbed depths, that accrued to man's feelings, emotions, sentiments. Nor is this merely a theoretical conclusion, as R. Otto's study of the nonrational element in the *Idea of the Holy* rather abundantly indicates.' *Insight* 532/555. See also 546-47/570: '...[the] unrestricted openness of our intelligence and reasonableness not only is the concrete operator of our intellectual development but also is accompanied by a corresponding operator that deeply and powerfully holds our sensitive integrations open to transforming change ... man's explanatory self-knowledge can become effective in his concrete living only if the content of systematic insights, the direction of judgments, the dynamism of decisions can be embodied in images that release feeling and emotion and flow spontaneously into deeds no less than words.' In 'Dramatic Artistry in the Third Stage of Meaning,' I have spoken of the sensitive operator in terms of psychic energy and have related my understanding of the sensitive dynamism to Jung's.

19 On the sublations here referred to, see Lonergan, *Method in Theology* 241-43. What I am seeking is a way to render moral and religious self-appropriation as much a matter of explanatory self-knowledge as is the intellectual self-appropriation aided by *Insight*. I am suggesting that we can develop a psychological self-mediation that would display the ground of one's being as a moral and religious subject, by uncovering the symbols that awaken and fail to awaken one's affective responses, and by enabling one to trace the story of the transvaluation of symbols in one's sensitive orientation.

20 See Lonergan, *Method in Theology* 267-69.

21 Strictly speaking, intellectual conversion has two meanings for Lonergan. There is a sense in which, as Lonergan says, the church reached intellectual conversion at the Council of Nicea. That is, a particularly vexing and critical problem was resolved by the exercise of human intelligence as orientated beyond the *priora quoad nos* to an affirmation of the *priora quoad se*, even though the latter affirmation involves prescinding from the familiarity of images that correspond to the content of one's affirmation. Thus the meaning of the Nicene definition of consubstantiality was expressed by Athanasius: 'All that is said of the Father is also to be said of the Son, except that the Son is Son, and not Father.' See Bernard Lonergan, *The Way to Nicea: The Dialectical Development of Trinitarian Theology* (Philadelphia: Westminster, 1976, to be included in Collected Works of Bernard Lonergan, vol. 9) 47. But this exercise of human intelligence was not mediated to itself by cognitional analysis. The Nicene definition issues from intelligence in act, but is not accompanied by a reflective account of what precisely

one is doing when one is so using one's intelligence. The second and most proper meaning of intellectual conversion is the change in one's being brought about by cognitional analysis. Thus Lonergan in *Method in Theology* equates intellectual conversion with this explanatory self-understanding in the third stage of meaning. Intellectual conversion is a liberation from long-ingrained habits of thought and speech about one's knowledge, a liberation 'that is to be had only when one knows precisely what one is doing when one is knowing.' See *Method in Theology* 238-40.

22 Explanatory understanding is not critical grounding but critical mediation. Moral and religious conversion are self-grounding, self-authenticating. Explanatory understanding of them would move beyond descriptive phenomenology to a formulation based on insights that fix terms and relations by one another: that is, beyond the *priora quoad nos* to the *priora quoad se*.

23 The third stage of meaning is the epoch in the history of consciousness upon which we are called to enter in our time, an epoch in which meaning is controlled neither by practicality nor by theory but by a differentiation of consciousness that occurs through explanatory self-understanding on the part of human interiority. See Lonergan, *Method in Theology* 93-96. As intellectual conversion, so psychic conversion can have two meanings. The first is analogous to the intellectual conversion *in actu exercito* manifested in the Nicene treatment of consubstantiality. It is manifest in many religious and literary documents and in the lives of countless men and women even in the first, commonsense stage of meaning. It corresponds to the first meaning of genuineness in Lonergan's treatment of this topic in *Insight* (see 475/ 499-500). The second and proper meaning, however, is the third-stage meaning I am giving to the term in this paper: the release of the capacity to disengage in explanatory fashion — with terms and relations fixing one another — the dynamic process of one's spontaneous symbolic sensitivity on the move. As such, it is dependent on intellectual conversion and *per consequens* on moral and religious conversion. See Lonergan, *Method in Theology* 243, for a treatment of intellectual conversion as following upon religious and moral conversion.

24 Ibid. 77.

25 On feelings as intentional, see Lonergan, *Method in Theology* 30-33.

26 On the need for a heuristic structure of psychotherapies, see Bernard Tyrrell, '"Dynamics of Christotherapy" and the Issue of a *De Jure* Psychotherapeutic Pluralism' in *Lonergan Workshop* 3:125-47.

27 This proposal is obviously not without its difficulties. First, two leading proponents of a hermeneutic of dreams, Freud and Jung, are dialectically opposed to one another as far as their interpretive principles are concerned. Secondly, I will disagree with both Freud and Jung. Thirdly, a leading philosophical investigator of Freud, Paul Ricoeur, has relegated dreams to the lowest level of symbols, the level of sedimented symbolism with nothing but a past. See Paul Ricoeur, *Freud and Philosophy* (see above, chapter 1, note 7) 504-506. Fourthly, many psychologists have turned from the depth therapy that works with dreams to the height therapies that concentrate on conscious but unobjectified cognitional and existential orientations. Nonetheless, Bernard Tyrrell, an advocate of the height-therapy approach, has indicated that my position emphasizing depth approaches and his concentration on height therapies are complementary. See his paper referred to in the previous footnote. While I concur with Tyrrell's judgment, I also admit that, before the dream can function as central to an explanatory mediation of affectivity, and so of existential subjectivity, its function in the infrastructure of primordial immediacy will have to be both clarified and vindicated. Several of my own papers are contributions to this task, most notably 'Dramatic Artistry in the Third Stage of Meaning' (above, chapter 7).

28 I have argued this rather major claim in the last-mentioned paper. To verify and affirm the claim for oneself, however, one must be thoroughly familiar with the dimensions of one's subjectivity which Lonergan has disclosed. My statement of the function of dreams departs somewhat from that presented by Lonergan in *Insight* 194-96/217-20, though it is consonant with his few remarks on dreams in *Method in Theology*. In a public dialogue session at the 1977 Boston College Workshop, Lonergan indicated agreement with my restatement of the position of *Insight* on the dream.

29 C.G. Jung, 'The Transcendent Function' (see above, chapter 2, note 14).

30 On the distinction of dreams of the night and dreams of the morning, see Lonergan, 'Dimensions of Meaning' (see above, chapter 2, note 7) 242. The distinction is, I believe, not so much temporal as

existential. Dreams of the night are occasioned by somatic disturbance. In dreams of the morning, 'the existential subject, not yet awake and himself, still is already busy with the project that shapes both him himself and his world.' Ibid. Lonergan here draws from Ludwig Binswanger and Rollo May.

[31] This is an expression that frequently appears in the Chinese book of oracles, *I Ching* or *Book of Changes*. On the *I Ching* and Christian discernment of spirits, see Vernon Gregson, 'Chinese Wisdom and Ignatian Discernment,' *Review for Religious* 33:4 (July, 1974) 828-35.

[32] On universal instrumentality, see Bernard Lonergan, *Grace and Freedom: Operative Grace in the Thought of St. Thomas Aquinas*, ed. J. Patout Burns (New York: Herder and Herder, 1971) 80-84.

[33] The distinction of archetypal and anagogic meaning is Northrop Frye's, and appears in *Anatomy of Criticism* (see above, chapter 3, note 45) 116-38. I have drawn on it in an effort to provide a needed differentiation of symbols beyond that arrived at by Jung. For Jung, the self is 'a borderline concept, expressing a reality to which no limits can be set.' C.G. Jung, *Psychology and Alchemy* (see above, chapter 6, note 68) 355. Such a notion is inflationary. Anagogic ciphers of absolute transcendence are images of God's action or call, not properly speaking of the self.

[34] The notions of finality, development, genetic method, and genuineness are explained by Lonergan, *Insight*, chapter 15. I have related them more amply to psychic energy in 'Dramatic Artistry in the Third Stage of Meaning.'

[35] For Heidegger's retrieval — some would say mauling — of the transcendental imagination from Kant's first critique, see Martin Heidegger, *Kant and the Problem of Metaphysics* (see above, chapter 2, note 60).

[36] See Lonergan, *Insight* 472-75/497-99.

[37] See C.G. Jung, 'On the Nature of the Psyche' (see above, chapter 5, note 14). The mediating role of the psyche is located heuristically by Lonergan, for whom human development is a matter of the appropriate interlocking of organic, psychic, and intellectual development. 'In the organism both the underlying manifold and the higher

system are unconscious. In intellectual development both the underlying manifold of sensible presentations and the higher system of insights and formulations are conscious. In psychic development the underlying neural manifold is unconscious and the supervening higher system is conscious ... Organic, psychic, and intellectual development [in the human subject] are not three independent processes. They are interlocked, with the intellectual providing a higher integration of the psychic and the psychic providing a higher integration of the organic.' Lonergan, *Insight* 467/492; 469-70/494.

38 Ibid. 474/498-99.

39 Paul Ricoeur, *Fallible Man* (see above, chapter 1, note 5).

40 Lonergan, *Insight* 475-78/499-503.

10 Psyche, Evil, and Grace

In the theological method proposed by Bernard Lonergan, the issue of authenticity, of the integrity of knowing, morals, and religion, is the foundational question of theology.[1] And it is an issue that is solved, not within theology, but outside the arena of scholarly research and systematic construction and elaboration. The *question* of authenticity, the problem of one's own integrity as a religious and moral, intellectual and aesthetic being, as a Christian person, surely is raised by performing the various tasks that are constitutive of the theological enterprise. Or, at least, the question is meant to be raised, and must be raised, if the theologian is not to be a compartmentalized subject — something quite other than a differentiated subject — and if theology is to be both an intellectually coherent enterprise and an agent of resistance against cultural corruption and decline. As we all know, however, the fact that theology is reflection on religion, and that Christian theology is reflection on the Christian religion, is in itself no guarantee that engagement in the theological enterprise will not contribute more to one's own alienation, first from oneself, but also from one's tradition and one's historical community, and ultimately possibly even from the founding events, the acts of God, that constitute the origins and the continuing history of the Christian community. Alienation in theology, alienation as a result of theologizing, theologizing as an alienating set of operations, are distinct possibilities. In our time, they are obvi-

337

ous realities. And the root of their possibility and of their
reality lies, oddly enough, in a non-event, in the failure to
raise or pursue the questions of authenticity that are
prompted by the very materials that one subjects to investigation in performing the various tasks that constitute the
theological enterprise.

Now, the non-event of not raising and pursuing relevant questions is precisely what Lonergan calls basic sin.[2]
The question of the possibility of sinfulness in the theological community precisely as theological thus suddenly
and surprisingly becomes the core issue in a theology that
would not be alienating, that would resist cultural corruption in its many forms. This question is the obverse of the
question of authenticity that spontaneously arises, and that
is often with equal spontaneity repressed, in the performance of theological tasks. The complexities of the issue
are compounded by the fact that this question, which arises
within theology, which can be discussed within theology,
and whose answer can and must be objectified within theology if the theologian is to give an account of the foundations of his or her positions, cannot itself be resolved within
theology. Such a strange set of circumstances can function
as an excuse against raising the question itself, and when
it so functions, of course, appeal is being made to reality
itself for warrant against facing reality. The existential
complications of being a theologian are very intricate
indeed.[3]

I   Psyche and Spirit: Image and Question

Any instance of the non-event of failing to raise relevant questions could have served well to situate our discussion of psyche, evil, and grace. But the instance that I
have chosen brings the issue close to home, and serves as
evidence for the very points that I wish to make in this

paper. There is no better way, it would seem, to invite a readership made up of theologians to reflect on the question of authenticity than to pose the question itself, not simply as a theological problem, but as an issue on whose resolution the intrinsic worth of what the readers are doing as theological practitioners stands or falls. One can construct a theology of theology itself; and that is precisely what I am inviting those who read this essay to begin to do; for I have begun by raising the issue of the sinfulness of theologizing itself, when such theologizing is not the work of one who is perseveringly intent on the question of integrity, not just in his or her work as a theologian, but in his or her life as a human being. But even in a theology of theology, the resolution of the question is an extra-theological event.

I cannot offer here the theology of theology that such reflections are meant to tease out as a distinct and largely unfaced question. What I hope is out on the table at this point in my essay is the problem of evil in all the banality of its 'roots.' It is the problem of evil that I wish to elaborate more fully in the course of this short paper. Moreover, what we are here concerned with is clearly not the question of physical evils, but of evil within the world mediated by meaning and motivated by values: with the moral evils whose root is the non-event of non-questions.

Despite the fact that I am not here offering the theology of theology that my instance of what is meant by 'evil' encourages and suggests, I propose to keep my suggestions within the context established by that instance, not because the possible import of what I am saying is limited to the existential complications of being a theologian, but because I have worked out my notion of the psyche, and of its religious involvement, within the overall context of attempting to make a contribution to the questions of theological method, theological foundations, and

theological responsibility for interdisciplinary collaboration, as these questions have been clarified by Lonergan.
My conviction, not simply as a theologian but more cen-
trally as a human being responsible for the constitution of
myself, has been that the issue of authenticity, of integrity,
of good and evil, is not fully treated by the methodologist
of theological performance, even when it is properly acknowledged in its theological significance, until it issues
not only in a cognitional theory, a foundational account of
ethical intentionality, and an objectification of the transcendent exigence for the knowledge and love of God, but
also in a psychology, where that term is used quite precisely to designate, not just any account of human interiority, and certainly not any explanation of human behavior that methodologically prescinds from interiority, but
an explanatory account precisely of that dimension of interiority itself that we properly call *the psyche*.

The psyche is sensitive consciousness. It is the sequence of sensations, memories, images, emotions,
conations, associations, bodily movements, and spontaneous intersubjective responses. It is the first level of conscious intentionality, the level at which are presented the
materials that are sublated by successive levels of spiritual
inquiry giving rise to human understanding, to judgment
within that world mediated by meaning that issues from
understanding, and to decision within the world motivated
by the desire for what is good.[4] It will not do to restrict
one's account of authenticity to a consideration of self-
transcendent performance at the intellectual, rational, and
existential or moral levels of consciousness. There may be
potentially an epochal transformation of consciousness that
is introduced by Lonergan's invitation to bring the operations of intentional consciousness as intentional to bear
upon these same operations as conscious.[5] But that transformation is advanced when the thematization of the sub-

ject extends to the objectification of the aesthetic stream of sensitive consciousness. Without this extension, transcendental method risks the derailment not only of one's theology but also of one's life into an isolation of spirituality from organism and psyche, and so from the spontaneous intersubjectivity that is the infrastructure of community and history. Whether a person will so extend the methodological exigence or not is a decision that one makes, not as a theologian, but as a human being. But so too, whether or not one heeds Lonergan's invitation to the self-appropriation of one's intelligence and rationality is equally a decision made in the existential context of deciding what one must do to participate in the divinely originated intention of redeeming the time — our time. In either case, the question *faced* in theology is *answered* only in the dramatic setting of world constitution and concomitant self-constitution.

There is, then, a psychic conversion that is required if the theologian's performance is to bear fruit in the construction of true positions and the systematic organization of what one holds to be the case. Psychic conversion is the opening of the preconscious collaboration of imagination and intelligence in their task of providing the imaginal materials that are needed if one is to have those insights, make those judgments, and execute those decisions through which one's life can become a work of dramatic art.

The movement from observation through insight and judgment to decision Lonergan has called the creative vector in human consciousness. In spatial terminology, it is a movement from below upwards. The process of conversion, however, is a work of healing before it is one of creating, and the healing vector in consciousness moves from above downwards.[6] The gift of God's love meets the believer at the fifth level of consciousness,[7] the level on which, if the great mystics are correct, most of us experience our-

selves operating far more rarely than is God's desire. The
love of God transvalues our values and so effects and promotes a moral conversion of the fourth level of consciousness, the level on which we evaluate, deliberate, and decide. The orientation of evaluative consciousness to what
is good changes the horizon of our understanding of the
world, through the eye of love that is faith.[8] It inspires the
sustenance of the process of knowing through which questions keep coming until issues are really settled, and cease
coming when it is reasonable to affirm on a given point,
'This is so.' But intellectual conversion, and even its philosophic extension into intellectual self-appropriation, is not
the end of the healing of consciousness from its native disorientation and division — especially, it is not the end of
the division or duality of consciousness. For there is an
aesthetic infrastructure to all conscious intentionality. It
easily is dissociated from the process of spiritual inquiry at
the existential, rational, and intellectual levels. The dissociation, radically considered within the dialectic both of
the subject and of history, is, when viewed under the rubric of self-alienation, ultimately a function of what subjects want and do not want. For subjects can flee insight,
shun truth, and avoid responsibility as radically and as in-
tensely as they can desire to know and to love. Then, of
course, subjectivity is in trouble. And the dimension that
is most in trouble is sensitive consciousness, the aesthetic
psyche, merely empirical luminosity.

Empirical consciousness, the psyche, is, on this account, a register of the fidelity or infidelity of the human
spirit to the laws of inquiry. But in itself, and considered
both concretely and abstractly, the psyche is more darkness than it is luminosity. It is not unconscious, and to
that extent it is luminous. But in itself it throws no more
light on the truth of things than does the extroverted biological consciousness of a cat. The luminosity of conscious-

ness is the light of understanding, which confers meaning; the light of judgment, which affirms that the meaning is true; the light of decision, of freedom, which decides for what is good, for what is better, for what is imperative. The sensitive stream of psychic consciousness, as such, is the movement of biological, neural life become conscious. It is energy become psychic. It is life become present to itself. But the deepest *human* desire and the most awesome *human* fear, however violently they may be experienced at privileged moments by the sensitive psyche, are a function, not of that psyche itself, but of spiritual intentionality in its thirst for understanding, for truth, for responsible or right action. Because of our ontological constitution as compounds-in-tension of organism, psyche, and spirit, we are invested with the task of seeking and finding direction in the movement of life. The direction is given for us not simply by the movement of life itself, as it is for a lower animal, whose finality is species being, but by the *meaning* we find when we ask and pursue the right questions, by the *truth* we affirm when we grasp that the evidence is sufficient to pronounce judgment on a given issue, and by the course of action we pursue when we *freely choose* what is good, better, imperative. The search for direction in the movement of life, then, demands *the integration of spirit and matter* in the compound that is the human person. And the *medium* of this integration is the sensitive *psyche*, which is the movement of life itself become conscious, but also by participation the operator of the search itself, at least insofar as it dynamically provides the materials that one needs for insight, judgment, and choice. The sensitive psyche of a subject constituted *as subject* by spirit participates in intelligence, rationality, and moral responsibility.

The matter is doubly compounded. First, by refusing to understand, affirm, and decide, and more radically by refusing to face relevant questions, one will not find direction in the movement of life. This means that the movement of life itself, as psychically experienced in sensitive consciousness, will be the victim of one's antecedent non-question, refusal, negation, basic sin. The psyche becomes fragmented into dissociated complexes. The primary dissociations occur in the realm of affect, but the dissociated, conflictual affects can become reassociated with new and at times incongruous ideational or representational components. For affect must and will find its way into consciousness, with or without its appropriate representational complement. In the limit, there results a nonsequential and disharmonious cacophony of psychic resonances on the part of a tortured, victimized sensitive consciousness.

The second and most agonizingly complicated compounding of the problem, however, is the relation of this dialectic of the subject to the dialectic of history. For, to treat only one aspect of this immense problem — a problem, by the way, which would constitute the anthropological core or general categories of a theology of history — the victimization of one's own psyche can be the result, not of one's own non-questioning, but of the basic sin of others. We are all born into a world whose social reality is only partly intelligible and more or less partly a surd. To the extent that communities, states, nations, civilizations fail to face the great crises that determine whether they will survive, the absurd component increases, along with the number of subjects whose sensitive psyche never had a chance, not so much because of the unwillingness of their carriers, as in virtue of the unwillingness or the psychic crippling of other non-makers of the social surd.

Let us prescind for present purposes, though, from any further compounding of the issue. The central point is that there is a human drama reflected in the story that each person has to tell. The life of the subject is not simply a matter of structured operations unfolding on successive levels of inner and outer sense, understanding, judgment, and decision. For permeating all of these operations, each of which moves further inward to the still point of the center of one's interiority, are *feelings*, which are the *permanent psychic concomitant of intentional human operations*. Psychic conversion is the operator of the self-appropriation of this psychic concomitant.

The self-appropriation of feelings is not easy. It is no more easy than the self-appropriation of operations. As operations intend objects, though, and so as operations are known, not by a *species* of themselves, but by a *species* of their objects,[9] so the feelings that permeate operations are involved *dramatically* in the intentional relations of insight, judgment, decision, and prayer to the objective correlatives of these intentional operations. Perhaps *that* intentionality, precisely as dramatic, provides us with a clue as to where to look for materials to get us started on psychic self-appropriation. However, the story of intentionality is best told in symbols, in those symbols evoked by the very feelings that attend the story, which are also the symbols that will evoke similar feelings in those who listen to one's story — or, if not similar feelings, and perhaps much better than similar feelings, that will evoke in the other an *insight* into my story.

Every story, though, may be a cover story, as Lonergan once said to me in a private conversation. And in an age when every intellectual seems to be accusing those who do not agree with him or her of *mauvaise foi* or false consciousness, we do indeed have reason to question the naivete of 'theologies of story.' But let us not judge too hastily. Johann-Baptist Metz, hardly a systematic slouch, has found it reasonable to write a 'short apology of narrative,' and his intention to mediate story-telling and remembering with theological argumentation is appealing.[10] But there is a question that Metz does not seem prepared to answer, and so he does not ask it: where are we to go for those symbols that will tell our story *as it is?* For symbols that, at least in their empirical presentation, if not in their subsequent interpretation, are not distorted by any resistance to understanding or decision? For those symbols that will even reveal a resistance to understanding or decision in one's very interpretation and narration of one's story?

The heart of the debate between Freud and Jung in modern depth psychology can, I believe, be understood by examining their respective answers to this question. For they both valued the empirical presentations afforded us in our dreams as a source of self-understanding or, in the terms that I am employing in this essay, as materials that would enable one to tell one's story as it is, to tell a true story about one's life. But for Freud, even the dream is a lie, a distortion, that can be unmasked only by sifting it through an interpretive screen that is the product of scientific rationality; whereas for Jung the dream is a true story of precisely what is going on. It could even reveal the artificiality and mendaciousness of the Freudian or other interpretive screens. Transposing Jung's option into my own context drawn from Lonergan, some dreams are an irrefutable commentary on the integrity of one's assumptions, insights, judgments, decisions, and, underlying these, on one's fundamental spiritual orientation. They offer precisely those materials that one may need to reverse one's assumptions, change one's insights, balance or challenge one's judgments, and transform one's decisions, so that one's life follows more closely the path of integrity.

I have treated the debate between Freud and Jung more extensively elsewhere.[11] Space permits me to indicate here only that I agree with Jung on this point. And the source of my agreement, I believe, is not that I wish it were so, as a Freudian would surely suspect, but that I have discovered of my own dreams that it is so. It is to the realm of the dream that one can often turn for the elemental symbols that narrate the drama, the psychic experience, of one's various human desires, and that, for the existential adult, portray one's engagement in the ground theme of every mature story. That ground theme is the dialectic of willingness and refusal with respect to insight, reasonable judgment, responsible decision, and the inevitable call to faith in transcendent reality.

But this Lonergan framework, it will be argued, is itself an interpretive screen. It may be no less distorting than other such screens. I can answer no more fully regarding both Lonergan's position and my extension of it to psychology than does Lonergan: try it out and judge for yourself. Is this or is it not what goes on in the data of your own consciousness? Surely more nuance is needed. Surely there are rich insights that can be mined from the Freudian corpus. But where is the more adequate heuristic outline for understanding the data to be found?

2   Jung and the Psyche

The Jungian understanding of psychic energy, then, is more accurate than the Freudian construct of libido, at least on the fundamental question of the autonomous differentiability of human sensitive intentionality. But one is not going to find in Jung more than a partial resolution of the drama of the ground theme of one's story. For Jung's vocabulary, if not his intention, makes the whole story a story of one's *psyche*, and that it is not. It is a story of one's *person*, *told* by the psyche, which itself is but one dimension of the self or subject. Jung is under the perduring

dominance of the Kantian epistemology, according to
which the soul or, better, spirit of the human subject is an
unknowable thing-in-itself that can only be postulated as
the ground of an equally postulated freedom and of a destiny that in the West we have called immortality. That this
Kantian epistemology is inadequate has been argued from
many sides, the most notable of which are probably the
neo-Thomist and the Hegelian. But what is frequently
overlooked is the source of the Kantian error, namely, the
primacy attributed to epistemology itself. Or, if this source
is not overlooked, another mistake is made of assigning
the primacy rather to metaphysics, as in the neo-Thomist
response to Kant. Then, however, what results is the posing of a de jure *assumption* in mortal conflict with a de jure
question. And the fundamental issues are not de jure but
de facto questions about the subject: what am I doing when
I am knowing? when I am setting values and deciding in
their regard? when I am taking an existential position in
regard to the mystery that beckons to the vertical self-transcendence of faith? By bringing the operations of conscious
intentionality to bear as intentional upon these same operations as conscious, one comes to an objective knowledge of the spiritual dimension of the human person,[12]
and to a precise delineation of the ground theme of the
story both of the self and of history. And far from being a
postulate that practical reason needs for its functioning,
the knowledge one comes to is a 'virtually unconditioned,'
subject to refinement and development and further
contextualization, but not to fundamental revision or in-
consequential relativization.[13] The ground theme, which
is thus *the point* of the drama of feeling and of the stories of
those existential dreams in which that drama achieves
nonmendacious objectification, is the emergence or failure of emergence of the subject as an integral performer
of intelligent, rational, responsible, universally willing op-

erations in that context of history in which one finds oneself. The ground theme of the human story is the theme of the dialectic of willingness and refusal to understand, to judge reasonably, to decide responsibly, and to answer the divine call to ultimate holiness. It is the drama of self-transcendence or self-enclosure. It is the drama of detachment, on the one hand, and either attachment or cynical indifference and moral renunciation, on the other hand. The structure of conscious intentionality, and the fact that that structure can be radically violated — both being realities that do not need to be postulated, because they can be unconditionally affirmed by a reasonably judging person — provide the interpretive grid for the understanding and existential negotiation of the symbols that elementally objectify one's own participation in that ground theme. The science of depth psychology is thus set on a new foundation by intentionality analysis. Conversely, intentionality analysis is enriched and brought to fundamental completion by the new psychology, which is an understanding of the psychic element that permeates all human intentional orientation.

To develop a psychology prescinding from such a standpoint is to misconstrue human teleology, and so to contribute, not to the promotion of the operations that, theologically viewed, are our cooperation with God's saving purpose, but to the contraction of spirit into its psychological manifestations. The teleology of the psyche can be understood only in terms of the psyche's orientation to the spirit; and the spirit, as Kierkegaard saw so brilliantly, posits in its concrete detail the synthesis of the psychic and the organic.[14] Concretely, this means that one understands the *drama* of life only when one understands it as the drama of insight, of judgment, of decision, and of prayer; that is, only when one understands it as a drama posited by spirit. For all his insistence on the teleological point of view as the basic assumption for understanding the psyche — the decisive point of Jung's relative adequacy in relation to Freud — Jung did not adequately thematize this teleology in terms of the psyche's participation in the ultimate constituents of its own drama: human intelligence, human rationality, human decision, and human destiny as supernatural participation in the life of an absolutely transcendent God. For Jung the teleology of the psyche is objectified as intrapsychic. To *act* upon such an understanding, to live on its basis, is to take the way, not of self-transcendence, but ultimately of self-enclosure. It is to opt for a natural resolution of the irreconcilable dialectic of good and evil that constitutes every human story.[15] In Jung's case, the option takes the form of insisting that the dialectic is, after all, naturally reconcilable, that good and evil can be reconciled in and by the psyche, that the issues of good and evil are themselves relative to one's perspective, and that a perspective beyond good and evil can be pursued and reached. However subtly it may be proposed — and Jung is slippery — the proposition that one can so engineer one's development as to achieve a position beyond good and evil is, I fear, the most diabolical of modernity's nihilistic fantasies.

It is not sufficient, then, to argue persuasively that teleology is more adequate than reductionism in understanding psychological data. Of course it is. But one must also determine heuristically *for what end* the psyche strives in its upwardly directed dynamism. Toward what is it directed? What is it seeking? What *in fact* really does constitute the flourishing of the psyche? Unless one has first elaborated an account of the self-transcendent intentionality of knowledge, of morality, and of religion, one is apt to miss the point concerning the psyche. And intentionality is, in its immanent ontological intelligibility, not psychological, but spiritual. The orientation of a human psyche is an inclination to participate, as the drama-constituting component, in the life of insight, of reflection, of the affirmation of truth, of free and responsible decision, and of partnership with God in the tasks imposed by the divine solution to the problem of evil. These are the operations through which human subjects constitute a world in which human beings can live. And concomitant with world constitution there is self-constitution. Thus these are also the operations through which a subject constitutes himself or herself, and such self-constitution has as a determinate constituent feature the ineradicable issue of the natural irreconcilability of good and evil. These are not opposites in the fashion of contraries, as are spirit and matter, consciousness and the unconscious, or the masculine and feminine dimensions of the androgyny of interiority. They cannot possibly complement one another. They are contradictories. Jung's attempt to reconcile them psychically is as futile as Hegel's to harmonize them speculatively.[16] And the results of Jung's misplaced intrapsychic dialectic will be as unintelligible and self-contradictory as the vagaries of post-Hegelian world-constitutive praxis.

3   *Gratia Sanans*

The issue of evil is ultimately not psychological but spiritual. It is grasped, in so far as we can 'grasp' it, only by understanding that the nonintegrity of intelligence, of rationality, of responsibility, and of orientation to the divine is constituted by a self-enclosure of what are meant to be self-transcendent operations. And yet there *is* such a thing as *psychic* resistance to self-transcendence. Lonergan's cognitional analysis shows that the flight from understanding can be the result of the interference of purely *psychic* desire with the proper march of the spiritual desire to know. More existentially, there is a duality to human desire, and it is this duality that establishes the dialectic of one's personal development. Lonergan describes the duality as follows:

> Intellectual development rests upon the dominance of a detached and disinterested desire to know. It reveals to a man a universe of being, in which he is but an item, and a universal order, in which his desires and fears, his delight and anguish, are but infinitesimal components in the history of mankind. It invites man to become intelligent and reasonable not only in his knowing but also in his living, to guide his actions by referring them, not as an animal to a habitat, but as an intelligent being to the intelligible context of some universal order that is or is to be. Still, it is difficult for man, even in knowing, to be dominated simply by the pure desire, and it is far more difficult for him to permit that detachment and disinterestedness to dominate his whole way of life. For the self, as perceiving and feeling, as enjoying and suffering, functions as an animal in an environment, as a self-attached and self-interested center within its own narrow world of stimuli and responses. But the same self, as inquiring and reflecting, as conceiving intelligently and judging reasonably, is carried by its own higher spontaneity to quite a different mode of operation with the opposite attributes of detachment and disinterestedness. It is confronted with a universe of being in which it finds itself, not the center of reference, but an object co-ordinated with other objects and, with them, subordinated to some destiny

to be discovered or invented, approved or disdained, accepted or repudiated.[17]

The stretching of sensitive, psychic desire to that detachment Lonergan calls universal willingness.[18] And such charity is the fruit of the gift of God's love. The disproportion of the two sources of desire in the human animal is the ontological condition of the possibility of basic sin and moral evil.[19] It founds a moral impotence that makes sustained development and undistorted human communication impossible.[20] Only the absolutely supernatural, divinely originated solution to the problem of evil can ground the intrasubjective and intersubjective collaboration through which the effects of sin are offset in the life of the individual and in human history.[21] God's redeeming purpose is at work in the psychological, social, historical, and intellectual life of men and women, healing the disproportion of sensitive and spiritual desire that grounds the possibility and even the statistical near-inevitability of evil. That healing reaches to sensitive desire itself, stretching it to agapic love. The psyche is brought to a participation in the divine solution to the problem of evil through the grace that heals. That grace enables the psyche's collaboration in the creative movement of human intentionality in its operations of understanding, judging, and deciding; and it is precisely through these natural operations, elevated to sustained integrity by grace, that the human subject cooperates with God in redeeming the time.

Psychic sensitivity, we have seen, attends the operations of spiritual intentionality; feelings are the permanent psychic concomitant of intentional operations. This means that, for these intentional operations to be consistently self-transcendent in their search for intelligibility, truth, and value, the psyche must be brought precisely to that degree of detachment that Lonergan calls universal willingness.

Then the individual is enabled to live the life of simple giving and receiving, of real reciprocity, of self-transcendent individuality, without ulterior motives, available for the performance of his or her own tasks in redemptive history without losing oneself in the psychic resonances that nonindividuated relationships always entail.

4   Jung and Theology

This description bears some complementarity to some of Jung's descriptions of what he would call the goal of the process of individuation.[22] The culmination of this process lies in the experience of the self, and at times this is detailed as an experience of oneself as a self-contained and self-possessed totality, whose very integration enables one to operate simultaneously as a self-transcending subject of distinctively human operations. The self for Jung is a higher and deeper authority than the ego, which is the center of one's conscious personality. In the self, the opposites of spirit and matter are joined. One comes to abide at 'the still point of the turning world.'[23]

But what is that still point? What is that place where the deeper center is found from which the ego receives its strength to live in a detached fashion? Is it ultimately myself, or is it God? Is it nature, or is it grace? What is that supraordinate authority that Jung calls the self? Does Jung perhaps predetermine the answer to that question by calling it the self? Christian tradition does not call it that, but maintains that the still point is not just my self; it is rather the region where God dwells in my innermost being. 'I live, now not I, but Christ lives in me' (Galatians 2.20). 'And I will pray the Father, and he will give you another Counselor, to be with you for ever, even the Spirit of truth, whom the world cannot receive, because it neither sees him nor knows him; you know him, for he dwells with you, and will be in you' (John 14.16-17). 'If a man loves me, he will keep my word, and my Father will love him, and we will come to him and make our home with him' (John 14.23). In Lonergan's words: 'There lies within [our] horizon a region for the divine, a shrine for ultimate holiness. It cannot be ignored. The atheist may pronounce it empty. The agnostic may urge that he finds his investigation has been inconclusive. The contemporary humanist will refuse to allow the question to arise. But their negations presuppose the spark in our clod, our native orientation to the divine.'[24] The innermost region of our interiority carries us *beyond* interiority. It is the center, yes, but that center is a temple, where the gift of God's love is poured forth into our hearts by the Holy Spirit who has been given to us (Romans 5.5). That temple, that shrine, cannot be contracted into the self without distorting its own reality and the reality of the subject who lives from the conviction that the still point is nature, pure and simple.

The last works of Jung, and the writings of some of his closest disciples,[25] are reluctant to accept this interpretation of the still point. They want to reduce the scriptural and traditional Christian terminology about this center to merely figurative language, and to explain the still point in terms, not of grace, but of nature. Christ, in St. Paul's 'I live, now not I, but Christ lives in me,' becomes merely a symbol of the self, and what St. Paul really means, they say, is 'the ego is no longer the center of my being, for I have found the self.'

Under this conception, the self can still function as the image of God buried in the human psyche. But then, the image of God will have to be altered from the way in which Christian tradition has understood it. For the self is not simply good, but also evil. And evil is treated as explicable within the order of nature. The integration of the self thus involves the natural reconciliation of good and evil. It also entails positing evil in the image of God, and in fact in God if indeed the image of God mirrors a real transcendent being. And Christ needs to be complemented by his other half, by the other son of God, Satan. The natural reconciliation of good and evil supplants the Christian aeon's establishing of a division and conflict between these two dimensions of reality. Evil is as substantive as good, and wholeness consists in their reconciliation within the order of nature.

Clearly, at this point, we have arrived at a 'mysticism' that departs radically from the Christian conception of the path toward the union of the soul with God. In these ultimate results, the Jungian myth is, I am convinced, a radically anti-Christian vision of human life and destiny. For on the inner journey, as in every other fundamental option in human life, the ultimate choice becomes one of self or God. Jung's *conceptual* choice is ultimately for self. And that formulation of things is too clearly apt to determine the *existential* option of others in such a way as to lead them along the path to a psychological *cul-de-sac* where one is trapped on the endless treadmill of self-analysis. At this point Jung's psychology must be so critically transformed as to propel it beyond this impasse, an impasse which threatens otherwise to derail the genuine achievements of Jung into just one more ideological justification of our basic alienation from the inner law of our self-transcendent intentionality.

The issue of psychic conversion, then, as an issue of personal integrity, involves the appropriation of the psychic undertow of all intentional operations. As such, the issue, and the psychology that results from meeting it, are dependent upon the self-appropriation of intellectual, moral, and religious spirituality. The heuristic structure of the orientations of the human spirit is uncovered, I believe, in the writings of Lonergan. As we saw at the very beginning of the present paper, the self-appropriation of these orientations meets an exigence that arises, among other *loci*, in the responsible performance of theological operations, but that can be settled only existentially in the extratheological context of one's development as a human subject. The point of insisting on the need for psychic conversion in the enterprise of self-appropriation should be clear: the subject is a compound-in-tension of organism, psyche, and spirit; the tension is experienced psychically, for the psyche is the meeting ground of organism and spirit, and as such has orientations in both directions, orientations whose conflict is adequately mediated only by the objectification of the tension between organic limitation and spiritual transcendence. Psychic conversion, which I have defined as the opening of the preconscious collaboration of imagination and intelligence to the imaginal materials issuing from the organism through the psyche to the spirit, enables this objectification by disclosing to the willing subject the symbolic representations of the affective component of the human search for direction in the movement of life. The issues of sin and grace have a twofold relation to the psyche, both aspects of which can be mediated by psychic conversion to the self-appropriating subject. First, sin is most radically the non-event of not raising further pertinent questions. The failure of questioning has inevitable psychic effects, whose discovery can enable one to acknowledge and avow the wrong. Second, the very condition of the possibility of the non-event that is basic sin lies in the disproportion of the duality of human desire, a disproportion still well captured in the definition of man as a rational animal. Psychic conversion enables the objectification of that disproportion itself as it is reflected in the psyche's 'ownmost' productions. For the sensitive psyche of a unified being that is also in part spirit will by ontological necessity be the dimension in which the disproportion comes to expression in consciousness. By releasing intelligence and freedom to communication with the psyche's experience of the duality of human desire, psychic conversion enables the identification of the concrete incidents of disproportion in one's own unfolding story, thus providing the spirit with materials it can employ, if it pursues the relevant questions, in effecting the synthesis of psyche and organism in their participation in the human drama of the search for direction in the movement of life. The authentic synthesis, finally, while the work of spirit, is effected only when that 'work' is itself converted into faithful participation in a solution to the problem of evil that, to be a solution, is and must be divinely originated, and so grace. The account of psychic conversion, consequently, is *theologically* foundational.[26]

Notes

[1] Bernard Lonergan, *Method in Theology* (see above, chapter 1, note 3) chapter 11.

[2] Bernard Lonergan, *Insight* (see above, chapter 1, note 37) 666/689.

[3] Theodor Adorno has reminded us that talk of authenticity can itself be alienating, because privatizing, jargon. He has in mind Martin Heidegger, for whom the alienating question, I believe, is not that of authenticity itself, but the preliminary question of Being, or better, the inadequate heuristic structure for raising the question of Being. Heidegger's *Kant und das Problem der Metaphysik* (see above, chapter 2, note 60), which may well be the foundational work of his entire corpus, displaces the tension of transcendence and limitation whose admission into consciousness constitutes the possibility of authenticity. In brief, the horizon of Being is simply *not* constituted by the time-instituting *Einbildungskraft*. For its real constitution, see Lonergan, *Insight*, chap-

ter 12. On the tension of limitation and transcendence, see ibid. 472-79/ 497-504. I have tried to consider this tension in terms of temporality in *Psychic Conversion and Theological Foundations* (Scholars Press, 1981) 117-22, 139-41.

[4] On the levels of conscious operation, see Lonergan, *Method in Theology*, chapter 1. Lonergan's definitive breakthrough to the beginnings of an explanatory account of human inquiry is presented in *Insight*, chapter 11.

[5] Lonergan, *Method in Theology* 14.

[6] See Bernard Lonergan, 'Healing and Creating in History' (see above, chapter 6, note 88).

[7] See Bernard Lonergan, *Philosophy of God, and Theology* (see above, chapter 5, note 87) 38. [This is the way I formulated the fifth level in writing this article; I would now want to say that the gift of God's love *creates* a fifth level of consciousness. R.D.]

[8] Lonergan, *Method in Theology* 115-18.

[9] Bernard Lonergan, *Verbum:Word and Idea in Aquinas*, ed. David Burrell (Notre Dame: University of Notre Dame Press, 1967) ix.

[10] Johann-Baptist Metz, 'A Short Apology of Narrative,' in *Concilium* 85: *The Crisis of Religious Language*, eds. Johann-Baptist Metz and Jean-Pierre Jossua (New York: Herder and Herder, 1973) 84-96.

[11] See 'Dramatic Artistry in the Third Stage of Meaning' (above, chapter 7).

[12] On the spiritual, see Lonergan, *Insight* 517-20/541-43; on knowledge of this dimension, ibid. chapter 11; on this knowledge as objective, ibid. chapter 13.

[13] Ibid. chapter 11.

[14] Søren Kierkegaard, *The Concept of Dread*, trans. Walter Lowrie (Princeton: Princeton University Press, 1957) passim.

[15] For a dramatic, elemental dramatization of this option, see Jung's own account of the dream that preceded the composition of his rationalization of the option in *Answer to Job*. The dream is narrated in C.G. Jung, *Memories, Dreams, Reflections* (see above, chapter 3, note 49) 217-19.

[16] See Paul Ricoeur, *Freud and Philosophy* (see above, chapter 1, note 7) 527.

[17] Lonergan, *Insight* 473/498.

[18] Ibid. 623-24/647.

[19] See Paul Ricoeur, *Fallible Man* (see above, chapter 1, note 5).

[20] Lonergan, *Insight* 627-30/650-53.

[21] Ibid. chapter 20.

[22] See C.G. Jung, 'Commentary on "The Secret of the Golden Flower" (see above, chapter 5, note 25) esp. 44-45.

[23] T.S. Eliot, 'Burnt Norton,' *Four Quartets* (New York: Harcourt, Brace, and World, 1971) 15. Thus William Johnston is enabled to make positive use of Jung in his study of Zen and Christian mysticism, *The Still Point* (New York: Harper and Row, 1971).

[24] Lonergan, *Method in Theology* 103.

[25] See especially Marie-Louise von Franz, *C.G. Jung: His Myth in Our Time* (see above, chapter 4, note 23).

[26] The argument of this paper has been telescoped into what for many may be an extremely cryptic statement. I have tried not simply to restate what I have argued elsewhere, but to reshape my previous considerations into a new configuration. But, because of the possible difficulties and seeming unfoundedness of what I here propose in the form of conclusions, perhaps I may be allowed to refer the reader once again to the article mentioned in footnote 11 and to indicate that the backbone of my entire argument may be found in my book *Subject and*

Psyche (see above, chapter 2, note 21). Chapter 2 of this book indicates where one might turn for criteria on psychic conversion.

The Lonergan framework of my argumentation is, I fear, something that I will have to afford myself the luxury either of assuming in readers or of encouraging them to explore on their own, as there is simply no question of repeating that mammoth enterprise before starting on my own. I might add regarding Lonergan, however, that the framework that he provides for ethical and religious self-appropriation is purely heuristic, while that afforded in his writings for cognitive self-appropriation contains a wealth of concrete detail. Even here, though, one is hardly left off the hook. The crucial issue is not met by parroting Lonergan's examples, but by supplying the concrete details of the questions one has oneself pursued in the course of the development of one's own knowledge. I have argued that psychic conversion supplies the concrete details for religious self-appropriation. See 'Psychic Conversion' (see above, chapter 2).

11 Jungian Psychology and Lonergan's Foundations: A Methodological Proposal

The archetypal psychology of Carl Gustav Jung has for several decades aroused considerable interest in the Christian and Jewish theological communities.[1] For the past seven years, I have been attempting to meet some of the fundamental issues that are at stake in the dialogue among theologians and Jungian psychologists. The present paper represents a synthetic statement of the cumulative advances in my own thinking over this period.

Protestant theologian Bernard Loomer has written that 'theology is subject to what has been disclosed in the concreteness of individuality.'[2] The extensive work in theological methodology done by the Roman Catholic theologian Bernard Lonergan enables us to recognize that Loomer's prescription is not simply a description of our contemporary theological situation, but expresses an inevitability. A historically conscious age, mindful of cultural pluralism and relativity, is becoming aware of the structuring role of the theologian as subject in the development of any theology at any stage of the history of consciousness. Theology is subject to the theologian who constructs it, and the theologian is subject to what has been disclosed in one's intellectual, moral, religious, and psychic individuality. For any theologian to articulate the foundations of theology is for that theologian to discover and appropriate the self as an intellectual, moral, religious, and psychic subject of self-transcendent operations in the cognitive and existential orders.

In this light, the potential significance and fruitfulness of the Jungian maieutic of selfhood for a methodologically grounded theology becomes clear. The whole point of the Jungian-guided process of conscious individuation lies in the discovery and appropriation of the psychic constituents of one's concrete subjectivity, as these are revealed in the elemental symbols of dreams, twilight imaging,[3] and associative fantasy. Jungian psychology, it seems, can function for the theologian at the level of psychic self-appropriation in a manner analogous to the functioning of the intentionality analysis of Lonergan at the level of intellectual self-appropriation. As Lonergan's cognitional theory helps one to answer the question, What am I doing when I am knowing? so Jungian psychological analysis promotes the self-appropriation of what one has done and is doing to create a work of dramatic art out of the materials of one's life: a human story with a meaning, with a direction, and with the integrity that comes from heightening and expanding one's consciousness through negotiating the various complexes of affect and image that constitute one's sensitive participation in the historical drama of life, and in the dialectic of history itself. In each instance, with Lonergan as with Jung, there is a disclosure of the concreteness of individuality, and so an appropriation of a portion of the foundations of one's affirmations and systematic understanding as a theologian.

In this paper, I will presume that the cognitional-theoretic disclosures of Lonergan and their significance for the self-appropriation of theology's foundational subjectivity are sufficiently public as to need no further exposition. Within the context set by the methodological gains that I find to accrue from Lonergan's work, I will attempt to specify the complementary significance of Jungian psychology. My paper will treat, first, a series of methodological considerations and, second, an indication of the changes that must occur in Christian theology and in Jungian psychology if the two are to prove mutually enriching.

1　Eight Methodological Considerations

I begin with methodological considerations, because I find that it is here that the principal difficulties have arisen in the incipient and often aborted dialogues between theology and Jungian psychology. Before we can establish the precise pertinence of Jung's psychology for the concreteness of individuality that is theology's foundational reality, we must determine just what it is that we are about in such an exercise.

1.1　Theory and Praxis

First, then, when we are talking about Jungian psychology, we are referring only derivatively to a set of categories that feature in a conceptual system — ego, shadow, persona, anima, animus, archetypes, collective unconscious, etc. Jungian psychology is primarily a praxis of psychological analysis through which the experiential base of such categories is disclosed. It is against this base that these categories are to be judged for their relative adequacy as disclosive of psychological reality. Jungian psychology is a set of existential and interpersonal exercises through which one embarks upon a journey through 'inner space' that promotes the conscious and self-knowing individuation of the concrete subjectivity that one is. In this sense, Jungian psychology parallels, but in a quite distinct medium of communication, the set of exercises for the appropriation of one's intelligence and rationality in act that Lonergan presents in *Insight* as cognitional theory. And the theologically foundational role of Jungian psychology, like that of Lonergan's work in transcendental method, is not primarily but only derivatively categorial, conceptual, and theoretical. Here as elsewhere, praxis grounds theory. In the case of Lonergan, the praxis of understanding grounds the theory of understanding. In the case of Jung, the praxis of individuation grounds the theory of individuation. And for the theologian, the praxis of Jungian analysis grounds any attempt at correlating or mediating theological and depth-psychological categories. The question of the pertinence of Jungian psychology for theology must be pushed back one step, to become the question of the pertinence of Jungian analysis for the disclosure of the concreteness of the theologian's individuality. That question can be answered only by reflection on the concrete praxis of Jungian analysis.

Through the medium of analysis, then, one discovers in an explanatory fashion the factors that have been at work either consciously or with relative unconsciousness or non-differentiation in the development of the person one has become. One negotiates these factors or complexes with the deliberate intention of integrating them through conscious dialectical procedures into the creation of one's own work of dramatic art. One objectifies in narrative form one's ongoing development as a conscious human subject in relation to one's own psychological depths, to the significant others in one's life, to the cultural and political drama of one's age, to the universe of being, and to the transpersonal mystery one discovers and relates to along the way.[4] Theologically pertinent questions inevitably arise in the process, but the process itself is required if the contributions of Jung to the construction of theological foundations, positions, and systematics are to bear fruit.

1.2 *The Existential Subject*

Secondly, Jungian psychology is pertinent for the objectification of *the existential portion* of theology's foundational reality. Theological foundations are understood by Lonergan to consist in an objectification of intellectual, moral, and religious authenticity or conversion. From such an articulation, one derives the categories that one will employ in one's theology, whether it be in the work one does to interpret, judge, and evaluate the past — research, interpretation, history, and dialectic — or in one's assuming responsibility for speaking *in oratione recta* to one's contemporaries — doctrines, systematics, and communications. The categories are twofold. General theological categories are shared with other disciplines. Special theological categories are proper to theology. Both sets are to have a transcultural base, which is, however, always objectified in culturally relative formulations. The base of general theological categories is the basic method of conscious intentionality itself, the interlocking set of terms and relations that constitute the unity of empirical, intelligent, rational, and existential consciousness. The base of special theological categories, in Christian terms, is found in God's gift of love. The historically conditioned objectification of the twofold base constitutes theological foundations.

The data, then, for theological foundations are found in the operations of one's own *knowing* and *choosing* and in the process of one's *development as a religious subject*. The data in one's *knowing* are retrieved and systematized in the objectification that is possible by the time one has reached chapter II of Lonergan's *Insight*. But, as Frederick Crowe has indicated, the data on one's *choosing*, on one's existential subjectivity, are not so easily retrieved.

We can quite easily practice experiencing; we have only to open and close our eyes repeatedly. We can practice understanding, though not so easily; we have to make up problems and puzzles, or find them in a book. To practice judgment is still more difficult; in the nature of the case the judgmental process has to be slow and thorough, concerned with the real world instead of the fictitious one of artificial problems, and so cases for practice do not come readily to hand. But when we turn to decision it seems that cases for practice are excluded on principle. If it is a real decision, it involves me existentially, and then it is no mere 'practice'; if it is a mere exercise, an example chosen for the practice, then it is no real decision, for it does not involve me existentially.[5]

The same may be said, a fortiori, for the retrieval of the data on religious conversion and development. When one is engaged existentially, one is not practicing operations so as to amass a field of data for self-appropriation. One is, rather, dramatically operating in such a way as to promote or to hinder one's very development as a person. The self-appropriation of one's moral and religious being is not achieved in the same manner as is the self-appropriation of one's intellectual and rational operations.

My second methodological consideration, then, has to do with the manner in which the theologian is to objectify the existential portion of theology's foundational subjectivity. What is existential also is dramatic, and so the appropriation of the existential is the construction, the weaving, the patterning, the telling of *the story that is one's life*. It is precisely here that we can locate the theological significance of the techniques that have been developed by twentieth-century depth-psychological analysis. These techniques are meant to bring the subject into personal possession of the existential and dramatic significance of one's personal history. The disclosure of this significance is meant, moreover, not only to bring one to a new series of decisions through which one's self-constitution may proceed more smoothly to the realization of one's unique selfhood, but also to mediate in explanatory fashion the positive or negative significance for one's development of previous existential, decisional moments in one's life. In the interpersonal maieutic of selfhood developed by depth psychology, we find a process of existential self-mediation that parallels what Lonergan's cognitional analysis does for the subject in the intellectual order. Through this existential maieutic one gains a control of meaning through interiorly differentiated consciousness that enables one to construct the dramatic narrative of one's moral and religious being. This control of meaning is analogous to that which issues from Lonergan's cognitional analysis, in that both investigations are explanatory of one's subjective interiority.

1.3   Freud and Jung

Thirdly, I must indicate what I find to be the relative superiority of Jungian analysis over Freudian psychoanalytic techniques for this existential self-mediation. The critical grounding of a preference for Jung over Freud lies for me in Lonergan's cognitional analysis itself, and more precisely in its vigorous and repeated arguments against reductionism and in favor of the relative autonomy of the sciences of sensitive psychology and of human consciousness from the biological, chemical, and physical sciences. In terms of the constitutive notions of the science of human psychology, the radical methodological difference between Freud and Jung manifests itself in their respective treatments of psychic energy or libido. But let me first locate their argument in a metaphysical framework.

Lonergan suggests that we identify energy with the metaphysical element, prime potency.[6] Characteristic of all development in the concrete universe of being proportionate to human experience, human understanding, and human judgment is a tension between limitation and transcendence. This tension is rooted in potency, that is, in the individuality, continuity, coincidental conjunctions and successions, and nonsystematic divergence from intelligible norms that are to be known by the empirical consciousness of a mind intent on explanatory understanding. Potency grounds tension because it is the principle both of limitation and of the upwardly but indeterminately directed dynamism of proportionate being that Lonergan calls finality. Prime potency is the principle of limitation of the lowest genus of proportionate being, and since each higher genus is limited by the preceding lower genus, prime potency is the universal principle of limitation for the whole range of proportionate being. Lonergan wants to conceive prime potency as a ground of quantitative limitation and to relate quantitative limitation to the properties verified by science in the quantity it names energy.

A methodological problem arises, however, when the object of scientific inquiry is the organism, or psychic sensitivity, or human intelligence itself, for in these instances, and increasingly as one moves from one to the next, 'measuring loses both in significance and in efficacy.' The loss in significance is due to the fact that these higher integrations in the universe are relatively independent of the exact quantities of lower manifolds. The loss in efficacy is due to the fact that the heuristic notion for explanatory understanding of organism, psyche, and intelligence is not some indeterminate function to be determined by the use of differential equations, but the general notion of development, for which quantitative measurement 'possesses no assignable efficacy.'[7] Thus, when the scientific intention is one of understanding human psychic systematizations of otherwise coincidental underlying manifolds of neurological events, quantitative techniques provide little or no assistance.

Paul Ricoeur has spotted a methodological inconsistency in Freud on precisely this issue. In his exegesis of Freud's early (1895) 'Project for a Scientific Psychology,' Ricoeur notes that, while Freud attempted to force a mass of psychical data into a quantitative framework, he specifies no numerical law or set of laws to govern his notion of quantity, which he understood at that time as 'a summation of excitation homologous to physical energy.'[8] In this and later psychoanalytic works of Freud, 'the quantitative framework and the neuronic support recede into the background, until they are no more than a given and convenient language of reference which supplies the necessary constraint for the expression of great discoveries.'[9]

The great discoveries, of course, are of another order than the quantitative. Despite Jung's relative imprecision of language compared to Freud, the operative heuristic notion in his thought for understanding human psychical reality approximates much more clearly the notion of development. Lonergan has defined development as 'a flexible, linked sequence of dynamic and increasingly differentiated higher integrations that meet the tension of successively transformed underlying manifolds through successive applications of the principles of correspondence and emergence.'[10] The principle of emergence states that 'otherwise coincidental manifolds of lower conjugate acts [events] invite the higher integration effected by higher conjugate forms.'[11] The principle of correspondence is to the effect that 'significantly different underlying manifolds require different higher integrations.'[12] With respect to Freud and Jung, these metaphysical principles mean that energic compositions and distributions emergent on the psychic level in the form of images and associated affects are not to be explained by moving backwards to one basic and unsurpassable desire whose real object is sexual and whose other object relations are displacements from the sexual object. Rather, there is to be affirmed a polymorphism of human desire, with a corresponding multiformity of energic compositions and distributions at the sensitively psychic level. For Jung, psychic energy is a surplus of energy from the standpoint of biological purposiveness. Its original orientation is upwardly but indeterminately directed. It is not tied to a destiny in reverse, and its changes in orientation are to be explained, not as relatively healthy or relatively neurotic *displacements*, but as *transformations*. Psychic energy has no determinate object from which to be repressively displaced. Transformation of energy occurs not by repression, but by a thoroughly natural process that occurs when the conscious subject adopts the proper attitude toward the process of energic composition and distribution — in Jungian terms, complex formation — that constitutes what for depth psychology is called the unconscious. This proper attitude is one of therapeutically tutored attentiveness. It is learned in the interpersonal dialogue of Jungian analysis. It puts one in touch with the upwardly but indeterminately directed dynamism of one's psychic finality that is headed toward the fuller being that Jung designates as wholeness or individuation. Thus Jung, in contrast to Freud, adopts a teleological orientation both in his theory and in the praxis of analysis that grounds that theory.

1.4 *Symbols*

Fourthly, Jung correlates the transformation of psychic energy with the process of elemental symbolization, and consequently provides a notion of and a familiarity with symbols that not only promote the subject's psychic self-appropriation or individuation, but also can provide the theologian with a useful hermeneutic tool and with the foundational possibility of critically grounding the use of symbols in the construction of one's own theological positions and systematics.

Freud and the early Jung regarded all fantasizing and dreaming as an intrusion of the pleasure-oriented, nonrealistic unconscious psyche into the domain of the reality principle or ego, and consequently as wishful thinking. But in Jung's mature position, fantasies and dreams are spontaneous products of a layer of subjective being that has its own distinct meaning and purpose. This purpose is to compensate for an unbalanced conscious attitude, or, in instances where the conscious attitude is already well integrated, to complement and confirm the ego's orientation to wholeness. Fantasies and dreams thus cooperate in the interests of the transformation of energy in the direction of the wholeness of the personality. They do not merely *point to* the transformation of energy, but *give* what they symbolize. They are not just symbols of transformation, but transforming symbols. Wholeness, then, is a generic goal of energic process that becomes increasingly specific through the transformation that occurs in and because of the symbolizing process, given the correct conscious attitude. As one deliberately enters upon the inner journey through the world constituted by one's elemental symbolizing, one comes into contact with the dimension of human reality whence have issued the symbolic productions of the mythopoetic imagination in the religions of human history.

1.5   *Jungian Psychology and Transcendental Method*

Fifthly, this release of what Jung calls the transcendent function, through which one establishes a bridge between one's ego consciousness and the symbolizing process of psychic energy, can be integrated with Lonergan's intentionality analysis in such a way as to render Jungian analysis not simply a parallel and complementary maieutic of selfhood, but an integral and constitutive feature of a truly transcendental method. The technique of this integration is quite simple: it involves extending the relations of sublation that Lonergan shows to obtain among the various levels of waking consciousness, so as to include dreaming consciousness in the analysis of intentionality. For Lonergan, empirical consciousness of the data of sense and of interiority is sublated by the intelligent consciousness that grasps relations among the data; intelligent consciousness is sublated by the rational consciousness that reflects on one's understanding so as to judge its adequacy to the data; and rational consciousness is sublated by the existential consciousness of the subject who is concerned to do what is good. The integration of the transcendent function in the intentionality of the human spirit toward the intelligible, the true and the real, and the good is effected by the recognition that consciousness begins, not when we awake but when we dream, and so a transcendental method that would approximate a retrieval of the dimensions of consciousness itself must acknowledge that the first level of consciousness really is the dream. Dreams are sublated into waking empirical consciousness by memory; into intelligent consciousness by the interpretation whose art one learns in the analytic sessions; into ra-

tional consciousness by critical reflection on one's interpretation; and into existential consciousness by one's quest
for integrity in one's decisions and actions. The finality of
the dream, then, is harmonious with that of the normative
order of inquiry: authentic cognitive and existential praxis.

These relations may also be understood by reflecting on Lonergan's discussion of the dramatic pattern of
experience in *Insight*. The dramatic pattern of experience
is that sequence of sensations, memories, images, emotions, conations, associations, bodily movements, and
spontaneous intersubjective responses that are organized
by one's concern to make a work of art out of his or her
living, to stamp life with a style, with grace, with freedom,
with dignity. The dramatic pattern is operative in a preconscious manner, through the collaboration of imagination and intelligence in the task of supplying to consciousness the materials one will employ in structuring the contours of one's life as a work of art. These materials emerge
into consciousness in the form of images and accompanying affects.

The preconscious collaboration of intelligence and
imagination in selecting images for conscious insight, judgment, and decision may be either authentic or inauthentic, open to truth or biased. The bias of the inauthentic
collaboration is an always individual blending of the dramatic bias that overwhelms consciousness by elementary
passion, the egoistic bias that excludes materials that would
challenge one's own narrowly conceived advantage, the
group bias that collapses the human good into what is expedient for one's group or class or nation, and the general
bias that despises the detachment of theoretical insight.
The authentic dramatic artist, on the other hand, is open
to receiving into consciousness the images that are needed
for the insightful, truthful, and responsible construction
of a work of dramatic art.

Dreams are a privileged instance of such images, for in dreams symbols are released in such a way that they are not prevented from entering into consciousness by the dramatic, egoistic, group, or general bias of waking consciousness or the ego. When we sleep, the distorted censorship of inauthentic imagination and intelligence is relaxed enough that the neural demands find an appropriate conscious complement in images that, were they negotiated by the waking subject, would provide some of the materials that are needed for the insights, judgments, and decisions through which one structures a work of dramatic artistry.

1.6   Psychic Conversion

Sixthly, the release of the internal communication that occurs through the habit of negotiating one's dreams intelligently, rationally, and responsibly can be understood in terms of a fourth modality of conversion beyond the intellectual, moral, and religious conversions that for Lonergan constitute theology's foundational reality. Jungian analysis promotes what I have called *psychic conversion*, which I understand as the release of the capacity for internal communication through the discovery, interpretation, and existential negotiation of the elemental symbols of dreams, through which neural process enters into conscious participation in the drama of one's life. If an objectification of conversion constitutes theological foundations, such foundations must provide an explanatory account of the elemental symbolization process with which the subject gains cognitive and existential familiarity through psychic conversion. A phenomenology of the sensitive psyche as operator of elemental symbols, or at least a heuristic structure of such a phenomenology, will provide a portion of theological foundations.

1.7   *Religious and Moral Self-appropriation*

Seventhly, such a development in transcendental method, if it is accurate, resolves a peculiar difficulty in Lonergan's account of conversion. Lonergan, it seems, is quite correct in speaking of religious conversion as generally occurring prior to moral conversion, and of religious and moral conversion as generally occurring prior to intellectual conversion. But religious and moral conversion are precritical. That is to say, while they are self-validating experiences, they also do not involve self-appropriation in the technical sense of explanatory self-knowledge. Intellectual conversion, on the other hand, is coincident with intellectual self-appropriation. It is acquiring 'the mastery in one's own house that is to be had only when one knows precisely what one is doing when one is knowing.'[13] Lonergan's account of conversion, then, leaves unanswered the question of how one gains religious and moral self-appropriation.

There are certain clues, however, in Lonergan's development of the notion of value that lead me to recommend psychic conversion as the key to religious and moral self-appropriation. For value, Lonergan says, is apprehended in *intentional feelings* before it is discriminated by questions for deliberation and affirmed in judgments of value.[14] And feelings enjoy a reciprocal relationship of evocation with *symbols*. 'A symbol is an image of a real or imaginary object that evokes a feeling or is evoked by a feeling.'[15] Thus to acquire the habit of internal communication through the cognitive and existential negotiation of the elemental symbols of one's sensitive psyche is to gain familiarity with the orientations and motivations of one's intentional feelings, and consequently is to disengage one's moral and, as the case may be, even one's religious orientation in a world that is not only mediated and constituted by meaning but also motivated by value. One's dreams are a story, told by the sensitive psyche, of one's dramatic participation as a morally and religiously authentic or inauthentic subject whose decisions and actions affect for better or for worse the constitution of the human world.

1.8   Political Significance

Eighthly, and finally, then, there is a political significance to the disclosures rendered possible by psychic conversion, and consequently a potential fruitfulness for political theology lies ready to be tapped in the maieutic of the psyche whose essential elements are provided some relative adequacy by Jung. The situations that provide the context of the subjective dialectic of waking consciousness and neural process are established by the dialectic of community and of history, whose twofold and opposed generative principles are, on the one hand, the biases, and on the other hand, the converted subjectivity of authentic persons. Psychic conversion promotes proximately the appropriation of the inner dialectic of the subject. But this dialectic makes no sense whatsoever unless the analysis of it sets it within the context of the dialectic of history. This means, then, that one's dreams gain an accurate interpretation only when the drama they reveal is placed in the environing context of the dialectic of progress and decline in history in which the subject is necessarily a participant. The theologian educated by the maieutic of the psyche is equipped for the kind of theological reflection, then, that brings to bear on the course of history itself the mediation of Christian faith with the contemporary dialectic of social, cultural, personal, and religious values.

2 Theological and Psychological Implications

The remainder of this paper deals with the effects of the above methodological positions on the doing of theology and on the praxis and theory of Jungian psychology. I begin with theology.

2.1 Theological Implications

In a paper delivered at the November, 1977, meeting of the American Theological Society, midwest division, Professor Walter Kukkonen of the Lutheran School of Theology in Chicago disengaged four areas of influence on theology that would follow from theology's encounter with Jungian psychology.[16] I have decided to list these influences as Professor Kukkonen mentioned them, and also to comment on them in the light of my own methodological position. The first of Kukkonen's recommendations has to do with theological method, the second with theological education, the third with theological categories, and the fourth with the theologian's consciousness or subjectivity.

2.1.1 Theological Method

First, then, a theology structured by a mind and heart informed by the Jungian maieutic of selfhood will have restored to its method, in Kukkonen's words, an element of madness: that is, of prophecy, of initiation, of the paradigmatic, of poetry, of love, of mysticism. What this means is that the grounding experiences of one's theology will be one's own numinous experiences, shimmering with the primal emotion of the elemental and the archetypal. These experiences are participatory, a share in the mystery of transcendence, precisely as mystery, that is, as ultimate

context and interpretive framework for the events of existence in the world. Religious experiences of awe and wonder, of incomprehensible and inarticulable transcendent
reality, will be restored to the position of being the founding experiences of a theological vision. For, as David Burrell
has expressed the matter, 'If one undertakes the inner journey to individuation, he cannot fail to meet God.'[17]

2.1.2 Theological Education

The implications for theological education are both
clear and far-reaching. Kukkonen limits his recommendations to specifying the introduction into seminary curricula
of practical training in pastoral dialogue. I want to expand
this suggestion, in light of my reliance on Lonergan, to
recommend extensive education of all theological students,
academic and ministerial, in the functional specialities of
dialectic and foundations, where the grounding experiences
of one's theological positions are retrieved in a dialogic
situation. What I add to Lonergan's position is that the
objectification of conversion, as mentioned above, will
profit immensely from depth-psychological analysis of a
Jungian variety.

2.1.3 Theological Categories

Theological categories, Kukkonen argues, will be
experientially grounded if the theologian is under the influence of the Jungian maieutic of his or her own selfhood.
I acknowledge that in theology itself one can find many
contributions to such an experiential grounding of categories, of which Lonergan's prescription for the derivation of categories is one of the more sophisticated. But the
point of introducing the Jungian maieutic into the foundational task is more profound: not only is experience
granted a role as ground of theology, but also the experience itself is deeply enriched when one allows oneself to

be introduced to the organizing principles or forms that guide one's activity, those principles that Jung calls archetypes.

2.1.4 The Theologian's Consciousness

Finally, and grounding the other influences of Jungian psychology on theology, there will be established the explicit connection of the theologian's consciousness with the elemental symbolic function that Jung called the collective unconscious. Through this connection, effected by what I have called psychic conversion, the theologian gains a hermeneutic tool for the interpretation of the religious expressions of other men and women at other times and places and in other cultures, and a foundational framework for introducing into one's own theological systematics the use of categories that are unapologetically symbolic, poetic, aesthetic, and yet explanatory, because derived from thoroughgoing interior self-differentiation.[18]

2.2 Psychological Implications

It remains that something must be said of the changes in Jungian psychology that will result from the encounter with a methodical theology grounded in transcendental method. The changes must be spoken of in two manners, for we distinguished above between the praxis of individuation and the theoretical system developed by reflection on that praxis.

2.2.1 Praxis

All human praxis is guided by heuristic notions through which one anticipates the objectives of one's operations. The praxis of individuation on the part of a theological consciousness tutored by the above methodological emphases on conversion will be in search of *self-tran-*

scendence. The heuristic notion that will govern the development of self-possession will shift *from wholeness to self-transcendence* or authenticity. Self-transcendence is fourfold: it is cognitive, moral, religious, and affective. The Jungian maieutic of the sensitive, symbolizing psyche will be particularly helpful in the pursuit of affective self-transcendence. The wholeness of the personality will be regarded from this standpoint as a byproduct of one's advance in authenticity, and will not be pursued for its own sake.

Affective self-transcendence is *detachment*, the inner freedom from both inner states and outer objects and situations that is the goal of authentic ascetical and mystical disciplines. Mysticisms, it seems, are twofold: there is an intentionality mysticism whose most appropriate expression is an apophatic theology; and there is a romantic mysticism that bogs down in the archetypal, the paradigmatic, the elementally symbolic, and that is ultimately tied to a pantheism or an atheism or an immanentism or a nature religion. In a romantic mysticism, the symbols of the psyche, however spontaneous and elemental and thus uncontrived they may be, in the last analysis cease to be exploratory of intentionality's reaching toward the nonrepresentable, and become ends in themselves. Their term is not *in re*, but *in se*. In an intentionality mysticism, on the other hand, detachment extends to symbolic productions themselves, to visions, dreams, and images, even when these are genuine results of the union of the subject with the world-transcendent goal of intentional striving. The key to the difference in the *praxis* of these mystical disciplines lies in the heuristic notions that govern them. The heuristic notion of an intentionality mysticism is absolute or vertical self-transcendence, while the guiding notion of a romantic mysticism has affinities with Jung's absolutization of the notion of wholeness.

Wholeness is for Jung best symbolized in mandala images. Mandalas, of course, are symbols of the integration of opposites, and they will continue to play this function in an individuation praxis governed by the heuristic notion of self-transcendence. But development is not only integration. *Integrators* of development are a function of *operators* of development.[19] And development, again, is 'a flexible, linked *sequence* of dynamic and increasingly differentiated higher integrations that meet the tension of successively transformed underlying manifolds through successive applications of the principles of correspondence and emergence.'[20] Clearly, when such a generic notion is used of conscious human development, the operative heuristic notion guiding the sequence is self-transcendence. The wholeness of the personality will be a byproduct of authentic intentionality.

Lonergan's term for affective self-transcendence in its full flowering is 'universal willingness.'[21] The term highlights well the referent in *existential consciousness* of such detachment. The affectively self-transcendent subject is one whose home is the universe of being and whose intentionality is oriented to the discovery and execution of a unique individual vocation within a universal order whose immanent intelligibility is not some statically fixed system but an emergent probability governed by classical, statistical, genetic, and dialectical laws. The discovery and execution of one's unique vocation in such an order is possible only by the implementation of the transcendental precepts that govern the operations of consciousness at each of its emergent levels: imperatives for attentiveness, for understanding, for rationality, for moral responsibility, and for faithful and self-sacrificing love. With each imperative, we are called to a more self-transcendent mode of being-in-the-world. The integration of our being as persons is a function of our fidelity to these imperatives.

The symbols of our dreams become from this perspective a narrative told by the sensitive psyche of an intentional human subject — a narrative whose dialectical theme is the emergence of the authentic historical agent, of the knower, the doer, the lover. Dreams are a cipher for the discernment of the 'pulls and counterpulls' experienced by the existential subject in search of authentic direction in the movement of life.[22] The praxis of individuation that emerges from a methodically grounded foundational subjectivity will sublate the dream into a conscious intentionality governed by the imperatives that are concomitant with one's capacities of empirical, intelligent, rational, moral, and agapic consciousness.

2.2.2 Theory

The Jungian *theory* of individuation will undergo a number of changes as a result of the encounter with the praxis that emerges from theological foundations. Many of the operative concepts in Jungian theory will suffer greater differentiation and clarification than was provided them by Jung. I limit my comments to three areas of necessary change that are particularly pertinent to theology.

First, we need a clearer delineation than Jung provides us of the tripartite constitution of the human person. For Jung the elements of this constitution are matter or instinct, psyche, and spirit or archetype. Matter and spirit Jung heuristically characterizes as psychoid, that is, to be understood by analogy with our understanding of the psyche. More precisely, though, what we need is a sharper clarification of the organic and spiritual dimensions of the person, and a concomitant delimitation of the referent of the term 'psyche.' Spirit must be more clearly differentiated from psyche, and the role of spirituality, which I take to include the operations of human understanding, judgment, decision, and agapic love, must be specified as it relates to the individuation process that is reflected in and promoted by the images of the psyche's dreams.

Secondly, the Jungian treatment of the symbolic significance of the person of Jesus Christ will not emerge uncriticized from the dialogue of theology and analytical psychology. For Jung, the person of Christ is represented as the hero who, by being faithful and completing his journey, became the Way for others to accomplish theirs; and Christ is also 'our nearest analogy of the self and its meaning,' 'the supreme symbol of the Self' (Kukkonen). Both aspects of the Jungian thought on Christ I find suspect from a theological point of view. The principal difficulty resides in Jung's notion of Christ as archetype of the self.

In his later writings on this issue, and especially in his book *Aion*, Jung provides us with an interpretation of Christianity such that, if individuation as Jung understands it were to be correlated with any specifically theological category from Christian tradition, it would be, not with such notions as conversion, justification, transformation in Christ, or redemption, but with the Origenistic notion of *apocatastasis*. For in *Aion*, we are presented with a notion of the self which is only partly expressed in the Christian imaging and understanding of Christ. The other half, as it were, of the self is expressed in the Christian imaging and understanding of Satan. These two halves of the self, Jung tells us, have been warring with each other during the astrological age of Pisces, but in the emerging age of Aquarius they will blissfully embrace in the movement of the individuated personality to a position beyond good and evil.

This, I believe, is pure wishful thinking in a quite Freudian i.e., Oedipal, sense. Sebastian Moore, in his recent book *The Crucified Jesus is No Stranger*, provides us with a far more helpful model of how Christ can be understood as a symbolic incarnation of the true self of human subjects. It is in his crucified condition that Christ embodies the self — the self that is killed, victimized, by the ego that is infected by the sinfulness of the denial of its own contingency. The Christian contemplative experience of entering into the Crucified has been, Moore says, also an experience of the emergence into life of the self that the ego has killed, an emergence that is empowered by the forgiveness of the sin of the ego meeting with love the murderous acts that victimized the self. With reference to Jung's derivative understanding of Christ as symbolic of the heroic quest, then, we might say that, if Christ is our way to God, it is only because more radically he is God's way to us, God's way of transforming what we have victimized and killed into the center of a life that stretches to the limits of agapic love. For Moore, we exist throughout our lives in the polarity of crucifier and crucified. The implications of Moore's model for the reworking of the Jungian theory of the final stages of the analytic process are substantial. In brief, Moore preserves from Jung a helpful insight into our customary misidentification of the locus of evil in instinct, but removes definitively the hopeless ambiguity of Jung's own treatment of evil in its relation to goodness.[23]

Thirdly, then, and with more specific reference to the problem of evil, Jungian psychology will have to make a distinction between two quite distinct dimensions of the transpersonal elemental symbolism that originates in what Jung calls the collective unconscious. I draw here on Northrop Frye for a distinction between the archetypal and the anagogic. As transposed from Frye's context to my own, archetypal symbols are taken from nature and imitate nature's processes: a helpful maternal symbol in one's dreams is an analogue of the personal mother in her nourishing and life-giving capacities. Anagogic symbols are taken from nature and from history, but they are not so much imitative as radically transformative of the dimension from which they are derived. They are the stuff of eschatology and apocalyptic, and they provide, I think, the inclusive symbolic horizon in terms of which all other elemental symbolic productions will receive their most adequate interpretation.

With such a distinction, one is enabled to differentiate those opposites that admit of natural reconciliation with one another and those whose contradictoriness is resolved only by a divinely originated solution. Among the former, for instance, are the opposites that join in the psychological androgyny — what may be called the masculinity of intentionality and the femininity of the psyche. The latter are the opposites of authenticity and inauthenticity. These never join, because of the radically unintegratable quality of that dimension of evil that, despite Jung's protestations to the contrary, is not superficially but most profoundly understood by such Christian theologians as Augustine and Thomas Aquinas as *privatio boni*. But this point would demand another article, and so I bring these suggestions to a conclusion on a note that will probably prove annoying to an orthodox Jungian, but that is, I am convinced, the locus where the dialogue among theologians and Jungian psychologists will become dialectical. But even the inevitability of dialectic on this point is evidence in favor of the natural irreconcilability of evil as *basic sin*[24] with graced authenticity.

Notes

[1] See James W. Heisig, 'Jung and Theology: A Bibliographical Essay' (see above, chapter 5, note 1).

[2] Bernard Loomer, 'S-I-Z-E,' *Criterion*, cited in Walter Kukkonen, 'The Beyond Within: Where Theology and Psychology Ought to Meet,' unpublished paper delivered at the November, 1977, meeting of the American Theological Society, midwest Division, Divinity School, University of Chicago.

[3] See Ira Progoff, *The Symbolic and the Real* (New York: McGraw-Hill, 1973).

[4] That all of these relationships are clarified in Jungian analysis can be verified only in practice. Gerhard Adler, in *The Living Symbol: A Case Study of the Process of Individuation* (Princeton: Princeton University Press, 1961), shows the clarification in the case of one individual's analysis.

[5] Frederick E. Crowe, 'Dialectic and the Ignatian Spiritual Exercises' (see above, chapter 5, note 109) 19.

[6] Bernard Lonergan, *Insight* (see above, chapter 1, note 37) 443/468-69.

[7] Ibid. 463/488.

[8] Paul Ricoeur, *Freud and Philosophy* (see above, chapter 1, note 7) 73.

[9] Ibid.

[10] Lonergan, *Insight* 454/479.

[11] Ibid. 451/477.

[12] Ibid.

13 Bernard Lonergan, *Method in Theology* (see above, chapter 1, note 3) 239-40.

14 Ibid. 31.

15 Ibid. 64.

16 See above, note 2.

17 David Burrell, *Exercises in Religious Understanding* (see above, chapter 4, note 24) 221.

18 This represents, I believe, an advance on Lonergan on symbols. He tends to view with suspicion the explicit use of symbolic categories in an explanatory systematics. I have dealt with the point more extensively in 'The Theologian's Psyche: Notes toward a Reconstruction of Depth Psychology' (above, chapter 6).

19 See Lonergan, *Insight* 464-67/489-92; 476-77/501-502; 532-33/555-56.

20 Ibid. 454/479.

21 Ibid. 623-24/646-47.

22 See Eric Voegelin, 'The Gospel and Culture,' in *Jesus and Man's Hope*, ed. D.G. Miller and D.Y. Hadidian (Pittsburgh: Pittsburgh Theological Seminary, 1971).

23 Sebastian Moore, *The Crucified Jesus Is No Stranger* (New York: Seabury, 1977).

24 See Lonergan, *Insight* 666/689-90.

12 Jungian Psychology and Christian Spirituality I: Christian Spiritual Transformation: Self-transcendence and Self-appropriation

This is the first of three articles on the subject of Jungian psychology and contemporary Christian spirituality. The present article will focus on the latter of these two items, on Christian spiritual transformation as this is understood at the present moment in the life of the church. By concentrating on two terms frequently employed in the works of Bernard Lonergan, *self-transcendence* and *self-appropriation*, I hope to provide a context for the next two articles, which will deal more extensively with Jung. This first article will treat, first, Christian spiritual transformation as *self-transcendence*; second, Christian spiritual transformation as growth in self-knowledge or *self-appropriation*; third, the levels of consciousness that can be discovered when one enters on the way of self-appropriation; and fourth, the relation of feelings and symbols to these various levels or dimensions of consciousness. This fourth topic locates that element of our interior lives in regard to which Jung's insights become pertinent for our spiritual self-understanding.

I have discovered that any such treatment of Jung as the present one eventually brings me into that form of discrimination which, in Ignatian spirituality, is called the *discernment of spirits*. Jung is a religiously controversial fig-

ure. Not only does my own treatment and evaluation of
Jung tend to arouse rather than quell the arguments that
surround his person and his work, but, more significantly,
my critical response to Jung always carries me to the heart
of the Christian exigence to differentiate the true call of
God from the subtle attractions of the forces of evil as
these two contrary tendencies compete for the allegiance
of men and women involved in the renewal of the contemporary church. Why this is so will, I hope, become clear in
the subsequent articles, especially in the final one. But
perhaps I can offer now some indication of the difficulty.

First, then, Jung *is* a religiously controversial figure.
The religious significance of his psychological insights is
variously interpreted. John A. Sanford and Morton Kelsey
are two well-known authors who have drawn on Jung to
promote and understand Christian self-discovery.[1] On the
other hand, James Hillman has maintained that Jung's
guidelines to 'soul-making' are of a completely different
order from the well-known paths to spiritual transformation in Christ and from the insights of the other major
religious traditions of the world.[2] Martin Buber entered
into direct conflict with Jung, claiming that the psychology of individuation and religious faith are diametrically
opposed orientations of the human spirit.[3] Jung himself,
as we shall see, gives some indications of his own that the
process of individuation will lead the *cognoscentes* to the
position of being able to dispense with all forms of traditional religious involvement; but he also attempted to offer his psychology as an aid to the pastoral care of souls.[4]

What is one to make of these differences and ambiguities? Obviously, some framework must be found to enable us to enter on the kind of process that Lonergan calls
dialectic and *foundations*: the process, namely, in which we
not only assemble and review alternative interpretations,
but also evaluate and compare them, reduce their affini-

ties and oppositions to their underlying roots, determine which, if any, of these roots stand in dialectical opposition to one another in such wise that only a radical transformation of the basic horizon can achieve reconciliation, and, finally, choose that basic horizon and those resultant positions and interpretations which we will make our own.[5] Such a framework is what I hope to offer in the present article.

Secondly, my own judgments and decisions regarding the potential spiritual fruitfulness of Jung's work are themselves controversial, at least in the sense that they will please neither Jung's detractors nor his enthusiastic followers. For I will sharply differentiate the process of Christian self-transformation from the way to individuation that Jung maps out for us. But I will also insist with equal force that there is much that we not only can, but indeed must, learn from him in developing both a theology and an ascesis of spiritual transformation in the context of the contemporary world.

Thirdly, the only final arbiter of the kind of discrimination that I find necessary is what we have come to call the *discernment of spirits*. Jung's theological ambiguities, and the alternative interpretations and evaluations that are offered of his work, are symptomatic of an underlying spiritual conflict that can be mediated only in the context of the dialectic of grace and sin, of the Standards of Christ and of Satan. David Burrell has indicated correctly that one cannot fail to meet God if one goes on the inner journey to individuation.[6] But one will also meet much that is not God, and that is even opposed to God. Not only does Jung not help one to discriminate these forces as they operate in one's psyche, but he also contributes to and even encourages the confusion that can be experienced in such moments that call for discernment, and thus mires one in the conflictual forces that wage an ultimate battle in the depths of one's psyche. Jung's work, if left uncriticized, leads one into a psychological *cul-de-sac* that can assume demonic proportions.

I   Christian Spiritual Transformation as Self-transcendence

There are many diverse and quite useful approaches to the understanding of spiritual transformation. I have chosen to focus on two terms that have been developed by Bernard Lonergan. Lonergan's thought has achieved a great deal of notoriety due principally, it would seem, to its difficulty. I have no intention here of repeating the subtle intricacies of his full argumentation. I will rather present in what I hope are quite understandable terms the *results* of that argumentation, and will deal with more subtle points only to the extent that they are necessary to clarify my basic position.[7]

I choose Lonergan's approach to the issue of Christian spiritual transformation for several reasons. First, it is the approach with which I am most familiar and the one that I personally have found most helpful. Secondly, Lonergan explicitly takes his stand in *human interiority*. And, when we are talking about either spiritual transformation or Jungian psychology, we are talking about the realm of interior experience, about the *data of consciousness*, about such events as insights, judgments, decisions, and, as we will see, dreams. All of these happenings are items that we experience. But we experience them interiorly. None of us has ever *seen* an insight or a feeling. But I trust, too, that none of us would claim that he or she had never *experienced* a feeling or an insight, never judged that some proposition was true or false, never made a decision. Moreover, I hope that we all know the experience of *wanting* to understand, wanting to be reasonable in our judgments, wanting to be responsible in our decisions. For it is in the realm of that *desire*, and in being faithful to that desire, that Lonergan locates what it is to be an authentic human person. But our experience of these events and of this desire occurs, not in the realm of outer sense, but in the domain of human interiority. It is in interiority that, through these events of understanding, judging, and deciding, we 'process' reality. Sensations come in; language goes out; but between sensations and language there is, as Lonergan has formulated it in some recent lectures, the mysterious 'little black box' of our interiority. The workings of that little black box are the domain that we concentrate upon in Christian spiritual theology, in Jungian psychology, and in any attempt such as the present one that would relate spirituality to psychology.

I should mention, in addition, two other advantages that accrue from employing Lonergan's framework for understanding interiority. First, his stress, as I have already indicated, is on human *desire*, and desire is the area of our being that is illuminated by the explorations also of the great depth psychologists, including Jung. Secondly, and most importantly, Lonergan emphasizes that spiritual development is not something that occurs in some realm that is isolated from the insights that we have into the events of our everyday life, from the judgments that we make as to the truth or falsity of the most mundane propositions, from the anxieties we feel and the decisions that we make regarding our orientation and actions as beings-*in*-the-world. God's saving purpose is a will to save the world itself, to redeem the time of our lives, as Eliot would put it. It is not a dimension of reality that is totally extrinsic from the events of understanding, judging, and deciding that we experience every day. On the other hand, our relation to God is not to be collapsed into a secularistic denial of the supernatural character of grace. Rather, grace is offered *in* its supernatural character within the events of our everyday lives. So the perspective offered by Lonergan is neither a fundamentalism or extrinsicism that denies the this-worldly character of our lives, nor a secularism or immanentism that neglects the absolutely transcendent origin and finality of the relationship to the divine in which we stand at every moment of our lives.

What, then, is Christian spiritual development? Lonergan's treatment of this question is provided at the end of a lengthy analysis of human cognitional and moral development that concludes with the realization that the flowering of human potential, the sustained development of the human person, the solution of such social ills as injustice, alienation, and the dominance of totalitarian aspirations in both the West and the East today are impossible on the basis of human resources alone. We are confronted with a *problem of evil* in our development as human persons and in the social organization of human affairs. This problem is rooted in our very constitution as human subjects, in our finitude, in the tension between our always limited possibilities and our aspirations to transcend these limitations.

I will not go into the intricacies of Lonergan's analysis of the roots of moral impotence. Suffice it to say that he argues persuasively that we are faced with a problem of evil that we are powerless to resolve. If there is going to be a solution to the problem of evil, it must come in the form of redemption. Either there is a divinely originated solution to the problem of evil, or there is no solution at all. If God exists, if God knows of our plight, and if God is good, then there is a divinely originated solution that is offered to our freedom, one that we can accept or reject, one that, if we accept it, will involve us in a whole new area of growth and transformation, an area which we would not even know in any explicit way if God had not come to meet us. This distinct area of development is related to our cognitional and moral development. It is not the product of our knowing and our choosing. It is not something that we vainly imagine, or that we produce by wishful thinking. Rather, it is offered to our knowledge and our freedom as a *gift*. And if we accept it, it transvalues our values, and provides a new context for our knowing, a new atmosphere or environment that enables us to be truly intelligent in our questioning and genuinely reasonable in our judgments. This new context is *faith*, which Lonergan defines as 'the eye of love,' the eye of the love that is ours, that is the atmosphere in which we live, when we know ourselves as unconditionally loved by, and rooted in, the love that is God's alone.[8]

The divine solution to the problem of evil, then, is God's gift of love that is poured forth into our hearts by the Holy Spirit who has been given to us.[9] Our desire for this love is a natural desire: with Thomas Aquinas, Lonergan insists that we have a *natural* desire for the vision and love of God.[10] He insists, too, that our subjectivity is mutilated or abolished unless we are stretching forth towards God:

> There lies within [our] horizon a region for the divine, a shrine for ultimate holiness. It cannot be ignored. The atheist may pronounce it empty. The agnostic may urge that he finds his investigation has been inconclusive. The contemporary humanist will refuse to allow the question [of God] to arise. But their negations presuppose the spark in our clod, our native orientation to the divine.[11]

Being in love with God, then, is for Lonergan the basic fulfillment of the deepest human desire, that desire that he calls 'conscious intentionality.'

> That fulfillment brings a deep-set joy that can remain despite humiliation, failure, privation, pain, betrayal, desertion. That fulfillment brings a radical peace, the peace that the world cannot give. That fulfillment bears fruit in a love of one's neighbor that strives mightily to bring about the kingdom of God on this earth. On the other hand, the absence of that fulfillment opens the way to the trivialization of human life in the pursuit of fun, to the harshness of human life arising from the ruthless exercise of power, to despair about human welfare springing from the conviction that the universe is absurd.[12]

God's love is offered to all men and women at every time and place. This universality of God's self-communication (a notion that he has in common with Karl Rahner) Lonergan speaks of in terms of God's *inner word*, the word that God speaks in the solitude of our hearts, drawing us to God's own self. But this love is also embodied, incarnate, revealed for all to see, in the *outer word* of the life, preaching, death, and resurrection of Jesus.[13] 'And I, if I be lifted up from the earth, shall draw all to myself.'[14] The disciples of Jesus through the centuries constitute that community whose task it will be until the end of time to give *explicit witness* in external words and deeds to the offer of divine love as the only resolution of the otherwise hopeless human dilemma of personal incapacity to grow, of social injustice and alienation. As another superb contemporary thinker, Eric Voegelin, has labored for thirty years to argue, no social order that is not permeated with the love of the unseen measure that Christians call God can be just or humanly fulfilling.[15] In language current among those who have followed recent deliberations within the church, faith and justice are inextricably linked in the mission of the disciples of Jesus in the world.

Christian spiritual transformation, in this context, is thus a matter, first, of a process of conversion that involves a growing intimacy with the source and fountain of redemptive love, an intimacy that takes the form of being ever more patterned after the example of Christ; and, second, of a growing commitment and ability to participate in the mission of Christ, which is also the mission of that community whose task it is to render explicit to the whole world the fact that, in Jesus the Christ, God has definitively revealed the saving action that God is always working in the world. To be in love with God is also to be *sent* by God. To grow in the love of God is also to grow in participation in the mission — the saving and revealing mission — of Jesus.

Christian spiritual growth thus involves a number of elements: (1) one comes to a developing familiarity with God, so that one is able ever more readily and ever more easily to find God and to participate with God in God's redemptive work after the pattern of Christ, the suffering servant of God; (2) one grows in the ability to discern precisely what it is that God wants of oneself and of one's community, and in the willingness to do what it is that God asks, confident that what one is doing is not one's own work but God's; (3) summing up all of what this development involves, one grows in *self-transcendence*. This is the first key term that I take from Lonergan. One grows in self-transcendence until, in the saint, there is reached a point of the union of one's own understanding, reason, and desire with the knowledge and love of God, a union that can only be broadened and heightened, deepened and enriched, but not gone beyond; and a point of self-abnegation and humility that rejoices in sharing the lot of the poor, despised, and humiliated Son of God himself, in his mission of establishing the reign of God on earth. Christian spiritual transformation is a matter of continual conversion to self-transcendence, within the community of the disciples of the Lord that is the church, until there is reached the point where one's understanding, one's judgments of fact and of value, one's desires, and one's choices, while not ceasing to be one's own, are a participation in the understanding, the judgments, the desires, the choices of God working in and through oneself and one's community, to continue and to spread the redemption of the world that only God can effect.

If, then, we are talking about Christian spiritual development as a transformation of our insights, our judgments, our desires, and our choices, we are speaking of it as fundamentally a transformation of our *interiority*, of our basic horizon. The difference that God's solution to the problem of evil makes in the social world, in the world of economics and politics, in the world of institutions and organizations, is a *function* of the difference it makes in persons, in the unity of personal consciousness, in people's vision and choices. Christian spiritual development, considered most radically, is a transformation of one's understanding and of one's willingness, so that these two are brought into harmony and cooperation with God's redemptive purposes in Christ Jesus and through the community of his disciples. The transformation, once again, is in the direction of *self-transcendence*, so that, by accepting God's offer of both salvation and vocation, one becomes ever more God-centered and Christ-centered in one's apprehensions of value and in one's decisions, in one's pursuit of meaning and truth, and in one's affective engagement with other persons in the dramatic situations that constitute the stuff, the setting, the stage of one's own personal story and of history itself.

2 Christian Spiritual Transformation as Self-appropriation

Now, besides 'self-transcendence,' there is another term that Lonergan uses when he speaks of development. That term is *self-appropriation*. Self-appropriation is a matter of self-knowledge, of self-discovery, of self-understanding. One can be quite self-transcendent, quite loving and generous, quite genuine in one's relations with others, quite sincere about wanting to understand things correctly, without being very adept at *intricate and precise* self-knowledge.[16] One can be, in Lonergan's terms, quite religiously and morally converted without being *intellectually converted*.[17] Intellectual conversion is a matter of knowing *precisely* what one is doing when one is pursuing understanding, reaching for truth, tying to decide in responsible fashion. Many people genuinely try to understand, and succeed in doing so, without being able to say *precisely* what they are doing when they understand, how their insights are related to their sensations, their questions, their beliefs, their images, their concepts, their feelings. One can also be quite religiously and morally converted without being what I have called 'psychically converted.' *Psychic conversion* is a matter of knowing what one is feeling, of being able to tell one's story, and to tell it as it is. One can have a quite genuine and even beautiful life of feeling without being able to tell what he or she is feeling, how *this* feeling is related to *that*, how both feelings are related to the objects they intend, how one's feelings are related to one's images and symbols, to one's questions and insights, to one's beliefs and ideas. In other words, one can have a quite profound and genuinely self-transcendent interiority without being able to articulate one's inner life with any notable clarity and precision. We all know wonderful and holy people who are quite unsophisticated when it comes to self-knowledge, or who will put their self-knowledge in very commonsense terms — people who make at times heroic decisions, but who, when asked *why* they made this or that decision, or what went on in their minds and hearts which led them so to decide, can answer only, 'I don't know; it just seemed to be the right thing to do.'

Such genuine self-transcendence without self-appropriation is by no means to be disparaged. It is the condition of most good and holy men and women down through the ages, the source of most that is good in human history. But there are factors at work in our age that seem to indicate that self-appropriation, in addition to self-transcendence, is becoming ever more necessary if one wishes to choose responsibly, to judge reasonably, to inquire intelligently, or just if one wishes to know what God wants and does not want.

Perhaps there was a time when commonsense wisdom and homespun practicality were enough for most people. Perhaps, too, there was a time when the only addition to common sense that some people needed was a good dose of theoretical understanding that was basically in harmony with the gospel. But there are a number of indications that would seem to argue persuasively that we are now living in a world where self-transcendence, backed up by a commonsense framework, or even by a cogent and brilliant theory, is simply not enough; where religious and moral conversion must be complemented by intellectual and psychic conversion; where self-transcendence must be aided and helped, complemented and augmented, by self-appropriation, by precise and even technical self-knowledge, by an ability to articulate just what is going on in one's 'little black box.' If this be the case, then spiritual transformation today is a matter not only of growing self-transcendence, but also of ever more precise and technical self-knowledge.

What are some of the indications that would back up this conviction that I share with Lonergan? Let me talk first about the insufficiency of common sense, and then about the ambiguity of theory. And let me do so within the context of the Church's recent pronounced recognition that the *promotion of justice* is a constitutive element in the preaching of the Gospel.

The paper that issued from the 1971 Synod of Bishops, 'Justice in the World,' and the statement of Pope Paul VI, *Octagesima Adveniens*, mark the beginnings, I believe, of a substantial leap forward in the Church's social, political, and economic insight and praxis. One of the few public statements that Pope John Paul I had a chance to make was to the effect that we need a new and worldwide economic order. The achievement of that order, I believe, is going to demand that we take our stand, and that we enable others to take *their* stand, not on practical common sense, and not on theory, but on the *self-appropriation* of our interiority and especially of our orientation to value.

Why do I say this? Well, let us treat common sense first, however briefly. One of the characteristics of practical common sense is that it not only is incapable of treating complex, long-range, and ultimate issues and results, but also that it resentfully brushes aside and ignores any attempts to raise questions that are concerned with such issues. It has the world's work to do, and it cannot be bothered by questions that would take time away from doing that work.[18] The person exclusively operating from practical common sense is concerned only with 'getting the job done.' Everything else — motivation, rationale, social organization, interpersonal communication — is oriented to that end. The question of whether the job is worth doing at all, or whether the most expedient way of doing it is also the most authentic way, is a bother, yes, but more than that, it is a threat, a subversive question that could overturn the entire project. Rejection precisely of such kinds of questions is what is responsible for the fact that our objective world situation today can be characterized in terms of opposed totalitarianisms: the totalitarianism of the multinational corporation, predicated on the assumption of the need of automatic progress and expansion; and the totalitarianism of the communist state, rooted in the assumption that class conflict can bring the social order into harmony with what is right. Both myths neglect the fact that there are religious, personal, and cultural values that must be pursued in an integral fashion if there is to be a *just* social order that *really* provides for the basic needs of all the members of a society. In both systems, however much theory may be involved in their establishment, we see operative the bias of practical common sense against the kinds of questions that must be asked if the job is to be done, not only expediently, but also humanely, genuinely, authentically. The question of *integrity* is, not just overlooked, but actively repudiated and repressed.

Nor is *theory* sufficient to reestablish the significance of that question. For there are theories that support the question, but there are other theories that discredit it. The theories of B.F. Skinner or of orthodox Freudian psychoanalysis are just as coherent, just as thorough, just as all-encompassing, and, for many, just as convincing, as are the theories of a Christian philosophy and theology.

The church's reliance on theory as the ground of praxis arose in the Middle Ages, more specifically with scholastic philosophy. One of the interesting things about that period, though, is that there were not many theories from which to choose, and there was not all that much to be learned in order to piece together a convincing theory. Even the disputes in the world of theory did not touch, as they do today, on the really basic issues, such as the existence of God, the fact of revelation, the ethical end of the human person, the value of a virtuous life, and so on. Right down into the Renaissance, there was so little to be learned that it was possible for one person to be at once an artist, a natural scientist, and a person of practical affairs — and we have Leonardo da Vinci to prove it.

The need for specialization to master one tiny dimension of reality is a distinctly modern phenomenon. And while one is spending most of one's time specializing in one's own area, one's contemporaries are adding theory upon theory in *their* specialized domains. And these theories sometimes contradict one another on the most fundamental issues, on issues that *every* developing adult must confront. But how is one to take a stand, if one has to devote all of one's energies to his or her specialization? There are issues on which we *must* judge and on which we *must* decide if we are to live a human life. Yet there is simply too much to be learned before we can judge and decide. Unless we find a ground *beyond* theory — for it will not do just to fall back on common sense — our situation becomes one of hopeless relativism. It is my contention that this ground beyond theory lies in the self-appropriation of human interiority.

This point about the need for a quite technical self-appropriation can be developed at great length; we do not have space to do that here. The point I wish to make in the present context is that *only* through such self-appropriation can one discover the precise relation that obtains between religious, personal, and cultural values, on the one hand, and the social value of a just economic and political order, on the other hand. And one needs to discover these relations, not simply in the abstract, as through some theory of value, but in the concrete order in which one is called upon to judge, to decide, and to act. And so I return to my general statement: *Christian spiritual transformation is a matter of self-transcendence that, at a certain point, calls for a movement to self-appropriation.* Christian spiritual development is a matter of ongoing conversion, and ongoing conversion means today not only religious and moral, but also intellectual and psychic conversion.

3   The Levels of Consciousness

There are five levels of operations that one discovers when one enters upon the project of the self-appropriation of interiority.[19] Inner and outer sensations, memories, and images constitute the level of empirical presentations. These empirical presentations are organized by understanding, which is a second level of consciousness. For example, if you are reading without any understanding of what I am saying, you are operating at the first, empirical level of operations. If you are reading *and* understanding what I am saying, your understanding is organizing the empirical representations into some kind of intelligible whole. You are processing what you see by the operations that go on in your 'little black box.' You are operating not only at the first, but also at the second level of operations. If, moreover, you not only *understand* what I am saying but are also trying to *judge* whether it is correct or not, you have added a third level of operations, where we either assent to, or disagree with, something we have understood.

These three levels of operations are what make us to be human knowers. Lonergan calls these levels *experience, understanding,* and *judgment.*

But we are not just *knowers.* There are times in our lives when, after we have made a judgment, 'This is true,' a further question arises, 'What am I going to do about it?'

Then we have to *decide*. And decision constitutes a fourth level of operations.

Finally, there is another whole dimension of interior reality that is not dealt with by speaking of the empirical, intelligent, rational, and decisional levels of consciousness. There is a fifth level of consciousness that is a matter of being addressed by, and in relation to, God. There is the experience of mystery. There is the reality of falling in love with God. There is prayer, worship, mystical experience, the dark night of the soul, the living flame of love, the search for and discovery of the holy, the gift of the divinely originated solution to the problem of evil.

Religious self-appropriation, obviously, is a matter of articulating what is going on at that fifth level of consciousness. The means of discovering oneself in one's relation to God are many: there are spiritual direction, retreats, various methods of keeping a journal, and so on. But what is important for us also to appropriate is the manner in which experience at that fifth level of consciousness has an effect on other levels. The influence of God's grace moves downward in our consciousness. It changes our values (fourth level), so that it provides us with entirely new orientations for our decisions, and enables them to be more self-transcendent. It changes our view of the world, our vision, the way we understand and judge things (second and third levels), and provides us with a determination to understand thoroughly and to judge reasonably; and it brings about a harmony and peace at the level of inner sensations, a peace that 'the world cannot give,' so that our inner being and our bodies rest securely in the love of God.

4   **Symbols, Feelings, and Drama**

Such is the pattern of interiority that is discovered when one enters upon the way of self-appropriation: five levels of consciousness, each related to the other, whether we move from below upwards, or from above downwards.

And now, finally, we are able to locate with precision the region where Jung's discoveries become significant for spiritual development, especially for self-appropriation. For all of the operations that we are talking about — sensing, imagining, remembering (first level), inquiring, understanding, putting our understanding into words (second level), reflecting, weighing the evidence, judging (third level), deliberating, deciding, acting (fourth level), praying, worshipping (fifth level) — all of these operations are permeated by *feelings*. We have feelings about the objects of all of these operations. The operations themselves are always dramatic. When you try to understand, it is because you are confused. When you succeed in understanding, the confusion ceases and you experience satisfaction, maybe even excitement. When you want to know whether you understand correctly, it is because you are not satisfied with just a set of bright ideas; you want to get things right and not just go about spouting opinions. When you have to make a decision, the drama of the situation stands out clearly. Some decisions can be agonizing. *All* decisions have a great deal of affectivity accompanying them, for we are dealing in decisions with questions of value. And value is something we feel before ever we judge about it or act on it.[20] Finally, fifth-level religious experience has those peculiar sets of feelings that we call 'consolations' and 'desolations.' In sum, we are not just structured conscious operators. We are also the subjects of a drama, precisely in and through these operations. There is a *story* to our operating, because there are feelings that permeate all of those operations.

Let us focus a bit more on this drama, because it is more complicated than I have so far indicated. In addition to the desire to understand, there is also a *flight* from understanding (second level). I can flee insight just as passionately as I can pursue it. Moreover, I can resist the truth just as strongly as I can intend it (third level). I can try to escape responsible decision and live a life of ease or of drifting or of hiding my talents, just as persistently as I can conscientiously examine every situation to find the best course of action (fourth level). I can flee contact with God just as passionately as I can seek to find God and do God's will (fifth level)

There are feelings that permeate not only genuine performance at each of the five levels but also *inauthentic* actions at each step of the way. The ultimate drama of my life, in fact, is this drama of *authenticity* and *inauthenticity*. The authentic person is the person who pursues understanding, who seeks truth, who responds to what is really worth while, and who searches for God and God's will. The inauthentic person is the person who flees understanding, who runs from the truth, who resists further questions about his or her decisions, and who tries to escape God. And those feelings never go away. They are present in the entire drama. They are precisely what make it so dramatic.

What, then, are feelings? Feelings are *energy*-become-conscious. Feelings are a matter of psychic energy. Feelings are the basic sensitive component of every human operation. Feelings make of spirituality a *story*. To know one's feelings is to begin to tell one's own story. Feelings are the drive and momentum of the life of the human spirit. Feelings join the spirit to the body in a conscious unity.

There is one further aspect to this matter. Feelings always enter consciousness through being connected with *some* representation. Now the most basic form of representation lies in symbols. A *symbol*, Lonergan says, is an image of a real or imaginary object that evokes a feeling or is evoked by a feeling;[21] we can extend this to mean that there is never a feeling without a symbolic meaning; never a symbol without a feeling. To *name* one's feelings is to discover the dynamic images, the symbols, that are associated with them. To have *insight* into one's feelings is to understand the symbolic association. To *tell one's story* is to narrate the course of one's elemental symbolizing. And where does one's elemental symbolizing occur in its purest form, untainted by the biases that, in waking life, can lead us to distort our story? The place of elemental symbolizing is in our dreams. It is in the dream that we first are conscious, and it is in the dream that we find a 'story' going forward that we cannot distort without being aware that we are doing so. If we want to know our 'story' — the story of insight, the story of judgment, the story of decision, the story of prayer — we can find it in our dreams. There is a psychic conversion that puts us into contact with that story. It affects us deeply once it has occurred. For it enables us to judge ourselves in our waking life as authentic or inauthentic in our pursuit of understanding, in our seeking of truth, in our decisions, and in our search for God.

In the next article I will situate Jung's psychology of individuation within this context of the discussion of self-transcendence and especially of self-appropriation. In the third article, though, I will use this same framework to criticize Jung's psychology. For Jung did not have an accurate understanding of the structure of our operations as human subjects — our understanding, our judgments, our decisions, and our search for God. His basic philosophical and theological standpoint did not take its stand on a notion of authenticity as self-transcendence. And this basic flaw renders his contributions to Christian spiritual development very ambiguous until these contributions are transposed into some such context as I have tried to indicate in the present article.

Notes

1 See, for example, John A. Sanford, *Dreams: God's Forgotten Language* (see above, chapter 6, note 1); *Healing and Wholeness* (New York: Paulist Press, 1977); Morton Kelsey, *Dreams: The Dark Speech of the Spirit, A Christian Interpretation* (see above, chapter 6, note 1); *Encounter with God: A Theology of Christian Experience* (see above, chapter 6, note 1).

2 See James Hillman, *The Myth of Analysis: Three Essays in Archetypal Psychology* (see above, chapter 4, note 8). I quote from p. 21: 'The spiritual-director models of *guru*, rabbi, of Ignatius or Fenelon, of Zen master, are only substitutions on which we lean for want of surety about the true model for psychology.'

3 See Edward C. Whitmont, 'Prefatory Remarks to Jung's "Reply to Buber,"' in *Spring: An Annual of Archetypal Psychology and Jungian Thought* (1973) 188-95; and C.G. Jung, 'Religion and Psychology: A Reply to Martin Buber,' ibid. 196-203.

4 Compare C.G. Jung, 'Is Analytical Psychology a Religion?' (notes on a talk given by Jung, in *Spring*, 1972, pp. 144-48) with Jung's 'Psychotherapists or the Clergy,' in C.G. Jung, *Modern Man in Search of a Soul* (New York: Harcourt, Brace, and World, 1933) 221-44.

5 Bernard Lonergan, *Method in Theology* (see above, chapter 1, note 3) chapters 10 and 11.

6 David Burrell, *Exercises in Religious Understanding* (see above, chapter 4, note 24) 221.

7 There are, of course, dangers in such a procedure, for the reader can easily take the results of Lonergan's explorations as a series of concepts that could dispense one from the task of insight into oneself. There are no shortcuts to the self-appropriation to which Lonergan invites one. But precisely because there are no shortcuts, I can only ask the reader interested in pursuing the process to go to Lonergan's works themselves.

8 See Bernard Lonergan, *Insight* (see above, chapter 1, note 37) chapters 18 and 20; *Method in Theology*, chapter 4.

9 Romans 5.5.

10 See Bernard Lonergan, 'The Natural Desire to See God,' in *Collection* (see above, chapter 2, note 7) 81-91.

11 Lonergan, *Method in Theology* 103.

12 Ibid. 105.

13 Ibid. 112-15.

14 John 12.32.

15 See Eric Voegelin, *Order and History*, four volumes to date (Louisiana State University Press, 1956-1974). 1993 note: A fifth volume, incomplete, was published posthumously in 1987.

16 See Lonergan, *Insight* 475/499-500.

17 On intellectual conversion as self-appropriation, see Lonergan, *Method in Theology* 238-40.

18 See Lonergan, *Insight* 225-42/250-67.

19 On the levels of consciousness, see Lonergan, *Method in Theology*, chapters 1 and 4.

20 Ibid. 31-33.

21 Ibid. 64.

13 Jungian Psychology and Christian Spirituality II: The Jungian Psychology of Individuation

The significance of Jungian psychology for spiritual theology lies in the fact that Jung is concerned with understanding and promoting a development in the realm of human interiority. The interest in Jung on the part of Christians concerned about their own spiritual transformation is thus not surprising.

In the previous article, I argued that Christian spiritual development is a growth, first, in self-transcendence, but, secondly, also a development in self-knowledge or self-appropriation. I located the area where Jung's discoveries aid this development. Permeating the whole range of the operations of human interiority, which Bernard Lonergan has shown to unfold on five levels, there is the dramatic life of feeling, which makes of our inner lives as human subjects a story. Getting in touch with one's story is a matter primarily of identifying the affective component of all our human operations. This task can be greatly aided if we learn the art of *symbolic identification*. The privileged place of symbols in human consciousness occurs precisely in those domains that Jung explored so fully: our dreams, our spontaneous waking fantasies, and our engagement in the techniques of what Jung called active imagination.[1]

To the material included in the previous article, I wish now to add the caution that it is easy to get *stuck* in the symbols and images that emerge elementally in our dreams. Let me recall a dream of my own that occurred precisely at the time when I was engaged in writing a doctoral dissertation whose whole point it was to explore the relations between the conscious intentionality so thoroughly elucidated by Lonergan and the depths of the psyche studied by Jung.

At the time of this dream, I was in Zürich, Switzerland, where I had gone to complete work on my dissertation. I had been there better than a month, had attended lectures at the C.G. Jung Institute, had immersed myself as much as possible in the atmosphere breathed by Jungians, and had reached a point of rather complete frustration with my efforts to articulate a series of relationships that I already knew obtained in the domain of human interiority, but whose intelligible connecting link I had not yet discovered. In the dream, I am descending a flight of stairs, and am clearly intending to go down into the basement of a very large house. The house, incidentally, resembled the building in which I was living in Zürich. I have almost reached the ground floor of the building, when I meet none other than Bernard Lonergan coming up the same flight of stairs. He stops me in my descent, looks at me very intently, and says, 'If you really want to see some images, come with me.' He takes me *up* the flight of stairs, to what appears to be the top floor of the house, and leads me into a large auditorium. We select a pair of seats next to one another, with Lonergan sitting to my right. Immediately a movie begins to be shown on a screen in the front of the room, and we begin to watch it.

The images that were provided me in this dream were precisely the material that I needed for the insight for which I had been searching, the insight into the connecting link between intentional consciousness and the psyche. The point of the dream is, at least in part, that the images of the psyche are not to be negotiated down in the basement, that is, in the lower reaches from which they emerge. Rather these images are to be allowed to be processed by the levels of consciousness; and their ultimate significance lies in their relevance for the uppermost level (the top floor) of human subjectivity, that is, for the operations of that existential level of consciousness whose task it is to evaluate, deliberate, discern, decide, and act. The images that emerge from the depths of the psyche are materials for insight, judgment, and decision. Thus they must be interpreted; the interpretation must be judged to be sound; and the self-knowledge thus gained is to be employed as one moves to existential self-determination in free decision. The dream contains, too, a warning regarding the need for an existential and aesthetic distance from the images themselves if one is going to be able to negotiate freely these elemental symbols. The detached and disinterested desire to know and the self-transcendence of existential deliberation are prerequisites for the proper negotiation of the psyche's elemental symbols. To attempt to negotiate the symbols from the inappropriate proximity of the lower reaches from which they emerge is, in fact, the stuff of madness: the overwhelming by psychic processes of the human spirit's capacities for intelligent inquiry, critical reflection, and responsible deliberation.

One further introductory point may prove helpful. I find it significant that the dimensions of intelligent, rational, and existential consciousness, on the one hand, and of elemental symbolism, on the other hand, are two quite distinct though not separate factors in the processes of human interiority. I find it both convenient and ontologically correct to refer to the first set of determinants of interiority as *spirit*,[2] and to the second as *psyche*. And I add to this pair a third constituent of the self, the organism, whose processes, precisely as organic, constitute what depth psychologists have been calling *the uncon-scious.* The metaphysical implications of this notion of the human compound that is the self or the subject are too complicated for us to investigate here,[3] but the distinctions thus established will prove helpful in our subsequent remarks.

I now wish to proceed in the present article to outline in heuristic fashion the Jungian understanding of the inner journey that one ventures on when one begins to appreciate the immense significance that accrues to one's spontaneous, elemental symbolizing.

1   The Individual and the Collective

Jung's term for this inner journey is 'the process of individuation.' In one of his writings he calls individuation 'the process of becoming one's own self.' I quote Jung more thoroughly: 'Individuation means becoming an "individual," and, insofar as "individuality" embraces our innermost, last, and incomparable uniqueness, it also implies becoming one's own self. We could therefore translate individuation as "coming to selfhood" or "self-realization."'[4] The Jungian stress, of course, is on that dimension of the self that I have referred to as the psyche, that is, on the complexes of feelings and symbols that permeate all our operations as human subjects. Individuation is a process of discovering, exploring, attending to that dimension of our being that is properly called psychic. Through this exploration, one comes to, one becomes, oneself, and one does so precisely by discovering a superabundance of meaning, beyond rational comprehension, that enables one to live what Jung called the 'just-so' life.[5]

The implications of this notion of individuation are important. If one must explore and successfully negotiate the psychic dimension of one's being in order to become one's own self, this must mean that the same psychic dimension of one's being can also alienate one from one's self. There must be tendencies in the psyche that would lead one astray, away from the path that leads to oneself. These tendencies must be confronted head-on and be overcome. This is the point of speaking of a *process* of individuation, of insisting, too, that such a process is incumbent on more and more people in our age if they are to come to a satisfactory sense of meaning in their lives, and if civilization and its values are to be preserved from destruction. And so it is that Jung speaks of two tendencies in the psyche that can lead us astray, that can, in the terms established in the previous paper, encourage the surrender of our own desire for accumulating insight, for the unconditioned, and for dedication to what is really worth while. One can identify with *collective consciousness*, or one can surrender to or be inflated by the *collective unconscious*. In either case, one is not assuming responsibility for self-constitution and world constitution, is not fulfilling one's unique vocation within the universe.

1.1   The Ego and the Persona

The dimension of the psyche that must find its way to the self, Jung calls the *ego*. The ego is the set of psychic complexes — constellations of images, ideas, feelings, and capacities — that constitute what in Lonergan's terminology would be called differentiated consciousness. The ego is constituted by the range of performance in which we feel at home as conscious operators, that is, in which we know ourselves to be competent to understand, pass judgment, and make decisions. The individuation process depends on the establishment of a relatively well-developed ego, that is, on a realistic sense of one's own areas of competence in the social and professional world, in the life of the family, in the world of the 'other.' The ego will develop further and will be transformed in the process of individuation, but for that process to begin, there must be a solid base in a relatively self-esteeming ego. The development of this base is the task of the first half of life.[6]

Even a well-developed ego, however, does not constitute an individuated personality. The journey to individuation, as an explicit and consciously assumed responsibility, remains a task for the afternoon of life. Closely connected with the ego, and in some respects undifferentiated from it in the course of its normal development in the first half of life, is another aspect of psychic experience that Jung calls the *persona*. The persona is the face that we turn outwards in the process of the socialization of the ego, the outer mask that we wear before others. Its development depends for its integrity on the kind of social recognition that we have received from others from very early on in life, on what we have had to do to secure the esteem of others, and consequently our own self-esteem. It is very easy for the ego to identify with the persona, particularly if the parents have not communicated to the child the inner sustenance to enable him or her to be relatively well-centered in a sense of one's capacities. The differentiation of the ego from the persona is a first, and often a lengthy, task to be accomplished in the process of individuation. One's social role, the network of one's external relations with others, the recognition granted one by the significant others in one's life may have been very important in the formation of one's ego. But one is *not* one's role in society, nor is it appropriate that one receive one's identity as a person — as a subject of intelligent, rational, and moral operations, and as a carrier of affective intentionality — from one's social role. The differentiation of ego from persona means, however, not that one is to abandon one's social role or position, but that one is to cease receiving one's identity from it. 'Who I am' is a far more extensive and rich story of experiences, feelings, insights, judgments, decisions, and religious commitments than 'what I do.'

Ego-persona identifications can take many forms, and their resistance to differentiation depends on the extent to which one was forced to turn outwards in one's development for a source of self-esteem. Moreover, one does not need to be what we call a task-oriented person (as opposed to a person-oriented task?) in order to stand in need of serious work at differentiating ego from persona. The common element in all forms of ego-persona identification is that one tends to identify oneself in terms of *who one is for others*, whether functionally or interpersonally. Ernest Becker's well-known book *The Denial of Death*, though reliant more on Otto Rank than on Jung, is in part a helpful treatment of the inveterate human tendency to seek self-esteem from one or other form of collective identification, even if only one other person.[7]

Breaking ego-persona identifications can be very difficult. Jung's experience of the process of individuation in his own life story involved, for instance, an extremely painful course of events that led him to dissolve the false identity he had assumed from his associations with the Freudian circle and from Freud's projections upon Jung, which, if maintained, would have prevented Jung from developing in his own way and would have locked him into an amalgamation of social and professional relationships that would have blocked the emergence of his distinct perspectives on psychological reality. To bring the issue closer to home, the problem of ego-persona differentiation can be very acute in religious life, and in fact wherever community living is pursued as a desirable goal. True community is based on shared meanings and values. But in religious life it involves also living and working together for the same apostolic ends. The complexities of common life and of corporate apostolic work are such that the temptation is ever present to identify too exclusively with one's job or function or with the opinion held of oneself by others — an opinion that in many cases may have been formed in a previous stage of one's development as a person or as an apostolic religious, and that does not take into account one's subsequent growth and cumulative discovery of the Lord's unique call upon one's talents and resources. While the solution to the self-alienation that can develop from such identification is not the kind of self-assertion or individualism that is clearly contrary to the union of minds and hearts to which one commits oneself by religious vows, only the gift of discernment in a context of obedience and mission can resolve such difficulties. The full reciprocity of genuine community involves keeping channels of communication open on all sides when a decision is being made concerning the disposition of a man's or a woman's apostolic energies. Religious who are too caught up in functional or interpersonal ego-persona identifications can all too easily introduce into their decision-making processes a variety of 'shuttle diplomacy' that is destructive of community life and apostolate.

Ego-persona identification is a relatively minimal instance of identification with collective consciousness. The latter can assume far more distorted and bizarre forms, as in the hypnotic surrender of an educated nation to a Hitler or of the masses to a Mao, or in the mass hysteria by which the residents of Jonestown submitted unto self-destruction to a religious madman who already had successfully persuaded them to abdicate whatever capacities for insight, judgment, and moral decision they still possessed before coming under his demonic spell.

1.2   *The Ego and the Collective Unconscious*

Let us employ further the last-mentioned example, and add that the madman, Jim Jones, was identified in his ego consciousness, not with collective consciousness, but with what Jung would call 'an archetype of the collective unconscious' — with, it would seem, the very image of God.

Jung's term 'the collective unconscious' is perhaps unfortunate. For it makes us think of an 'already down there now' real thing, a kind of Platonic world of Ideas, but now located in the depths rather than the heights. Spatial imagery is deceptive when we are speaking of psychic reality, and yet we *do* need some imagery to get us started on the road to insight, and the imagery of mysterious depths does seem, in fact, to be that employed by dreams themselves to indicate the unconscious. In fact, though, what Jung means by the collective unconscious is the innate or inherited tendency of human neurophysiology to achieve conscious representation at times in the form of powerful images that are invested with a primal force that is not personally or even culturally determined but that seems to convey a significance that is crosscultural or universally human. The images released from these depths have a universally meaningful appeal, because they seem to express themes that characterize the human drama wherever and whenever it occurs.

The experience of archetypal images, which has its own time in the natural course of the process of individuation, and which is not to be hastened or artificially induced, is an event fraught with significance. It brings with it an integrating, healing sense of the transpersonal meaning of one's existence within the context of the immense universe of being. And yet the power of archetypal images is also their danger. For one can begin to identify with an archetype, either by the submergence of one's ego in the imaginal undertow of conscious existence, or by the inflation of the ego through the conscious appropriation, rather than negotiation, of an archetypal image.

The natural time for the negotiation of the archetypal world in the process of individuation occurs, in general, *after* not only the dissolving of ego-persona identifications but also the withdrawal of the projections of the shadow and the encounter with the contrasexual opposite, that is, with the anima or animus. The shadow represents the dimensions of one's own being that are awkward, undifferentiated, and even downright malicious or evil, the dimensions that ego consciousness chooses not to admit to belong to oneself. The shadow is projected onto another person or onto a group, who then become scapegoats upon whose shoulders the sins of the ego-centered subject are laid. The encounter with and negotiation of the shadow marks the beginning of coming to terms with the unconscious, but still in its personal dimensions. The withdrawal of the shadow projections leads in the natural rhythm of things to the discovery of the contrasexual opposite, whose successful negotiation is the gateway to the discovery and experience of the archetypal images.

If the archetypal images are *appropriated* by the ego, rather than being negotiated as irretrievably other, and if one succeeds in convincing others of one's superhuman significance, one has started a movement of mass hysteria. Thus, for example, Jung's psychology provides a way of understanding the events that occurred in Germany's succumbing to the influence of Hitler. Germany had been defeated in the First World War. Its economic life after the war was in shambles, its cultural heritage in a state of confusion, its moral values in disarray, effective political leadership lacking. There appears on the scene a man held in the grip of a myth and proclaiming himself and his myth as the solution. The myth is the result of Hitler's identification with forces released into his conscious life from the neural depths. He is the savior, proclaiming a myth of racial superiority. To identify with an archetype is to distort not only one's ego, but the archetype itself. Moreover, the German people were in search precisely of a way out of their individual and national malaise. And they shared our common propensity to find the solution 'out there,' instead of taking the journey to a heightening and expansion of consciousness. So they projected what can be authentically found only in interiority onto an external figure who has identified himself with what in itself is rather a symbol of an inner reality. The projection gives rise to a collective consciousness, with which they identify their own ego consciousness, under the dominance of a figure who has appropriated for himself the power of a primordial energic constellation and, in the process, distorted that constellation itself. The people then projected onto a scapegoat, the Jews, the source of their own frustration, that is, the collapse of their own meanings and values. The inner source of their collective confusion, waywardness, frustration, powerlessness, despair — the enemy within — is projected onto a group that is different, that represents a set of experiences, meanings, and values that they find alien, mysterious, threatening. The external group, in this case the Jewish race, is 'mythicized,' by being identified with the inner source of confusion, the shadow.

A leader, then, creates a cult by identifying with an archetypal image and by persuading others to project onto himself the same image, thus surrendering to the power with which they have invested the leader the use of their own intelligence, rationality, and moral responsibility. The same process lies behind the formation of the various cults springing up in the United States today. The conditions are ripe: economic anxiety, loss of national purpose, break-down of long-cherished meanings and values, and so forth. Jung saw the United States as a potential scene of the same kind of aberration that occurred in Germany; for its materialism and practical denial of ultimates leaves it empty, ready to be victimized by inflated personalities held in the grip of some demonic power.

From this perspective, too, it is possible to interpret one of the strangest facts recorded in the Gospel; namely, the fact that Jesus 'strictly charged the disciples to tell no one that he was the Christ' (Matthew 16.20; see Mark 8.30 and Luke 9.21). The experience of Jesus at his baptism by John marks the beginning, let us assume, of his personal coming to terms with an extraordinary identity and mission. And what he wrestled with in the desert experience is the temptation to identify in an inflated fashion with the energic power represented in the title 'Son of God' and so to distort the meaning of this elemental symbolic constellation. Such temptation is precisely demonic. Is it any wonder, then, that he forbids the disciples to proclaim him as the Messiah, that is, to project upon him an energic symbolic constellation that belongs to their own religious interiority, and so to distort the meaning of the constellation by converting it into a mass movement? Walter Kasper conjectures that it is likely that, at his trial before the Sanhedrin, Jesus *did* admit to being the Messiah, but only when it was no longer possible for that admission to be distorted by projection and converted into the instrument of a demonic and violent quest for political power on the part of his followers.[8] In order to *be* in reality what he is, he has to *resist* identifying himself with the energic force of that reality and to *forbid* his disciples from engaging in the distortion that would result were they to project upon him their own interior image of the Christ.

Primordial or archetypal images, then, are invested with immense power. It is crucial that they be negotiated from a distance, as other, if one is not to lose one's way on the journey to individuation. And it is equally crucial that they not be projected onto an external other or a group. Perhaps some more mundane examples of the latter necessity will help to clarify its meaning and importance.

As we have seen, Jung insists that we all bear in our psychic repertoire an image of the opposite sex, who is at the same time the carrier of our own contrasexuality. The image is built up, in its concrete details, as a result of one's own experience of the opposite sex. Thus it takes different forms in different people. For some men, the anima is determined too exclusively by their own mothers. For others, the anima is a plaything, or a vessel of hidden wisdom, or an emasculating power whose influence they must resist with all their force. We tend to project the anima or animus onto real people and to relate to these persons as embodiments of the image. The anima is an inner reality, and when she is discovered and negotiated as such, she can be a source of guidance on the journey to the self. But her reality as inner is dissipated by projection onto a real woman, whose own reality is itself distorted by becoming the bearer of one's idealization.

Perhaps the most complicated and painful human relationships are those in which one party is the carrier of the projections of the primordial images of the other, and vice versa. People who have accomplished a great deal in a long lifetime, who have taught others important truths, have frequently to suffer being the recipients of the projection of the archetypal images of the Wise Old Man or the Wise Old Woman. The fact that they may even appear as such in our dreams does not entitle us to treat them in that way in our external relations with them. Nor, for that matter, does it entitle *them* to be so treated!

People in the helping professions — in psychiatry, medicine, pastoral ministry, education — are often the recipients of archetypal projections. A transference relationship develops, in which the dependent person overinvests in the helper. What is worse, a countertransference can develop, in which the helper invites the projection, needs it, wants it, and is in turn projecting this need or desire upon the person being helped. Then what Hegel referred to as a master-slave dialectic develops, a network of intersubjective events that is extraordinarily painful for both parties, who more often than not have very few clues as to what is really going on.

2   The Reconciliation of Opposites

A notion that became ever more important in Jung's mature thought about the process of individuation involves the progressive reconciliation of the opposites in one's being. The steps we have seen thus far come to be interpreted in accord with this notion. Thus the first reconciliation is between the ego and the complexes that constitute the personal unconscious. In the course of the development that occurs in the first half of life, one's psyche tends to become more or else one-sided in its differentiation. One's development occurs along the line of least resistance, which itself is a matter of one's superior function. That is, one finds success and social approval by differentiating one's consciousness in one of the four functions: thinking, feeling, sensation, and intuition. If thinking constitutes one's superior function, feeling will be one's inferior function, and vice versa. So too, if sensation is one's superior function, intuition will be one's inferior function, and vice versa. The shadow is constellated around one's inferior function. The other two functions will be more or less differentiated, and so will function either as auxiliary to the superior function or as contributing to the shadow, or as allied with both the inferior and the superior function. The first step toward the reconciliation of the opposites involves the relativization by the ego of the supremacy of the differentiated function, so as to grant to the other functions more of a prominent place, or at least more recognition, in one's conscious life.

Next, there is required the reconciliation of one's ego with its contrasexual counterpart. Meeting the opposite here and successfully negotiating it, without identification or appropriation, leads to a psychological androgyny that moves one along the way to wholeness. The contrasexual element is also the key to the journey through the world of the archetypes, where one finds the transpersonal meaning of one's life and story: both the myth that one has been leading and the myth that is one's own to lead. The inner journey through this transpersonal source of significance leads one eventually to the reconciliation of ego and self. The self is the deeper center of the psyche, and also the totality of the entire psyche. Its symbols are symbols of centering and of wholeness: the mandala, the quaternity, the cross in the circle, and so forth.[9] Once again, the important procedure is not that the ego identify with the self, but that it negotiate the self's higher authority, that it receive from the self, that it recognize that the ego is not the center of the psyche and yet that the ego is responsible for the restrictive shaping of psychic possibilities contained in the totality of the psyche, in the self.

There is one other area of reconciliation treated by Jung: the reconciliation of *good and evil*. Jung starts from the correct position that the ego tends to regard as evil whatever it finds strange, and thus despises many of the complexes of the unconscious that are not evil at all, but that can and should be negotiated and attended to on the path to individuation. He proceeds from that assumption, however, to a relativization of the issue of the struggle between good and evil, to a position that good and evil can be reconciled in the same manner as ego and unconscious, or masculine and feminine, or ego and self. Evil becomes in Jung's thought a substantive reality; it becomes as real as the complexes themselves. And in this way it becomes relativized as evil. The upshot of this position, as we will see in the final paper, involves the formulation of positions on God and Christ that are unacceptable from a Christian standpoint. But let me suggest in concluding this paper where the principal difficulty lies.

The reconciliation of opposites for Jung is located too exclusively within the psyche. It is more accurate to say that the basic set of opposites in the constitution of the human person is that of spirit and matter. These opposites are reconciled by negotiating the psyche, which shares in both. But the problem of evil remains: it is a *spiritual* problem, not a psychological one. It is resolved, as I suggested in the first paper, only by the reception of the gift of God's love, which transforms the human spirit in a movement that extends downwards into the psyche. But the basic transformation is at the level of decision, where one's values are transformed in such a way that one chooses and wants to choose the good, one opts for self-transcendence. The option has effects on the psyche. But it is an option that one makes, not down in the basement of the psyche and its complexes, but at the level of spiritual intentionality in the existential mode as the latter is transformed by God's grace, so that it comes more and more to opt for, to choose, the good that carries one beyond oneself.

Notes

1 On active imagination, see Rix Weaver, *The Old Wise Woman* (New York: C.G. Jung Foundations, 1973).

2 On the spiritual, see Bernard Lonergan, *Insight* 517-20/541-43.

3 See ibid. 467-79/492-504; 514-20/538-43.

4 C.G. Jung, 'The Relations between the Ego and the Unconscious' (see above, chapter 5, note 5) 173.

5 See C.G. Jung, *Memories, Dreams, Reflections* (see above, chapter 3, note 49) 325, for a description of the experience leading to this awareness.

6 See C.G. Jung, 'The Stages of Life,' in *The Structure and Dynamics of the Psyche* (see above, chapter 2, note 14) 387-403.

7 Ernest Becker, *The Denial of Death* (see above, chapter 4, note 4), especially chapters 7 and 8.

8 Walter Kasper, *Jesus the Christ* (New York: Paulist Press) 106.

9 C.G. Jung, 'Concerning Mandala Symbolism,' in *The Archetypes and the Collective Unconscious* (see above, chapter 3, note 40) 355-90.

14 Jungian Psychology and Christian Spirituality III: Psychology and Grace

The previous article gives us some indication of the potential overlapping or correlation of Jungian psychology and Christian spirituality. The withdrawal of projections mentioned previously correlates well with the Ignatian notion of removing inordinate affections and attachments from one's life, so as to be able to give oneself in spiritual freedom to God and to God's will for oneself. Jung's talk of the withdrawal of projections onto people, things, and situations is a contemporary and psychological way of expressing both this Ignatian insight and the *via negativa* which the great mystics such as St. John of the Cross emphasize as so central to the spiritual life.

A psychological understanding of the development and flowering of human affectivity, then, *is* pertinent to our spiritual self-understanding. There are, in general, two extreme positions on the relation of psychology and spirituality that must be avoided.

The first extreme is a reduction of spirituality to psychology, so that religion is 'nothing but' a more or less complex psychological mechanism. Such an understanding is to be found in the works of Freud, who is prevented from properly understanding even the sensitive psyche itself because he does not admit the spiritual dimension of the human person, to which the psyche is oriented. The

rational affirmation of spiritual reality is, of course, quite a
sophisticated philosophical achievement. But one alternative to such an affirmation is to conceive the human person
as consisting only of psyche and organism, and to explain
psyche by moving backwards to the organism. Then
spirituality is reduced to psychology, and psychology to
organic instinct.

The second, and opposite, extreme is one of divorc-
ing spirituality from psychology so completely that discernment itself becomes impossible. Spirituality becomes
a separate realm of human activity that is not integrated
with psychological reality. This tendency, once perhaps
pronounced in Christian spirituality, is still to be found;
there still are spiritual theologians for whom the relationship of spirituality to the life of affectivity is negligible.
Such an orientation, when put into practice, leads to a
split consciousness and a compartmentalized life. The orientation itself is perhaps often rooted in both a fear of the
complexities of affective self-knowledge, and in an epistemological conceptualism that finds little relation between
the concepts of spirituality — grace, the supernatural, self-
denial, the following of Christ — and the concepts of psychology. But it is the task of spiritual theology to mediate
these two conceptual worlds, the one with the other, by
taking its stand in interior experience, which is the dimension to which both sets of concepts refer if they are talking
about anything real.

It may well be that Jung will prove more helpful for
spirituality and spiritual theology in the negative way suggested in the previous paper, that is, in helping us to recognize inordinate projections and disoriented affections,
than in orienting us positively to the God of Christian faith
and to Christ. On the issues of the psychological orientation to God and the psychological meaning of the Christ

of faith, Jung, I find, is quite deficient, and his thought derails him from the appropriate orientation to the reality of God. I propose to treat these problems in the present paper.

One of the insights of scriptural spirituality and of the major theologies of the Christian tradition concerns the incomprehensibility of God. God's ways are not ours.[1] 'Where were you when I laid the foundations of the earth?'[2] 'I will be who I will be.'[3] 'How unsearchable are God's ways.'[4] According to St. Thomas Aquinas, even in the direct vision of God, God will remain for us an incomprehensible mystery.[5] The denial of God's ultimate incomprehensibility involves one in some form of what has been called *gnosis*. The incomprehensibility of God comes to its sharpest focus in our own experience of the mystery of inevitable and uncontrollable suffering, the only response to which, as Karl Rahner says, is to 'let ourselves fall into the incomprehensibility of God as into our true fulfillment and happiness,'[6] precisely as Christ himself surrendered in the hour of his most intense darkness. Nothing is more difficult than this surrender to what we cannot understand. And one of the ways of resisting this surrender — the way, I suggest, which Jung manifests in some of his very late works — is to deny that God is all good, to think of God as a unity of good and evil, to see Christ as the representative only of God's goodness, and Satan as the symbol of the evil in God. From such an understanding, it is only a short step to the affirmation of oneself as superior to God and to assigning to oneself the task of reconciling the good and evil in God by reconciling the good and evil in the self which is the image of God. Such seem to have been Jung's final conclusions on the ultimate religious problematic, and any treatment of the relation of Jungian psychology to Christian spirituality must face these issues head-on.

I   **The Integration of Spirit and Matter**

In our previous article we summarized the Jungian understanding of the process of individuation as a matter of reversing false identifications of the ego with collective consciousness and with the collective unconscious; of withdrawing projections, whether they be in the realms of the shadow, of the anima or animus, or of archetypal symbols; and of ceasing to allow oneself to be swayed and derailed by the projections others may have placed on oneself. As the process of individuation goes forward, then, what happens is that the individual emerges as a conscious unity in his or her own right, with a self-possession in the realm of affectivity that enables one to live the 'just-so' life, the life of simple giving and receiving, of real reciprocity, of self-transcendent individuality, without ulterior motives, available for the performance of his or her own tasks in the world without losing oneself in the psychic resonances that non-individuated relationships always entail. The culmination of the process lies, ideally, in what Jung calls the experience of the self. For me, this is an experience of oneself as a self-possessed, integrated totality, whose very integration enables one to operate simultaneously as a self-transcending subject of the operations of insight, judgment, decision, communication, collaboration, love, and prayer. The self-possessed person is not a self-enclosed person, but is an independent agent of self-transcending action in the world.

Such a state of integration is hard to describe. Jung himself probably comes closest to succeeding in his work, 'Commentary on the "Secret of the Golden Flower."'[7] But may it not be the case that the best descriptions are still found in the great religious documents of world history? In the Bible, for instance, St. Paul says: 'I have learned, in whatever state I am, to be content, I know how to be abased, and I know how to abound; in any and all circumstances I have learned the secret of facing plenty and hunger, abundance and want. I can do all things in him who strengthens me.'[8] In the Sermon on the Mount, Jesus says: 'Do not be anxious about your life … Seek first God's kingdom and God's righteousness, and all these things will be yours as well. Do not be anxious about tomorrow, for tomorrow will be anxious for itself. Let the day's own trouble be sufficient for the day.'[9] In other religious traditions we find other ways of expressing similar states of being. The *Bhagavad Gita* speaks of acting, but renouncing the fruits of one's action;[10] the *I Ching* says: 'If one does not count on the harvest while plowing or on the use of the ground while clearing it, it furthers one to undertake something.'[11] Mystics of various traditions speak of a state of detachment from inner states and outer objects, where detachment is not unrelatedness but free, non-demanding relatedness, where one is no longer preoccupied with compulsive plans or with the images of things, because one lives from that deeper center where the soul is at one with God, that shrine for ultimate holiness which is the innermost mansion of the soul. 'I live, now not I, but Christ lives in me.' Thus Jung can speak of a higher and deeper authority than the ego. The ego is not identified with this authority, but receives from it, so that a person is enabled to forge his or her life and work with all the energy at one's disposal, and at the same time to give one's life and work over to God to let God do with it whatever God chooses, making no demands at all. So, too, Lonergan can speak of a condition of universal willingness, where one's whole life is dominated by a detachment and disinterestedness that comes from a vision of reality in which one's ego is no longer the center of reference, but is rather subordinated to some universal destiny governed by the providence of God.[12] And T.S. Eliot's *Four Quartets* concludes by speaking of

> A condition of complete simplicity
> (Costing not less than everything)
> And all shall be well and
> All manner of thing shall be well
> When the tongues of flame are infolded
> Into the crowned knot of fire
> And the fire and the rose are one.[13]

The fire of spirit and the rose of the earth are one; the opposites of spirit and matter are joined, at peace and harmony with one another. The culmination of the process of individuation is a reconciliation of the opposites in the human person. In what is perhaps his most important scientific paper, Jung comes very close to identifying the ultimate opposites in human personality with spirit and matter, to be joined by negotiating the psyche, which shares in both.[14] And as long as his thought is interpreted in this way, it can prove very helpful in the development of a spirituality that leads one to the point of union with God, of dependence on God alone, that is the fruit of the mystical journey. Thus, finally, William Johnston, one of the finest spiritual writers of our time, can make good use of Jung in his excellent book *The Still Point.*[15]

2   The Still Point

But what is that 'still point' of the turning world, that place where the deeper center is found, from which the ego receives its strength to do all things in the one who strengthens it? Is that 'still point' myself, or is it the place of the indwelling of God in my soul? Is it ultimately self or God? *Is it nature or is it grace?* Is it *in* human interiority or beyond interiority? What is that supraordinate authority that Jung calls the self? Does Jung predetermine the answer to that question by calling it the self? Christian tradition does not call it the self. It declares emphatically that the 'still point' is not just me, but is rather the region where God dwells in my innermost being. 'And I will pray the Father, and he will give you another Counselor, to be with you forever, even the Spirit of truth, whom the world cannot receive, because it neither sees him nor knows him; you know him, for he dwells with you, and will be in you.'[16] 'If a man loves me, he will keep my word, and my Father will love him, and we will come to him and make our home with him.'[17] The innermost region of our interiority is, in the Christian mystical tradition, no longer ourselves, but the place of grace, where the gift of God's love is poured forth into our hearts by the Holy Spirit who has been given to us.[18] It is what Lonergan calls the region for the divine.

The last works of Jung, and surely too the writings of some of his closest disciples,[19] are reluctant to accept such an interpretation of the innermost center of our being. They evince a desire to reduce the scriptural and traditional Christian terminology about this innermost center to merely figurative language. They want to explain the 'still point' in terms, not of grace, but of nature. Christ, in St. Paul's 'I live, now not I, but Christ lives in me,' becomes merely a symbol of the self. What St. Paul really means would be something like, 'The ego is no longer the center of my being, for I have found the self.' Edward Edinger, in his book *Ego and Archetype*, explicitly speaks of St. Paul's conversion as an example of the encounter with the self.[20] The relation of the human person to God is immanentized, so that it becomes a relation of ego to self. Prayer, then, is literally reduced to talking to one's self. It is not to be ridiculed for that reason, for it is psychologically important for the ego to be in relation to the self.

I propose to examine a dream of Jung's shortly before he wrote his most controversial work, *Answer to Job*, where these problems come to explicit formulation. I will offer of this dream a Christian theological interpretation, one with which orthodox Jungians will most likely not be happy, but one that at least establishes the issue on which, I believe, a Christian adaptation of Jung centers.

In the portion of this dream that is most relevant to our consideration, Jung is in a large hall with his father. The hall is a high, circular room with a gallery running along the wall, from which four bridges lead to a basin-shaped center. The basin rests on a huge column, and forms the round seat of a Muslim sultan, who from this round seat speaks to his councilors [sic] and philosophers, who themselves sit along the wall in the gallery. The scene is, as Jung says, 'a gigantic mandala,' that is, a symbol of the self. To quote Jung:

> In the dream I suddenly saw that from the center a steep flight of stairs ascended to a spot high up on the wall — which no longer corresponded to reality. At the top of the stairs was a small door, and my father said, 'Now I will lead you into the highest presence.' Then he knelt down and touched his forehead to the floor. I imitated him, likewise kneeling, with great emotion. For some reason I could not bring my forehead quite down to the floor — there was perhaps a millimeter to spare. But at least I had made the gesture with him. Suddenly I knew — perhaps my father had told me — that that upper door led to a solitary chamber where lived Uriah, King David's general, whom David had shamefully betrayed for the sake of his wife Bathsheba, by commanding his soldiers to abandon Uriah in the face of the enemy.[21]

And what Jung says about this portion of the dream is the following:

> When I was in India, the mandala structure of the *divan-i-kaas* (council hall) had in actual fact powerfully impressed me as the representation of a content related to the center. The center is the seat of Akbar the Great, who rules over a subcontinent, who is a 'lord of this world,' like David. But even higher than David stands his guiltless victim, his loyal general Uriah, whom he abandoned to the enemy. Uriah is a prefiguration of Christ.[22]

In what follows it is important to remember that this dream prefigures Jung's writing of his *Answer to Job*, which vividly portrays his conviction that God is ambivalent, that God is not the highest good, as Christianity would have it. But let me first say how I interpret this dream, and then we will examine Jung's understanding of it.

Jung was always fascinated by the mandala as a symbol of wholeness. When he saw the council hall of the sultan in India, it had to make a deep impression on him, and this impression remained in his memory, ready to be released into consciousness once again as a way of portraying the wholeness that, he believed, was the goal of the process of individuation. The mandala, then, symbolizes the integrated self, which is both center and totality of the personality. As center, it is the sultan, the higher authority, the king in the middle of the round room, giving out his orders to his ministers who surround him, and who together with him constitute the totality. But this higher authority is in itself nature; it is this-worldly. The sultan is a 'lord of this world.' This higher authority is the 'greater personality, the inner man,' which has an impact 'upon the life of every

individual.'[23] Jung's father, who himself had been a cler-
gyman and whose faith had always dissatisfied Jung, tells
him that there is a still higher authority, the highest presence, beyond the door at the top of the flight of stairs, at a
spot high up on the wall which, Jung says, 'no longer cor-
responded to reality,' that is, which was otherworldly. The
relation to this highest authority, this highest presence, is
embodied in the innocent suffering of the Just One, here
Uriah, whom Jung sees as a prefiguration of Christ. The
mystery of the suffering of the innocent points beyond
nature and calls one to the response that Jung's father shows
in the dream, the response of touching one's forehead to
the floor, the response of letting oneself fall into the
incomprehensibility of God as into true fulfillment and
happiness, a response similar to Job's at the end of the
book to which Jung tried to compose a response. In this
voluntary acceptance of innocent suffering — what in
Christ we call the law of the cross — evil loses its power,
and we are elevated into a relationship that transcends the
dimensions of nature, a relationship beyond the perfect
symmetry of nature's finest achievements. Jung's father is
telling him that there is an otherworldly, supernatural
authority, a highest presence, revealed in the mystery of
the Christ, and before whose dominion the self has to be
stretched to the point of adoration, submission, and
ultimate silence. *That* is the real answer to Job, the answer
that Job himself came to, the answer *of* Job when God
questioned him: 'Where were you when I laid the
foundations of the earth?'

Interestingly, earlier in the dream, Jung's father had
been reading from Genesis, and expounding eloquently
on it, but Jung found his father's words incomprehensible,
even though he marveled at them. And what is it that Job
answers when confronted with the incomprehensibility of
God? 'I have uttered what I did not understand, things too

wonderful for me, which I did not know ... I had heard of you by the hearing of the ear, but now my eyes see you. Therefore I despise myself, and I repent in dust and ashes'[24] — I touch my forehead to the floor in adoration.

The dream reflects, I believe, Jung's ambivalent attitude to that final step in coming to the point, the condition, of complete simplicity. There is a fascination with the wholeness of the mandala, of the self, of nature, that prevents him from granting that the mandala is *not* self-enclosed, that there is a small door that opens from the center of the self, through the mystery of suffering, onto the incomprehensibility of a God in relation to whom we have to adopt the final posture of Job himself. But, 'Something in me,' says Jung, 'was defiant and determined not to be a dumb fish.'[25]

3   The Mystery of Evil and the Incomprehensibility of God

What that defiance, that millimeter to spare, meant in terms of Jung's final religious testament is not difficult to discover. There is an option made to limit our understanding of the deepest dimensions of our selves to the contours of the mandala-shaped council hall; there is expressed in Jung's defiance a desire *not* to transcend the realm of nature in order to come to the end of our journey to individuation, *not* to acknowledge the small door that leads beyond the self and its wholeness and into the dimension of the otherworldly and incomprehensible, a desire *not* to surrender *gnosis* to faith, since the aspect of reality that beckons us to this opening of the self-beyond-itself is the mystery of suffering. The inclination not to be opened beyond oneself, not to fall into the incomprehensibilty of God, is an inclination to resent the fact that the final step in the journey is not our own doing, not even the doing of the deeper center of the self, but the activity of God, an activity that is not fully comprehensible in natural terms. This God who opens us through suffering to God's own incomprehensibility as to our happiness and fulfillment is then viewed as evil as well as good. The attitude adopted toward God is one of anger. This means for Jung that Christ cannot be the full embodiment and revelation of this God, for Christ is only good. Satan, too, must be viewed as a revelation of God, as the fourth person in the Godhead. In his late book *Aion*, Jung reverts to astrological speculation in order to explain where the history of the image of God is heading. We are, Jung says, at the end of the astrological age Pisces, an age symbolized by the warring fishes, and we stand at the beginning of a new age of Aquarius, whose symbol is the *Anthropos*, the human being in whom the opposites are reconciled. Christ and Satan are the warring fishes, and in the age of Aquarius they will be reconciled, through the emergence of Anthropos, the realization of the individuated self. This means that human beings are helping God to find God's own self, to get beyond God's own inner contradictions. We have to redeem God from God's own unconsciousness. The overcoming of evil, then, is reduced to a matter of achieving greater consciousness; through this process evil and good come to be relativized, and so capable of being integrated with one another. We are encouraged to adopt a different attitude to evil: not to reject it, but to give it a place in our lives. Then the final opposition, that of good and evil, will be overcome, and the image of God will lose its fearsome aspect of incomprehensibility precisely in the process through which the self comes to integration.

Christian theology would offer an alternative interpretation of the same issues. Most radically, it would suggest that we must make the option not to limit the deepest dimensions of the reaches of our intentionality to the contours of the closed mandala, but must acknowledge the small door that leads beyond the self and onto the otherworldly dimension of the incomprehensibility of God. It *is* in the limit situations of suffering, loss, and ultimately death that we are beckoned to this opening of the self. And *not* to open oneself to the mystery of God in these situations is evil, a denial of our creaturehood, what Ernest Becker would call a *causa sui* project,[26] a desire to be God. It is faith, not *gnosis*, that enables us to fall into the incomprehensibility of God as into our true happiness and fulfillment. The mystery of evil is rooted, not in God's incomprehensibility, but in the radical depotentiation of moral agency that Christian tradition has called original sin, and even more radically in that whole dimension of reality that St. Paul was struggling to articulate when he spoke of 'principalities and powers.' Christ is the incarnation of God's saving purpose in our regard, the full and explicit sacrament of the divinely originated solution to the problem of evil. Satan is the expression of all the enmity toward God in the world that will not surrender to God's incomprehensible purpose, and that wants the control that comes from being the cause of oneself, the control that refuses faith and chooses *gnosis*. Christ and Satan are irreconcilable enemies, in the same way as is expressed in the fact that one cannot both surrender and not surrender at the same time, cannot both touch one's forehead to the floor and still leave a millimeter to spare. The astrological speculations about the age of Aquarius are themselves pure myth posing as science, and so *gnosis*. For a scientist such as Jung to turn to such speculations represents a disreputable neglect of the evidence. And the evidence found in the conditions of the contemporary world hardly inspires us to believe that, by some natural course of events, all contradictions and enmities are about to come to an end, and the human race about to achieve a har-

mony with itself and with nature through a natural reconciliation of good and evil. The requirement for peace and
justice in our world is still the same as it always has been:
accepting the divinely originated solution to the problem
of evil that comes to us in Christ Jesus; allowing God to
transform us into agents of love and justice and reconciliation; and *bearing the suffering* that the powers of evil will
unleash on us because of our option. The age of martyrs is
anything but over. The overcoming of evil, then, is not a
matter only of coming to greater consciousness, even if
self-appropriation is a moral demand of our time. And
achieving greater consciousness will not relativize good and
evil, but rather will sharpen our ability to differentiate what
is worth while from what is worthless, seductive, malicious.
The process of coming to greater consciousness is a process of *conversion*. It involves a more discerning rejection
of what is evil, not a compromise with evil in our lives.
Good and evil remain contradictories. They cannot be integrated, as can spirit and matter, or the masculine and
feminine dimensions of the personality, which are not
contradictories, but *contraries*.

The ground of the individuation process, then, must
be the gift of God's love, and the eye of that love which is
faith. And the goal of the process is not properly symbolized in the utterly closed mandala with no opening onto
the absolutely transcendent. The symbolic significance of
Christ is clear: in the moment when the powers of darkness are unleashed against him *because* he is from God, he
surrenders to the incomprehensible reality that lies beyond
that small door at the furthest dimensions of the self, and
he comes in victory through that door into the highest presence, to the right hand of that good God who in Christ
has proposed once and for all a redemptive solution to the
problem of evil.

Notes

1 Isaiah 55.8.

2 Job 38.4.

3 Exodus 3.14.

4 Romans 11.33.

5 See Karl Rahner, 'Thomas Aquinas on the Incomprehensibility of God,' in *Celebrating the Medieval Heritage: A Colloquy on the Thought of Aquinas and Bonaventure: Journal of Religion* 58: Supplement (1978), ed. David Tracy, especially p. S114.

6 Ibid. passim.

7 C.G. Jung, 'Commentary on "The Secret of the Golden Flower"' (see above, chapter 5, note 25).

8 Philippians 4.11-12.

9 Matthew 6.25-34.

10 *The Bhagavad Gita*, trans. from the Sanskrit with an introduction by Juan Mascaro (Baltimore: Penguin Books, 1962).

11 *The I Ching or Book of Changes*, the Richard Wilhelm translation rendered into English by Cary F. Baynes (Princeton: Princeton University Press, 1967) 102.

12 Bernard Lonergan, *Insight* (see above, chapter 1, note 37) 623-24/646-47.

13 T.S. Eliot, *Four Quartets* (see above, chapter 2, note 15) 59.

[14] C.G. Jung, 'On the Nature of the Psyche' in *The Structure and Dynamics of the Psyche* (see above, chapter 2, note 14) 159-234.

[15] William Johnston, *The Still Point: Reflections on Zen and Christian Mysticism* (New York: Harper & Row, 1971).

[16] John 14.16-17.

[17] John 14.23

[18] Romans 5.5.

[19] See Marie-Louise von Franz, *C.G. Jung: His Myth in Our Time* (see above, chapter 4, note 23).

[20] Edward Edinger, *Ego and Archetype* (New York: C.G. Jung Foundation, 1972) 76.

[21] C.G. Jung, *Memories, Dreams, Reflections* (see above, chapter 3, note 49) 218-19.

[22] Ibid. 219.

[23] Ibid. 221.

[24] Job 42.3-6.

[25] Jung, *Memories, Dreams, Reflections* 220.

[26] Ernest Becker, *The Denial of Death* (see above, chapter 4, note 4) 115-23.

15 Primary Process and the 'Spiritual Unconscious'

This paper presents some terminological suggestions that go beyond my earlier formulations of psychic conversion. These earlier articulations are all included in an integrated and systematic fashion in *Psychic Conversion and Theological Foundations*.[1] This paper is primarily concerned with the same reorientation of depth psychology that was the focus of these earlier reflections, but adds, I hope, some new precision.

The terminological suggestions I wish to make have to do with a reconstruction of the Freudian notions of primary and secondary process[2] and of the notion of a 'spiritual unconscious' developed by a Jungian, Roger Woolger.[3] I will treat first the Freudian categories; second, the meaning of Woolger's 'spiritual unconscious'; and I conclude with an account of the sense in which this dimension can be called 'unconscious,' indicating briefly the manner in which its retrieval might affect two ways of understanding another dimension of the 'unconscious,' the psychic dimension. I refer to the work of Ernest Becker and Carl Jung.

1 Primary Process and Secondary Process

There is a paradoxical feature in the structure of reductionist theories. We will witness one instance of it in

447

discussing Freud. While it is true that reductionist accounts
have the character of describing 'higher' activities as 'nothing but' more basic activities or their 'reflexes,' the basic
level itself is conceived too narrowly. For example, the
Marxist notion of the base and superstructure of society
not only has the superstructure become 'nothing but' a
reflex of the base; also, not enough is included in the base
itself. Thus, primordial intersubjectivity is more or less
overlooked, and both the political dimension of society and
also the commonsense level of cultural values are projected
into the superstructure, when in fact they belong to the
base. As a result, what *does* belong in the superstructure —
namely, scientific, scholarly, artistic, philosophic, and
theological objectifications — is deprived of its autonomy
and denied its place as a significant contributor to the
integrity or distortion of the base.

An analogous difficulty can be found in Freudian
psychoanalytic theory. In the present essay I will limit discussion of this difficulty to Freud's notions of primary and
secondary process. I was led to a reorientation of these
notions by reflecting on several phrases in the introduction to Bernard Lonergan's *Insight*. There we are told that
the effort of the book is to attain 'greater concreteness on
the side of the subject.'[4] The reader is invited to locate 'in
the pulsing flow of life'[5] the various elements discovered
by a careful reading of the book. This 'pulsing flow of life'
includes such elements as insight, reflective understanding and judgment, existential freedom culminating in decisions, and even the supernatural life of grace. None of
these elements (only some of which would be admitted by
Freud even to exist) is to be excluded from primary process and relegated to a secondary process that develops
only because the aims of the primordial desires are inevitably frustrated. The basic question regards what one will
include among the primordial desires. If the desire to un-

derstand correctly, or, more compactly, the desire to find and hold to what Eric Voegelin has called the direction that can be found in the movement of life[6] is to be included in the primary process of the pulsing flow, then the categories that to date have served as the basic terms and relations of depth psychology, including Freud's primary and secondary process, have been incorrect. No depth psychology, including those less reductionist than Freud's, adequately accounts for the relation to the sensitive flow of the psyche on the part of the elements of intentionality that Lonergan would have us discover. I suggest that we reconceive 'primary process' as the pulsing flow of life in which we can find not only the dynamics uncovered by Freud and others but also the operations whose self-appropriation is the aim of *Insight*; and that we reconceive 'secondary process' as all more or less successful scientific and commonsense attempts to articulate primary process: all attempts (to adapt Lonergan's terms) to bring the operations of conscious intentionality as intentional to bear upon both *the operations* and *the states* of conscious intentionality as conscious.[7] Thus 'secondary process' would be a category applicable to Freudian psychoanalytic theory as well as to Lonergan's intentionality analysis. Both have disengaged something of the truth about primary process. A higher synthesis would integrate these discoveries with one another. But what I am emphasizing at the moment is that what Lonergan has disengaged belongs as much to primary process as what Freud discovered, and that a recognition of this fact would alter the significance and structure of psychoanalytic theory. In Lonergan's own words:

> On the empirical level, it is true, process is spontaneous sensitivity; it is intelligible only in the sense that it can be understood. But with inquiry the intelligent subject emerges, and

process becomes intelligent; it is not merely an intelligible that can be understood, but the active correlative of intelligibility, the intelligence that intelligently seeks understanding, comes to understand, and operates in the light of having understood. When inquiry comes to a term, or an impasse, intelligence intelligently yields place to critical reflection; as critically reflective, the subject stands in conscious relation to an absolute — the absolute that makes us regard the positive content of the sciences not as true and certain but only as probable. Finally, the rational subject, having achieved knowledge of what is and could be, rationally gives way to conscious freedom and conscientious responsibility.[8]

To the preceding affirmations, moreover, we must add the important assertion that 'secondary-process' articulations of primary process, whether scientific or commonsense and whether more or less successful, reverberate back upon primary process, influence it, and either distort or facilitate it. This assertion not only explains the frequently remarked phenomenon that patients in Freudian analysis will tend to have Freudian dreams; those undergoing Jungian analysis, archetypal dreams; and so forth. It also throws into relief the extreme importance of getting things right when it comes to self-understanding. Primary process in its totality may be understood with Voegelin as the search for direction in the movement of life. The normative order of that search is unpacked in Lonergan's intentionality analysis. When secondary-process apprehensions of primary process in its twofold intentional and psychic constitution are correct, the self as it is and the self as it is understood to be 'are operating from the same base along the same route to the same goal.' When secondary-process apprehensions of primary process are mistaken, the self as it is and the self as it is understood to be 'to a greater or less extent, are operating at cross-purposes. Such a conflict is inimical to the development' of the person.[9]

Personal development, moreover, is a dialectical process that affects the level of primary process itself. There is a dialectic of the subject whose basic terms and relations constitute the transactions between neural demands for conscious representation and psychic integration, on the one hand, and the repressive or constructive censorship of dramatically patterned intentionality, on the other hand.[10] This dialectic is one instance of the general law of limitation and transcendence that constitutes all development in the concrete universe of proportionate being.[11] Mistaken apprehensions of primary process will distort that dialectical process by displacing in one direction or another the tension, the poised equilibrium, the taut balance, of limitation and transcendence. The pulsing flow of life, the search for direction in the movement of life, primary process, is a duality. In *Insight* we are afforded an opportunity to 'unravel an ambiguity and to eliminate an ambivalence'[12] that affects our *cognitive* activity. But we are also invited to understand the duality of our knowing as a manifestation or instance of a more wide-ranging and inclusive tension that informs our living in its entirety: the heightened tension that, on the side of the object, is the opposition between the world of sense and the world mediated by meaning and motivated by value; and, on the side of the subject, is the opposition between a center in the world of sense and an entry into the universe of being.[13] This tension constitutes the pulsing flow of life; it constitutes the very structure of primary process. But its integrity depends on the accuracy of those acts of self-understanding constitutive of secondary process.

The duality of primary process is ontologically grounded in a *threefold* constitution of the person. The person or 'self' in its entirety is a unity of living organism, sensitive psyche, and spiritual intention of the intelligible, the true and the real, and the good. Consciousness is a duality, but no ontological dualism underlies this duality; but dualist ontological conceptions of the human person typically fail to recognize the distinct function of the sensitive psyche. As we will see later, even such a sensitive and perceptive reorientation of the psychoanalytic tradition as Ernest Becker's falls down on this point; whereas one of the distinct merits of Jungian insight, at least at one point of its development, is its insistence on the threefold constitution of the human person[14] — even though Jung did not yet draw these distinctions precisely enough.

The sensitive psyche, then, participates in both organic·process and spiritual activity, and mediates the tension of the two. Neural process receives a higher and conscious integration at the level of the psyche. But the same psyche is constellated into a variety of patterns of experience[15] correlative to a variety of realms of meaning,[16] which are the objectives of spiritual intentionality. The tension of primary process is thus *experienced* at the level of the sensitive psyche. Precisely as sensitive, psychic experience is bounded both by the dynamics of what Heidegger has disclosed as the dimensions of primordial time[17] and by the ecology of human spatiality. But the psyche also participates in the operations of conscious intentionality: every act of inquiry, insight, reflection, judgment, deliberation, decision is accompanied by corresponding sensitive and affective elements. And the objectives of conscious intentionality are *not* restricted by time and space. The latter are *within*, not inclusive of, the objectives of human cognitional and existential praxis — the real and the good.[18]

The tension experienced by the psyche is an opposition between being at home in a habitat and being at home in being. The opposition cannot be eradicated by choosing either alternative over the other. Genuineness lies in admitting the tension itself into consciousness and self-understanding,[19] so that one lives out of the balance of limitation and transcendence rather than by displacing the balance to one pole or the other. Psychologically, opting to dissolve the tension in favor of a habitat is to invite the dynamics of depression; and choosing to flee the limitations of a habitat is to soar into schizophrenic fantasy.[20] All one can do is admit the tension in its fullness into one's development (primary process) and into one's understanding of one's development (secondary process), to admit it precisely as a dialectic, and as that kind of dialectic in which the linked but opposed principles of change 'are modified [not eliminated] by the changes that successively result from them.'[21] We might call this a dialectic of contraries, as opposed to a dialectic of contradictories. In the latter the issue at stake is one of choice between two mutually exclusive opposites (for instance, the true and the false, the good and the evil). But both poles of a dialectic of contraries are to be affirmed, each in its proper relation to the other. In this instance, any genuine dialectic of contradictories would involve the choice of either the balanced development of the dialectic of contraries or the distortion of the poised equilibrium of limitation and transcendence.

In the terms being suggested here, any attempts to continue to unfold the implications of the notion of a generalized empirical method are secondary-process efforts at articulating the dynamics of the pulsing flow of primary process. Fred Lawrence has specified the core genuineness of secondary process: 'The key to method is ... the subject as subject ... To do 'method' calls ... for a release from all logics, all closed systems or language games, all concepts, all symbolic constructs to allow an abiding at the level of the presence of the subject to himself.'[22] Lawrence's 'key to method' explains perhaps why method so conceived was for so long such an improbable emergence in the development of human consciousness. To abide at the level of the presence of the subject to himself or herself, to abide beyond all representation, is a rare achievement. And to *represent* what is experienced in that abiding, and to do so not just descriptively but with explanatory precision, is the kind of differentiation that, borrowing Eric Voegelin's terms, we might describe as a 'leap in being.'[23] Now we are confronted with the question of the probability of survival of what has already emerged: with the step by step, question by question implementation of the integral heuristic structure of proportionate being.[24] My own option has been the dialectical integration into 'method' of the findings of those who have specialized in exploring the psychic rather than intentional dimensions of primary process. Is not this the next step in attempting to augment the probability of survival of 'interiorly differentiated consciousness,' which is a distinctly secondary-process achievement?

This integration, however, must be critical and dialectical, because I am convinced that in the last analysis an adequate science of psychic depths is dependent on a correct analysis of human intentionality. If the major representatives of depth psychology to date have not been equipped with such an analysis, then at one point or another their apprehensions are mistaken, and their psychologies become, in Voegelin's terms, psychologies of passional motivation, the psychologies of pneumopathological subjects, rather than psychologies of orientations.[25] In contrast, a psychology of orientations would start by elucidating the participation of the sensitive psyche in the intentionality of the human spirit. Mistaken apprehensions will be found to reverberate back upon primary process to distort it by displacing the integral tension of limitation and transcendence in one direction or another. Most of the remainder of this paper will be devoted to analyzing some instances of such misapprehension and to reflecting on their implications.

Before I proceed to this analysis and reflection, though, let me make one comment: what has been said thus far is significant for understanding the four conversions — religious, moral, intellectual, and psychic — that constitute the foundational dimensions which can be explicitated as a result of abiding at the level of the presence of the subject to himself or herself. In the third stage of meaning, intellectual and psychic conversion refer both to the integrity of cognitional and psychic process (primary process) and to the *self-appropriation* of cognitional and psychic process (secondary process), but I contend that they affect secondary process most immediately; whereas religious and moral conversion (along with prephilosophic instances of cognitive integrity and constructive censorship regarding neural demands) affect primary process most immediately.

2   The Spiritual Unconscious

I turn next to the category of the spiritual unconscious. The term 'spiritual unconscious' appears in a paper by Roger Woolger that attempts to come to terms from a Jungian perspective with the anti-imaginal mysticism of Simone Weil.[26] Woolger adopts the term from Roberto Assagiolli's *Psychosynthesis*, and integrates it into Jungian thought by suggesting that the *mundus imaginalis* called the collective unconscious by Jung should be understood as 'that region of the soul where psychic contents become contaminated and transformed by the spirit to take on the primordial and numinous character of the archetypes.'[27] Woolger's model is obviously influenced by Jung's programmatic essay 'On the Nature of the Psyche,'[28] where the psyche's archetypal images are distinguished from the 'psychoid' (that is, to be understood by analogy with the psyche) archetypes-as-such. The latter belong to the 'spirit factor' in its tense interplay with the instinctual factor. The spirit releases the images as a result of a tension constellated between itself and its polar opposite but equally 'psychoid' dimension, instinctive process. For Woolger instinct maps out the Freudian psychoanalytic path when it is considered independently of its tension with the spirit factor.

From what Woolger says expressly, I infer that when the psychoanalytic path is regarded as the exclusive explanatory principle for understanding primary process, it is an abstraction, a substitution of a part for a whole, a contraction of reality into a framework that cannot contain it, a distortion not only of the whole but also of the part that is supposed to include the whole. Jungians in general, and Woolger in particular, will acknowledge that there is more to primary process than what Freud and his followers will admit. Included in this 'more' is Jung's 'spirit factor' or what Woolger calls 'the spiritual unconscious.' What is most important about Woolger's essay as written by a Jungian is that he correlates this factor neither with the psychoanalytic path nor with the Jungian archetypal path, but with the mystical purification of the dark night of the soul. Here 'the capacity to produce or meditate upon images appears to have irrevocably dried up.' Woolger's critique of available psychologies thus extends even to Jungian formulations, where the dark night is frequently understood as an archetypal process. A Jungian explanation, says Woolger, would grant to archetypal images 'wider explanatory power than they warrant.' The dark night is more adequately understood as 'a state which may include visionary experience but which is not to be exclusively identified with it' nor to be understood in the archetypal terms that do go a long way in elucidating visionary events. Even the Jungian designation 'psychoid' for this factor, Woolger says correctly, betrays 'an insufficient distinction between the psychological and the spiritual.'[29] The confusion to which Woolger is pointing haunts and plagues practically all Jungian writing on spirituality and religion.

Woolger's paper is most significant coming from a Jungian. As might be expected from one with such commitments, it would (and quite correctly, I believe) point out to theologians and spiritual directors with apophatic inclinations that the archetypal world *is* a terrain to be explored and transformed if spiritual development is not to risk becoming schizoid. 'Not for nothing is the traditional antidote for spiritual pride, humility — the practice of being grounded in one's *humus*.'[30] But the paper also represents an admission that, while Jung correctly locates more in 'primary process' than Freud does, he still does not acknowledge enough, at least in a sufficiently differentiated fashion. The archetypal *mundus imaginalis* is not an ultimate resting place in interior development.

Thus Woolger suggests the potential contributions of the Jungian archetypal path to the recovery of the spirit: 'Unless the spirit enters into the psyche to transform mundane imagination into vision or numinous dreams, spirit remains unknowable or unconscious in a more absolute sense than our unconsciousness of personal memories [the psychoanalytic path], and even of archetypal images [the Jungian path].'[31] In Lonergan's terms, the Jungian archetypal path is one road towards a recovery of the subject, in precisely the fullness of the dimensions Lonergan has disclosed, from neglect and truncation.[32] Archetypal experience is a road toward entrance into the universe of being intended by the human spirit. It presents data for questions that, if pursued, would reveal the subject to himself or herself as a pure question for complete intelligibility, unconditioned truth, and unqualified goodness: these data, precisely as psychological, display the intermediate status of the psyche in the human constitution, the openness of the psyche to the spirit, the participation of the psyche in more than sensitive process, the tension of limitation and transcendence.

But in this present essay I am attempting to affirm that intentionality analysis is needed to ground an adequate psychological analysis: more existentially, that pneumopathology is in the last analysis the ground of psychopathology. And Woolger speaks more to this point when he maintains that whether or not one is going to be able to transcend the Jungian *mundus imaginalis* into the mystical detachment from inner states and images and from outer objects 'may … depend on whichever *philosophies* we adopt consciously or unconsciously from our cultural heritage.'[33] That is to say, the spiritual effect (primary process) of an exploration (secondary process) of psychic process is intimately dependent upon one's implicit or explicit philosophical position (secondary process) regarding the intentional objectives of the human spirit (primary process). Primary process depends on secondary process. The self as it is depends on the self as it is understood to be. Secondary process reverberates upon primary process, for better or for worse. Woolger does not say but does imply that one difficulty with the Jungian school is the lack of an adequate philosophy to ground and properly locate the further contributions to secondary process that Jungian analysis potentially provides.

In several other writings I have made much of a dream that Jung relates in his autobiography.[34] He had this dream just before writing *Answer to Job*, which is perhaps his most controversial work and definitely the work that reveals most clearly Jung's own inability to transcend the *mundus imaginalis* of the archetypal psyche to the universe of being that is unrestricted by the dimensions of time and space. In the dream Jung refuses to follow his father's counsel to touch his forehead to the ground in adoration of the highest presence beyond the mandala-shaped temple of his own psyche. It indicates both the inability and its pneumopathological roots in as graphic and direct a manner as one could possibly conceive. The point that I want to make here is that the *philosophical* heritage that was available to Jung — Kantian in epistemology and German-idealistic in metaphysics — is intimately related to this supremely existential, primary-process inability and refusal. Without accurate philosophy the Jungian path does not and cannot cross the threshold between the psychological and the spiritual. Such confusion and inaccurate secondary-process *objectification* of what one is doing and where one is heading when one is traveling the archetypal path through the *mundus imaginalis* distorts the journey itself, and ultimately the primary process of life. Without a therapy of pneumopathology, psychopathology cannot be healed. It is simply redistributed over and over again, as a result of variations on the pneumopathological theme.

As an ultimate issue, the secondary-process element caught in a vicious circle with the aberrations of primary process becomes the final product of unchecked counterpositional affirmations: the problem to be remedied becomes the course of action to be recommended.[35] In this case, incredible as it may appear, psychopathology is lionized in further developments of Jungian thought and made into a condition to be indulged in.[36] The roots of such an affirmation in pneumopathology can be seen, I believe, in the casual acceptance of epistemological and moral relativism, and in the recommendation now found in some Jungian literature of a new polytheism as the appropriate mytho-religious sensibility for postmodern humanity.[37] The intention of integration which is still clear in Jung's own writings and which remains the potential key within the Jungian corpus for unlocking the door of Jung's psychic cul-de-sac (however inadequately its real exigences and roots may have been articulated by Jung himself) is now being abandoned by some of Jung's followers, who would maintain that it is the one mistake Jung made. It is true that one cannot both remain on the way to the integration of self-transcendent subjectivity and follow Jung into the prison house of the self explicitly chosen as the alternative to vertical transcendence. But, while this choice is Exhibit A of pneumopathology, it should not be viewed as discrediting the very intention of integration. It only manifests one of the possible derailments of this intention, and perhaps the source of all the others. I would argue that Jung's dream was telling him precisely this, but he, the great interpreter, could not see it. Instead he wrote *Answer to Job*, a great affirmation of pneumopathology.

Now, I want to reinterpret what Woolger calls the spiritual unconscious more precisely as the *conscious but unobjectified* (primary process) exigences of human intentionality for the intelligible, the true and the real, and the good, which have been forgotten and repressed because of the inherited philosophies of our day (secondary process). A correct secondary-process understanding of the *mundus imaginalis* and of the journey through and beyond it — an accurate science of depth psychology — is dependent on a critical retrieval of that conscious but unobjectified intentionality. As Woolger's essay suggests, the dependence is mutual to a certain extent. The retrieval of intentionality can also be aided by a journey through the *mundus imaginalis*, especially in the sense that the latter has the dramatic potential of providing a defensive circle around both the secondary-process events of self-appropriation and the primary-process events of authentic cognitive and existential praxis. But it has this potential only when the archetypal events are acknowledged as *data to be understood correctly* and to be brought to bear upon the decisions leading to existential praxis only through this correct understanding.

Consequently, what Woolger calls the spiritual unconscious is in fact human consciousness itself: not of course in the Jungian sense, where consciousness is ego perception, but in Lonergan's sense of consciousness as experience, consciousness as structured into empirical, intelligent, rational, existential, and religious dimensions, each of them permeated by the strictly psychological components of inner sensitivity. These strictly psychological components are determined as to their quality by the dialectics of the subject and of community,[38] whose explanatory principle lies ultimately in the minor and major unauthenticity[39] of the intentional levels of consciousness. Kierkegaard understood this issue of authenticity better than most twentieth-century psychologists (but more compactly than we are now prepared to do under Lonergan's tutelage): spirit posits the synthesis of the psyche and the body; that is, spirit determines in large measure what the relation of the psyche will be both to the body and to itself.[40] To move beyond Kierkegaard, spirit is not only radical existential freedom and its dread-filled vocation to determine the synthesis of the psychic and the bodily and the synthesis of the temporal and the eternal; spirit is also inquiry, insight, conceptualization, formulation, reflection, grasp of the virtually unconditioned, affirmation and negation; and existential freedom itself is historical responsibility for both short-range and long-range cycles in the dialectic of community.[41]

It is very important to grasp this relation of spirit to psyche, especially in any attempts to come to grips with both the contributions and the possible derailments of contemporary depth psychology. One's experience of the *mundus imaginalis* is not a matter of fatalistic destiny or even of what Woolger calls 'our individual destinies;'[42] instead, it is a function of and cipher for the appropriation of spiritual authenticity or inauthenticity. A dream such as Jung's to which I referred earlier does not have to be an overwhelming experience that propels with deterministic necessity an *Answer to Job* that simply objectifies religious pathology. Such a dream provides data for the questions that in virtue of understanding will ultimately lead to a decision as to whether or not *this* state of affairs is what one wants to accept as the truth about oneself. Such a decision could *alter* the *mundus imaginalis*, and *the change would be reflected in subsequent dreams*. That is to say, the experience of the *mundus imaginalis* is a function of the spiritual authenticity or inauthenticity of the five-storeyed intentionality of the human subject as the subject responds in one way or another to the transcendental exigences of consciousness in their dramatic exchanges with neural demands. Jung's spirit factor as transforming the contents of the *mundus imaginalis* really consists precisely in the exigences of the levels of conscious intentionality explicated by Lonergan; and in the dialectic of grace and sin that constitutes the ultimate drama of the operations at each level of conscious intentionality. Whether one remains stuck in the *mundus imaginalis*, as Jung's dream tells us he did, or transcends it through the release of the psyche's potential wisdom toward a mystical union with the complete intelligibility, absolutely unconditioned being and truth, and unqualified goodness of God is not to be accounted for by some Jungian *heimarmenê*. Contrary to Jung's dream and Jung's personal myth, spiritual destiny is not determined by constant rotation within the order of nature. The Jungian doctrine of the *coincidentia oppositorum* conflates the *contraries* of consciousness and the unconscious, masculine and feminine, and so on (where the doctrine is correct) with the *contradictories* of good and evil, by subsuming the latter into the former. This confusion reveals that the choice (conceived of as ultimate) of the realm of rotary, cyclical, quadripartite symbols, which is precisely what is reflected in Jung's dream, is actually the choice of the demonic.[43] But our argument on the relations of primary and secondary process leads us to affirm this: whether implicitly or explicitly one remains in or transcends the bondage of the spirit to the demonic is in large part a function of 'whatever philosophies we adopt consciously or unconsciously from our cultural heritage.'[44] 'The hopeless tangle ... of the endlessly multiplied philosophies, is not merely a *cul-de-sac* for human progress; it also is a reign of sin, a despotism of darkness; and men are its slaves.'[45]

Let me conclude this section by making it clear that I am not challenging Jung's clarification of rotary and quadripartite symbols such as the mandala precisely as symbols of integration. In Lonergan's terms, I am challenging the Jungian preference for the self as integrator over the self as operator. In addition to the symbols of the self as integrator there are symbols of the self as operator. For example, in Jung's dream, the father, his words and actions in adoration of the highest presence, and the small opening to the beyond guarded by the innocent victim of human sin (Uriah the Hittite) are symbols of the self (and of more than the self) as operator. In this case the quadripartite symbols of the integration of a previous stage of development are to be dissolved in favor of new differentiations that will lead, through the tension of limitation and transcendence, to more expansive but still temporary plateaus of well-rounded integration. 'One and the same reality is both integrator and operator; but the operator is relentless in transforming the integrator.'[46] 'The higher integration is not only an integrator but also an operator.'[47] And how can it be otherwise, if 'everyone by the dynamic structure of his being is oriented into ... the sphere of the ulterior unknown, of the unexplored and strange, of the undefined surplus of significance and meaning'[48] that constitutes the *permanent*, because unrestricted, primary field for the affect-laden images that result from the penetration of sensitivity by the operator? To insist on the self as integrator at the expense of the self as operator is not only to displace the tension of limitation and transcendence in the direction of limitation (with corresponding distortions of the transcendence pole). More ultimately, it may at times be a choice of a humanism in revolt against the proffered supernatural solution to the problem of evil.[49] While no one may dare judge another or even oneself on this point, it is penetratingly clear that the symbols of Jung's dream and the terms of his argument in *Answer to Job* revolve around precisely this question. In Lonergan's words:

> ... the heightened tension, which would result from a supernatural solution, would not lack its objectification in the dialectical succession of human situations. Hitherto, the dialectic has been conceived to rest on a bipolar conjunction and opposition. Within each man there are both the attachment and interestedness of sensitivity and intersubjectivity and, on the other hand, the detachment and disinterestedness of the pure desire to know. From this conjunction of opposites there follow (1) the interference of the lower level with the unfolding of inquiry and reflection, of deliberation and decision, (2) the consequent unintelligibility of

situations, and (3) the increasing irrelevance of intelligence and reasonableness to the real problem of human living.

But when this problem of evil is met by a supernatural solution, human perfection itself becomes a limit to be transcended, and then, the dialectic is transformed from a bipolar to a tripolar conjunction and opposition. The humanist viewpoint loses its primacy, not by some extrinsicist invasion, but by submitting to its own immanent necessities. For if the humanist is to stand by the exigencies of his own unrestricted desire, if he is to yield to the demands for openness set by every further question, then he will discover the limitations that imply man's incapacity for sustained development, he will acknowledge and consent to the one solution that exists and, if that solution is supernatural, his very humanism will lead beyond itself.[50]

3 Spirituality as 'Unconscious' and the Redistribution of the Archaic

Despite the fact that what Woolger is calling the spiritual unconscious is in fact consciousness itself in its native orientation toward the intelligible, the true and real, and the good, there is some warrant in the contemporary situation for referring to this orientation as unconscious. More precise, of course, are Lonergan's descriptions of the neglected, truncated, immanentist, and alienated subject.[51] For just as what depth psychology elucidates is in large part not strictly speaking unconscious but unobjectified, so too what Lonergan has succeeded in clarifying is the previously unobjectified or inadequately objectified structure of intentional consciousness itself. But in present parlance, the term 'the unconscious' refers, for better or for worse, to the forgotten and repressed dimensions of the human subject. The point I would make in retaining the term 'the spiritual unconscious' is just that spirituality has been forgotten and repressed and that the distinction between the psyche and the spirit has been relegated to oblivion, largely though not exclusively through the ministrations of depth psychologists. The full dimensions of spirituality are overlooked even by many theologians who write books and teach courses on 'Christian spirituality.' How often, for instance, do these books and courses mention understanding and judgment, let alone unpack their dynamics, when speaking of spirituality? Let us, then, grant a certain descriptive usefulness to the term 'the spiritual unconscious,' even if it is not a precise expression from a strictly technical point of view.

Jung has written that the self is the reality that it is most important for 'modern man' to understand.[52] One can agree with him on this point, and even with many of the specific reasons that he offers for this conviction, and still argue, as I am doing here, that the self, even in its archetypal manifestations, cannot be correctly understood from the standpoint of an uncriticized Jungian psychology. As we argued above, even the properly psychological dimensions of the self, both as data and as understood, depend on an analysis of cognitive and existential intentionality. Without this critical foundation, such an understanding as Jung would offer, despite its genuine contributions to the full position on the subject, will eventually be submerged in an immanentism whose very sophistication constitutes a high potentiality for self-destructiveness and historical irresponsibility.

The personal, immanently generated affirmation of the spiritual as distinctly real demands not only a fairly high degree of philosophical sophistication but also a *periagogê*, a conversion, that is appropriately called intellectual. The same affirmation, though not always immanently generated, however, *was* a constituent element of the Western cultural heritage until modern times, as a result of belief in the classic philosophical tradition rooted in the Platonic and Aristotelian conversions. In Roman Catholic circles, that effective history continued well into modern times, but at the expense of explicit relation to the specific intellectual, political, and historical problems of modernity. At the present time, neither a fidelity to the classical breakthrough nor a responsible negotiation of the contemporary problems is particularly obvious. If anything, the spirituality of personhood is at a further remove for Catholics today than it was several decades ago when they were assured the opportunity to affirm at least the values resident in a quite specific intellectual tradition, if not what they had immanently grasped as virtually unconditioned. The prospects for a reversal of the neglect, truncation, immanentization, and alienation of the subject are not particularly encouraging, when religious communities and educational institutions that still claim nominal allegiance to a particular tradition have in fact succumbed to the major surrender of intelligence — the factor most responsible for the acceleration of decline. Are we perhaps even further removed today from any responsible participation in history than the earlier recipients of an indoctrination into a culturally outmoded formulation of a basically quite worthy tradition?

Be that as it may, for many of us the work of Bernard Lonergan has succeeded in helping us begin to retrieve in a contemporary fashion what Voegelin would call the engendering experiences of that tradition. Much of my own work has been devoted to trying to bring Lonergan's achievement to bear on one of the principal and uniquely modern sources of data on the subject, the science of depth psychology, and this paper has been arguing that in order to do this effectively one must insist on an objectification of a forgotten dimension of subjectivity quite analogous to depth psychology's objectification of what it calls the unconscious. A mere turning to the psyche's *mundus imaginalis* is not sufficient for that understanding of the self which would begin to reverse the cycle of decline. In fact, as Voegelin has grasped better perhaps than any depth psychologist, the *mundus imaginalis*, the myth, is itself dependent on the extent to which consciousness has been differentiated. A differentiated consciousness will have a quite different *mundus imaginalis* to which to turn from that of an undifferentiated consciousness. It is not sufficient to affirm that there is needed a psychic conversion, a *conversio ad phantasma*, through which the symbolic can be appropriated. It is just as important to articulate that conversion correctly. For that conversion to proceed from and contribute to an accurate understanding of the self, in fact for it to be a genuine conversion at the secondary-process level, there is required a knowledge of the realities of intelligence, rationality, and moral responsibility. Much of what Polanyi called the tacit dimension and which he seems to have claimed must always remain tacit[53] has in fact been objectified, and need no longer remain silent. The role of spirituality in the pulsing flow of life, and so as a constitutive dimension of primary process, has been demonstrated. It can now be brought to bear upon the rest of primary process in an endeavor to reorient the findings of depth psychology. As I have argued elsewhere, the full disclosure resulting from this recovery of the subject who has been neglected, truncated, immanentized, and alienated by 'enlightenment' rationality would constitute what we may call, borrowing a term from Paul Ricoeur, a semantics of human desire.[54]

The intentional dimensions of consciousness, of course, are not the only elements of the subject that have been rendered 'unconscious' by that instrumentalization of reason in the service of power which constitutes so much of modern culture. Depth psychology *has* begun the task of retrieving other dimensions, such as the realm of the archaic, that enlightened moderns would claim has been eliminated, but in fact has only been differently distributed.[55] Depth psychology has exposed as an illusion the belief that the archaic has been eliminated. I conclude by examining briefly how the recovery of the 'spiritual unconscious' would affect two different depth-psychological approaches to exposing this illusion.

For Ernest Becker,[56] the illusion is a denial of the contingency of the death-doomed animal body and a flight into cultural lies that we create in order to proclaim our self-sufficiency. For Jung, the illusion is a neglect of the compensating factors of the multiform psychic unconscious on the part of the hypertrophied ego and *persona* of 'culturally normal' consciousness; these factors, when either attended to and appropriated (the personal unconscious) or negotiated in their autonomy (the collective unconscious) promote a progressive and cumulative reconciliation of opposites heading toward a condition of personal wholeness; and as one moves toward psychic wholeness, the archaic, precisely because it has once again been acknowledged, is transformed, redistributed, and reoriented.

As I said earlier, Jung's approach has a distinct advantage over Becker's in that it begins to transcend the radical dualism that for Becker still remains the lesson that psychoanalysis has to teach us. For Jung the psyche begins to be articulated as a factor distinct from the body and the spirit and mediating these 'psychoid' opposites; whereas for Becker, the person is conceived as a duality of body and 'self,' due in part to a misunderstanding of Kierkegaard.

On the other hand, Becker's reconstruction of depth psychology has one advantage over Jung's approach. Becker says what almost every depth psychologist either neglected or refused to say: in the last analysis, religious faith is the only possible operator of whatever authenticity we are able to achieve. I have already called attention to the theoretic ambiguities of Jung's position regarding vertical transcendence, and, more pointedly, to his autobiographical revelation of a possible existential refusal of such transcendence. *Answer to Job*, the least ambiguous of Jung's pronouncements, is in fact a reflection of the primordial temptation, You shall be as gods — in some respects, even superior to God. And this temptation is precisely what Becker labels the multiform *causa sui* project which is the source of our cultural lies and the springboard of our destructiveness.

What I want to do now is to see what happens to Becker's position and then to Jung's, if we accept the basic thesis of this paper: that the spiritual exigences of conscious intentionality are as much a constituent dimension of primary process as is 'the archaic.'

Becker's thesis is that the repressed fear of death is the mainspring of human activity, 'activity designed largely to avoid the fatality of death.'[57] This thesis determines all of Becker's principal contentions. From it he derives an understanding, among other things, of the almost universally false or cheap heroics of humanity, of our hopeless self-absorption, of the pathetic means we employ to secure our self-esteem, of culture as a system of false heroics, of our evasion of the intensity of personhood (an evasion that we call 'character'), of schizophrenia as an inability to lie, and of depression as a bogging-down in character defenses. The root of the malaise is not psychological but ontological: the human person is a mixture of the irreconcilable opposites of an animal body and a symbolic

self-consciousness. 'The two dimensions of human existence — the body and the self — can never be reconciled
seamlessly.'[58] The child experiences the impossibility of
identifying exclusively with either dimension, and emerges
from the earliest years with 'a face that one sets to the
world,' but that 'hides an inner defeat.'[59] And 'there is no
real difference between a childish impossibility and an adult
one; the only thing that the person achieves is a practiced
self-deceit — what we call the "mature" character.'[60] The
main task of most lives becomes the denial of one's bodily-
based contingency and fragility by buying into a cultural
system of heroics while maintaining the illusion that one
is creating one's own existence. This task shows itself in
many forms: our yearning for freedom from contradictions
and ambiguities; our buying into the artificial certainties
of our culture; our difficulty with sexual differentiation;
our misuse of religion as a support for our personal and
cultural lies; our slavishness to other persons; our impossible attempts at romantic and creative denials of our
unsurpassable dependency on the rest of reality; the dynamics of neurosis, psychosis, and perversion.

The figure who seems to Becker to have come closest to understanding the only possible resolution of the
duality is Kierkegaard, who, in his portrayal of the knight
of faith, comprehends clearly what an existence disciplined
in the school of anxiety would be. But — and here is the
rub for Becker — such faith is not our own doing; moreover, there probably is no superiority to be discerned if we
place Kierkegaard's *life* as a believing Christian over against
Freud's as an agnostic.[61] Neither escaped the character lie
of the *causa sui* project, even though Kierkegaard saw correctly that one must abandon this project completely, give
the meaning of one's life over to God, and live 'centered
on the energies of his Maker,'[62] while Freud never was
able to analyze away his own bondage to the dimensions

of the visible world and his attempts to deny that bondage through the drivenness of his dedication to his own cause.

Despite my admiration for the courage that Becker displays in an 'enlightenment' academic milieu by insisting on the complementarity of religious insight with the discoveries of the most penetrating human scientists of our day, and despite the fact that one cannot help but be moved profoundly by his prophetic denunciations of what we are doing to earn self-esteem — 'everything painful and sobering in what psychoanalytic genius and religious genius have discovered about man resolves around the terror of admitting what one is doing to earn his self-esteem'[63] — Becker's basic thesis still represents something of the pneumopathological narrowing of modern perspectives that it is attacking. Voegelin argues that the fear of death is, in fact, not repressed by modernity, but cultivated by the imperial entrepreneurs of Leviathan in order to win submission from their subjects.[64] Elsewhere he insists that the anxiety of existence is more profoundly a horror of losing attunement with the silent voices of conscience and grace than it is a fear of biological extinction. The deliberate elevation of the fear of death into an absolute is in fact one way of obliterating these other voices from persons, culture, and society. What is required is attunement to their differentiated nuances. For then it will be apparent that what has really been repressed and to this extent rendered 'unconscious' is the very question that was rationally differentiated in classical Greece, and that enabled the effective proclamation of the Gospel in Hellenistic culture and continues to enable that proclamation wherever the question remains alive: the experience of life as a movement with a direction that can be found or missed.[65] The modern forgetfulness is radically the forgetfulness of the question of attunement, a question which, while spiritual, is responsible for the unrest in the psychic dimensions of the pulsing flow of life, in living energy become psychic and human and so requiring a higher systematization and integration in the explicit reachings of conscious intentionality for proportion with the measure disclosed in the silent voices of conscience and grace. Ultimately Becker cannot arrive at such a position because he does not distinguish — and on this, he misinterprets Kierkegaard — between this psychic unrest and the intentional or spiritual question in which it participates.

Jung does acknowledge, at least incipiently, the threefold — organic, psychic, and spiritual — constitution of human primary process. Precisely because he does so, he is able to reformulate 'the archaic' in the more appropriate terms of the primordial and the numinous. Still, as we have seen, his understanding does not reach adequate differentiation. His retrieval of the relationship between experiencing and symbolization is an immanentization of the cosmological horizon, a horizon whose problems are carefully pinned down by Voegelin:

> Acts of symbolization are still badly handicapped by the bewildering multitude of unexplored facts and unsolved problems. Not much is really clear beyond the experience of participation and the quaternarian structure of the field of being, and such partial clearness tends to generate confusion rather than order, as is bound to happen when variegated materials are classified under too few heads.[66]

The recovery of what, for better or worse, I have here called the spiritual unconscious will enable us to complement Jungian psychology with the distinction offered by Northrop Frye in a different context between the archetypal and the anagogic.[67] The imagination participates in nature and imitates it (archetypal). But because it participates as well in a spiritual intention of an objective that is not restricted by space and time, it is able to contain the whole of nature and in fact the whole of proportionate being in the symbols that 'make sensible to human sensitivity what human intelligence reaches for or grasps,'[68] in 'the image that symbolizes man's orientation into the known unknown,' in the 'symbols that unlock [sensitivity's] transforming dynamism and bring it into harmony with the vast but impalpable pressures of the pure desire, of hope, and of self-sacrificing charity.'[69] No depth-psychological semantics of desire will be adequate if it cannot account for such realities. As Jung recognized the reality of dimensions of elemental symbolization that could not in principle be accounted for in Freudian terms, and as he had the courage in his own situation to develop an alternative psychology to account for these dimensions, so now we must acknowledge the reality of dimensions that cannot in principle be accounted for in Jungian terms. The terms in which they can be understood are provided by Lonergan's recovery of the 'spiritual unconscious,' and we must now accept the challenge of developing an alternative psychology that moves toward the understanding and therapeutic transcendence of psychopathology on the basis of the understanding and healing of pneumopathology.

Notes

1 Robert M. Doran, *Psychic Conversion and Theological Foundations: Toward a Reorientation of the Human Sciences* (Chico, CA: Scholars Press, 1981).

2 Sigmund Freud, *The Interpretation of Dreams*, vol. 5 in Stan-

dard Edition of the Complete Psychological Works of Sigmund Freud, ed. James Strachey (London: Hogarth, 1958), especially chapter 7.

3 Roger Woolger, 'Against Imagination: The *Via Negativa* of Simone Weil' (see above, chapter 5, note 94).

4 Bernard Lonergan, *Insight* (see above, chapter 1, note 37) xxv/19.

5 Ibid. xix/13.

6 Eric Voegelin, 'The Gospel and Culture,' in *Jesus and Man's Hope*, ed. D.C. Miller and D.Y. Hadidian (Pittsburgh: Pittsburgh Theological Seminary, 1971) 59-101.

7 Bernard Lonergan, *Method in Theology* (see above, chapter 1, note 3) 14.

8 Ibid. 16.

9 Lonergan, *Insight* 475/500.

10 Ibid. chapter 6.

11 Ibid. 472-79/497-504.

12 Ibid. xx/15.

13 Ibid. 473-74/498-99.

14 C.G. Jung, 'On the Nature of the Psyche' (see above, chapter 5, note 14).

15 Lonergan, *Insight* 181-89/204-12.

16 Lonergan, *Method in Theology* 81-85.

17 Martin Heidegger, *On Time and Being*, trans. Joan Stambaugh (New York: Harper and Row, 1972).

[18] See Lonergan, *Insight* 379-80/403-404. For all the wealth of his disclosure of the dimensions of time, Heidegger is not correct in affirming time as the horizon of Being. 'Interpretations of being ... in terms of space and time are mere intrusions of imagination.' *Insight* 379/404. Thus it is not surprising that Heidegger grounds the primordial time that for him is the horizon of Being in the transcendental imagination he retrieves from the first edition of Kant's *Critique of Pure Reason*. See Heidegger, *Kant and the Problem of Metaphysics* (see above, chapter 2, note 60).

[19] Lonergan, *Insight* 475-79/499-504.

[20] See Ernest Becker, *The Denial of Death* (see above, chapter 4, note 12) chapter 10.

[21] Lonergan, *Insight* 217/242.

[22] Fred Lawrence, 'Self-knowledge in History in Gadamer and Lonergan,' in *Language, Truth, and Meaning*, ed. Philip McShane (Notre Dame, IN: University of Notre Dame Press, 1972) 203.

[23] Eric Voegelin, *Israel and Revelation*, vol. 1 of *Order and History* (Baton Rouge: Louisiana State University Press, 1956) 10.

[24] Lonergan, *Insight* 391/416.

[25] Eric Voegelin, *The New Science of Politics* (Chicago: University of Chicago Press, 1952) 184-87.

[26] See above, note 3.

[27] Woolger, 'Against Imagination' 267.

[28] See above, note 14.

[29] Woolger, 'Against Imagination' 265.

[30] Ibid. 268.

[31] Ibid. 270.

³² See Bernard Lonergan, 'The Subject' (see above, chapter 3, note 1).

³³ Woolger, 'Against Imagination' 270, emphasis added.

³⁴ C.G. Jung, *Memories, Dreams, Reflections* (see above, chapter 3, note 49) 217-21.

³⁵ See Lonergan, *Insight* 226-32/251-57.

³⁶ James Hillman, *Re-Visioning Psychology* (see above, chapter 4, note 8). Pertinent to Hillman, though without mentioning his work, are the following comments from Ann and Barry Ulanov:

'We can find symbolic meaning in almost anything — without committing ourselves to anything. By that failure of commitment we incline too much toward the nonego side. There is no concrete living in history: rather, history functions only to occasion the uncovering and investigation of new fantasy wrappings. We may feel in some way reconnected to religious symbols through the discovery of parallels between them and personal psychological experience, but no bridge is built that way between individual meaning and collective tradition. The result is that we feel both psychologically and spiritually lonely, set apart from others and our inner selves. And too much spiritual isolation of this sort leads to madness.

'Unbalanced emphasis on the symbolic approach leads to a rootlessness of the ego in the nonego realm. Nowhere is one decisively committed, for better or for worse; ... the individual person [is] divested of his or her concrete self. Personal problems then cease to lead to new perceptions and transformations of personality, pleasurable or painful. Instead, we come to view even our most intimate problems and possibilities as new "manifestations" of the psyche's life ... Individuality has come to be seen as merely a thin layer wrapped around a core of psychic meaning.' Ann and Barry Ulanov, *Religion and the Unconscious* (Philadelphia: Westminster, 1975) 113.

Hillman's position is a function of his otherwise valuable clarification of the notion of anima, a distinct advance upon Jung. See his articles entitled 'Anima' in *Spring: An Annual of Archetypal Psychology and Jungian Thought* 1973: 97-132 and 1974: 113-46.

³⁷ David Leroy Miller, *The New Polytheism* (Dallas: Spring Publications, 1981).

³⁸ Lonergan, *Insight* , chapters 6 and 7.

[39] Lonergan, *Method in Theology* 79-80.

[40] See Soren Kierkegaard, *The Concept of Dread*, trans. Walter Lowrie (Princeton: Princeton University Press, 1944).

[41] Lonergan, *Insight* 226-42/251-67.

[42] Woolger, 'Against Imagination' 270.

[43] See Northrop Frye, *Anatomy of Criticism* (see above, chapter 3, note 45) 161-62.

[44] Woolger, 'Against Imagination' 270.

[45] Lonergan, *Insight* 692/714.

[46] Ibid. 476/501.

[47] Ibid. 532/555.

[48] Ibid.

[49] Ibid. 728/749.

[50] Ibid.

[51] See Lonergan, 'The Subject' (see above, chapter 3, note 1).

[52] C.G. Jung, *Aion* (see above, chapter 5, note 48) 266.

[53] See John Apczynski, 'Integrative Theology: A Polanyian Proposal for Theological Foundations,' *Theological Studies* 40, 1 (1979) 23-43.

[54] Paul Ricoeur, *Freud and Philosophy* (see above, chapter 1, note 7) 5-7.

[55] See Charley Hardwick, 'Psychoanalytic Groups and the Teaching of Religion,' *Journal of the American Academy of Religion* 45:2 Supplement (June, 1977) 501-27.

[56] Ernest Becker, *The Denial of Death* (see above, chapter 4, note 4).

[57] Ibid. ix.

[58] Ibid. 29.

[59] Ibid.

[60] Ibid. 46.

[61] Ibid. 258.

[62] Ibid. 257.

[63] Ibid. 6.

[64] Eric Voegelin, *The New Science of Politics*, chapters 5 and 6.

[65] See Voegelin, 'The Gospel and Culture.'

[66] Voegelin, Israel and Revelation 3.

[67] Northrop Frye, *Anatomy of Criticism* 95-128.

[68] Lonergan, *Insight* 548/571.

[69] Ibid. 723/744.

16 Affect, Affectivity

The role of the affections in the spiritual life is treated by major authors in the tradition, but contemporary developments enable us to attain greater precision.

Bernard Lonergan distinguishes nonintentional from intentional feelings. Nonintentional feelings correspond to what some psychologies call *affects*, as distinct from feelings, while the term *feelings* is used by these psychologies to refer to what Lonergan calls intentional feelings. *Affectivity* is used here to cover both realities, and for the sake of clarity we will employ Lonergan's distinction.

Nonintentional feelings include such states as anxiety and fatigue, which have causes, and such trends as hunger and thirst, which have goals, but they are nonintentional, inasmuch as they do not arise out of an apprehension or representation of their causes or goals or of any object. They occur, and from their occurrence one diagnoses the cause or goal. Intentional feelings, though, are responses to apprehended objects. The major classes of objects to which they respond are, on the one hand, the satisfying or dissatisfying, and, on the other hand, values. The two classes of objects are not mutually exclusive, for what is satisfying may also be truly worth while; but they are also not mutually inclusive, for what is genuinely worth while may also be disagreeable. What distinguishes value from the merely satisfying is that value carries us to transcend ourselves, and on that basis Lonergan distinguishes vital, social, cultural, personal, and religious values in an ascending order.

Such a link between feelings and values renders feelings of crucial importance in discernment and decision-making. Ignatius of Loyola speaks of three times or moments of election or decision. The times reflect different affective states of the subject, and in each instance affectivity is a criterion of both the method to be employed and the course of action to be chosen. In one of these times (the second), one is agitated and experiences alternations of consolation and desolation; a decision is reached precisely by monitoring these experiences in the practice of what Ignatius calls the discernment of spirits. In another time (the first), one has been so moved by God as to have no doubt concerning what one is to do. And in the third time, one already is tranquil and so is antecedently disposed to employ more rational means, such as weighing the pros and cons of the various alternatives.

These moments are exhaustive of all possibilities. Either there are no further questions about what is to be done (first time) or there are (second and third times). And if there are, either one is moved affectively in diverse and conflicting directions (second time) or one is not (third time). If a person is in the second time, when affective apprehension is only of *possible* values, one should choose what leads to equanimity. If one is in the third time, a test of the genuineness of a decision is that one preserves and deepens the equanimity that enabled one to employ this method in the first place; and the first time is so clear precisely because it places one in such a state of equanimity that there is no need for further deliberation; the apprehension of values in feelings is, and is known to be, an apprehension of what is genuinely worth while and to be done.

The criterion both of what method is to be employed and of what course of action is to be chosen thus lies in an affective dispositional state referred to by Ignatius as equanimity or equilibrium. When one is in the second time, what *leads to* such a state is to be followed, and what *leads away from* such a state is to be rejected. When one is in the third time, such a state sets the very conditions for employing more rational methods of decision-making, and the choice is to be confirmed by perseverance in such a state; and the first time is one in which one is placed in such a state by the action of grace.

The practice of discernment, of course, is engaged in independently of such moments of decision. Discernment is a matter of noticing constancy in, or departure from, the state of equilibrium that makes affective self-transcendence possible. Self-transcendent affective response, in fact, may be correlated with the dynamic equilibrium that is the criterion for both the method and the object of choice. What calls for further comment, then, is the constitution and origination of this equilibrium of self-transcendent feeling.

Such an equilibrium is constituted by the creative tension or functional interdependence of the linked but potentially opposed principles of (1) limitation rooted in the body and (2) transcendence rooted in the spirit. The human person is an incarnate spirit, and the authenticity of the person is a function of one's perseverance in the tension of matter and spirit. That tension is *felt* in the sensitive psyche, and these feelings are ciphers, indeed criteria, of one's genuineness. What the tradition has called concupiscence is our tendency to distort the tension of matter and spirit in either direction. Sin is capitulation to that tendency. Grace is needed to preserve us in the inner harmony felt in the psyche as equanimity or equilibrium.

The origination of such equanimity is complex, but besides more or less normal favorable circumstances in a person's life, another ground may be found in the experience that Ignatius calls consolation without a cause. Karl Rahner has interpreted this expression to mean consolation with a content but without an apprehended object. In this sense, consolation without a cause is a peculiar instance of a nonintentional feeling, in that it does not arise from the apprehension or representation of an object but occurs by divine causation without any such apprehension. Its occurrence is a ground or condition of equilibrium, and therefore a factor in the sustained exercise of authentic personhood. It is identified by Bernard Lonergan with the dynamic state of being in love with God, which is the basic fulfilment of our conscious longings. In proportion to the consistency of that state, one's affectivity is of a single piece. Religious and affective development converge in their finality when the goal of each is acknowledged to be a dynamic and habitual state of being in love.

Such a perspective enables the integration of spirituality with a reoriented science of psychology. Many of the techniques discovered by contemporary psychologies can be employed in the spiritual life to enable one to discover, name, and negotiate one's affective dispositions and responses. Under these perspectives, taking cognizance of, and assuming responsibility for, one's affective orientation is partly constitutive of one's development as a spiritual person.